Libraries, Digital Information, and COVID

Chandos
Digital Information Review Series

Series Editors

David Baker and Lucy Ellis

Chandos is pleased to publish this major series of books entitled Digital Information Review. The series editors are Professor David Baker, Professor Emeritus, Plymouth Marjon University and Dr Lucy Ellis, Honorary Research Fellow, Exeter University; Associate, David Baker Consulting.

The Chandos Digital Information Review series aims to be a summary and a summation of the key themes, advances and trends in all aspects of digital information and explores the impact on the information world. The emphasis is on both the key current topics and future developments; an international perspective is taken throughout. Each publication in the series has a dynamic set of contents that respond to and, more importantly, anticipate digital information futures. The relevant chapters are written by experts in the field, drawing widely from Europe, North America, Australasia and South East Asia.

New authors - we would be delighted to hear from you if you have an idea for a book. We are interested in short practically orientated publications (45,000 words) and longer theoretical monographs (75,000-100,000 words). Our books can be single, joint or multi author volumes. If you have an idea for a book please contact the publishers or the Series Editors: Professor David Baker (david@davidbakerconsulting.co.uk) and Dr Lucy Ellis (lucy@davidbakerconsulting.co.uk)

Chandos Digital Information Review

Libraries, Digital Information, and COVID

Practical Applications and Approaches to Challenge and Change

Written and edited by

David Baker
Lucy Ellis

CP
CHANDOS
PUBLISHING

ELSEVIER   An imprint of Elsevier

Chandos Publishing is an imprint of Elsevier
50 Hampshire Street, 5th Floor, Cambridge, MA 02139, United States
The Boulevard, Langford Lane, Kidlington, OX5 1GB, United Kingdom

Notices
Knowledge and best practice in this field are constantly changing. As new research and experience
broaden our understanding, changes in research methods, professional practices, or medical treatment
may become necessary.

Practitioners and researchers must always rely on their own experience and knowledge in evaluating
and using any information, methods, compounds, or experiments described herein. In using such
information or methods they should be mindful of their own safety and the safety of others, including
parties for whom they have a professional responsibility.

To the fullest extent of the law, neither the Publisher nor the authors, contributors, or editors, assume
any liability for any injury and/or damage to persons or property as a matter of products liability,
negligence or otherwise, or from any use or operation of any methods, products, instructions, or ideas
contained in the material herein.

Library of Congress Cataloging-in-Publication Data
A catalog record for this book is available from the Library of Congress

British Library Cataloguing-in-Publication Data
A catalogue record for this book is available from the British Library

ISBN: 978-0-323-88493-8 (print)

For information on all Chandos publications
visit our website at https://www.elsevier.com/books-and-journals

Publisher: Stacy Masucci
Acquisitions Editor: Glyn Jones
Editorial Project Manager: Chiara Giglio
Production Project Manager: Surya Narayanan Jayachandran
Cover Designer: Alan Studholme

Typeset by SPi Global, India

Contents

Part One   Immediate challenges

Part Two   Analysis and opportunities for new behaviours

Section A   How we learn?

Section B   Supply of information

Section C   Psychological effects—Adjustment or radical alteration?

Part Three   Re-shaping society and the future

List of figures and tables

List of figures

List of tables

Forewords

Perspective from North America

In March 2020, as it became clear that COVID-19 would be a pandemic of a scale not seen in most of our lifetimes, universities around the world had to decide how to react. Some closed and sent all their students home, some scaled back services, and ultimately most of them moved many if not all of their courses into a digital environment, emptied the dormitories, and sent their staff and faculty off to work from their homes.

But for the university libraries, this was just the beginning. Not all students are able to return home, so how do we serve their needs? How do we move from print to electronic reserves on a suddenly even tighter budget? Can we provide the video resources needed by faculty who used to walk a DVD into the classroom? What about the student who has neither a home computer nor access to the Internet? There were more questions than answers, but we are librarians: We made it work. We consulted and discussed, and came up with the answers we needed at the time. And, of course, we started talking to each other. Groups with plans already in place for online discussions changed to currently relevant topics such as supporting students online or staff working from home.

My initial introduction to this book began with an invitation to participate as a panellist on the September 2020 Asia-Pacific eBook Forum, *COVID-19 and the Future of Libraries: Accepting the Challenge and Recognizing the Opportunities,* led by the authors of this book. The webinar was a great chance to talk through issues, services, and future plans with librarians in the United States, Hong Kong, and Australia, and led to the opportunity to say a few words in this handbook of information on the library world's operational response to the COVID-19 pandemic, analysis and new behaviours coming out of that response and new directions for libraries now and in the longer term.

Fortunately for all of us, there are scholars presumptuous enough to jump in and begin studying, analyzing, and publishing on a current event even as it continues. The book in your hands or on your screen is history in motion. David Baker and Lucy Ellis didn't wait until the pandemic had run its course, spend 6 months on a book proposal, and another 2 years gathering chapters. This is crucial since *Libraries, Digital Information, and COVID* is meant to be a handbook, a primer, a manual, a reference to be used as we all deal with the ongoing issues around services, staffing, and budgeting during and immediately after a cultural event that will change the future of our work.

A quick browse of the Table of Contents tells us that the chapter contributors come from all parts of the globe providing a truly international viewpoint. There are case studies, thought pieces, and data analyses. Topics range from instruction to acquisition to library as space. In addition to the contributed chapters, the authors have gathered relevant material, led global webinars, and interviewed leaders in the library field and in other sectors to provide analysis of the chapters.

So dive in! Browse some case studies or specific chapters relevant to your needs. Read about the future of libraries in Nigeria, assessment of student satisfaction in Lisbon, or scientific production in Mexico—all within the context of the pandemic. Don't miss the first and last chapters which pull together the strategic themes. Then pass the book on to a colleague, and keep the discussion going.

Diane Bruxvoort
Dean of Libraries at the University of North Texas

Perspective from Canada

For over a year, coronavirus shocks have negatively submerged every sector—public and private—around the world. Counterintuitively, readers of *Libraries, Digital Information, and COVID: Practical Applications and Approaches to Challenge and Change* may conclude that libraries have actually benefited from their painful adjustments to the pandemic.

This book shows the agony of coping with new ordeals related to the virus in addition to dealing with the acceleration of current trends within the ecosystem. The impact of technology and virtual access were testing libraries in areas such as resources, skills, and information management before February 2020. COVID-19 applied boosters to the speed of those challenges.

The intricacies of managing online teaching and learning were familiar to many. The rapidity and magnitude of the shift, however, augmented difficulties in accessing and disseminating trusted information. Cybersecurity concerns multiplied as well. As always, financial pressures increased. Then, COVID-19 piled on the problems related to the "health" of physical spaces and employee/user safety. Every contributor has experienced those pains as well.

David Baker and Lucy Ellis's extensive, well-timed review of the various responses to COVID-19 by libraries and digital information providers gives valuable insights for practitioners. Moreover, it provides a platform for future experiments in adaptation. The diverse narratives in this timely book indicate that the virus moved institutions along routes they were previously exploring. Plus, it enabled libraries to continue leading cultural change in their institutions and their countries.

This book provides an overview of library "petri dishes" across the globe. It gives librarians, access architects, and information data managers insights into different solutions. It represents a source of exemplars of "best" practice or maybe, at this point, several "possible" practices to solving shared problems. Each reader will find sufficient "takeaways" to help with future approaches.

In addition, some chapters explore the sociological impacts of the virus on library mandates. Again, many of these trends were apparent before—such as the wedge driven between advantaged populations and the vulnerable by information technology and privileged access. This book opens the discussion on other policy issues that organizations at all levels of the education sector will need to address: for example, the availability and reliability of research and information. Having opened those policy doors, libraries will be instrumental in exploring courses of action in the "new normal."

Libraries, Digital Information, and COVID was conceived and executed by David Baker and Lucy Ellis as an outgrowth of their wide-ranging work on strategic information management and human communication. Professor Baker has published extensively on libraries, information management, and learning sciences. He has consulted broadly on technology, digital and hybrid library development, and content development in several countries. Besides teaching, Dr. Ellis has undertaken consultancies in a wide range of higher education issues. She has also been a reviewer for *Information and Learning Sciences* (Emerald). Their recent work in the Asia-Pacific region on best practice and qualitative benchmarking in these areas stimulated this book's release.

It is fitting that Elsevier is publishing a book on these topics and in this format. Given its history since the 1500s, Elsevier has shown flexibility in publishing and adaptation to world events. More recently, its tack to sponsorship of groundbreaking work by leading researchers to advance science and health supports this kind of release.

Every practitioner and policy formulator in information and access management; library services and management; collection development and protection; and verification of scientific data will find useful lessons in this book. They will recognize and share the pain of their colleagues as they find pathways to solutions.

Phyllis Clark
Chair, Royal Canadian Mint; Director, Bank of Canada (2012–18);
Vice-President, Finance and Administration, University of Alberta (2002–16)

Perspective from a UK University student

Introduction

The COVID-19 pandemic continues to present severe and widespread challenges across the globe, leaving virtually no industry, organization, or population untouched. Higher education institutions (HEIs) in particular have had to adapt to an ever-changing set of circumstances, often in radical and fundamental ways. When lockdown was announced in the United Kingdom in March 2020, all face-to-face teaching was suspended immediately, and new, effective, but remote, methods of delivery had to be devised and implemented almost overnight. University libraries were forced to shut indefinitely, leaving many thousands of staff and students in dire, unprecedented predicaments, with many not reopening in some form until well into the 2020–21 academic year.

The following is a commentary on the impact of, and response to, the many pandemic-related challenges faced by HEI libraries, from the perspective of a university student. Three principal themes will be considered in turn: First, the immediate consequences of the pandemic on library operations, in terms of student experience, and second, the actions put in place by libraries to adapt to the "new normal" will be evaluated. Third, I will consider library provision post-pandemic, and how university libraries might learn from this period of upheaval and transformation.

The immediate consequences of the pandemic

Perhaps the most obvious, most critical, impact of library closure was the inevitable restriction of access to only those resources which could be provided online. With many undergraduate finalists and research postgraduates facing looming dissertation or thesis deadlines, this presented a severe limitation as many, particularly in the arts and humanities, rely on key literature and source materials which may not possess digital surrogates. A key issue here is that students who would usually use library computers may not possess adequate IT equipment or infrastructure themselves to access online resources from home. Although this may only be pertinent to a select group of students, it is significant for those that it does affect, who are more likely to be from lower-income backgrounds, and is therefore not to be overlooked. Even though "no-detriment"-type grade assurances were made by virtually all universities, and UKRI-funded doctoral students were granted thesis deadline extensions, in many ways this could not make up for what was felt by some to be a gaping hole in requisite resources. While academic safety nets may have assuaged the worries of some students whose goal is simply to receive their degree with a satisfactory classification, viewing assessment just as a "means to an end," others doubtless felt robbed of their ability to achieve their best in what was meant to be their crowning academic achievement.

Equally, for many students undertaking major independent research projects, library access is perceived to be practically the only educational provision received in return for payment of tuition fees. Some might argue that this already represents poor value for money, so when libraries were forced to close, there were widespread calls for wholesale tuition fee rebates, and frustration when these were not, on the whole, answered. Concurrently, many students have had to continue paying for private accommodation which they are barred from inhabiting; ensuing financial worries and despair at the situation have contributed to rising levels of anxiety, exacerbating what has become a mental health crisis among the student population. Although this is really part of a much bigger problem, the library plays a key role in the delivery of university education, so it is considered by the student body crucial that it offers good value for money—even when only accessible remotely—if tuition fees are to remain unchanged over the course of the pandemic.

University libraries' dual purpose as both a resource centre and study space means that their closure completely disrupted normal working patterns for many students, displacing them around the country to environments with less favourable working conditions, or perhaps caring responsibilities or limited access to IT resources. During the spring exam season, which usually takes place around May (when in 2020 the first wave of the pandemic was at its peak in the United Kingdom), the usual insatiable demand for study space in the library is indicative of the fact that many people struggle to focus to produce coursework or prepare for examinations, at home. As I discuss in detail in my thought piece in Chapter 31, the library provides the perfect environment for studying, and is in fact something many students rely on as part of their perennial exam preparation routine. Being denied access during this critical period meant a complete overhaul of exam technique for some, whereas for others it meant they had a safe space taken away from them or had nowhere to access the Internet.

The true impact of the pandemic on teaching, learning, and research may not become clear until after the return to normality, but ultimately it is unlikely that the amount of disruption directly creditable to library closure will be particularly significant (c.f. virtual lectures or curtailment of laboratory work). For the vast majority of students, particularly in the sciences, documents that at one time would have needed to have been sourced from a physical library are now exclusively online resources, thanks to a steady migration over recent years. Therefore, a combination of this ongoing shift to digital, rapid imposition of effective mitigations (as discussed in the following section), and a relatively short timescale before most libraries were able to reopen, meant that much of the potential negative impact was felt to be successfully avoided.

Adaptations and mitigations

Although many of the traditional day-to-day operations such as lending and IT provision were suspended, the ongoing digitization of resources meant that libraries were already generally well placed for remote provision. The pandemic has presented a clear validation of the digital migration philosophy and provided what some may consider a long overdue impetus to expand and accelerate the process. Where digital surrogates existed, with ready availability of licences and subscriptions for online books, journals, and databases meant that online access to core resources could quickly and easily be purchased by institutions; where digital versions were unavailable, services such as "scan and deliver," where library staff email scans of book chapters and journal articles directly to students, could be extended. And in any case, course reading lists could be quickly updated for the next academic year to consist solely of resources which could be accessed virtually to ensure that everyone had equal access to materials. In this sense, it is lucky that lockdown began when it did, when teaching at most universities had almost concluded for the year.

As Antunes, Lopes, and Sanches illustrate in Chapter 14, replacement digital resources and services are found almost universally to be satisfactory substitutes. This lends further credence to the argument that migration to a more digitally facing library as part of Education 4.0 is effective, necessary, and desired by primary users. Virtual resources are already the norm in the sciences, so digitalization would also contribute to remedying a disparity across faculties which has unfairly disadvantaged those in the arts and humanities over the course of the pandemic. However, many argue that there is no real substitute for physical resources; at a time when everything is accessed via a computer, and students are expected to attend many hours per week of virtual lectures, seminars, and tutorials, "screen fatigue" has become an important and widespread issue. While having every requisite resource available digitally provides unprecedented flexibility and ease of access, there is an argument for at least keeping the option of having print media available as well.

When libraries reopened in autumn of 2020 for the new academic year, sweeping changes to layout, protocol, and organization took place for compliance with new COVID-safety regulations. Social distancing requirements mean that study space capacity is much reduced, and advance bookings for study sessions and even slots to browse and borrow are mandated. While these are important and necessary, and it is in many ways miraculous that libraries are able to reopen at all, this is far from ideal from the student perspective. Typically, demand is such that study slots are booked up days in advance, meaning that students must plan their study routine ahead. While for some students this might be useful as an organizational aid, others find that it obstructs their natural flow of learning or research; where before a spontaneous trip to the library to browse or to study may provide a useful spark of inspiration, this is now no longer an option. Limitations on the number of timeslots one can book, and the time at which they take place, also mean that the normal working habits of some, like colloquially named "night-owls," are unfeasible. There are also reports of increased stress among students as a direct result of scarcity of study space availability; as an example, to address this, the Durham University Library has recently moved the time that new timeslots are released from midnight to 6.30 p.m. "to help support student wellbeing."

In summary, in terms of adapting resource accessibility, much of what was enacted has simply been to extend tried-and-tested methods by expanding existing digitalization programmes. Although inevitably this presents difficulties where digital surrogates do not exist, this has been minimally disruptive since students are already largely used to accessing and using virtual resources anyway. The main source of difficulty has really been in relation to the lack of available physical space, particularly when students don't have suitable working environments at home. While there is seemingly no obvious solution to this issue, this ultimately represents a relatively minor, and hopefully temporary, inconvenience to most.

To the future

The COVID-19 pandemic has brought about huge transformations in the way that we use libraries and access data. As Brenton and Tury touch on in Chapter 10, the library's role in HEIs may well be at a turning point, and the way that we view it is in the process of considerable change—is the library a physical space, an information access point, or in fact the group of people that uses it? The university library's traditional prominence in campus life means that for many, it embodies the intangible sense of community which plays such a crucial role in the university experience. Having this hub, which provides not only an academic but a social environment too, taken away, echoes the theme of social isolation which has pervaded the pandemic, and has highlighted the importance many students attach to the library. It is clear that the library, however it is defined, will continue to be central to student life for many years to come.

The question is, however, which adaptations have worked well, and are therefore worth keeping, and which have not? From the student perspective, the key benefit in terms of library provision that the pandemic has brought about is increased flexibility. Centralized resources accessible 24/7 from anywhere in the world facilitates much more versatile modes of teaching, learning, and research, particularly benefiting those who may previously have had accessibility difficulties: those with disabilities or caring responsibilities, for example. It is therefore imperative that extensive virtual resource provision is adopted on a permanent basis; most would regard a return to prepandemic provision as a step in the wrong direction.

While a greater shift to a digital-first or digital-only culture is to be welcomed, the pandemic has also demonstrated the importance of university libraries as physical study space. Most will look forward to the time when libraries can operate at normal capacity again, without the need for prebooked slots, but others would welcome the ability to continue to reserve study spaces in advance so they can be sure of a seat during periods of peak occupancy. In response to this, perhaps a hybrid approach could be explored where some areas of a library remain unreserved, but others require advance booking.

Ultimately, as long as university libraries continue to provide abundant, high-quality study space, while retaining the flexibility in resource access developed in response to the pandemic, they will continue to serve the student body well. To provide good value for money for fee-paying students, it is paramount that libraries are given the resources they need to match advances made in teaching as we move to more digital or blended modes of learning, given their key role in the delivery of higher education.

Conclusion

As a result of the COVID-19 pandemic, students in higher education have seen their entire way of life thrown into disarray, having had to acclimatize to a profoundly different and challenging set of circumstances from what they are used to, and adapt to novel methods of learning and research. However, technological advances have meant that university libraries have been able to continue to provide many key services almost as normal, becoming central access points for virtual resources, and minimizing disruption to learning. Digital libraries' essential role in remote education highlights their importance in our increasingly digital culture, and as long as they can continue to adapt to the needs of the student body, they will remain relevant, useful, and loved.

Ted O'Hare
Durham University, United Kingdom

Preface—What is in this book

Part One - Immediate Challenges

Operational responses
New services
Physical protection and hygiene
Librarian roles
Staff engagement
Public libraries
Supply chains
Discoverability
Project delivery
Professional identity

Chapter 1:
Context for the book

Part Two - Analysis and Opportunities for New Behaviours

Data repositories
Scientific production
Physical spaces
User reaction
Special needs
Library branding
Emotional context for learning
Developing countries
Digital divides
Publishing
Library acquisition strategies

Chapter 31:
Summative analysis`

Part Three - Re-shaping Society and the Future

Risk evaluation
Public libraries
The future of working
Off-site working
Moving teaching online
Forecasting
Value for money
Digital space
Accelerative change
Collections development

Contributors to this book

By invitation, 45 leaders in the field have contributed chapters for this book, representing work carried out in China, Denmark, Finland, France, Germany, Greece, Mexico, Nigeria, Portugal, Spain, Sweden, the United Kingdom, and the United States of America. This multinational perspective will be valuable to the reader as it gives an understanding of the organizational characteristics and constraints that have shaped responses to the pandemic.

Contributing authors are those who have been at the "sharp end" of delivering information services and systems throughout the COVID-19 crisis, and their chapters represent the views and behaviours of subject specialists and academic communities. A further group of authors contributed thought pieces which were commissioned to provide stimulating statements, reflections, predictions, ideas, and viewpoints.

The Chandos Digital Information Review Series, of which this is the latest volume, aims to be a summary of the key themes, advances, and trends in all aspects of digital information, and explores the impact on the information world. The two Chandos series that sit alongside it are *Advances in Information* and the *Information Professional* Series. *Digital Information Reviews* captures key themes, advances, and trends. It is about the process of adding things together, a methodology for identifying the matters of our time, and the ways of thinking that define us.

Sector interviews

As part of our research for this book, we looked to gain a wide range of views, information, and experience about how different sectors are responding to the challenges of COVID as a way of summarizing best practice not just for the library and information sector, but also for public service provision in general. The results of the interviews and their wider interpretative context can be found highlighted in boxes in Chapters 1 and 31.

Twelve leading professionals were interviewed from the United Kingdom, New Zealand, China, and Australia from the sectors of data science and artificial intelligence, national infrastructure provision, higher education, digital strategy for museums and galleries, health and social care, public libraries, business change consultancy, IT services, and commercial online education.

Delphi exercise

The key themes in this book are reinforced and augmented by the results of a Delphi exercise undertaken for this publication which are presented in text boxes in Chapters 1 and 31. "Delphi is a qualitative method of forecasting by developing expert consensus about a topic through a series of anonymous mailed questionnaires...The Delphi method has been employed in technological forecasting, planning, and a variety of other areas" (Baker, 2004, p. 82). A total of 23 panellists took part in the exercise from a wide range of backgrounds relating to digital information provision and libraries (for a full list of panellists, see *Acknowledgements*). The core panellists were from the Asia-Pacific (APAC) region of the world, and their invited participation was a result of their attendance at the Elsevier 2020 series of e-book Forum webinars (Elsevier, 2020). The APAC panellists were primarily from universities and higher education institutions and consultancies specializing in, amongst others, arts, chemistry, technology, nuclear research, agriculture, engineering, business and management, and maritime studies. One panellist is an expert in digital strategy and development in the museums and archives sector, and one is a university librarian in Nigeria as well as a leader in the National Institute for Policy and Strategic Studies.

A series of questions was developed according to the main themes of this book and are shown in Appendix A: Delphi questions. The answers to these questions were collated and turned into a series of statements which were then sent back to the participants for further comment. These responses were then summarized and analyzed.

David Baker
Lucy Ellis

References

Baker, D., 2004. The Strategic Management of Technology: A Guide for Library and Information Services. Chandos, Oxford.

Elsevier ebook webinar, 27.10.2020. Elsevier, Singapore. https://www.brighttalk.com/webcast/18191/450635/apac-ebook-forum-2020-covid-19-the-future-of-digital-information-for-libraries.

Contributors

Stephen Akintunde National Institute for Policy and Strategic Studies, Kuru, Plateau State, Nigeria

Maria Luz Antunes ESTeSL (Instituto Politécnico de Lisboa); APPsyCI—Applied Psychology Research Center Capabilities and Inclusion, Lisboa, Portugal

Jeremy Atkinson Jeremy Atkinson Consultancy, Cardiff, Wales, United Kingdom

Otmane Azeroual German Centre for Higher Education Research and Science Studies (DZHW), Berlin, Germany

David Baker Professor Emeritus, Plymouth Marjon University, Plymouth; David Baker Consulting, West Yorkshire, United Kingdom

Emma Bond University of Suffolk, Ipswich, United Kingdom

Sam Brenton University of London, London, United Kingdom

Ellen Buck University of Suffolk, Ipswich, United Kingdom

Victoria F. Caplan The Hong Kong University of Science and Technology (HKUST), Clear Water Bay, Hong Kong

Diana L.H. Chan The Hong Kong University of Science and Technology (HKUST), Clear Water Bay, Hong Kong

Lucy Ellis David Baker Consulting, West Yorkshire; University of Exeter, Exeter, United Kingdom

Melissa Fulkerson Elsevier, Cambridge, MA, United States

Amanda Glimstedt Gothenburg University Library, Gothenburg, Sweden

Martin Hamilton MartinH.Net Un Limited, Loughborough, United Kingdom

Graeme Hawley National Library of Scotland, Edinburgh, United Kingdom

Scott Henderson Imover Consultancy Ltd, Hebden Bridge, United Kingdom

Carl Gustav Johannsen University of Copenhagen, Copenhagen, Denmark

Paul Kirkham Institute of Contemporary Music Performance (ICMP), London, United Kingdom

David Kjellin Gothenburg University Library, Gothenburg, Sweden

Carlos Lopes APPsyCI—Applied Psychology Research Center Capabilities and Inclusion; ISPA—Instituto Universitário, Lisboa, Portugal

Juan D. Machin-Mastromatteo Autonomous University of Chihuahua, Chihuahua, Mexico

Richard Maidment-Otlet EdTech and Marketing Consultant, Bristol, United Kingdom

Rosanna Mann Independent Consultant, ACU, London, United Kingdom

Rob May ABE Global, London, United Kingdom

Sarah Mears Libraries Connected, London, United Kingdom

Katarina Michnik Gothenburg University Library, Gothenburg, Sweden

Valentini Moniarou-Papaconstantinou Dept. Archives, Library and Information Studies, University of West Attica, Athens, Greece

Anna Nunn University of Suffolk, Ipswich, United Kingdom

Andy Phippen Bournemouth University, Bournemouth, United Kingdom

José Refugio Romo-González Autonomous University of Chihuahua, Chihuahua, Mexico

Rick Rylance University of London, London, United Kingdom

Tatiana Sanches APPsyCI—Applied Psychology Research Center Capabilities and Inclusion; UIDEF, Instituto da Educação, Universidade de Lisboa, Lisboa, Portugal

Joachim Schöpfel GERiiCO Laboratory, University of Lille, Lille, France

Lucy Shackleton Independent Consultant, ACU, London, United Kingdom

Yi Shen Independent Researcher, Blacksburg, VA, United States

Daniella Smith University of North Texas, Denton, TX, United States

Bulcsu Szekely LUT University (Lappeenranta-Lahti University of Technology LUT), Lappeenranta, Finland

Javier Tarango Autonomous University of Chihuahua, Chihuahua, Mexico

Sandra Tury University of London Worldwide, London, United Kingdom

Evgenia Vassilakaki European Insurance and Occupational Pensions Authority (EIOPA), Frankfurt, Germany

Tim Wales Brunel University London, Uxbridge, United Kingdom

Jane Winters University of London, London, United Kingdom

Sayeda Zain Mont Rose College of Management & Science, London, United Kingdom

Author biographies

Stephen Akintunde is a systems analyst at the National Institute for Policy and Strategic Studies, Nigeria's apex think tank. He is University Librarian at the University of Jos, Jos, Nigeria. He has served as Chairman of the Nigerian University Libraries Consortium and Country Licensing Coordinator of Electronic Information for Libraries (EIFL), and is a member of the Steering Committee of Supporting Research Community, Association of Commonwealth University Libraries. He was for several years a resource person at the United Nations Economic Commission for Africa Committee on Development Information (CODI) and later the Committee on Development Information, Science and Technology (CODIST), especially the Knowledge, Libraries and Information Services track. He is well published in journals and books. He has held leadership positions in the Nigerian Library Association and is a member of the American Library Association, the Chartered Institute of Library and Information Professionals, and the International Sociological Association.

Maria Luz Antunes is a researcher in the APPsyCI (Applied Psychology Research Center Capabilities & Inclusion) at ISPA (Instituto Universitário), Lisboa, Portugal. She began her career at the Library of the Portugal Bureau (European Commission, 1988) and coordinates several health libraries: one specialized in family medicine and another in health quality. Since 2000, she has been the head librarian at the ESTeSL Library. She is the manager of the institutional scientific repository and the editorial manager of two scientific journals: *Revista Portuguesa de Medicina Geral e Familiar* (since 2014) and *Saúde & Tecnologia* (since 2008). Her publications are mainly on health literacy, information literacy, and open science.

Jeremy Atkinson has wide-ranging experience and expertise in the leadership, management, and development of academic library services. He has worked as a library and information services consultant for the past 8 years, with a number of high-profile clients, including Jisc, SCONUL, and individual UK universities, including work on open access, repositories, and copyright. He previously had overall responsibility for the strategic and operational management of library and information services at the University of South Wales. He has also held posts at the University of Northumbria, Cardiff University, and Manchester Metropolitan University. Jeremy has produced a wide range of publications and conference papers on topics, including change management, electronic resources, library collaboration, and quality assurance. He is also the editor of three recent books published by Chandos/Elsevier: *Technology, Change and the Academic Library* (2020), *Collaboration and the Academic Library* (2018), and *Quality and the Academic Library* (2016).

Otmane Azeroual is a researcher at the German Institute for Higher Education Research and Science Studies (DZHW), Berlin, Germany. After studying business information systems at the University of Applied Sciences—HTW Berlin, he is undertaking his doctorate in computer science at the Otto von Guericke University of Magdeburg and at the University of Applied Sciences—HTW Berlin. His areas of research include database systems, information systems, data quality, business intelligence, big data, open data, cloud computing, text data mining, IT security, and industry 4.0.

David Baker has published widely in the field of library and information studies, with 20 monographs and over 100 articles to his credit. He has spoken worldwide at numerous conferences and led workshops and seminars. His other key professional interest and expertise has been in the field of human resources, where he has also been active in major national projects. He has held senior positions at several institutions, including as Principal and Chief Executive of Plymouth Marjon University and as Emeritus Professor of Strategic Information Management. He has also been Deputy Chair of the Joint Information Systems Committee (JISC). Until recently, he was a member of the Board of Governors of the Universities of Northampton and South Wales. He is Chair of the Board of the Institute of Contemporary Music Performance. He is a leader in the field of library and information science.

Emma Bond is Director of Research, Head of the Graduate School, and Professor of Socio-Technical Research at the University of Suffolk. She has extensive research experience focusing on online risk and vulnerable groups, especially in relation to domestic abuse, revenge pornography, sexual abuse, and image-based abuse. Emma has 20 years of teaching experience on social science undergraduate and postgraduate courses, and is Senior Fellow of the Higher Education Academy. Her research on virtual environments, mobile technologies, and risk has attracted much national and international acclaim, and she has been interviewed for BBC Breakfast, ITV, The Today Programme on Radio 4, Woman's Hour on Radio 4, Channel 4's Sex Education Show, and for various national media channels in the United Kingdom, America, and Canada.

Sam Brenton is Director of Education, Innovation, and Development at the University of London, where he is responsible for devising, designing, and developing the University's distance learning programmes, which serve some 48,000 students in more than 180 countries. He has over 20 years of experience of technology-enhanced learning, learning technologies and distance education, and deep knowledge of the strategy, implementation, pedagogy, and practice of online teaching and learning. Prior to joining the University of London, he was Director of Digital Learning at Cass Business School. Previously, he was Director of the Learning Institute at Queen Mary, University of London, and he has also worked with various online learning firms in the private sector.

Ellen Buck leads the Centre for Excellence in Learning and Teaching, and the Directorate of Learning and Teaching at the University of Suffolk. Ellen is responsible for implementing the university's Learning Teaching and Assessment strategy, which includes the development and delivery of progressive learning models, and curricula which are inclusive in design, research informed, and employer engaged. This includes the provision of support, guidance, and a range of blended CPD activities. Ellen began her career as a professional librarian in the civil service before moving into the higher education sector. She has extensive leadership experience and has overseen a number of transformational projects for the university, including the development of block and blend pedagogies, and review and procurement of the institutional online learning environment and library management system.

Victoria F. Caplan is the Head of Information Instruction and Collection Services (IICS) at the Hong Kong University of Science & Technology Library. A member of the library's senior management team, she oversees the library's work in promoting and providing information literacy instruction and information services to the HKUST community. After joining HKUST in 1992 as a cataloguer, she soon found her métier in public services. From 1996 to 2002, she served in the Media Resources & Microforms section, and 2002–12 as the Access Services Manager. Since becoming IICS Head in 2012, she worked to develop library instruction and link users to HKUST collections via many services. She received her BA in East Asian Studies from Yale, her MSc from the University of Illinois at Champaign-Urbana, and an MPhil (sociology) from the University of Hong Kong.

Diana L.H. Chan has been the University Librarian at the Hong Kong University of Science & Technology (HKUST) since 2012. She received her Bachelor of Business Administration at the Chinese University of Hong Kong and Master of Library Science from San José State University, United States. She started her library work in the United States and Canada before returning to Hong Kong. Ms. Chan has published 20 journal papers, book chapters, and a book, and presented 50 conference papers on various library topics, including strategic management, staff development, space development, learning commons, institutional repositories, consortia collection development, research support services, and shared ILS. She has served as the Chair of JULAC (Joint University Librarians Advisory Committee in Hong Kong) in 2015/2016, also in the JULAC Access Services Committee, JULAC Consortiall Committee, Hong Kong Monographic Acquisitions Committee, Hong Kong Public Libraries Advisory Committee, Guangdong Higher Education Library Committee, Hong Kong Library Association, and many university-wide committees.

Lucy Ellis is a consultant and research associate within higher education. Published In 2021 she was coeditor and author with Professor David Baker of *Future Directions in Digital Information: Predictions, Practice, Participation*. She holds a PhD in experimental phonetics from Queen Margaret University in Edinburgh and was the recipient of a British Academy scholarship to study linguistics at the University of Cambridge. She has worked as a senior lecturer and programme leader at Plymouth Marjon University and as a project development consultant. She holds an honorary research fellowship with the College of Humanities at Exeter University.

Melissa Fulkerson has held various leadership roles in marketing, sales, and products at Elsevier since 2009; the common thread has been a passionate determination to expand awareness of STEM books into libraries and to consumers. She has extensive experience in the e-book industry, having created and maintained partnerships with key channel partners aimed at ensuring breadth of availability in library choice for content acquisition. She has been an invited speaker and contributed to published works in the area of digital technologies and accessibility. She is passionate about the intersection of reading, research, and education, and is based in the United States.

Amanda Glimstedt has held the position of teaching librarian at the Gothenburg University's Social Science Libraries since 2018 and is team coordinator for the Social Sciences Libraries' teaching team. In addition, she works with research support, with particular focus on literature reviews. Amanda holds an MLIS and has previously worked as a teacher and programme coordinator at the Swedish School of Library and Information Science (SSLIS) at the University of Borås. Her academic and professional interests focus primarily on learning, literacies, pedagogy, and the university library's pedagogical function, particularly in relation to digital tools and environments, as well as researchers' information practices and scholarly publication.

Martin Hamilton is a widely published writer, public speaker, strategist, and change agent. His work focuses on helping people and organizations to understand the impact of near-future trends and technologies. Martin has worked extensively with senior teams in various organizations to help them develop their innovation strategy, and supported a large number of start-ups to scale up their business. Martin has worked in and around the intersection of research and industry for some 30 years, doing everything from researching next-generation Internet protocols to running a supercomputer centre.

Graeme Hawley is Head of General Collections at the National Library of Scotland, where he is responsible for 20th- and 21st-century publications. From a collection of over 14 million printed things, this collection has grown extensively since 2013 with the further addition of 5 million published collection items and 10 million archived websites. His team of curators are responsible for curating this collection, from the selection of collection content to interpretation activities, research collaborations, and audience engagement. He is on various subgroups of the Legal Deposit Libraries Implementation Group in the United Kingdom. He has worked at the National Library of Scotland since 2002 and is a chartered member of CILIP.

Scott Henderson is an IT and business transformation consultant with over 30 years of experience in the delivery of large-scale projects in the UK Public Sector within local and central government organizations. He has had a long and varied career, including working with the National Health Service and various UK government offices such as the Department for Work and Pensions, the Ministry for Justice, and the Cabinet Office. He also has much experience in the private sector, including the major banks HBOS plc, Lloyds Banking Group, and Barclays. He is a keen author, having contributed to previous published works and won a poetry competition on the subject of "accidental love." A strong advocate of leveraging digital solutions, Scott is passionate in believing that many positives can be taken from the current pandemic for individuals, businesses, and the planet in general.

Carl Gustav Johannsen is Emeritus Professor at the University of Copenhagen. He has written and contributed to more than 20 books and several international articles, conference papers, and reports on different public, academic, and special library issues. Recently, he has, in particular, focused on innovative staff design, like the staffless or open public library model, and also on the various roles that the users today play in modern public library environments as clients, citizens, guests, customers, and creative partners. He has also contributed to the library history literature, especially on special library issues.

Paul Kirkham is owner and Chief Executive of the Institute of Contemporary Music Performance (ICMP), a London-based independent provider of higher education for students of popular music. Paul acquired the institute in 2003, following a 15-year career as a senior business executive with a major multinational company, during which time he managed large and complex companies all over the world. In recent years, Paul has overseen a major programme of investment and development at the ICMP, which now enrols over 1000 full-time students across a range of undergraduate and postgraduate courses. The ICMP's reputation has been built on providing high-quality, specialist education and training, deploying the best teachers and industry practitioners in state-of-the-art facilities, and engaging extensively with the music industry in the development of career opportunities for graduates. In addition to his role at the ICMP, Paul is also Director at GuildHE, one of the United Kingdom's two formally recognized representative bodies for providers of higher education.

David Kjellin is a librarian at the Social Sciences Libraries, Gothenburg University, where he teaches information searching and works with support for researchers, in particular systematic reviews.

Carlos Lopes is currently Director of the Documentation Center, Assistant Professor at ISPA, and Guest Professor at Universidade Nova de Lisboa. In addition, he is integrated researcher at the Applied Psychology Research Center Capabilities & Inclusion (APPsyCI) and Director of the Graduate Program in Health Literacy: models, strategies and intervention at ISPA-Instituto Universitário. He has developed research in the areas of health literacy, electronic resources, and the development of digital skills. His current research interests include information literacy (digital resources), learning processes in higher education, and health literacy programmes. He was a member of Scielo PORTUGAL (2006–17) and has published several papers in national and international journals and book chapters, and presented his research at national and international conferences. His main research interests are information literacy and research resources inserted in the teaching-learning processes of university students.

Juan D. Machin-Mastromatteo is a full-time professor and researcher at the Universidad Autónoma de Chihuahua (UACH) in Mexico and a member of the National Researchers System. He holds a PhD in information and communication science, a master's degree in digital library learning, and a bachelor's degree in library science. He has more than 18 years of work experience in archives, libraries, higher education, and professional development. His lines of research include information literacy, action research, evaluation of scientific production and bibliometrics, open access, information architecture, and digital libraries. He has published over 60 peer-reviewed and indexed articles, 7 books, and 19 book chapters, and has presented his papers in 60 international conferences. He is Associate Editor for *Information Development* (SAGE) and *Digital Library Perspectives* (Emerald), and is Editorial Board Member for the *Journal of Academic Librarianship* (Elsevier). From 2015 to 2020, he published the regular column Developing Latin America in *Information Development*. He is peer reviewer for 20 scientific and indexed journals, for which he has evaluated over 250 manuscripts.

Richard Maidment-Otlet has a deep understanding of EdTech implementation and marketing in the education and research sectors, built on many years of experience at director level at Jisc. He has extensive practical leadership experience in brand strategy, implementation, and re-branding bringing Jisc together under one brand. He has also been the lead on many of Jisc's flagship activities, including Europe's leading EdTech conference, Digifest. He was also the lead on Jisc's Libraries of the Future campaign. With a doctorate in education (EdD), his research experience is focused on EdTech and the student experience in tertiary education. This has enriched his understanding of the practical and real-life issues and implications of technology changes across the institution.

Rosanna Mann is a social researcher with 10 years of experience embedding evidence into policy design and delivery. She has a research background in higher education and has worked for a range of government departments. Her chapter has been written on behalf of the Association of Commonwealth Universities (ACU), which is accredited by the United Nations and the Commonwealth. It is an international organization dedicated to building a better world through higher education. With over 500 member universities across 50 countries, the ACU's international network spans more than 10 million students and over a million academic and professional staff.

Rob May has worked in the education and social impact sectors for 20 years. He is currently the CEO of ABE, a not-for-profit multinational skills development organization and examination board specializing in business and entrepreneurship education. With a special interest in entrepreneurship in emerging economies, Rob has frequently advised on policy development and has appeared as an expert commentator in the media across Africa, Southeast Asia, the Caribbean, and the United Kingdom on issues ranging from exams policy to economic development to geopolitical affairs. In 2019, Rob was honoured as a Friend of UNESCO by Princess Victoria Adejoke Orelope-Adefulire of Nigeria for his work on actualizing the UN Sustainable Development Goals.

Sarah Mears is Programme Manager for Libraries Connected (formerly Society of Chief Librarians). Her role includes developing projects which deliver quality, innovation, and workforce development for public library services in England, Wales, and Northern Ireland. Prior to this, Sarah was Library Services Manager for Essex County Council. Sarah was Chair of the Association of Senior Children's and Education Librarians for almost 4 years. She is Director and one of five founders of Empathy Lab, a not-for-profit organization that works with schools, libraries, and authors to build children's empathy skills through the creative use of literature. In recent years, Sarah has been commissioned by the British Council to train librarians and teachers in Pakistan and Bangladesh. She has also presented at librarians' conferences in Turkey and in Belgium. Sarah was awarded an MBE for Services to Children and Young People in the Queen's Birthday Honours in June 2018.

Katarina Michnik has a PhD in library and information science. The focus of her doctoral thesis is how the social legitimacy of public libraries may be challenged and strengthened in digital contexts. Katarina is particularly interested in the role and use of libraries in digital societies, and how information is searched for, disseminated, and evaluated through different online tools, including social media. Katarina is now working as an academic librarian at the University of Gothenburg. Her current research project is on PhD librarians' roles and situations at academic libraries in Sweden.

Valentini Moniarou-Papaconstantinou is Emeritus Professor at the Department of Library Science and Information Systems of the Technological Educational Institute of Athens, now the Department of Archival, Library and Information Studies, University of West Attica, Athens, Greece. She taught information organizations management and collection management, and has given lectures on these topics in courses hosted by various organizations in Greece. Her research interests include a theorization of changes in the information field and information services management, LIS students' educational choices and their learning careers, as well as the understanding of information technology acceptance by LIS students. She has given talks and presentations at several international conferences, and her research publications have appeared in international journals such as *Education for Information, Aslib Journal of Information Management, Library and Information Science Research, New Library World, Library Management, Program, Library Review*, and *Journal of Librarianship and Information Science*.

Anna Nunn is currently a graduate trainee librarian at the University of Suffolk. In her role, she supervises the library front of house and helps ensure the smooth running of the service. As her traineeship progresses, she will assist with collections development and teaching provision. Anna is currently undertaking a postgraduate qualification in information science at Northumbria University; her specific research interests include information literacy, information inequality, and information-seeking anxiety. She graduated from the University of East Anglia in July 2018 with a bachelor's degree in English literature. While studying, she was an occasional library and information advisor with Suffolk Libraries. Anna joined the Department of Library and Learning Services at the University of Suffolk in 2018 as a library assistant, and was shortly thereafter seconded into the post of Library Services Assistant.

Andy Phippen is Professor of Digital Rights at Bournemouth University, United Kingdom, and is Visiting Professor at the University of Suffolk, United Kingdom. He has specialized in the use of ICTs in social contexts and the intersection with legislation for over 15 years, carrying out a large amount of grass roots research on issues such as attitudes toward privacy and data protection, Internet safety, and contemporary issues such as sexting, peer abuse, and the impact of digital technology on well-being. He has presented oral and written evidence to parliamentary inquiries related to the use of ICTs in society, is widely published in the area, and is a frequent media commentator on these issues.

José Refugio Romo-González is a full-time professor and researcher at the Universidad Autónoma de Chihuahua (UACH) in Mexico and a member of the National Researchers System. He holds a PhD in administration; is a PhD candidate in education; and holds master degrees in quality and innovation management, information and knowledge management, marketing, administration, and sciences. He also holds a bachelor's degree in agricultural engineering. He was a technical advisor for the Ministry of Agriculture and Hydraulic Resources at the State of Aguascalientes (Mexico) and evaluated investment projects at the Bank of Mexico in Puebla. He has authored diverse articles, books, and book chapters. His lines of research include evaluation of scientific production and communication, information literacy, and knowledge and innovation management.

Rick Rylance is Emeritus Professor and Dean of the School of Advanced Study at the University of London. Prior to that, he was PVC for Research at London, Director of the Institute of English Studies, CEO of the Arts and Humanities Research Council (AHRC), and Executive Chair of Research Councils UK (RCUK), in which capacity he was heavily involved in early debates about open access publication. He held decanal roles at Exeter and Anglia Ruskin universities, and chaired several public bodies in research and education. He has published widely on 19th- and 20th-century literary topics as well as *Victorian Psychology and British Culture 1850–1880* (2000) and *Literature and the Public Good* (2016). He is presently writing the *Oxford English Literary History of the Mid-Twentieth Century*.

Tatiana Sanches is a researcher in the Unit for Research and Development in Education and Training of the Institute of Education (UIDEF, University of Lisbon). She also collaborates with the APPsyCI (Applied Psychology Research Center Capabilities & Inclusion) at ISPA (Institute of Applied Psychology—University Institute). Currently, she is Head of the Documentation Division at the Faculty of Psychology and Institute of Education (University of Lisbon). She has been working in the field of public libraries since 1993 (initially in a professional-technical position and then as a librarian) and of university libraries since 2007. Her research is on topics such as information literacy, university libraries, library management, and academic writing, among others, having already published several books, chapters, and articles, both nationally and internationally.

Joachim Schöpfel is Associate Professor in information sciences at the University of Lille, France, and a researcher at the GERiiCO laboratory. He is a consultant in scientific communication at the Ourouk consulting bureau, Paris. His research fields are scientific information and academic publishing, research data, and open science.

Lucy Shackleton has a background developing and influencing policy in local, national, and international contexts, across science, higher education, and international relations. She led European and international engagement for Universities UK, including in the immediate aftermath of the Brexit vote. She has also held positions at King's College London and the London School of Economics and Political Science. Her chapter has been written on behalf of the Association of Commonwealth Universities (ACU), which is accredited by the United Nations and the Commonwealth. It is an international organization dedicated to building a better world through higher education. With over 500 member universities across 50 countries, the ACU's international network spans more than 10 million students and over a million academic and professional staff.

Yi Shen holds a PhD in information studies from the University of Wisconsin-Madison and was Associate Professor at Virginia Tech. She undertakes quantitative and qualitative social informatics research on topics such as data science practice and scholarly information behaviour; data management, stewardship, and reproducibility; and intelligent infrastructure, transdisciplinary landscape, and library innovation; as well as global engineering education and cross-cultural competency. Her previous appointments include the NSF-funded International Research and Education in

Engineering postdoctoral researcher at Purdue University and the Council on Library and Information Resources postdoctoral fellow at Johns Hopkins University. Shen has led data landscape mapping and research environment assessment efforts, and has instrumented socio-technical empirical research to identify and address disciplinary and transdisciplinary research engagement and data mobilization challenges. Shen has served on various national and international committees and advisory boards, and is currently Associate Editor of Higher Education Pedagogies. Her academic record is available at http://johnshopkins.academia.edu/YiShen.

Bulcsu Szekely is a researcher at Lappeenranta-Lahti University of Technology (LUT), formerly Lappeenranta University of Technology in 2005. His research interests are concentrated on supply chain management, logistics IT systems, eLearning platforms, and academic project coordination. He has published one book and two scientific peer-reviewed articles as a single author, and coauthored several other articles as well as conference papers. He is an experienced researcher with a demonstrated history of working in the research industry with organizations such as the Turku Chamber of Commerce, University of Vaasa, and Haaga-Helia University of Applied Sciences Ltd. Mr. Szekely is a member of the International Society for Professional Innovation Management (ISPIM) and has been recently invited to join the Association of Certified E-Discovery Specialists (ACEDS).

Daniella Smith is an associate professor in the Department of Information Science at the University of North Texas. She has been a faculty member since 2010 and is the current Associate Director of the Information Science PhD programme. She is the author of the book *Growing Your Library Career with Social Media* from Chandos Publishing (2018).

Javier Tarango is a full-time professor and researcher at the Universidad Autónoma de Chihuahua (UACH) in Mexico and a member of the National Researchers System. He holds a PhD in education and a master's degree in information science and in organizational development. He has been the president of five international conferences (Transborder Library Forum, 2005; Mexican Librarianship Conference, 2008; Trejo Foster Foundation Institute, 2012; International Symposium of Higher Education, 2013; International Conference on the Digital Divide and Social Inclusion, 2014; the UNAM-IIBI Information and Society Seminar, 2018). He is a member of the Institute Agustín Millares Carlo of Documentation and Information Management at the Universidad Carlos III Madrid. His lines of research include evaluation of scientific production and communication, knowledge and innovation management, and information literacy.

Sandra Tury is Associate Director of Online Library Services at the University of London Worldwide (UoLWW), where she has worked since 2005. She is responsible for developing and managing the university's online library service which supports over 48,000 students and faculty from over 180 countries of the world. She is also a dissertation tutor on two distance learning masters programmes. Sandra holds a doctorate in information science (information-seeking behaviour in distance learning) from City University of London, an MSc in information technology, and a bachelor's degree in library and information studies from Loughborough University. She has extensive experience of managing and developing resources to support teaching learning and research, with particular strength in e-resources, library management systems, resources discovery tools, and authentication systems, and has recently led the Implementation of the "Summon" Resource Discovery tool, the Open Athens Single Sign-On, and the embedding of Information Literacy into a number of UoLWW programmes.

Evgenia Vassilakaki is an SNE in IT project management at the European Insurance and Occupational Pensions Authority (EIOPA). She was awarded a doctoral degree in May 2011 from the Department of Information & Communications at Manchester Metropolitan University, Manchester, United Kingdom, on Multilingual Information Retrieval and Users' Information Seeking Behaviour. For the past 10 years, she has taken part in research projects in various contexts, including business administration, public/private sector, cultural heritage, and the refugee crisis. These projects were on a national level (i.e., THALIS DOCCULTURE, Consultant to Greek Ministry of Education) and European level (i.e., CrossCult H2020, Erasmus + Lib(e)ro, Europeana "Rise of Literacy") and involved different positions of responsibility and role, for example, as member, coordinator, team and work package leader, and deputy and member of a management board. Her research interests lie in information-seeking behaviour, LIS roles and information services offered, information literacy, and multilingual information retrieval and access. She has published in international peer-reviewed journals such as *Library and Information Science Research*, *New Library World*, *Library Management*, *Program*, and *Library Review*.

Tim Wales has been Head of Library Services at Brunel University London, Uxbridge, United Kingdom, since January 2020. In the previous decade, he held research/academic library leadership positions at Rothamsted Research, the University of West London and London Business School, after "earning his stripes" as a manager at Royal Holloway, University of London, a subject librarian at the Open University (Milton Keynes), and a researcher at a boutique investment bank. His first job after graduating from the University of East Anglia was as a trade journalist in the furniture industry before he completed his MSc in information science at City, University London. Tim has written on a diverse range of professional topics, including library strategy, business librarianship, library technologies, information literacy, and veterinarian information-seeking behaviour. He is a chartered member of CILIP, a fellow of the Higher Education Academy, and an editorial board member of the *New Review of Academic Librarianship*.

Jane Winters is Professor of Digital Humanities and Pro-Dean for Libraries and Digital at the School of Advanced Study, University of London. She has led or codirected a range of digital projects in partnership with GLAM institutions, including Big UK Domain Data for the Arts and Humanities (with the British Library) and Traces Through Time: Prosopography in Practice across Big Data (with The National Archives of the United Kingdom). She is a coinvestigator for the Towards a National Collection foundation project Heritage Connector. Jane's research interests include digital history, born-digital archives (particularly the archived web), the use of social media by cultural heritage institutions, and scholarly communication. She has published most recently on non-print legal deposit and web archives, born-digital archives and the problem of search, and the archiving and analysis of national web domains.

Sayeda Zain has been working in higher education for more than 20 years. She worked for the British Council in Pakistan for 7 years as a UK Education Manager. She is currently working as Dean of Studies at Mont Rose College in London. She has four master's degrees: PGCert Learning and Teaching from the Anglia Ruskin University, United Kingdom, 2019; MSc International Management from University of Wales Newport, United Kingdom, 2008; MSc Strategic Human Resource Management from University of Glamorgan, United Kingdom, 2007; and MBA from Al-Hajvery College of Business Administration, 1994. She has a Level 8 qualification in Strategic Direction and Leadership from the Chartered Management Institute, and is also a fellow of Advance HE. She has completed a high-impact leadership course from the University of Cambridge Institute of Sustainability Leadership and strategic alignment course from the University of Oxford. She is a member of the Mont Rose College Board of Governors and the Academic/Quality Assurance Board. She initiated the formation of the MRC Research Centre and the associated research journal published biannually since 2015.

Acknowledgements

The editors are especially grateful to all who made this book possible: the authors of the chapters for their contributions and their enthusiasm for the project; to all those who contributed Thought Pieces: Diana Harris, Sarah Mears, Hannah Myers, Ted O'Hare, and Cliff Wragg.

We are grateful to all Delphi panellists: Stephen Akintunde, Rissa Amper, Amir Reza Asnafi, Agnes S. Barsaga, Chris Batt, Prasanna Iyer, Jay Jani, Nandkumar Kamat, B.U. Kannappanavar, Salma Khan, A. Mallikarjuna, Arthur Bryan C. Mariano, Shaharima Parvin, Pushpanjali Shriram Patil, Gurunath Ramanathan, Syuqran Rohaizad, Septi, Tejas Shah, B. Siva, Akhmad Syaikhu, Bulcsu Szekely, J. Varadharajalu, and Upasana Yadav.

Thanks are due to our interviewees: Chris Batt, Coral Black, Alice Colban, Anne Goulding, Scott Henderson, Louise Jones, Stuart Lee, Maja Maricevic, Chris O'Gorman, Tony Staneff, and Alan Wilson.

We would also like to thank Glyn Jones for his support in establishing the book proposal, to Zachary Smith for the index and abbreviations list, and to Chiara Giglio and Surya Narayanan Jayachandran at Elsevier for their help in the preparation and production of this book.

David Baker
Lucy Ellis

Abbreviations

ACU	Association of Commonwealth Universities
AI	artificial intelligence
ALC	active learning classroom
APC	article processing charges
APPsyCI	Applied Psychology Research Center Capabilities and Inclusion, Lisboa, Portugal
BAME	Black, Asian, and Minority Ethnic
BAU	business as usual
BBC	British Broadcasting Corporation
BHO	British History Online
BIREME	Latin American and Caribbean Centre on Health Sciences Information
BUL	Brunel University London
CASEL	Collaborative for Social, Emotional and Academic Learning
CDL	controlled digital lending
CILIP	Chartered Institute of Library and Information Professionals
CLA	UK Copyright Licensing Agency
CNAC	Copyright Negotiating and Advisory Committee
CORD-19	The US COVID-19 Open Research Dataset
COVID-19	coronavirus disease 2019
CPAG	Child Poverty Action Group
CTS	CoreTrustSeal
DSA	data seal of approval
DZHW	German Institute for Higher Education Research and Science Studies, Berlin Germany
EIOPA	European Insurance and Occupational Pensions Authority
eLib	Electronic Libraries Programme
EOSC	European Open Science Cloud
ESTeSL	Instituto Politécnico de Lisboa, Lisboa, Portugal
ETL	Edinburgh Tool Library
FAANG	Facebook, Apple, Amazon, Netflix, and Google
FAIR	findable, accessible, interoperable, reusable
HCQ	hydroxychloroquine
HE	Higher Education
HEI	Higher Education Institution
HELMET	Helsinki Metropolitan Area Libraries
HEPI	Higher Education Policy Institute
HF	Hackspace Foundation database
HKUST	Hong Kong University of Science and Technology
HNCs	Higher National Certificates

ICMP	Institute of Contemporary Music Performance
ICPSR	Inter-University Consortium for Political and Social Research
ICSU	International Council for Science
ICT/s	Information and Communications Technology/ies
ICTRP	International Clinical Trials Registry Platform
IFLA	International Federation of Library Associations
IPL	International Poverty Line
ISB	information-seeking behaviour
ISPA	Instituto Universitário, Lisbon, Portugal
JICA	Japan International Cooperation Agency
LGBT	Lesbian, Gay, Bisexual and Transgender
LGBTTQQIAAP	Lesbian, Gay, Bisexual, Transgender, Transsexual, Queer, Questioning, Intersex, Asexual, Ally, Pansexual
LIS	Library and Information Science
LMS	Library/Learning Management System
MAP-1	multilevel antimicrobial polymer
MOOC	Massive Online Open Course
MS	Microsoft
NFER	National Foundation for Educational Research
NGO	Non-Governmental Organisation
OECD	Organization for Economic Cooperation and Development
OfS	Office for Students
OFSTED	Office for Standards in Education
OLL	The University of London's Online Library
ONS	Office for National Statistics
OSCCA	Office for Student Complaints, Conduct and Appeals
PCs	personal computers
PIAAC	OECD's Survey of Adult Skills
PLE	principle of least effort
PPE	personal protective equipment
RRS	Residual Risk Score
SAS	School of Advanced Study
SCONUL	Society of College, National and University Libraries
SEL	social and emotional learning
SES	socioeconomic status
SES	Student Experience Survey
SSHRC	Social Sciences and Humanities Research Council
SSRN	Social Science Research Network
STEM	Science, Technology, Engineering and Mathematics
STI	Science, Technology, and Innovation
TNA	The National Archives (of the United Kingdom)
UCM	Complutense University of Madrid
UIDEF	Instituto da Educação, Universidade de Lisboa, Lisboa, Portugal
UN	United Nations
UNC	University of North Carolina at Chapel Hill
UNESCO	United Nations Educational, Scientific and Cultural Organisation
UNICEF	United Nations Children's Fund
UNPF	United Nations Population Fund
UOS	University of Suffolk

VLE	virtual learning environment
VPN	virtual private network
WDS	World Data System
WFH	working from home
WHO	World Health Organization

Libraries, digital information, and COVID: Practical applications and approaches to challenge and change

1

David Baker[a,b] *and Lucy Ellis*[b,c]
[a]Professor Emeritus, Plymouth Marjon University, Plymouth, United Kingdom, [b]David Baker Consulting, West Yorkshire, United Kingdom, [c]University of Exeter, Exeter, United Kingdom

1 Introduction

The world has been turned upside down by COVID-19. It is one of the most serious health emergencies the world has faced in the past 100 years. The virus has affected—and will continue to affect—every aspect of human activity. The pandemic has already resulted in serious social, organizational, logistical, economic, and political problems that require both immediate and longer-term solutions. COVID-19 will not disappear any time soon; nor will it be the last major threat of its kind that humanity will face in the future.

This book describes the significant and often devastating effects that have already been experienced—and will continue to be experienced—all around the globe. It tells of the way in which individuals, organizations, sectors, and countries have responded, often with significant success in difficult circumstances; and of the opportunities that are being created and seized for innovation and development in ways and at a pace that few would have predicted until that fateful discovery in Wuhan in late 2019 changed our world forever. Each and every chapter provides a range of perspectives on the present and likely future impact of the pandemic and its aftermath, including academic, public, and special libraries, those which support teaching and those which are focussed on research. There is a strong emphasis on experiences in different countries, in both northern and southern hemispheres, and Third-world contexts are considered.

The focus here is on libraries and digital information, though the range of contributions commissioned and selected for this book is deliberately broad, given the all-encompassing nature of COVID-19, its effects, and the likely long tail of recovery from the pandemic. Not only are experiences and exemplars drawn from a wide range of environments, scenarios, and sectors, but the case studies specific to library and information provision that underpin much of this publication have a much wider relevance and potential application that just their core constituencies. As Jeremy Atkinson notes in Chapter 29, strategies and solutions that work for libraries may have relevance for retail and service sectors, and vice versa.

This has been an unprecedented crisis, and it's been completely global – all facing essentially the same problem.

> Tony Blair, quoted in Times Higher Education 7 January 2021

2 Immediate operational responses

Part One looks at the immediate responses to the pandemic and reveals a remarkable—but not entirely surprising—degree of commonality—the "re-massification" to which Graeme Hawley refers in Chapter 28. While the decision-making processes and the detailed timings varied from sector to sector and country to country, physical access to library buildings and services was almost universally barred at some point and for some time during the earlier phases of the pandemic. Limited reopening has subsequently been allowed in some cases, depending on in-country approaches and the relative severity of infection, transmission, and death rates. Often, however, offering (at least some) physical access has been followed by further (total) closure as governments have periodically imposed lockdowns in light of deteriorating conditions. Some library users were hit especially hard, as Lucy Shackleton and Rosa Mann (Chapter 16), Daniella Smith (Chapter 23) and, in a different context, Jane Winters, relate.

> *It is the nature of research libraries that they will hold rare or unique printed materials, often alongside special collections. These became immediately inaccessible when libraries closed.*
>
> Jane Winters, Chapter 8

This book, nevertheless, demonstrates that while COVID-19 and its effects were not well or easily anticipated, as noted by Carl Gustav Johannsen in Chapter 5 and Rob May in Chapter 15 ("the pandemic exposed both the weaknesses of conventional continuity planning practices"), many library systems were well prepared, in part because of the ongoing trend towards digital and hence remote access and the often-significant investment in e-resources over many years, as catalogued in Chapter 7, among others. This is not to underestimate the significant "effort and ingenuity" involved in responding "with almost no notice" to the needs of users and staff alike (Jane Winters, Chapter 8). Chapters 2 and 3, in particular, describe how two academic libraries—one in Hong Kong and the other in the United Kingdom—approached the provision of access and services—both physically and remotely—as soon as the pandemic hit. Diana Chan and Victoria Caplan stress the crucial importance of adaptability, flexibility, and good communication as they adopted a series of proactive measures to reach a "new normal" in delivery, while at the same time ensuring the health and safety of both staff and users. Similarly, Carl Gustav Johannsen (Chapter 5) gives a frank account of the Danish public library system's response to COVID-19 to date, while Sarah Mears (Chapter 24) focusses on the work and potential of public libraries in the United Kingdom, with special reference to families, children, and young people.

In March 2020 as the UK's public library buildings closed, public libraries swiftly transformed, moving events and activities to their online platforms, and improving access to electronic books and resources. Children's events and activities were the first to be delivered digitally, demonstrating libraries' determination to maintain contact with children and to keep them engaged with purposeful activity, books and reading. From early years rhyme times to lego clubs, reading groups and challenges, author events, crafts and performances, libraries demonstrated endless creativity. Whilst restrictions are in place libraries have continued to develop their online presence, improving quality and range. As we look to a post COVID-19 future, the creative potential of blended physical and digital activity is exciting.

However, there is growing concern about the children who are being left behind – those who do not have access to digital resources, who have missed out on learning and social development, whose families are struggling with poverty and those who are experiencing anxiety, loneliness, and poor mental health.

Sarah Mears, MBE, Programme Manager, Libraries Connected, United Kingdom

It could be said that library and information services, their leaders, and their staffs, have, to date, "had a good COVID crisis" (Chapter 3). They have responded efficiently, effectively, speedily, innovatively, imaginatively, ingeniously. Libraries around the world coped and coped well, including through cooperation, collaboration, and transition, especially where a flexible approach was adopted. They have not only provided exemplars for other libraries, but also for other sectors. Librarians have balanced the needs of the users and their staff's needs (Chapter 23, for example) and been seen as leaders beyond the library, with their essential key skills proving valuable within their wider communities. Much has been learned that will be well applied in the future. Resilience and commitment have been in abundant evidence.

There was more than one point of urgency in the immediate response to the pandemic. One was in relation to the everyday users and communications with users on the decision to close. Dealing with impacts on users and any reactions to the closure was one of the priorities. At the same time, staff support and safety was a priority. Dealing with messages about the unfolding situation, staff safety, job security, business continuation etc demanded huge attention. Also running alongside these priorities was the problem of the security of collections. Keeping collections safe and secure was vital and some collections needed great care. All these issues were co-occurring.

Senior manager, national library, United Kingdom

[The organization's] immediate priority was survival, since it is anticipated that there will be 18 months - two years of reduced income. Innovation and new development work was therefore stopped. Subsequently, the position taken … has been one of projecting confidence and optimism and providing support for when the virus is under control and we arrive at a future.

Senior UK library professional

Priorities were set by a twice-weekly business continuity planning meeting in IT. This looked at anything that came up. There was an action plan, a risk register, feedback from other meetings such as a bronze operational group, bronze strategic decision-making group and a silver group. There was a spin off group for making exams happen. At the service level there was service continuity planning already in existence. This helped in that there was a clear governance structure to deal with it. The structure held up due to good leadership, good communication and everyone rallied round. Reacting to government announcements has not been easy.

Senior IT manager, UK university

The immediate response of the sector was, in general, not organized. Health libraries immediately supported Health and Social Care workers with the information they needed for research and practice; while public libraries remained open to begin with, but then had to close and switch to digital. School libraries supported teachers to figure out how to deliver online teaching, while in the corporate area, information professionals were an active part of helping companies to keep running.

Senior library professional, United Kingdom

This has not been a universal experience, however. Akintunde's study (Chapter 26) talks of the "battered" services that now exist in sub-Saharan Africa and the toll which COVID-19 has already taken on them, but also, as Rob May stresses in Chapter 15, there has been a determination in many Third-world countries to be creative in their response to the pandemic.

Some publishers' willingness to vary their supply and funding models have also been welcomed, though possible changes in pricing structures in the longer term (as well as more immediate price increases and variations) are worrying many librarians, as exemplified by comments in many chapters. Sam Brenton and Sandra Tury (Chapter 10) focus in particular on current and likely future difficulties with regard to copyright and digital library development. Witness Martin Hamilton's comment in Chapter 27 about the amount of publicly funded research that is still inaccessible and Sam Brenton and Sandra Tury's concerns regarding future e-book purchases (Chapter 10). As Tim Wales stresses (Chapter 3), the development of future costing, pricing, and publishing policies and frameworks is becoming pressing. Melissa Fulkerson responds from a publisher viewpoint in Chapter 17. Andy Phippen and Emma Bond (Chapter 22) and Evgenia Vasilakaki and Valentini Moniarou-Papaconstantinou (Chapter 7) underline the crucial role libraries have to play in tackling not only the pandemic but also the "infodemic" that has taken hold, while Otmane Azeroual and Joachim Schöpfel (Chapter 18) review how the pressing need—in the light of the pandemic in particular—for trustworthy data repositories can best be achieved. In this context—and in terms of the pandemic more broadly—libraries have not been slow to set up COVID collections for the future, as for example at the National Library of Scotland (Chapter 28).

The trustworthiness of libraries, museums and archives is going to become much more important with the advent of fake news, anti-vaxxers etc. People now value the fact that they can 'visit' the library, or the museum without physically going there.

Former public sector chief executive

The library has been working hard on preserving the pandemic experience for future generations. There has been a great deal of collecting. There have been special COVID collections, especially online ones. There has also been a lot of work on the website and social media and different informal projects. There will be no shortage of COVID collections, scholarly or otherwise.

Senior manager, national library

3 New operating models

The basic assumption underpinning the responses described in part One has been that provision of access to collections and delivery of services (the "lockdown library") will largely be done remotely and therefore, wherever possible, digitally, especially in academic libraries, according to Atkinson (Chapter 29), though "click-and-collect" services, allowing access to physical stock, have also been available, as have bookable slots for entry to buildings to use library materials. Indeed, such a move was inevitable as part of a broader movement towards remote working, studying, teaching, learning, and living. Even in specialist research subject areas, at least secondary material was available online and therefore still accessible (Chapter 8).

As Jane Winters points out in Chapter 8, the challenge—and, indeed, the opportunity—has been not only to aim for "business as usual" in library provision but to go beyond basic access and service provision through creative approaches wherever possible. Locking down physical provision has forced libraries to build on the best and most relevant of existing delivery and services, and created opportunities for innovation, a theme that permeates this book.

Lucy Shackleton and Rosanna Mann (Chapter 16) talk of "the great pivot online" though the extent to which this has happened to date—and is likely to continue to happen—varies considerably depending on the wealth of particular countries or income groups, as Carl Gustav Johannsen (Chapter 5), Stephen Akintunde (Chapter 26), and Sarah Mears (Chapter 24) all point out. "The digital divide is one of the very biggest issues that will have to be solved. A solution is not on the horizon" (Delphi participant), despite the significant investment over many years now, as Rob May points out in Chapter 15, though Sam Brenton and Sandra Tury (Chapter 10) believe that the barriers to equitable digital provision are not insuperable. It is more than digital divides, though: it is economic, educational, social, and more, as Graeme Hawley concludes (Chapter 28), though Rob May (Chapter 15) notes that "COVID-19 has in one sense had a levelling effect, as access to technology, money, and resources was unable to guarantee consistency and quality in education provision, whether the student was living in Surrey or Suriname."

In Chapter 21, Evgenia Vasilakaki and Valentini Moniarou-Papaconstantinou provide a useful list of the main transitions, summarized here as:

- Shift to teleworking
- Promotion of existing online information services—e-journals, e-books, databases, material from digital libraries, and institutional repositories
- Greater use of websites, social media accounts, e-learning platforms
- Support for online requests for digitization
- Online distribution of material

- Development and promotion of online information literacy programmes and courses
- Enhancement of users' digital information competencies
- Response to the need for information on COVID-19
- Support for users in the identification of fake news

In addition, some systems, such as the School of Advanced Study (SAS) at the University of London (Chapter 8), prioritized discoverability, the building of virtual communities of interest and the co-creation of a knowledge base as a way of replacing the loss of physical access to libraries.

All this has quickly resulted in new operating principles (such as those noted by Paul Kirkham in Chapter 25) and implementation models, as described in detail in later chapters, including with reference to specific libraries, both public and academic. Ellen Buck and Anna Nunn (Chapter 11) talk of the "lift and shift" of existing provision from physical to virtual, though Sam Brenton and Sandra Tury (Chapter 10) describe the time and effort in creating a full digital library as well as the fundamental need for robust and resilient infrastructural capacity to meet significantly increased demand—something that was not always available, as noted in many contributions to this book, including Chapter 16, by Lucy Shackleton and Rosa Mann.

COVID-19 has affected roles and responsibilities in that teaching online is different and consideration has to be given to how this is approached. While teaching postgraduates online is normal and unproblematic, teaching undergraduates this way is a challenge due to lower levels of engagement. It's a case of finding different ways to engage the students and 'scaffolding' them more. Moving teaching online does not 'transfer' from face to face in the same way as it does with postgraduates.

Senior academic, New Zealand

Amanda Glimstedt, David Kjellin, and Katarina Michnik (Chapter 4) also stress the resource-intensive nature of going digital, not least the rapid rise in the need for bandwidth through teleworking, along with a whole range of other infrastructural considerations, including the need for greater cybersecurity.

One of the biggest challenges of all was the fact that the IT infrastructure was only scaled for 10 – 20% staff working remotely. Overnight, systems had to be adapted for mass working at home. There were risk factors which had to be urgently dealt with and major concerns turned out to be unfounded, namely in terms of resilience of the IT system. Senior members of council staff had to focus on COVID-related priorities which meant that staff on lower management tiers were tasked with finding solutions to ensure the programmes of work continued to plan. People just got on with it and did it. This exercise re-defined the project timescale of what can be achieved in an 18-month programme.

Senior IT consultant, United Kingdom

Similarly, while Carl Gustav Johannsen (Chapter 5) notes that the closure of buildings and hence the transition to remote working have had a positive effect on productivity and—provided the organization has put appropriate facilities and support in place (Henderson, Chapter 9)—staff wellbeing, he also remarks that digital only cannot provide everything required of the public library, at least for the foreseeable future. The same is likely to be true of other types of library provision, as discussed later in this book.

4 Digital developments: From place to space

So the balance between the physical and the digital is changing rapidly, and will continue to transition, with educational establishments, at least in the west, delivering digitally, though many authors think that there will be a rebalancing back towards physical provision as the effects of the pandemic recede. It will be some time before physical provision and delivery is fully trusted again, however.

> *Physical visits to campus have reduced to such an extent that campus seems empty (to one-third of pre-COVID levels; even though 50% of seating is available). The 'Commons' area is now a Zoom zone at 70 per cent occupancy allowing students to actively participate in online learning without worrying about disturbing others. It is not expected that physical presence on campus/f2f teaching will return for a while. Areas such as The Makerspace and Digital Scholarship Lab are oriented to physical presence because of the need to use equipment, but people are just not coming onto campus.*
>
> *University librarian, South East Asia*

> *The University has used the IT tools that are already available to alleviate the worst effects of COVID-19. Zoom is used a lot and also the i-conferencing software. The Centre for Academic Development and the Information Technology Services have been helpful. Lectures have been recorded and flipped classrooms are supported by Blackboard. Physical space has been used differently during the pandemic. For instance, a Zoom room has been set up with optimal equipment and good lighting.*
>
> *Senior academic, New Zealand*

The serious need for sustainable off-premises (digital) access has been evident from the start of the present crisis. While offering a physical space to read and study will remain important, recent events have triggered a significant shift towards off-site working and study, making online access to information crucial. Libraries were already providing extensive access to digital information; the new forms and use of materials described here and throughout this book all serve to eliminate the need for direct contact in physical space. Further mass digitization of material is an obvious way forward, though it is not without its challenges in the Humanities in particular.

> *Of the three types of institutions, museums have been the most cautious about providing their digital collections to aggregators since maintaining the museum's brand/identify may support both the overall intellectual integrity of the collection and also, sometimes for commercial reasons. In order to provide high quality, trustworthy resources on the Internet, you have to do it properly. For all institutions there is increasing communication with communities and outreach work is often very good, however broader cooperation is problematic through lack of resources and risks of losing control. If material is digitized then it is for everybody. As an example, there was a project to get all the history of the ports of the UK together in one place which was exciting because it made sense. It's a holistic way of thinking about resource disclosure. Examples such as DPLA (Digital Public Library of America) and Europeana are developing this approach and some institutions in the UK are involved in the latter project. The vast majority of museums, libraries and archives are paid for by the public through taxes and public funds. This provides the potential to start a process of change and make an attempt to remove the hang-ups about losing territory, etc. The Arts Council gives money to the Museums*

Association in the form of the Digital Innovation and Engagement Fund. This makes no mention of collaboration but talks about individual museums doing things. The British Library recently led a study on the possibility of public libraries developing shared and integrated online services, but so far, no practical actions have followed, to my knowledge.

Former public sector chief executive

It would seem that even physical environments will be predicated on evolving systems of digital information, as some of our most critical needs are met by remote delivery of goods and services. Intensified financial pressure will also shape the future, with a reassessment of the value (and not just the commercial value) of information, discussed later in this book and summarized in the final chapter.

The replacement of much of the physical library experience, with digital because of the pandemic, has led to a reflection on the value-add of face-to-face. It has been recognized that in spite of it being possible to have a good library experience without face-to-face, there is a basic value in the social infrastructure of a 'safe place'.

Senior library professional, United Kingdom

Digital publication, as Graeme Hawley (Chapter 28) points out, is also changing, partly in relation to environmental and societal changes and partly as a result of not only the technological developments described here but also ones which are still to be fully developed and implemented. In response to all these challenges, will there be a massification of provision through increased cooperation and collaboration, or further demassification and atomization, perhaps the key question posed by Hawley? As has often been the case in the recent past at least, the legislative is not always running in parallel with the technological.

One aspect of the crisis that has not been discussed enough is the difficulty for online services due to the antiquated legal and copyright systems that we have. A lot more could have been done if the legal and copyright systems worked. This will be a legacy of the pandemic. The problem is not the technology, it's what you are allowed to do with it.

Senior manager, national library, United Kingdom

5 Acceleration

There is no doubt, however, that many activities have benefitted from going online, and the pandemic has merely speeded up the transition. Going digital can save at least the end-user time and effort and provide greater access to a broader spread of resources and services. As a result, much provision has experienced a significant increase in demand by being offered across the Internet.

The national conference happened just before the first national lockdown. Subsequent events were online and the business model was changed for events. This has gained more participants as it is cheaper and easier to attend. A recent event on cyber security had double the delegates (over 1,000) that would have attended if the event had been face to face.

Chief operating officer, national infrastructure provider, United Kingdom

Graeme Hawley introduces the concept of accelerative change in Chapter 28. Will COVID-19 be seen as a catalyst or a break? It is too early to answer this question: On the one hand, the move to digital provision has speeded up significantly of late; on the other, there are already concerns about the availability of the resources that will be required, post-pandemic, with a possible economic depression looming, to sustain the present pace and nature of developments. Technological trajectories and financial constraints are just two of the variables that will need to be considered. However, some form of "fast-tracking" or even "turbo-charging," as Rick Rylance puts it (Chapter 20) of existing developments and trajectories, seems inevitable for some time to come, as evinced by the contributions to this book.

COVID has had the effect of accelerating the move to digital-first for disciplines which had not been so advanced in this direction, even though electronic was already preferred. Now the libraries only purchase print if there is no digital.

University librarian, South-East Asia

Some changes made were already in train, such as the reorientation and restructuring of library services, and COVID-19 has merely hastened the new moves. Some user groups in particular—such as researchers in certain contexts —seem to have found the transition to online relatively straightforward (Chapter 16). Other changes have been more rapid and even discontinuous: not so much transition as disruption. What is not yet clear is the extent to which new and perhaps "interim" arrangements become permanent, though later chapters in particular forecast what the "new normal"—if there ever is a "normal" in the future—might look like.

Some of the changes which were accelerated because of the pandemic, will be retained, as for example: the option for staff to WFH some of the time, and working on tasks normally outside their areas of responsibility; delivery of more library courses and information resources online; the Research Advantage programme; the move from provision of a PC Suite to provision of laptops to students. Tech-enabled new opportunities will be actively explored from now on.

University librarian, Australia

Likely scenarios and planning approaches are considered in the second and third parts of this book especially and summarized in Chapter 31. It is evident, nevertheless, that significant change is inevitable, and many libraries are already planning for the longer term in respect of what will remain as now, what will be newly introduced, what will be revised, and what will be curtailed. What is obvious, however, is the speed with which libraries—like their parent institutions, sectors, and countries more broadly—can identify and implement change when they are forced to do so.

It is salutary to acknowledge just how much can be developed in a relatively short space of time during a crisis and embedded into normal operations afterwards. The obvious question 'why didn't you offer these earlier?' is an uncomfortable one to answer for a library director.

Tim Wales, Chapter 3

6 The human dimension

This book focusses not only on the library and the digital. Inevitably, it also considers the human dimension of the pandemic. Libraries have a duty and an opportunity to respond to the social as well as the economic and cultural challenges that COVID-19 has brought. This consideration must take account of future staff development as much as user provision, hence the inclusion of content on children, young people's and students' libraries as well as the needs of library and information professionals, both now and in the future.

The social impact of what is happening now is unknown, but there could be an analogy with shopping on the high street, which was already in trouble pre-pandemic and has been decimated by periods of lockdown. The increasing shift to online shopping is unlikely to diminish in the future. The Agrarian Revolution in the Neolithic age involved a shift from hunter-gatherer to harvester. This is a useful analogy to apply to museums, libraries, and archives [MLAs]. There is a long tradition of MLAs serving their users based on the hunter/gatherer model; you had to visit the institution to acquire the material you need. The same was true of shopping. For many, the shift is now towards harvesters shopping online. Will we lose any value intrinsic to the effort of going to find information by shifting from the hunter-gatherer mode? Probably not, partly because we have already made the shift.

Former public sector chief executive

The full scale and severity of the situation nationally would come to me in the days that followed, but I suppose my initial reaction to being furloughed, albeit partially, was 'Why me?'. Were my skills considered less important than someone else's? In an ever-growing digital age, where the old image of the cardigan-clad book-reading library colleague still prevails, was I perceived as obsolete? Or even, in an environment where databases now do most of the retrieving for us, were my honed research skills a luxury they felt they could temporarily do without?

I admit I tend to take these things personally, but in hindsight, I realise choosing to furlough anyone can't have been an easy task for the management, and nothing was done without deep consideration. Theirs is a position I certainly don't envy.

I feel the use and prevalence of technology has been on the rise for years – in all sectors of life, not just information services. Social networks replacing school reunions. Online ordering replacing hours-long marathons around shopping centres. The changes were slow but sure: user numbers increasing as time went on. Then, the pandemic struck the world, and adopting these new ways became borderline mandatory for all. Video calls have replaced the conference and classroom, and online gaming the night out with friends.

Libraries were not immune from this transformation. I have attended workshops both as a library employee and a library user which took place through an online meeting. My familiarity with online resources has greatly increased in a situation where both users and books are under lockdown. Since my return to full-time work, my role, too, is slowly evolving to incorporate even more research duties. Moving away from physical stock has given me the opportunity to grow as a professional.

I and other information workers are still offering the key services we always have, just in different ways. In truth, I am grateful for this technological revolution, as it has allowed both my personal and working life to continue with some semblance of normality.

Hannah Myers, Walker Morris, Leeds, United Kingdom

A Tale of two students

This is the story of the effects of the COVID 19 pandemic on the work of two part-time doctoral students at a UK university. The first, we'll call her Helena, had finished her empirical research and was in the process of writing up with a submission date of 31ˢᵗ October 2020. The second, Ingrid, had already carried out a limited amount of face-to-face research when the pandemic caused lockdown in the UK as well as the European country where she was based.

As their doctoral supervisor I was inundated with material from the university about what the virus meant for our students. If you'll pardon the use of the term in these circumstances, it was 'overkill', such that many of us began to skim read, at best, the material coming out. The gist of it was that all doctoral students, whether their work was affected significantly by the virus or not, should include in their thesis a section on the effect of the virus.

Helena, a primary school teacher, went into lockdown in March like the rest of the UK. She has three children, one at primary school and two at secondary school. The youngest has special needs and required a considerable amount of Helena's time in order to do the online schooling. The elder two worked well on their own most of the time but, as a teacher, Helena wanted to work with them some of the time as well. With her research completed, and no work of her own to do, Helena was able to continue to write up her research in the same way as before. In June her youngest returned to school, but Helena was not allowed to because she has severe underlying health issues such that catching COVID could have been dangerous. After Easter, all her children went back to school but she was still not allowed back. The effect of COVID, therefore, was that she had many extra hours to write up, and overall she gained from the situation. Now, how many of you would be recommending that she include this stroke of good fortune in her thesis?

For Ingrid the situation was very different. Ingrid works from home, running her own company. She has three children, two away at university and a third who lives at home, has severe autism and needs 24hr care. Usually he is at school but with the pandemic his school was closed. Ingrid was able to employ someone to look after him for some of the day but the rest of the time she was the carer. Ingrid's participants were unable to attend the training programmes which were the subject of her research because these were all cancelled. Therefore, it follows that Ingrid could not do any interviews. It is unlikely that the company where her research is being carried out will go back to face to face training any time soon and online training will be materially different, especially since the research surrounds issues of gender equality in training programmes. Ingrid's interviews will also have to be online or by phone. Understanding these circumstances Ingrid has been granted a six-month extension for her research, and will certainly be making out a case for COVID-19 to be taken into account when submitting her thesis.

Diana Harris, Consultant Doctoral Supervisor, Open University, United Kingdom

What is important here is that organizations take due and best account of their greatest resource—their people. There is much evidence—as discussed in this book—that this has largely been the case to date.

The pandemic has shown that [the organization] can go further, faster and it has been useful to see this. Opportunities have been gained through the situation and it has helped us to find other ways of achieving what is wanted. Some of the team have been far more productive working from home, although what "normal" will look like for them in, say, six months' time, is unknown at present. The loss of the social side of work affects some staff more than others. Changes in professional identity are unknown – home working may change this. Interacting with others is different. The emotional context for learning and working is important.

Chief Executive, major educational supplier, United Kingdom

7 Conclusion

This chapter has summarized the main themes and concepts of this book and introduced many of the authors represented in the later part of this publication. It has set the overall context within which library and information services have had to operate during the COVID-19 pandemic and enumerated the key challenges to which they have responded. It is clear that while the threats have been common to most sectors, many library systems around the world have not only responded well but seized the opportunities to develop or re-engineer services to best effect, often in difficult circumstances. None of this has been easy, given the lack of obvious precedent. There is no doubt that many library users have suffered deleterious consequences of COVID, despite librarians' best efforts, and it will take some time for the situation to return to some kind of stability, if ever. Much trust has been lost and needs to be regained; many questions remain unanswered; existing models are breaking if not broken; future resourcing levels are in doubt. Nowhere is this uncertainty more evident than in the current debates over "place versus space" and digital or physical, or both. Future root-and-branch rebalancing will be necessary. Accelerative change is here to stay in some form. The rest of this book aims to chart a way forward.

Part One

Immediate challenges

Working towards a "new normal": HKUST's innovations and adaptations in response to COVID-19

2

Diana L.H. Chan and Victoria F. Caplan
The Hong Kong University of Science and Technology (HKUST), Clear Water Bay, Hong Kong

1   Introduction

The year 2019–20 was unprecedented, as the COVID-19 virus has turned the world upside down. The first case in Hong Kong was confirmed on January 23, 2020. At the time of writing, the virus is still haunting us in its third wave. Relatively speaking, the number of COVID cases in Hong Kong is smaller than in many places, with 5346 cases and 105 deaths as of early November 2020 (Centre for Health Protection, Hong Kong, 2020). Yet losing a single life in the pandemic is a tragedy in any place in the world. Across the world, the World Health Organization reports that 46.84 million people have been confirmed to have been infected, and 1.2 million have died (World Health Organization, 2020). These figures continue to skyrocket.

The pandemic in Hong Kong has caused enormous disruption. It closed schools and colleges. Classes have been moved online. For weeks, restaurants opened at night and only offered take-away dinners. Everyone must wear masks in public. Government workers have worked from home for months. Many businesses followed suit. There were periods when the infected cases went down, and people resumed work in their offices. Then another wave of cases hit, and offices closed again. It has been unsettling.

As of autumn 2020, the pandemic caused the Hong Kong University of Science and Technology (HKUST) Library to close for 85 more days than usual in 2020 and to make major adjustments to staffing, working methods, and user services. In this chapter, we will describe how HKUST Library adapted flexibly in the face of challenges brought on by the COVID-19 pandemic, to eventually reach a "new normal" in delivering collections and services to students, faculty, and staff, virtually and in-person.

2   Local context

The Hong Kong University of Science and Technology (HKUST) is a government-supported, PhD-granting university with over 16,000 students and 690 faculty members. In 2021, it will celebrate its 30th anniversary. In 2020, it was rated as first in the *World's Top 400 Young Universities 2020* (THE, World University Rankings, 2020).

Libraries, Digital Information, and COVID. https://doi.org/10.1016/B978-0-323-88493-8.00009-4

3 The Library's immediate response

In the greater China region, COVID-19 shutdowns began in late January 2020, which in Hong Kong was during the Chinese New Year holidays. By 25 January, HKUST's senior management decided to postpone the start of the spring semester. Not only did HKUST's Library close, but its labs also closed, classes moved online, as well as other university facilities. Most HKUST staff began to work from home, in line with the Hong Kong government's civil service staffing.

Good communication was essential. HKUST Library staff, working from home, had online meetings and WhatsApp messaging to plan and discuss. Senior library staff faced a long list of concerns and challenges when the Library was closed: How to allow users to check out books? How to disinfect books when they were returned? How to direct print users to digital resources? What self-services to introduce? When to re-open the library again? How to prioritize our resources?

To protect our users and staff, and to provide services, the Library adopted a series of proactive measures (the major ones listed below) creating the beginning of a new normal.

4 Physical protection and hygiene for users and staff

Smart antimicrobial coating—HKUST's senior management arranged for the whole library building, together with high traffic facilities, to be sprayed with a multilevel antimicrobial polymer (MAP-1) coating, invented by HKUST researchers. The coating is effective in killing viruses, bacteria, and even hard-to-kill spores with an effective period of up to 90 days (Reuters, 2020). All furniture, computer keyboards, and surfaces in the Library were sprayed to safeguard the health of staff members and the public. It was repeated after 3 months.

Installation of a Smart Fever Detection System—Another invention by HKUST researchers (HKUST News, 2020), the Library installed an automated thermal sensor system at the Library entrance. Using AI and real-time tracking technologies, the system tracks human faces and detects heat at the same time. Real-time video and thermal data is displayed on a remote tablet PC, which Library staff monitor. The system triggers an alarm if the human body temperature is over a certain temperature threshold, such as 37.5°C. Library staff can recognize an unwell person whose face is bracketed in red on the screen. Library staff can then take necessary actions such as not allowing the unwell person coming in the Library, advising them to go to the clinic, and so on. This system has also been implemented at other Hong Kong government and university facilities.

Masks worn at all times in the Library's public spaces—To enter the Library, all users and Library staff must wear a mask, and keep them on at all times in public areas and group study rooms. The Library's staff and security guards patrol regularly to remind users if they take the masks off. HKUST students and staff generally maintain good mask discipline and are cooperative, making it easier for this vital component of infection prevention to work.

Disinfection of returned books—In 2019, the Library bought a heavy-duty UV-C book wash to deal with mold issues. It proved to be an excellent purchase, because it allows Library staff to process books against COVID-19 when they are returned. A UV-C sterilizer was also provided for users before they check out a book.

More frequent cleaning—When the Library was opened, cleaning was more frequent and used stronger cleaning materials. The Library made disinfectant gels available at service points, and increased airflow for stronger ventilation. Water spigots on fountains were capped to prevent people drinking directly from the fountains, while bottle refilling remained available.

5 Social distancing for users and staff

Reducing seats to enable user distancing—Re-opening was done in phases, with reduced seating. When HKUST first re-opened the Library in late February, it was only two floors, with around 75% of the chairs removed to create more space between users. Since May, after the second re-opening, the Library administration has gradually opened the whole library building and is now at 60% seating capacity.

Roster for staff (staggered staffing)—Like the rest of HKUST, the Library adopted flexi-hours in work time and lunch breaks. For several weeks in spring 2020, staff worked in shifts, alternating work in office and work from home. Half of the restaurants on campus were closed. Staff brought their own lunches and no longer ate together. It was only in autumn, with relaxed social distancing rules in Hong Kong that staff could eat in group of two, later four, then six.

6 Virtual access

E-book approval plan—Before the pandemic, the Library had already put an e-approval plan in place for sci-tech books. Ordering and receiving them in e-format made convenient use for remote users. This proved to be timely and essential in this critical time. The e-journal usage jumped 21% in 2019–20. Thus, digital only was the most preferred plan.

Re-order highly used print books—By spring, HKUST had already made plans to start teaching remotely, with the expectation that some students from outside Hong Kong might have to study remotely for the whole semester. To prepare for fall 2020 course reserves, Library staff screened and prioritized heavily used titles, taking affordability into consideration, and re-ordered titles in e-format to serve remote users.

Controlled Digital Lending (CDL)—Internet Archive's Open Libraries has a CDL programme, with a lending library of 1.5M digitized books available to anyone with an email address and an Internet connection, using a simple signup. After consideration, HKUST Library staff checked our course reserve titles against their holdings. Ultimately, 5% of our print course reserves were matched, and staff built links to Open Libraries (http://openlibraries.online/) into our course reserves system.

7   New and special services for users

Material retrieval service—When the Library was closed, staff retrieved available books and DVDs on user requests and arranged pick-up through emails. The interlibrary loans and HKALL, a local consortium ILL, continued when the situation allowed. Policies were adjusted such as waiving fines and overriding renewal limits. In autumn 2020, we regularized the service, by enabling the request function in the integrated library system.

Virtual InfoDesk service and changes to counter services—In spring 2019, the Library replaced the face-to-face staffed information desk with a virtual service (telephone, email, WhatsApp, with staff "on call" if the user needed face-to-face interaction). This was fortuitous, because when the physical library closed, staff were able to keep the information service with the same roster, with no disruption. Library users were also already accustomed to it. Because of departmental changes and streamlining, the Media counter service had merged with the Circulation/Reserve service in autumn 2019. Circulation/Reserve continued with a skeleton staff, even during the "work from home" period when the Library was closed, answering questions, and fulfilling physical book and media requests. Once the Library re-opened, staff were given facial masks and shields and served patrons from behind a flexi-glass barrier.

Space for exam invigilation—Thirteen group discussion rooms were reserved for the teaching assistants of different courses to run online tutorial classes. The e-learning classroom was used by professors and teaching assistants to invigilate online examinations. The built-in camera in our iMac workstations with plenty supplies of headphones and microphones were the main attractions for their selection of this library venue.

8   User education and library events go online

Online information literacy classes—In spring 2020, 88 sessions of information literacy classes were offered via Zoom from February to May 2020. In autumn 2020, all library orientation, classes, and workshops are also being conducted via Zoom, with comparable attendance and feedback from the students. Librarian instructors met the challenges presented by being suddenly online with positive attitudes and can-do spirit. They all shared learning and tips on Zoom teaching and proactively acted as each other's teaching assistants. The "esprit de corps" helped get us through and even developed further. The work in blended and e-learning via Library Guides and e-learning videos also bore good fruits in this hard time.

Refresher sessions for faculty—Librarians offered multiple sessions via Zoom in both spring and fall semesters, to aid the use of the Library's e-resources for teaching and learning remotely instead via campus IP access. Since the pandemic also coincided with a revamp of the Library's Integration to the university's learning management system (LMS) called Library Toolbox (which allows faculty members or their teaching assistants to customize library search tools for their teaching within the LMS), we combined the two into a simple 30-minute session. Whether from the promotion, or the need for more e-resources integration, faculty used the Toolbox seven times more frequently in January–November 2020 than they did in the same period in 2019, and the number of times library resources were accessed via the Library Toolbox increased by 57%.

Talks on Zoom—Initially, some of the Library Talks and exhibitions scheduled for spring 2020 had to be postponed. However, starting in late March, the Library began to stage such talks via Zoom, with excellent attendance and very positive feedback. Similarly, in autumn 2020, the Library Talks have reached a large and appreciative audience. In October, we also launched our first exhibition opening ceremony via Zoom. Working with our Media Production and Technology Centre, the physical exhibition has also been turned into a dynamic virtual tour.

Research consultations on Zoom—The Library regularly collaborates on two courses (a Chemistry capstone course and a Humanities independent film class) which require individual or group research coaching. Instruction librarians were able to continue to provide these courses embedded coaching via Zoom, as well as some non-course coaching sessions.

9   Innovations become the "new normal": What we expect in the future

Throughout the world, people are wondering and even making projections about how higher education will respond and change in the face of the COVID-19 pandemic (EBLIDA Secretariat, 2020; Grajek and EDUCAUSE IT Issues Panel, 2020). Like many, we believe that some of the changes we have instituted in haste will become a new way of serving the teaching, learning, research, and information needs of our users in years to come. We expect that the trend for using e-resources, already strong before COVID, and intensified during the pandemic, will continue. We believe that delivering library instruction and a variety of cultural activities online as well as face-to-face will continue to be popular. At the same time, in the past few months, we have seen more patrons returning to study and research in the Library, so the need for Library as place, if perhaps a more spread out space, will continue.

References

Centre for Health Protection, Hong Kong, 2020. Latest Situation of the Coronavirus Disease (COVID-19) in Hong Kong. https://chp-dashboard.geodata.gov.hk/covid-19/en.html. (Accessed 4 November 2020).

EBLIDA Secretariat, 2020. A European Agenda for the Post Covid-19 Age: A Work in Progress. http://www.eblida.org/Documents/EBLIDA-Preparing-a-European-library-agenda-for-the-post-Covid-19-age.pdf. (Accessed 25 October 2020).

Grajek, S., EDUCAUSE IT Issues Panel, 2020. Top IT Issues Emerging From the Pandemic. https://er.educause.edu/articles/2020/11/top-it-issues-2021-emerging-from-the-pandemic. (Accessed 5 November 2020).

HKUST News, 2020. HKUST Researchers Develop a Smart Fever Screening System Offering a More Efficient Solution to Safeguarding Public Health. https://www.ust.hk/news/research-and-innovation/hkust-researchers-develop-sm. (Accessed 4 November 2020).

Reuters, 2020. HKUST Scientists Say New Antiviral Coating Can Protect Surfaces for 90   Days.   https://www.reuters.com/article/us-health-coronavirus-hongkong-coating-idUSKCN2290S5. (Accessed 4 November 2020).

THE, World University Rankings, June 24, 2020. Best Young Universities in the World. Times Higher   Education.   https://www.timeshighereducation.com/student/best-universities/best-young-universities-world. (Accessed 4 November 2020).

World Health Organization, 2020. WHO Coronavirus Disease (COVID-19) Dashboard. https://covid19.who.int/. (Accessed 4 November 2020).

Back to the future? Practical consequences and strategic implications of a UK academic library's COVID response

3

Tim Wales
Brunel University London, Uxbridge, United Kingdom

1 Introduction

The UK academic library sector at the time of writing (April 2021) has had a "good COVID crisis." It was one of the last professional higher education service providers to close on-campus services before the first UK lockdown and one of the first to restart them again ready for the 2020/21 student intake. A radical and rapid transformation was required in the intervening period for circumstances which no library disaster plan could have ever foreseen. Anything enacted was still subject to last-minute changes as government policies (and university interpretations of said policies) kept altering. And yet the sector coped, collaborated, and changed in response. Some library directors even took on broader institutional strategic roles such as heading up "Gold command COVID response teams" (thereby responding to a direct challenge to the academic library sector laid down by senior university managers in a previous study by Baker and Allden (2017)).

Nevertheless, the impact of the crisis on academic libraries' day-to-day operations and medium-to longer-term strategic planning should not be underestimated, even if the rapid development of various promising vaccines seems to offer a road "back to the future." This chapter considers the sector's response through the prism of the author's own experiences as Head of Library Services at Brunel University London (BUL), a mid-size, research-intensive, single-campus university in Uxbridge (Greater London), United Kingdom.

2 Exit the hybrid library, enter the lockdown library

When the UK government initiated its first national lockdown to help combat COVID-19 towards the end of March 2020, academic libraries were already in a strong position to support the remote needs of their students because of their (and the publishing sector's) multibillion pound investment in e-library resources and associated systems during the past two decades.

Libraries, Digital Information, and COVID. https://doi.org/10.1016/B978-0-323-88493-8.00021-5

An increased focus on reading list (and background reading) provision to cover the period leading up to summer examinations—whether by direct purchase, subscription, scans of third-party content under the aegis of copyright legislation and/or licensing bodies—offered business as usual (BAU) to students working remotely even if access to physical study spaces had stopped. In addition, emergency negotiations with the UK Copyright Licensing Agency (CLA—see https://www.cla.co.uk) via UK professional bodies such as the Copyright Negotiating and Advisory Committee (CNAC—see https://www.universitiesuk.ac.uk/policy-and-analysis/Pages/copyright-working-group. aspx) and the Society of College, National and University Libraries (SCONUL—see http://www.sconul.ac.uk) permitted temporary license extensions for the UK HE library sector to allow for additional copying to cover known gaps in the curriculum.

Looking back at that period one year on, the timing of the first UK lockdown was actually the "least worst" in terms of removing physical library access from undergraduate students as the bulk of teaching was already completed by then and undergraduate students (especially final-year students) were about to enter their examination revision period, having already borrowed most of the physical stock they needed. Postgraduate students (especially taught postgraduates needing to complete theirdissertations) were adversely impacted however and so they were the group most vociferously demanding immediate resumption of study space (and stock) access at the end of the first lockdown period in July 2020.

For libraries such as BUL therefore, there were only three *COVID-specific* strategic considerations[a] identified at the point of entering the first UK lockdown:

(1) How much financial resource should be reallocated to information resource budgets to finance the anticipated additional demand for e-book titles as well as the increase in simultaneous user licenses needed.

(2) Identification of those e-library resources or systems which were still predicated on an on-campus access model and therefore required some form of alternative remote access provision, e.g., Bloomberg and Eikon.

(3) The need to audit Library staff's IT needs to be able to work from home effectively (whether it be equipment, access to reliable broadband connections, or an alternative method of accessing the library management system from personal devices rather than via university VPN).

With hindsight, a fourth consideration—identification of, and planning for, additional new remote delivery or fetch services—could also have been initiated during April 2020, but this work started in earnest only once the new realities and limitations of reopening a physical library service in a COVID-secure way were apparent.

3   A new library operating model

Active planning for reopening BUL commenced in May 2020 with an initial cross-campus focus on identifying those service points requiring "sneeze-screens" to

---

[a] An even more significant strategic priority at this time, for example, was planning for the execution of a rapid demerger from Information (IT) Services to a new Student and Academic Services directorate from July 2020 with the subsequent recreation of separate Library Customer Services and Administration teams.

protect front-line workers from aerosol contamination as well as analyzing the impact of 1-m or 2-m social distancing measures on teaching space provision and class sizes. Library Services benefited early on from both strands of work, and once the 2-m principle, strongly advocated by BUL's Health & Safety (H&S) team, was accepted, this unlocked the space planning process within the Library building.

Crucially (and surely a first in academic librarianship history), the Cleaning Services team input became a *sine qua non* for all planning decisions relating to library provision as they had been tasked to produce detailed sanitization maps for every floor to show how they could provide regular and reliable enhanced cleaning processes for key touchpoint areas as well as for public washroom areas based on their staff rotas. The maps also included such details as the proposed locations of alcoholic wipe dispensers and wall-mounted hand sanitizers (both tools for self-service cleaning by users of each space). However, the single most impactful requirement around cleaning on library space in the end was the need for clear desks and decluttered floor plans to reduce the perceived contamination risk from the virus remaining on hard and soft surfaces. All of this planning activity provided a much-needed impetus to completely rethink BUL's helpdesk provision and location (a need anyway from the aforementioned demerger from Information Services) as well as address a backlog of office maintenance tasks.

Armed with information on 2-m distancing of study desks and associated cleaning regimes, it soon became apparent H&S would only formally sign-off a limited form of library study space provision on one floor of the Library to support summer examination revision and so a book fetch service was designed alongside such novel concepts as book quarantining and cinema-style prebooked seating reservations with numbered study desks. The latter requirement was helped enormously by one of our key system suppliers having had the strategic insight to rapidly develop a product based on their existing resource scheduler web products. Finally, UK building regulations required maximum building occupancies to be recalculated in light of the overall reduction in toilet facilities due to the 2-m social distancing principle.

Once the library was finally able to reopen in a limited capacity with a skeleton staffing model in the last week of July 2020, the BUL Student Union proved invaluable in addressing the inevitable complaints about lack of Library access from postgraduate students by cunningly suggesting that the limited capacity be allocated to them for a 2 week period once the examination period had finished. This bought additional time for Library staff to plan for a full reopening with unmediated access to shelves and a greater provision of study spaces as well as a gradual rollout from September of new remote services across Library operations. Table 3.1 gives a summary of the various new student-facing services that BUL introduced during the pandemic and, crucially, the last column indicates which of these will be retained post-pandemic. Although many libraries around the world will have been offering a combination of these even before the pandemic, it is salutary to acknowledge just how much can be developed in a relatively short space of time during a crisis and embedded into normal operations afterwards. The obvious question "why didn't you offer these before?" is an uncomfortable one to answer for any Library director.

Table 3.1 New Brunel University London Library services launched during the COVID-19 pandemic.

Service name	Description	Notes	Retain post-pandemic?
Free book returns for graduating students	Freepost returns via Clicksit (Collect+ network)	Designed to get 2600+ items taken off-site by final-year students in March	Yes, funding permitting
Click & Collect	Advance reservations service via Library catalogue (for all user categories)	Intended to reduce the number of short visits made inside the physical Library	Yes
Click & Post	Free postal loans and returns service via webform (for all user categories)	Brought in during lockdown 2. Built on previous service to disabled students but cost-free	Yes, funding permitted
Scan & Send	Scans of items held in Brunel stock (especially book chapters) to email (for all user categories)	Brought in lockdown 2 to augment document delivery service—but Click & Post type services reduced demand	No, merged with document delivery?
Mandatory prebooked seat reservations to access library building	Online seat bookings and check-ins using Springshare LibCal Seats module	Absolutely essential for Health & Safety sign-off Library reopening	Yes, but for selected Library seating areas
Off-site access to Bloomberg & Eikon financial data	A combination of advance online booking for virtual Bloomberg "seats" and an upgraded cloud access to Eikon	Prepandemic access was via on-site in-Library terminals only	Yes, but with reduced simultaneous users, depending on teaching model
Prerecorded library training/ information literacy sessions	Up to 1-h "lecture" sessions delivered by Academic Liaison Librarians for their discipline areas	Developed in Panopto, these were made for large-scale events with numbers too large for synchronous training. Also supported "flipped classroom" approach	Yes
Library training/information literacy sessions delivered via various videoconferencing platforms (MS Teams, Zoom etc.)	As above but carried out live	Multiple delivery channels were available (Zoom, Microsoft Teams, Blackboard Collaborate, Panopto). Hybrid in person/remote delivery sessions were not needed	Yes, depending on teaching model
Online self-guided tutorials (via Adobe Captivate)	Interactive, chunked, self-assessment guides on generic information literacy topics with audio track	Already used prepandemic for annual Library inductions, expanded to include plagiarism and referencing versions	Yes

Virtual drop-in sessions (via MS Teams or Zoom)	One-to-one appointments with Academic Liaison Librarians at specific times of the week	The online equivalent of a tutor leaving the office door open at specific times of the day for students	Yes
24/7 web chat enquiry support	A subscription service via Springshare LibAnswers 24-7 Cooperative and its knowledgebase, staffed by librarians around the globe	Many UK academic libraries already had this in place already but COVID amplified the need for this at Brunel	Yes
Enquiry Management System (EMS) via Springshare LibAnswers	Intended to streamline monitoring of 15+ library email boxes off-site with improved standardization, reporting etc.	A deceptively complicated project as it also necessitated tightening up of Library data handling and privacy policies	Yes
Shift from p-books to e-books/e-textbooks in reading lists	New subscriptions to e-book collections, direct purchase of titles, and increased funds for patron-driven acquisition (PDA) all used	This was already part of longer-term Library budget planning but the COVID pandemic brought it forward. However, gaps in e-books coverage have emerged rapidly, and PDA is not a panacea	Yes

4 New library policies

It was not just on the service delivery side that BUL was duty bound to try new initiatives. A unique combination of restricted building capacities, NHS Track & Trace requirements, the exigencies of the Brunel H&S team, and the reformation of the old Library Customer Services Team over the Summer of 2020 (reporting to the Head of Library Services) necessitated a review of Library policies and practices relating to access and behavior management.

First of all, there was an opportunity, in part due to the cessation of 24/7 Library opening, to redeploy the out-of-hours security personnel team to staff the Library's Reception Desk during normal opening hours. Not only did this help reduce the amount of day staff needing to attend campus at any one time as part of the COVID Secure operational plan, but it also better facilitated the enforcement of wearing face coverings within the Library and the inspection Brunel ID cards on entry. At a stroke, this solved the long-running abuse of a "temporary day pass" system that had been in place during pre-COVID times which was causing many problems and unnecessary work for front-line staff, e.g., enabling non-Brunel affiliated people to access the facilities unchallenged as passes were often swapped around.

However, the new entry policies did lead to a minority of aggressive and inappropriate student/staff confrontations at the Reception Desk even two-thirds of the way into the autumn term. These in turn exposed issues with existing Library CCTV coverage but, just as importantly, revealed gaps in Library regulations in terms of available sanctions for user misconduct. The former was addressed with the introduction of body cams for the security team, which could capture both sound and vision of incidents, thereby addressing the lack of neutral evidence available to University authorities when adjudicating between conflicting points of view of the same event. It also helped deter vexatious student complaints which were arising whenever Library security staff tried to enforce COVID regulations (especially the mandatory wearing of face coverings) with which a minority of students were displeased.

The latter issue was addressed by revisiting existing Library regulations with colleagues in BUL's Office for Student Complaints, Conduct and Appeals (OSCCA). A formal process for Library Services to referstudent misconduct to OSCCA under the auspices of existing University student conduct regulations was then able to be agreed for the first time.

The third example of a nascent policy emerging out of the pandemic relates to Library staffing policy around staff recruitment and expected working practices. Six months of homeworking and service continuity, especially on the scholarly communications side, gave new insight into management expectations around employment and presenteeism. If a long ($> 2\,\mathrm{h}$) commute were an understandable reason not to accept a job offer made prepandemic, what if the need for that commute and campus attendance was significantly reduced? Would that same job offer be accepted mid-pandemic? BUL Library Services had an opportunity to test this theory for real on a successful interview candidate and the answer was in the affirmative subject to certain understandable written guarantees that any such arrangements would continue even after the current Head of Library Services moved on. It also highlighted unexpected issues around the applicability of London Weighting in such working practices which needed unpicking with the Human Resources team.

5 Conclusion

The 2020 pandemic has brought to a head various matters that were bubbling away in the academic library sector during the past couple of years and which now need to be resolved urgently, the most important of which being e-textbook pricing models and associated funding. Some UK universities have already been investing heavily in e-textbooks during the past decade. For others, such as BUL, the restricted availability of e-textbooks through conventional library e-book purchasing platforms had only recently become apparent when trying to source content for the University's new online distance learning programme. Although the CLA's Digital Content Store (see https://www.cla.co.uk/digital-content-store) copyright clearing service has helped with chapter-specific content, sometimes the whole e-textbook is required as the set book for the course and the Library is still expected to finance it out of its information resources budget "bucket." A vigorous debate is now underway between publishers and libraries about how the HE sector can possibly afford such content (especially if it is the only content access option available). For a per student capita per annum pricing model is unsustainable from a Library resources budget perspective, when the amount in question could be *£50,000 per annum for just one book and one course alone*. How can we avoid e-textbooks ending up with the same excessive, upfront, committed pricing model that has been financing journal publishing for decades and crippling library budget and collection development decisions in the process without jeopardising academic publishing?

From a UK library leader's perspective, four initial reflections come to mind (and it would be interesting to revisit these again in a year's time to see if anything has changed):

(1) One of the most important reaffirmations that came out of the crisis was the value of professional academic library cooperation and coordination, whether through professional JiscMail (https://www.jiscmail.ac.uk/) mailing lists or through the aegis of professional bodies such as SCONUL. An excellent example of this in practice was an online UK library directors' discussion in April 2020, which flagged the problem for the sector of the thousands of books still on loan to (and, crucially, at home with) those final-year students graduating in 2020. This was definitely a matter that my leadership team and I had not even considered until that point as we were focused on BAU activities. Although SCONUL's subsequent efforts to set up a national purchasing agreement for freepost library courier services subsequently floundered, the fact that this issue was raised at all meant that an acceptable solution could be identified in time, ultimately rescuing 82% of BUL final year loans with a cost/benefit ratio of 1:16.

(2) Initial concerns about insufficient study capacity arising from COVID-secure provisions have proven to be overblown at the time of writing (at the end of the spring 2021 term). BUL has not witnessed queues for seats, unlike other large UK university libraries, and has never reached more than 50% of available capacity on any 1 day. This fact would seem to support the principal design philosophy underpinning library new build projects of the past two decades: the main student expectation of libraryspace is for a variety of *group* study environments that are configurable for multiple purposes, something which has been sadly impossible to provide for during this pandemic. Again, with the benefit of hindsight, some serious consideration of how best to support group study on the basis of approved student household bubbles may have mitigated some of the adverse effects of the pandemic on student experience and student mental health.

(3) Winston Churchill's (alleged) maxim of never wasting a good crisis has proved correct. At BUL, both the introduction of security team body cams and tighter access control policies would have been very controversial and time-consuming to implement prepandemic but are both now examples of the benefits of a crisis in changing conventional beliefs and norms in library operations to achieve rapid and acceptable change.

(4) The additional expense of providing the COVID services listed in Table 3.1, especially those requiring postal services (so often perceived as a barrier to implementation prepandemic), happily coincided with one-off VAT rebates to the UK academic library sector in the 2020/21 financial year (arising from a change in tax policy from May 1, 2020, announced in the UK government's Budget earlier in 2020—see https://www.gov.uk/government/publications/vat-zero-rating-e-publications/vat-zero-rating-e-publications). However, there is a real risk that any financial downturn in the UK HE sector arising from the pandemic (exacerbated or not by Brexit) may lead to a reduction in professional services' departmental budgets in the following two financial years from 2021/22 and thereby requiring an urgent reappraisal of the financial sustainability of these new services.

Finally, the fact that these new COVID-era services (alongside mass e-book provision) have increased stock turnover and utilization of obvious key texts while literally thousands of books lay unused and unscanned on university library shelves does again bring into question the persistence of the "just-in-case" approach to collection management in conventional UK academic libraries. Dare we return back to the once futuristic concept of a true "just-in-time" model in which the e-library is the norm, underpinned by a small backbone of national or specialist research libraries providing scanned or loan access to original, seldom used materials?

Acknowledgment

Thanks to Anne Hutchinson for her assistance with this chapter.

Reference

Baker, D. and Allden, A., Leading Libraries: The View From Above, 2017, https://www.sconul.ac.uk/publication/the-view-from-above, 2020, (Accessed 31 January 2021).

Further reading

Adobe Captivate, 2020. https://www.adobe.com/uk/products/captivate.html. (Accessed 18 April 2021).

Blackboard Collaborate, 2020. Blackboard. https://www.blackboard.com/en-uk/teaching-learn-ing/collaboration-web-conferencing/blackboard-collaborate. (Accessed 18 April 2021).

Bloomberg Terminal Access for Academic institutions during COVID, 2020. Bloomberg. https://data.bloomberglp.com/professional/sites/10/EDU-Remote-Access.pdf. (Accessed 18 April 2021).

Clicksit, 2020. http://www.clicksit.com. (Accessed 18 April 2021).

LibAnswers, 2020. Springshare. https://www.springshare.com/libanswers/. (Accessed 18 April 2021).

LibAnswers 24/7 Cooperative, 2020. Springshare. https://buzz.springshare.com/producthigh-lights/libanswers-platform/247-global-cooperative. (Accessed 18 April 2021).

LibCal Seats Module, 2020. Springshare. https://blog.springshare.com/2020/06/17/libcal-seats-module-safely-reopen-your-building-blog-series-part-one/. (Accessed 18 April 2021).

Microsoft Teams, 2020. Microsoft. http://www.microsoft.com/en-GB/microsoft-365/micro-soft-teams. (Accessed 18 April 2021).

Panopto, 2020. http://www.panopto.com. (Accessed 18 April 2021).

Refinitiv Eikon, Refinitiv, 2020. https://www.refinitiv.com/en/products/eikon-trading-software. (Accessed 18 April 2021).

SCONUL, 2020. http://www.sconul.ac.uk. (Accessed 18 April 2021).

Zoom, 2020. http://zoom.us. (Accessed 18 April 2021).

Teaching librarians' experiences in the first months of system change

Amanda Glimstedt, David Kjellin, and Katarina Michnik
Gothenburg University Library, Gothenburg, Sweden

1 Introduction

In this chapter, we describe our experiences of the first 6 months of the COVID-19-pandemic, as three teaching librarians at the University of Gothenburg, when almost all teaching was transferred from on-campus to online. Our purpose is to identify factors that seem to have an impact on the outcomes of academic librarians' teaching after a rapid transition to online teaching. We present three teaching cases, one successful and two unsuccessful. We discuss the choices we made, the reasons behind them, and what we have learned regarding pedagogical approaches, resources, and digital tools. By comparing these cases, we have identified the three factors that seem to have an impact: the level of active learning during the library teaching sessions, the time available to librarians for choosing, learning about and using digital tools online, and working relationships between teaching librarians and course coordinators.

2 The Gothenburg University Social Sciences Libraries teaching team

Gothenburg University Library consists of eight libraries where the Social Sciences Library, the Economics Library, and the Education Library together form an organizational unit—the Social Sciences Libraries. The unit's library teaching team currently employs 12 teaching librarians who work for 4 of the University's faculties: the Faculty of Social Science, the Faculty of Education, the IT Faculty, and the School of Business, Economics and Law. The team's overarching aim is to design and deliver subject-embedded sessions that are strategically placed within the programmes. Fulfilling this ambition requires deep collaboration between teaching librarians and course coordinators, and between teaching librarians and programme coordinators. However, establishing such a model as a norm is a long-term process, and many coordinators who contact the teaching team still have more traditional perceptions and expectations of what a collaboration with a teaching librarian might entail.

Digital developments have substantially changed educators' approaches to, and ways of, teaching. The traditional pedagogical approach, with its focus on the transmissive lecture, is no longer perceived as an obvious option; teaching activities are not necessarily equated with transferring oral information, but may be used for "adapting material to the interests of a particular group" or "helping students discover key

Libraries, Digital Information, and COVID. https://doi.org/10.1016/B978-0-323-88493-8.00023-9

concepts, principles or ideas" (Bates, 2019, p. 88). In line with this development, the Social Science Libraries' teaching team has, over the last few years, been moving away from traditional lectures, replacing them with active learning classroom (ALC)-inspired workshops, incorporating student-activating elements in order to scaffold interactive learning. Prior to the pandemic, the team created digital learning objects[a] for flipped teaching formats on a limited scale. When talking of the use of digital tools in teaching situations, we see it as important to not use *digital* and *online* as synonyms. Whereas online relates to something happening on the Internet, digital relates to the format; there are digital tools that can be used in both online and offline teaching environments, and digital tools that can only be used online.

3 Moving library teaching online: Three cases

In March 2020, the University severely restricted student access to all faculty buildings and moved almost all teaching operations online. The Social Sciences Libraries closed down two library branches and reduced opening hours at the third library. In September 2020, the branches that had been closed reopened but with reduced opening hours, study spaces and services and with the majority of the staff working from home most of the time. To complement email and telephone communication, library staff have primarily been using the video conferencing tool Zoom and Canvas, the newly implemented Learning Management System (LMS), to communicate with their users. Remote work can be challenging because of difficulties such as lack of a sufficiently fast connection and restricted access to computers at home (Mehta and Wang, 2020). In Sweden, a significant majority of the country's population has access to a stable Internet connection at home (The Swedish Internet Foundation, 2020). Furthermore, all academic librarians at the University have work laptops as well as access to a well-functioning IT infrastructure for off-campus work. All this means that remote working at the Social Sciences Libraries is usually not hampered by technical obstacles.

As courses at the University went online almost overnight, so did the activities of the library's teaching team. Over the first 6 months of the pandemic, the team has been developing new educational designs and experimenting with digital tools, trying to establish what constitutes high-quality online teaching. Between March and September 2020, the teaching librarians held sessions in various contexts and formats and with a range of outcomes. The next section of this chapter describes three teaching cases held during this period. Of these cases, one was perceived by us as successful, while the other two were deemed to be unsuccessful.

3.1 The successful case

Our successful case is a workshop held as part of a course in Criminology at the Faculty of Social Sciences, in mid-May. The course can be taken either as a freestanding element or as part of a Bachelor's programme. We were approached by the

---

[a] Digital learning object = a small, reusable resource of instructional media (Wiley, 2000).

coordinators 4 months before course commencement and were invited to a teachers' meeting. There was a discussion about the design of the course assignments in relation to information searching, as well as the content, format, and timing of our involvement in the course. One of the two course coordinators had previously been in contact with the library's research support services, prompting the contact with the teaching team.

3.1.1 The aim of the library's involvement

The library session was connected specifically to a course assignment that required the students to conduct a minor literature review. While the review was expected to relate to topics relevant to the course, the assignment was also set to prepare the students for the upcoming thesis course. The aim of the library's session was consequently twofold. It aimed, on the one hand, to support the students in achieving a specific learning objective of their course by developing the skills to locate relevant previous research for a literature review, and on the other hand, it aimed to provide the students with the methodological skills, knowledge, and understanding of literature reviews required later.

3.1.2 Format and content of the session

The design of the course as a whole was based upon the potential of constructivist learning and included several student-activating elements, such as flipped formats, peer feedback elements, and seminars. We and the course coordinators consequently agreed that the best format for the library's involvement would be a workshop in one of the University's ALC rooms. In line with the ALC concept, we decided to implement mini-lectures, individual tasks, and group activities as well as discussions during the session. We also decided to let the structure of the workshop mimic the steps of the literature review information search process. By participating, the students would be moving forward in their work on their literature reviews, as well as developing knowledge and skills relating to the literature review genre and to academic information searching. In order to reduce lecture time, the students were asked to read a chapter in a book on literature reviews in preparation. The course coordinators included the chapter in the compulsory reading list.

With the arrival of the pandemic, the then ongoing course went online. The months between the course going online and the date of the library workshop offered time for us to rethink the educational design at a relatively comfortable pace, drawing upon our previous knowledge and interest in educational development, a dialogue with the course coordinators, and the experiences gained through the rest of the work undertaken by the teaching team.

We decided to retain the original educational design with the combination of a flipped format and an ALC workshop, and to use Zoom for live interaction with the students. During the spring, the teaching team had started to experiment with the University's LMS, Canvas, as a potentially relevant learning space. Canvas as an arena offered the possibility both of communicating directly with students and of creating an online learning environment to be used to complement synchronous live workshops.

We asked for, and were given, a green light to create a multimodal digital learning object in Canvas,[b] to be used by the students during the workshop.

Following discussion with the course coordinators, the scheduled workshop time was also extended from three to six and a half hours. With the students working remotely, we were able to scaffold an extended pedagogical process which did not require our physical presence for the entire duration of the workshop. Making use of Canvas as a learning space, we allotted more time for the students to work on a total of five tasks. We focused the interactions via Zoom on a live demonstration, peer feedback sessions, and Q&A sessions, with the aim of optimizing opportunities for interactive learning in the online environment. The five tasks were intended to guide the students through the information search process, letting them document their progress and allowing for feedback.

On the day of the workshop, the Canvas module was opened up to the students after the start of the workshop. The students moved between the live elements in Zoom and the material and tasks in Canvas, participating actively in all elements, whether independently completing and submitting tasks, giving peer feedback, or asking questions. One of the course coordinators decided to participate in several elements, her presence potentially emphasizing the connection between the library session and the rest of the course for the students.

Throughout the workshop, the students' performances indicated that they had begun to identify and locate criminological research, meeting the specific learning objective the workshop was designed to support. Via the hand-ins, we noted a development during the day both in the students' skills and in their knowledge and understanding. In the final task, a noticeable improvement in the students' conception of both information searching in general and their research topic in particular became evident. Examples of this include insights into the scope of available research, revisions of research questions based on previous test searches, revisions of search terms based on new recalled articles or test searches, and reflections on the scope of searches identifying a need to broaden or narrow the search. At the end of the course, the course coordinators noted that students who took part in the library workshop also performed well in the review assignment. Overall, the active, multimodal format seems to have led students through a successful learning process, scaffolded by interactions with fellow students, librarians, and the course coordinator.

3.2 Two unsuccessful cases

We have chosen to present two unsuccessful cases since they represent different types of problems. The first case was a session on the topic of systematic literature reviews. It was held as part of a newly developed course in Social Psychology given as part of a Masters' programme at the Department of Psychology, in early April. The second case was a session on academic information searching processes, held in late September, as

---

[b] Materials included three videos (planning for a systematic review, using a systematic framework, and finding relevant search terms), a text presenting and explaining the differences between a number of search services and instructions for the tasks.

part of a course in Work Science, which forms part of a Bachelor-level programme at the Department of Sociology.

3.2.1 The aim of the library's involvement

The aim of the first case's session was to prepare the students for an examination assignment in which they were expected to undertake systematic literature reviews. The focus was requested by the course coordinator. In the second case, we initially conceived the aim of the library session as preparing the students for an examination assignment. However, it became clear that this was a misunderstanding and that the course coordinator instead expected a basic introduction to library services.

3.2.2 Format and content of the sessions

The first case was designed prior to the pandemic and was to contain short lectures on how to conduct literature reviews and on database presentations followed by a workshop in which the students were to work on their literature reviews, with our support. All this was planned for a physical classroom. The transition to online occurred shortly before the library session was scheduled, and we had to transfer it to an online environment in a very short time. Since the course was targeting international students, some of whom moved back home[c] during the first weeks of the pandemic, we decided to make the session as asynchronous and flexible as possible. The planned lectures and presentations were either recorded or presented in written form and published in the course's Canvas module. The students were expected to go through the asynchronous material on their own before attending a noncompulsory Q&A session in Zoom that replaced the planned workshop.

The new setup had fewer student-activating elements than had been originally intended. This was done deliberately as the librarian in charge had limited experience of using digital tools in online teaching. We also suspected that some of the students were not familiar with using digital teaching tools online since they had applied for an education programme on campus prior to the pandemic. With this in mind, we decided to minimize the student-activating elements to make the session as smooth as possible for everyone.

Only a few students took advantage of the voluntary Q&A session; overall, student activity was low and few students looked at the recorded clips. It subsequently became clear that this student group had in fact already been working with literature reviews in a previous course, something neither we nor the course coordinator were aware of. This is probably the main explanation for the lack of student engagement.

The session in the second case was held 6 months into the pandemic. This session had been planned from the outset with online in mind. Even though the session had been part of the course for several years, on this occasion both the coordinator and we were new to the delivery. The previous coordinator and the former teaching librarians had moved on to new assignments. During the planning phase, we had some email conversations with the new course coordinator, during which two communication failures occurred.

---

[c] Some of the students were thus in different time zones.

The first communication failure concerned access to Canvas. When giving us access to Canvas, the coordinator gave us the administrative status of "observer" rather than "teacher." This meant that we could access the course's Canvas modules but could not publish information ourselves. This hampered our ability to communicate with the students. The status was not changed despite repeated requests on our part. It is possible that the course coordinator did not know how to make the change or did not conceive of us as fully accredited members of the course teaching team.

The second communication failure concerned the aim of the library session. We were under the impression at an early stage that the course coordinator wanted the session to relate to an upcoming course assignment. With this in mind, we developed a student-activating workshop consisting of two group tasks. The students were, first, to formulate search terms relevant to the content of their assignment and, second, to search in selected databases for scientific articles that would be relevant to the course assignment. However, shortly before the workshop was scheduled, it became apparent that the course coordinator was expecting a basic presentation of library services with no pedagogical elements. Still, on the basis of our general knowledge and understanding of undergraduate students' needs in respect of academic information literacy, we decided not to remove the outlined content but instead to add a brief introduction to library services. The workshop was held live via Zoom, making use of the breakout room function for group tasks. At this stage of the pandemic, the different functions of the University's digital tools were being more extensively used both by teachers and by ourselves. We felt comfortable knowing that Zoom would be used in the course and would be a familiar tool and learning environment for the students, carrying only a low risk of technical difficulties that could interrupt students' learning processes.

On the day of the workshop, we soon discovered that there had been unexpected delays in the course setup. As a consequence, students had not received instructions for the upcoming assignment, threatening their perception of the relevance of the workshop as well as their learning during it. After some adjustments, however, we were able to commence the workshop and the students participated actively in all elements, formulating search terms and exploring the databases in accordance with the instructions for the tasks.

The course evaluation showed that the students felt the library session to be concrete and clear. They also stated that they had gained new knowledge and skills relating to academic information searching processes. The design of the session, therefore, seems to have supported the students' learning processes, despite the initial disruption and on-the-spot alterations. However, we consider this session to have been unsuccessful due to the miscommunication with the course coordinator. As a consequence of this, the library session never became an integrated part of the course.

4 Reasoning

The aim of this chapter is to identify factors that seem to have an impact on the outcomes of academic librarians' teaching after a rapid transition to online teaching. A lot has been written about the benefits and strengths of online teaching. According to many studies, online teaching is flexible (Davis et al., 2019) and offers more opportunities for study than on-campus education (O'Shea et al., 2017). At the same time, there are obstacles. Students may lack technical resources and skills, and may feel socially isolated and distanced from the teachers when studying online. Previous studies indicate that successful online teaching requires strategically planned work activities, active participation from both instructors and students, time, and use of both synchronous and asynchronous tools (Yuan and Kim, 2014). By comparing our cases, we were able to identify three factors that seem to have affected the outcomes of our teaching after the rapid transition to online teaching: the level of active learning during the library teaching sessions, the time available to librarians for choosing, learning about and using digital tools online, and working relationships between teaching librarians and course coordinators.

In the literature on online teaching, two terms recur: active learning and interactive learning. One way to define these terms as well as the relationship between them is to assume interactivity to be a critical part of active learning (Mehlenbacher et al., 2000). When comparing our cases, the differences in the level of activity stand out as a contributing factor to the success of the sessions. In the successful case, the whole course was based on active ideas and the library workshop itself was designed in accordance with the ALC concept. In comparison, the first unsuccessful case had no interactive elements, and while the second unsuccessful case included activating learning elements in terms of group tasks, it never scaffolded active learning in any deeper sense. This difference should be noted. However, a lack of active learning was not the major hindrances in our unsuccessful cases. In the first unsuccessful case, students did not participate because they had already been working with similar content on a previous course, and in the second unsuccessful case, the miscommunication between the course coordinator and us was the main issue.

Academic librarians have a plethora of digital tools to choose from. Depending on the activity, different tools may be used (Rysavy and Michalak, 2020). Some, such as Zoom, can be used for synchronic activities (cf. Mi et al., 2020). Others are primarily designed for asynchronous activities, with the Mentimeter as one example. Determining what digital tools are suitable for specific teaching situations requires experience. Mashiyane et al. (2020) show that even though there is a high level of awareness among academic librarians regarding different multimedia (digital) tools, the librarians themselves seldom use these technologies and therefore lack experience. The extent of library staff's earlier experience of working online seems to influence how smoothly an online transition goes (Rysavy and Michalak, 2020; Walsh and Rana, 2020). In our first unsuccessful case, the librarian in charge lacked experience of using digital tools for online teaching. Such a lack of experience is not unusual; in an online teaching context, the instructor has to handle technology-related issues, which requires skills and competencies that not all instructors have (Crawford-Ferre and Wiest, 2012; Moore and Kearsley, 2011; Davis, et al., 2019). There are other studies showing that, with time, inexperienced librarians became familiar with the digital tools they were expected to work with during the pandemic and thus discovered several benefits of online services (Walsh and Rana, 2020). Time to learn was a specific element that was missing in our first unsuccessful case.

The time factor is about more than simply having time for learning how to use digital tools. Developing the session design and creating the digital learning object, i.e., creating videos and publishing materials in Canvas, was, in a sense, more labor-intensive and time-consuming than we suspect would have been the case if we had instead opted for a simple format with a 1-h lecture live-streamed via Zoom (interspersed with tasks). This in turn points to the fact that the way in which our pedagogical approach should be translated to the online learning environment was not very obvious from the outset, and that we found this out through trial and error. Considering this, it is perhaps no surprise that the successful case took place several weeks into the pandemic and after the close-down of the University campus. We thus also believe that our pedagogical knowledge and skills will evolve even further, as the pandemic, and, consequently, online teaching, continues.

Another aspect identified in research as a determining factor in the outcome of a library session is the relationship between teaching librarians and course coordinators. Previous studies have established the necessity of aspects such as a shared fundamental understanding, a mutual respect and trust (Ivey, 2003), and ongoing communication, especially during the planning phase (Meulemans and Carr, 2013), preferably with librarians establishing themselves, and being perceived as, experts and equal to the university teachers (Gardner and White-Farnham, 2013). However, studies have often identified an unequal power balance that hinders the working relationships between teaching librarians and course coordinators (Julien and Pecoski, 2009; York and Vance, 2009). Our three cases do not offer us any indications as to whether our relationships with faculty members have been affected during the pandemic. However, we see that a weak relationship may impact the ability of teaching librarians to reach students and thus achieve the teaching outcome in an online environment. If teaching librarians are considered as fully accredited members of the course teaching team, and given "teacher" access to the online learning environment of an LMS, a teaching librarian has more possible tools and arenas for interacting with students than in an on-campus context. However, it is important to remember that interactions with students via the LMS is not in itself a decisive factor for the outcome of librarians' involvement in a course; in the first unsuccessful case, as well as in the successful case, we received access to Canvas on the same terms as the rest of the teaching group with two completely different teaching outcomes. It is therefore not easy to identify a digital tool as being responsible in itself for a particular outcome.

Judging from the successful case, well-considered and customized educational designs that are supporting active learning and are developed in collaboration between course coordinators and teaching librarians, certain levels of knowledge about the use of digital tools and ample time for planning all seem to be factors that support successful outcome of teaching after a rapid transition to online teaching.

5 Our concluding thoughts

Over the course of 2020, the teaching team at the Social Sciences Libraries has developed deeper insights into the prerequisites for scaffolding successful online teaching. As the three cases show, some of these prerequisites we can affect, but not all.

Specific pedagogical approaches, such as designs supporting active learning, can easily be perceived as a necessity for, and perhaps also as a sign of, successful online teaching. Interestingly enough, however, the major hindrances in our unsuccessful cases were not related to a lack of interactivity in the educational designs, nor even to the educational designs as such. In the first unsuccessful case, students did not participate because they had already worked with similar content on a previous course, and in the second case, the library session was not well enough integrated into the course due to communication failures between the course coordinator and us. As we perceive it, these issues, which are unrelated to the transition to online teaching, could not have been compensated for by more extensively interactive sessions. It thus seems that the transition to online teaching has not altered the traditional issues faced by teaching librarians. Instead, previously well-known imbalances in course coordinator-librarian relationships and individual perceptions among course coordinators shaping the ability of librarians to create strong premises for successful student learning have taken new forms, such as differences in perspectives regarding librarians' access to the LMS.

Based on our experiences, online teaching should not be understood as less resource intensive. Shortly after the transition, we learned that online teaching requires resources that are in some ways different from those needed for classroom teaching, but it does not require fewer resources. Rather, as we have learned, successful online teaching might need *more* time than classroom teaching. Creating a relevant, well-functioning educational design for online teaching takes longer, especially if the librarian is new to it as well as to digital tools. We have discovered that this is not always understood when hours are allocated for planned teaching sessions. From a short-term perspective, librarians might choose to create elements of their online learning in their spare time, or might be forced to work overtime. In the longer term, this may cause teaching librarians to opt out of teaching activities considered to be too time-consuming, for example, choosing to hold lengthy live lectures on Zoom rather than to create qualitative digital materials to be implemented in varied educational designs. With the potential value of varied active teaching formats clearly demonstrated in our successful case, this could be an unfortunate development for academic librarian teaching.

Looking beyond the intensive months of March-September 2020, the online transition has made the teaching team aware of the potential of online learning environments and of the possibilities offered by digital tools in an online teaching context, and has allowed us to develop new work skills. It has also led us to initiate new discussions about learning and pedagogy. It is very likely that these experiences will have stamped their mark on the teaching methods we use in the future, beyond the end of the pandemic.

In summary, our purpose for this chapter is to identify factors that seem to have an impact on the outcomes of academic librarians' teaching after a rapid transition to online teaching. We have identified three factors that seem to have an impact but have not discussed what a successful outcome of academic librarians' teaching means. Is a successful outcome dependent on extensive student participation, or on librarians being considered as partners rather than service providers by the course coordinators, or on the library session being integrated and contributing to the outcome of the course in question? Or perhaps on a combination of all of these? Thanks to the transition to an online teaching format, we have gained new perspectives on prerequisites for successful outcome of teaching, and our belief has been strengthened that success is a matter of a sense of meaningfulness; a successful library session is a session that is considered meaningful by all involved, course coordinators, students and teaching librarians alike. No matter if it happens online or in a classroom.

References

Bates, A.W.T., 2019. Teaching in a Digital Age: Guidelines for Designing Teaching and Learning for a Digital Age. BC Open Textbooks, Vancouver.

Crawford-Ferre, H.G., Wiest, L.R., 2012. Effective online instruction in higher education. Q. Rev. Distance Educ. 13 (1), 11–14. https://eric.ed.gov/?id=EJ1005834.

Davis, C., Greenaway, R., Moore, M., Cooper, L., 2019. Online teaching in social work education: understanding the challenges. Aust. Soc. Work 72 (1), 34–46. https://doi-org.ezproxy.ub.gu.se/10.1080/0312407X.2018.1524918.

Gardner, C.C., White-Farnham, J., 2013. "She has a vocabulary I just don't have": faculty culture and information literacy collaboration. Collab. Librarianship 5 (4), 235–242. https://digitalcommons.du.edu/collaborativelibrarianship/vol5/iss4/3.

Ivey, R., 2003. Information literacy: how do librarians and academics work in partnership to deliver effective learning programs? Aust. Acad. Res. Libr. 34 (2), 100–113. https://doi.org/10.1080/00048623.2003.10755225.

Julien, H., Pecoski, J.L., 2009. Librarians' experiences of the teaching role: grounded in campus relationships. Libr. Inf. Sci. Res. 31 (3), 146–154. https://doi.org/10.1016/j.lisr.2009.03.005.

Mashiyane, D.M., Bangani, S., Van Deventer, K., 2020. The awareness and application of multimedia tools for information literacy instruction at an African university. Electron. Libr. 38 (4), 711–724. https://doi.org/10.1108/EL-02-2020-0027.

Mehlenbacher, B., Miller, C.R., Covington, D., Larsen, J.S., 2000. Active and interactive learning online: a comparison of web-based and conventional writing classes. IEEE Trans. Prof. Commun. 43 (2), 166–184. https://doi.org/10.1109/47.843644.

Mehta, D., Wang, X., 2020. COVID-19 and digital library services—a case study of a university library. Digit. Libr. Perspect. https://doi.org/10.1108/DLP-05-2020-0030. ahead-of-print.

Meulemans, Y.N., Carr, A., 2013. Not at your service: building genuine faculty-librarian partnerships. Ref. Serv. Rev. 41 (1), 80–90. https://doi.org/10.1108/00907321311300893.

Mi, M., Zhang, Y., Wu, L., Wu, W., 2020. Four health science librarians' experiences: how they responded to the COVID-19 pandemic crisis. Coll. Res. Libr. News 81 (7), 330–334. https://doi.org/10.5860/crln.81.7.330.

Moore, M.G., Kearsley, G., 2011. Distance Education: A Systems View of Online Learning. Wadsworth, Belmont, CA.

O'Shea, S., May, J., Stone, C., Delahunty, J., 2017. First-in-Family Students, University Experience and Family Life Motivations, Transitions and Participation. Palgrave Macmillan, London.

Rysavy, M.D.T., Michalak, R., 2020. Working from home: how we managed our team remotely with technology. J. Libr. Adm. 60 (5), 532–542. https://doi-org.ezproxy.ub.gu.se/10.1080/01930826.2020.1760569.

The Swedish Internet Foundation, 2020. Meaningful Time Online and the Pros and Cons of Digital Society. https://svenskarnaochinternet.se/rapporter/svenskarna-och-internet-2019/the-swedes-and-the-internet-2019-summary/. (Accessed 30 January 2021).

Walsh, B., Rana, H., 2020. Continuity of academic library services during the pandemic: the University of Toronto Libraries' response. J. Sch. Publ. 51 (4), 237–245. https://doi.org/10.3138/jsp.51.4.04.

Wiley, D.A., 2000. Connecting learning objects to instructional design theory: a definition, a metaphor, and a taxonomy. In: Wiley, D.A. (Ed.), The Instructional Use of Learning Objects. Online version. Available: http://reusability.org/read/.

York, A.C., Vance, J.M., 2009. Taking library instruction into the online classroom: best practices for embedded librarians. J. Libr. Adm. 49 (1–2), 197–209. https://doi-org.ezproxy.ub.gu.se/10.1080/01930820802312995.

Yuan, J., Kim, C., 2014. Guidelines for facilitating the development of learning communities in online courses. J. Comput. Assist. Learn. 30 (3), 220–232. https://doi-org.ezproxy.ub.gu.se/10.1111/jcal.12042.

How the Corona pandemic influenced public libraries in Denmark

Carl Gustav Johannsen
University of Copenhagen, Copenhagen, Denmark

1 Introduction

On the evening of March 11, 2020, the Danish Prime Minister, Mette Frederiksen, announced a complete lockdown of Denmark, with effect from the following day. The country was then effectively shut down until May 8, when some parts of the public and private sector gradually began to open. Public libraries were closed for user access on March 13, but continued to offer digital services, in particular, e-books. Libraries gradually began to reopen a month later.

The shutdown was unexpected by the Danish library sector. Indeed, not one of the ten future challenges for public libraries in the 2020s identified by the experienced public library expert Jens Thorhauge referred to the possible effects of a pandemic (Thorhauge 2020, pp. 24–25). Instead, challenges such as climate change, economic and social inequality, civil society, and leadership challenges were regarded as the most important. One month later, Danish library journals were filled with reports from Corona-affected library services. Although the shutdown was unforeseen, later developments showed that the Danish public library system was able to meet the inevitable challenges.

The following account of the public library-oriented events and developments is primarily based upon the three main sources:

(1) Reports published by the Danish Library Association and published in the journal of the association: *Danmarks Biblioteker* (*Denmark's Libraries*)
(2) Reports made by Michael Moos-Bjerre (published July 1, 2020) as a consultant for the Danish Library Association
(3) Research report by two Danish sociologists (available online June 18, 2020).

2 Reports by the Danish Library Association

The year 2020 started unremarkably enough; it was announced in the year's first number of *Denmark's Libraries* that one of the most significant events to come would be the centenary of the first Danish public library law in 1920.

The April number of the same journal was dominated by the likely effects of the pandemic. The tone was optimistic and constructive. The secret weapon of the public

Libraries, Digital Information, and COVID. https://doi.org/10.1016/B978-0-323-88493-8.00033-1

libraries was their comprehensive digital resources, accessible from users' homes. The closure of physical services did not therefore mean the total interruption of public library provision in Denmark. On the contrary, various digital services were available covering different media such as e-books, e-books in English, audio books, films, digital courses, and reference services. Many libraries had already developed new digital online services and other Corona-related innovations, including new ways of printed book delivery.

Reports from libraries were published, telling how efforts were made to make the transformation as smooth as possible for users. Communication was considered essential; some libraries stressed that users should meet the new realities through personal and verbal communication, not through signs and posters (Niegaard, 2020).

The library cases presented by the Danish Library Association indicate that Danish public libraries facing the Corona lockdown challenges have applied the three different strategies:

(1) From analogue to digital library services
(2) Focusing on students
(3) Children and families: stimulating reading activities (Niegaard, 2020, p. 12).

Staff resources have been transferred from borrowing and user services to telephone and online services. In particular, staff were focused on the production of online content for the Facebook site and the homepage of the local library.

3 Economic challenges

The shutdown and the transition towards digital services resulted in economic challenges, mostly because digital services, compared with physical media, were priced and paid for differently. It was expected that the reduced access to physical libraries would lead to an increased demand for digital services. It was not fully anticipated that increased costs would be one of the results of the changes in user demand.

Because of different cost calculations in libraries between books and other physical materials, on the one hand, and digital materials, on the other, an increased demand for a physical book would not mean extra expenditures—but surely longer waiting times—unless the library decided to buy extra copies. Higher usage of digital materials would lead to increased expenditure, at least where authors are paid per view.

Danish public libraries had typically defined a fixed monthly quota for digital materials per user. The closure of physical libraries led to increased expenditures. From the authors' viewpoint, this mechanism was beneficial since it would lead to increased income. Lack of user access to the physical library also meant less income in terms of fees.

A small poll made by the Danish Library Association showed that loans via the digital platform for video films and DVD in the week March 16–22, 2020, had doubled to 55,000 shows per week from about 26,000 about a month earlier (Hartz Larsen, 2020, p. 7). A survey from March 23 to April 5, 2020, showed that many allowed increased user access to popular platforms as a result of greater demand (Hartz Larsen, 2020 p. 7).

COVID-related closures have also stimulated innovation such as the development of online live debates with authors, and courses delivered through live-streaming (Hartz Larsen, 2020, p. 7).

4 Moos Bjerre's 2020 survey for the Danish Library Association

The Moos-Bjerre survey was conducted in May-June 2020 as an online questionnaire survey with a sample of 1505 respondents aged 15 or over. This report focused on literacy and the importance of public libraries in the development of reading habits among children. A key theme was children's library use and its influence on later educational levels and trajectories. The probability of attaining a higher education level was 9% higher in the case of children who had been library users. It was particularly valuable to examine how the Corona-induced shutdown of public libraries influenced reading habits in families.

Moos-Bjerre's survey revealed that 23% of the respondents increased their reading of literature during the shutdown. Among library users, this rose to 28%. More interesting were the observations about the use of libraries' digital media. The results showed that 17% of respondents "fully agreed" or "agreed" that the closures had stimulated an increased use of digital literature platforms. Eight percent agreed that they had become more familiar with the use of e-books, though 67% did not agree. Ten percent either "agreed" or "fully agreed" that they were now more familiar with e-books. These results demonstrate how the close-down has been an opportunity to try out and acquire new reading habits and competencies. Every fourth Danish parent (23% of the total survey population) thought that the shutdown had inspired them to read more together with their children.

5 The sociologists' survey: COVID-19 has magnified existing inequalities

Another recent survey (Meier Jæger and Hoppe Blaabaek, 2020) showed that COVID-19 also had negative consequences by increasing existing inequalities in children's learning opportunities. Survey data on home schooling activities showed that socioeconomic differences that existed before COVID seemed to have increased during the lockdown. High-SES (socioeconomic status) families took out more digital and hard copy children's books before the COVID-19 lockdown than low-SES families. Since the pandemic, the baseline SES gradient increased: High-SES families consistently took out more digital children's books than low-SES families in each of the three phases of the COVID lockdown, documenting that inequality increased. Overall, the results suggest that COVID increased inequality in learning opportunities because better-off families were more successful in using libraries during the pandemic than worse-off families (Meier Jæger and Hoppe Blaabaek, 2020).

High-SES parents provided more academic support such as help with homework, computers/tablets, and motivational support for their children than low-SES parents. The study also includes information on daily borrowing of all types of materials from all Danish public libraries. Data on library usage has also been linked to information about the families that borrowed the materials. In total, the data included more than 55 million family-by-day transactions covering the months of February, March, and April 2020. The results indicate that digital delivery does not seem to promote social equality.

6   Libraries compared with other cultural institutions

The reopening of Danish public libraries began on May 18, with opportunities for users to borrow materials and later to use the physical library. However, in October 2020, the planned gradual reopening was reconsidered because of increased danger of infection. Indeed, the libraries were then re-closed from December 2020, for the time being until February 2021, because of increased spread of infection from 218 to 372 infected per 100.000 inhabitants from December 6 to 15, 2020, an increase of 70% (db.dk).

Museums and theatres were unhappy with the sequence of reopening. There are many reasons why authorities decided to reopen libraries before other institutions, including the distinction between low- and high-intensive meeting places as defined by Ragnar Audunson. The library is seen as a low-intensive meeting place, but one which offers opportunities to meet people with a different background from your own (Audunson, 2005).

7   Perspectives and lessons learned

The recent experiences of many private companies have showed that productivity and effectiveness were affected positively through increased homeworking, although some employees have missed the community spirit of the physical working place. In public libraries, a greater degree of remote working is likely to be less beneficial. On the other hand, digital provision has been shown to be a strong, future-oriented element in facing pandemic-like challenges. But there is an attendant problem of COVID socioeconomic imbalance. Similarly, the staff-less library model was not staff-less at all. Indeed, Denmark's many unstaffed libraries were not kept open during the COVID shutdown phase, because staff still play a significant role. Indeed, COVID has at least indirectly demonstrated the qualities of the physical library, and, most importantly, the vitality and innovative spirit of the public library idea and the value of library staff.

References

Audunson, R., 2005. The public library as a meeting place in multicultural and digital context: the necessity of low-intensive meeting places. J. Doc. 6 (3), 429–441.

Hartz Larsen, M., 2020. Bibliotekernes corona-aktiviteter/the corona-related activities of the libraries. Danmarks Biblioteker 2, 7.

Meier Jæger, M., Hoppe Blaabaek, E., 2020. Inequality in learning opportunities during COVID-19: evidence from library takeout. Res. Soc. Stratif. Mobil. 68. https://doi.org/10.1016/j.rssm.2020.100524.

Moos-Bjerre, M., 2020. *Opinionsmåling* 2020: *Moos-Bjerre for Danmarks Biblioteksforening.* Copenhagen https://www.db.dk/corona-og-bibliotekernes-digitale-tilbud-styrker-laeselysten.

Niegaard, H., 2020. Corona-ramte Silkeborg Bibliotek i fuld sving/Silkeborg Public Library hidden by corona in full swing. Danmarks Biblioteker 2, 10–13.

Thorhauge, J., 2020. 10 udfordringer til 20'erne/Ten challenges of the 20's. Danmarks Biblioteker (1), 24–25.

Digital information services provided by libraries during the COVID-19 pandemic: Case studies from the viewpoint of supply chain management

6

Bulcsu Szekely
LUT University (Lappeenranta-Lahti University of Technology LUT), Lappeenranta, Finland

> *Open science is like a love letter to the future. We cannot always anticipate the concrete opportunities that will evolve, but it is still important to do the right things now that will enable the use of data later.*
>
> **Susanna Nykyri, Head of Open Science Services at Tampere University Library, cited in Korhonen (2020).**

1 Introduction

The Finnish academic sector has long been under great pressure. Between 2015 and 2019, over 500 million euros has been cut from university budgets. The emerging scale of uncertainty as a result of COVID-19 is set to make the future even more uncertain. System agility has a key role in determining optimal solutions for managing uncertainties in time of crisis (Dai et al., 2020; Ivanov, 2020; Keeler, 2020; Krishnamurthy, 2020; Mehta and Wang, 2020; Shaw and Alexander, 2020; Schwab and Held, 2020). Traditionally, the evolution of value creation within research initiatives in Finland has been a linear one, part of a stable environment. Now, during the emerging crisis, at a time of turbulence, there is a great need for an interactive, trusted, open science approach in supply chains of research ecosystem (Haak et al., 2020; Keeler, 2020; Loima 2020; Mehta and Wang, 2020; Schwab and Held, 2020). In this chapter, five case studies are discussed within the specific context of industry-university collaboration. As the starting point of the analysis, core concepts are defined, and the theoretical framework is set forward. The aim is to highlight the opportunities and identify the limiting factors that reduce the extent to which existing potential within these scientific networks can be exploited. The focus is on the transition process toward an agile online learning center model. The metrics used are aimed at evaluating the degree of inclusivity, transparency, and collaboration within research projects in stimulating positive network effects (Haak et al., 2020; Soares et al., 2020).

Libraries, Digital Information, and COVID. https://doi.org/10.1016/B978-0-323-88493-8.00013-6

The information for this chapter was gathered by desktop research, visiting the libraries in question, acting as a client (the author has been a registered customer at the targeted academic libraries for more than ten years), using available services online and offline, talking to library service experts, exploring the websites of the associated universities from January to November 2020. In addition, a series of interviews was carried out with specialists from other universities, research institutions, and industry sectors. The main criterion when selecting specialists was that they were involved in university-industry collaboration in the field of digital supply chain management, as, for example, in smart data mobility projects.

2   Definitions

Supply chain management is about conveying materials, products, services, and related information between manufacturers and service providers in the most cost-effective way. A core element is the exchange of information which becomes crucial in the case of emergency operations. The speed with which information services are delivered within digital ecosystems and the transparency of process are of primary importance. In the context of the evolving emergency, systems thinking is a tool to help create data quality transparency and assist with the measurement of key performance indicators (Araz et al., 2020; Azeroual et al., 2018; Foreman et al., 2020; Wang, 2017). Agility indicates the extent to which a system is resilient and responsive (Dai et al., 2020; Mehta and Wang, 2020). An ecosystem is a cluster: an interconnected network of supply chains across industries (Ratten, 2020; VTT, 2012). A library network is defined as a research ecosystem knowledge supply center for universities. This research uses a qualitative case study approach combined with an interpretive action research methodology. As a researcher, the author interprets the environment as a social construction by judging specific organizational factors.

3   Lessons from the past—Digital information services for mitigating supply chain emergency

The COVID-19 pandemic has dramatically altered expectations of digital service systems in academic libraries. No one knows how long and how severe the overall impact of COVID will be for scientific communities in the future in either social or financial terms. Agile capabilities have a central role in responding to the emerging needs of stakeholders. Agility can lead to a situation in which information can be delivered more quickly, with higher reliability, and at a lower cost overall.

"Knowledge and best practice in this field are constantly changing. As new research and experience broaden our understanding, changes in research methods, professional practices may become necessary" (Baker and Evans, 2016). An event with a rate of unpredictability comparable with the current crisis is the 2011 tsunami in Japan. A lesson from this disaster is that with an unforeseeable chain of events, the need to integrate theory with practice becomes evident (FUURT, 2020; Haak et al., 2020; Loima 2020; Lovari and Bowen, 2020; Schwab and Held, 2020). Uncertainty is reflected in the use of virtual social forums, such as is happening now on BrightTALK. Collecting, analyzing, and disseminating transparent data while coordinating research projects via virtual channels becomes critical (Baker et al., 2020; Gul and Bano, 2020). In the future, organizations that coordinate digital space will have a key facilitative role. The challenge will be to mitigate the risk of disruptions to digital supply chains within the context of ever-growing uncertainty (Manners-Bell, 2020; Shaw and Alexander, 2020).

4 Case studies: Reflections upon current practices

Three Finnish academic libraries form this case study: Two are located in the capital and one in Karelia. **X** is the oldest and most prestigious academic library in Helsinki. The university with which **X** is associated, provides pharmacology education within the Faculty of Medicine, which also owns and operates a pharmacy network. **X** provides outsiders with a separate "guest" account to access all licensed digital resources. **Y** is an academic library in Espoo, Helsinki, and Mikkeli with one of the most diversified set of collections in Finland, established with the merger of three universities in 2010. Multidisciplinary studies are conducted, for example, with the Department of Bioproducts and Biosystems, Department of Neuroscience, Biomedical Engineering, and Department of Industrial Engineering and Management. There is a learning centre with rooms for video conferencing. **Y** is part of the HELMET (Helsinki Metropolitan Area Libraries) network of public libraries, covering the cities of Helsinki, Espoo, Vantaa, and Kauniainen. **Y** does not provide separate accounts for visitors, but does offer free access to the Internet via an open wireless network. **Z** is a brand new library network based in the cities of Lappeenranta, Lahti, and Kouvola. The university has two special features: it functions under a corporate model, and there is a university of applied science involved in the group structure. The library is one of Finland's EU Documentation Centers. **X** has the greatest potential to coordinate research in international healthcare supply chains, but **Y** has the advantage of large sets of engineering and digital supply chain resources at its disposal. Z does not address the digital access needs of people from outside the university because of the pandemic and the fact that the university is about to implement a new database management platform, with delays in the implementation process. Of the three libraries described, only X engaged actively with the author through a customer survey, which emphasized that "In 2021 the Library will start a customer panel for developing HELKA" (Library-network X, 2020). All three libraries are offering a wide range of services during lockdown, such as

- Online customer service,
- Remote access to electronic resources,
- Remote guidance on information seeking,
- Reference material for thesis writing,
- Pick-up service for printed material
- Webinars.

However, remote access is not available to external users, though it is still possible to place an interlibrary loan request online, for a fee, as with the other two libraries in this study. Library Z aims to leverage the value of digitization to the international academic community through a multiorganizational platform focusing on opportunities for industrial e-learning. The aim is to create an online community:

> To meet the needs of today's students, industries, and societies, the CEPHEI Project brings together four major elements: innovations in industry; links between universities and industry; a flipped learning approach; and a freemium model of education. This project is contributing to the scale-up of flipped and e-learning in the field of Industrial Innovation. Thus, the best university of tomorrow is one that is able to orchestrate the wide diversity in the supply of teaching materials, project-based learning in international multidisciplinary teams, and real needs of industry and society.
>
> *(Cephei Industrial E-Learning News, 2020)*

Despite its size, **Z** has well-founded resources for implementing a Massive Online Open Course (MOOC). With the help of the Cephei project, this institution has the ability to carry out massive online open conferences (Chechurin, 2020; LUT University News, 2018). This initiative started in October 2017. Online courses are accessible via the project website. However, there is no list available on past courses and material used during those events; nor is there any list of articles to access, view, download, or add for public use. By keeping data collection and analytical processes open, it would be easier to reproduce research undertaken and build upon findings in other settings. An interactive digital asset (metadata) management software would allow specialists to verify data and analysis, and so gain new customers internationally (Azeroual et al., 2018; Baker et al., 2020; Gul and Bano, 2020; Keeler, 2020; Khan Arnob et al., 2020; Young and Rossmann, 2015).

By implementing the FAIR (Findable, Accessible, Interoperable, Reproducible) principle, this online learning centre could become a digital workspace where it would be possible to trace down "open linked data" and transform sets to any set of "open linked knowledge" (Baker and Evans, 2016; Haak et al. 2020; Soares et al., 2020).

Library **W** is part of the largest research ecosystem in Finland with its centre in Espoo. It is operated by a nonprofit-limited liability company **A,** owned by the Finnish state through the Ministry of Economy Affairs and Employment, which is responsible for managing operations. During interviews, it was revealed that there is ongoing research cooperation with Oulu University on the data support needs of researchers. This research group orders high-value books for individual use on academic projects. The expert interviewed gave further details

> The COVID-19 pandemic has caused significant disruption to the way business operates. The many unknowns surrounding the virus, such as the duration of its spread or expectations for revenue growth, make planning for the future difficult. We need to confirm the financial conditions of information providers. We need reliable, trustworthy information sources and tools, and secure access methods to subscribed content.
>
> Negotiation skills are important for both subscriber and information provider. Mutual understanding of tailoring services helps to meet organizational needs. Reporting

skills will be crucial, to prove the importance of the source to the top management = ROI (return on investment). Information literacy skills: training and guidance increase awareness and usage. Transformative agreements allow access and publishing options for research outputs. Working from home makes our employees fully utilize our digital information services. Long-term agreements give steadiness. Open Access helps with budgeting and gives tools to disseminate research outputs.

Mergers or bankruptcies of information providers might bring competitive advantage for big publishers and cause price increases. Librarians share best practices and undertake benchmarking. Institutions strengthen national collaboration, publishing mutually agreed, national policies and recommendations. Joint procurement brings cost savings. For example, the FinELib consortium for Finnish universities, research institutions, and public libraries secures and improves the availability of electronic resources. Data management planning tool DMPTuuli helps us to create, review, and share data management plans that meet our and funder requirements. JUFO—Publication Forum is a classification of publication channels created by the Finnish scientific community to support the quality assessment of academic research. The research data storage service IDA is a continuous service for safe research data storage organized by the Ministry of Education and Culture.

(Expert A, 2020)

Company B, based in Frankfurt, is a research-oriented unit that belongs to a multinational German corporation. The focus is on smart mobility and smart city research in particular. They operate an online coordination platform to manage data and information across regions. In so doing, they build a digital workplace, a data hub to create individual mobility services. As an expert from this company stated:

Design mediates between human and technology, human and system, human and society, and thus plays a key role in mediating future technology. In the sense of universal design, a product can only be understood by as many people as possible if the interfaces are designed accordingly. This includes all levels of design: the structuring and weighting of information, the form, symbols, feedback, sound, surface, atmosphere. I am actually only interested in the idea that future mobility is not determined by the thought of vehicles and infrastructure, but rather by the idea that future mobility is thought of as software, similar to the way digitization is thought. Then I as a user can individually determine how I want to move around; independently, according to my own wishes. Cashless payment and cross-platform, individualized solutions are certainly the key. At the same time, in terms of design, such systems have the task of being understood by everyone and, above all, of conveying trust.

(Eckart, 2020)

B aims to create agile mobility as a service platform where inclusivity, transparency, and collaboration are key elements. In the same way, digital libraries can be seen as a hub for smart data mobility, facilitating researchers, companies, and students to work toward common goals of building new online community infrastructures.

There is a real need for new library information services in Finland to create an open innovation "one-stop-shop" research coordination and brainstorming platform to address better the emerging needs of stakeholders of universities and their industrial partners. A great amount of information is currently lost: Students and many researchers still use memory sticks and other external storage facilities for the information they gathered. When one loses a memory stick, libraries are not able to return the device to the owner. In most instances, the knowledge saved on this type of external database is lost. There is a demand for digital online repositories where one could work safely on a constant basis. Libraries could set up digital platforms using cloud solutions connecting universities in Finland, with agencies, hospitals, and pharmacies to form a network for managing disaster relief operations across Scandinavia and beyond (HUMLOG Institute, 2020; Ivanov, 2020; VTT, 2012). A robust, agile ecosystem could be centred within the interconnected virtual network of university libraries. Large, multinational digital infrastructure service providers such as Google could play a significant role in creating new hubs in cooperation with academic libraries. These virtual hubs could be of help in forming new communities that may become future customers of, or investors in, online interactive community platforms (Baker et al., 2020; Keeler, 2020).

Highly valuable sets of data remain hidden in university research networks in Finland. The adverse effects on research are potentially detrimental to value-added experiences of stakeholders of digital industry research communities. It can be argued that the ecosystems of the academic libraries in this case study are only to a limited extent collaborative, with a lack of transparency and inclusivity. The research companies examined are way ahead in terms of implementing open science principles. The firms studied offer novel value-added services for researchers and students in helping them to conduct research online.

Based on the case studies, COVID-19 caused a panic reaction: libraries focused more on intraorganizational issues while addressing the needs of their own researchers and students. One can argue that this policy militates against transparency and inclusivity, creating silos among project teams and other user groups.

5 Conclusions

It can be seen that the Finnish library networks featured in this chapter have much still to do to become interlinked, inclusive, and transparent. While there is some collaboration in serving users, fear of potential negative future impacts of COVID-19 on university budgets and a range of administrative barriers are potential blockages to the development of radical new service models (Loima, 2020; FUURT, 2020). The supply chain of value creation within publishing processes at these library networks is still a linear one, and the transition process toward an open science-oriented operation model has just begun (Chechurin, 2020; LUT University News, 2018; UNITE! University Network, 2020; VTT, 2019): The mindset change required is not there yet. The FAIR-principle should be embedded into projects so that supply chains within the research ecosystem could become agile. The library networks discussed in this case study could play a critical role in forming a novel agile research ecosystem enabling cloud-based digital workplace platforms. In the future, data access considerations related to user group policies and existing administrative barriers will need to be investigated fully.

References

Araz, O.M., Ramirez-Nafarrate, A., Jehn, M., Wilson, F.A., 2020. The importance of widespread testing for COVID-19 pandemic: systems thinking for drive-through testing sites. Health Syst. 9 (2), 119–123.

Azeroual, O., Saake, G., Wastl, J., 2018. Data measurement in research information systems: metrics for the evaluation of data quality. Scientometrics 115 (3), 1271–1290.

Baker, D., Evans, W., 2016. Digital Information Strategies: From Applications and Content to Libraries and People. Chandos, Oxford.

Baker, D., Ellis, L., Williams, C., Chan, D., Fulkerson, M., 2020. COVID-19: The Future of Digital Information for Libraries—Partnerships, Supply and Demand—Panel Discussion, Asia-Pacific eBook Forum 2020 webinar-presentation. Elsevier. https://www.elsevier.com/en-au/solutions/sciencedirect/apac-ebook-2020. (Accessed 19 April 2021).

Cephei Industrial E-Learning News, 2020. Welcome to the Cephei Community. Blog, May 3 https://www.cephei.eu/en/news/Blog/welcome-to-cephei-community/. (Accessed 20 April 2021).

Chechurin, L., 2020. Systematic Creativity and TRIZ basics, Online Courses, Course Information. Open Access https://www.cephei.eu/en/online-courses/1226317/systematic-creativity-and-triz-basics/. (Accessed 20 April 2021).

Dai, T., Zaman, H.M., Padula, W.V., Davidson, P.M., 2020. Supply chain failures amid Covid-19 signal a new pillar for global health preparedness. J. Clin. Nurs., 1–3.

Eckart, P., 2020. Perspectives from Prof. Peter Eckart—An Interview 15 October. IOKI, Blog https://ioki.com/en/perspectives-from-prof-peter-eckart/. (Accessed 20 April 2021).

Expert A, 2020. A Microsoft Teams—Discussion with Expert A From Company A—An Interview 29 October. Company A.

Finnish Union of University Researchers and Teachers (FUURT), 2020. Free Research and High-Quality Education That Support the Renewal of Society are Key Elements of Structural Change. Press Release, September 15 https://tieteentekijat.fi/en/free-research-and-high-quality-education-that-support-the-renewal-of-society-are-key-elements-of-structural-change/. (Accessed 26 May 2021).

Foreman, R., Atun, R., McKii, M., Mossialos, E., 2020. 12 Lessons learned from the management of the coronavirus pandemic. Health Policy 124, 577–580.

Gul, S., Bano, S., 2020. Smart libraries: an emerging and innovative technological habitat of 21st century. Electron. Libr. 37 (5), 764–783.

Haak, W., Chatterji, P., Decker-Lucke, S., Schlosser, S., Watson, S., 2020. Open Science Tools for Discovering, Promoting and Sharing Research, an Elsevier Library Connect Webinar—Presentation, October 22. https://www.elsevier.com/events/webinars/open-science-tools-for-discovering-promoting-and-sharing-research. (Accessed 20 April 2021).

HUMLOG Institute, 2020. Health Emergency Response in Interconnected Systems (HERoS). An ongoing EU Research Project, Coordinating partner: Hanken School of Economics, the Humanitarian Logistics and Supply Chain Research Institute (HUMLOG), Finland https://www.hanken.fi/en/departments-and-centres/department-marketing/humlog/research-projects/ongoing-projects/health. (Accessed 20 April 2021).

Ivanov, D., 2020. Viable supply chain model: integrating agility, resilience and sustainability perspectives—lessons from and thinking beyond the COVID-19 pandemic. Ann. Oper. Res. https://link.springer.com/article/10.1007/s10479-020-03640-6. (Accessed 26 May 2021).

Keeler, J.P., 2020. Using Innovation Intelligence to Unlock the Covid-19 Crisis, Webinar—Presentation. Academy by Patsnap, https://info.patsnap.com/on-demand-webinar-using-innovation-intelligence-to-unlock-the-covid-19-crisis. (Accessed 26 May 2021).

Khan Arnob, I., Kaliteevskii, V., Shnai, I., Chechurin, L., 2020. Analysis of students' performance in an online discussion forum: a social network approach. In: Arseniev, D.G., Overmeyer, L., Kälviäinen, H., Katalinić, B. (Eds.), Cyber-Physical Systems and Control. Lecture Notes in Networks and Systems, Springer International Publishing. https://www.springerprofessional.de/en/analysis-of-students-performance-in-an-online-discussion-forum-a/17452046. (Accessed 19 April 2021).

Korhonen, M., 2020. Open science is generating new understanding. Tampere Univ. Res. News. 6 April https://www.tuni.fi/en/news/open-science-generating-new-understanding. (Accessed 19 April 2021).

Krishnamurthy, S., 2020. The impact of COVID-19 on IT services industry—expected transformations. Br. J. Manag. 31 (3), 450–452. Free access https://onlinelibrary.wiley.com/doi/full/10.1111/1467-8551.12423. (Accessed 26 May 2021).

Library-network X, 2020. Customer Survey. https://elomake.helsinki.fi/lomakkeet/104161/lomake.html?rinnakkaislomake=Customer_survey_english. (Accessed 14 December 2020).

Loima, J., 2020. Socio-educational policies and Covid-19—a case study on Finland and Sweden in the Spring 2020. Int. J. Educ. Literacy Stud. 8 (3). Free access http://www.journals.aiac.org.au/index.php/IJELS/article/view/6201. (Accessed 26 May 2021).

Lovari, A., Bowen, S.A., 2020. Social media in disaster communication: a case study of strategies, barriers, and ethical implications. J. Public Aff. 20 (1). Special Issue.

LUT University News, 2018. International CEPHEI Project Aims to Build an e-Learning Platform That Follows Progress and Tests Knowledge. LUT University 2018, 24 August https://www.lut.fi/web/en/news/-/asset_publisher/lGh4SAywhcPu/content/international-cephei-project-aims-to-build-an-e-learning-platform-that-follows-progress-and-tests-knowledge. (Accessed 20 April 2021).

Manners-Bell, J., 2020. Supply Chain Risk Management: How to Design and Manage Resilient Supply Chains, third ed. Kogan Page Publishing.

Mehta, D., Wang, X., 2020. COVID-19 and digital library services—a case study of a university library. Digit. Libr. Perspect. 36 (4), 351–363.

Ratten, V., 2020. Coronavirus and international business: an entrepreneurial ecosystem perspective. Thunderbird Int. Bus. Rev. 62 (5), 629–634. Free access https://onlinelibrary.wiley.com/doi/full/10.1002/tie.22161. (Accessed 26 May 2021).

Schwab, S., Held, L., 2020. Science after Covid-19: Faster, better, stronger? Significance—R. Stat. Soc. 17 (4), 8–9. Free access https://rss.onlinelibrary.wiley.com/doi/full/10.1111/1740-9713.01415. (Accessed 26 May 2021).

Shaw, R., Alexander, D., 2020. COVID-19: How Can We Better Integrate Health and Disaster Management? A Workshop-Webinar Presentation. Elsevier Researcher Academy. 16 July 2020 https://www.journals.elsevier.com/international-journal-of-disaster-risk-reduction/news/covid-19-health-and-disaster-management. (Accessed 19 April 2021).

Soares, B.H., Assunção, P., Hoblos, A., Slade, B., 2020. Data Governance: How to move from Strategy into Practice with IDC and Novartis a TIBCO—Software Webinar Presentation December 3. https://www.brighttalk.com/webcast/17090/454456?utm_campaign=knowledge-feed&utm_source=brighttalk-portal&utm_medium=web. (Accessed 20 April 2021).

UNITE!—University Network for Innovation, Technology and Engineering, 2020. Bridging the Gaps Between Engineering, Science, Technology and the Grand Challenges of Society: UNITE! Ambitions for 2025, An EU—Project Co-founded by Erasmus+ Programme, Horizon. Framework Programme https://www.unite-university.eu/about-us. (Accessed 20 April 2021).

VTT, 2012. High-tech Hospital Forum—Summary in English: Projects and Cooperation Networks Relating to High-Tech Hospital Forum. VTT Technical Research Centre of Finland Ltd. http://htsairaala.vtt.fi/english.htm. (Accessed 26 May 2021).

VTT, 2019. OPEN MODE Project Co-develops New Logistics Solutions and Services for Consumers. VTT Technical Research Centre of Finland Ltd. Press Release 28.8.2019 https://www.vttresearch.com/en/news-and-ideas/open-mode-project-co-develops-new-logistics-solutions-and-services-consumers. (Accessed 19 April 2021).

Wang, J., 2017. Supply Chain Management for Collection Services of Academic Libraries— Solving Operational Challenges and Enhancing User Productivity. Chandos, Cambridge.

Young, S.W.H., Rossmann, D., 2015. Building library community through social media. Inf. Technol. Libr. 34 (1), 20–37.

COVID-19: Libraries' responses to the global health emergency

7

Valentini Moniarou-Papaconstantinou[a] and Evgenia Vassilakaki[b]
[a]Dept. Archives, Library and Information Studies, University of West Attica, Athens, Greece,
[b]European Insurance and Occupational Pensions Authority (EIOPA), Frankfurt, Germany

1 Introduction

The new type of coronavirus (COVID-19) began to spread rapidly all over the world forcing the World Health Organization (WHO) to define it as a pandemic on March 11, 2020. During the first wave, many countries (March till May 2020) implemented lockdowns of varying lengths, leading to the closures of nonessential services to mitigate the spread of the virus. In addition, they strongly recommended special measures to prevent transmission and spread. Working from home, online learning as the only mode at all levels of education, conversion of public or cultural events online, to name just a few examples, were introduced as a response to the "new normal."

Viruses tend to spread in waves with the first wave of infection often followed by a more severe one. At the time of writing, many countries, especially in Europe, are experiencing the second wave of COVID-19 (November 2020). The pandemic continues to affect the lives of individuals, families, communities, and organizations across the world, especially as the number of cases and deaths continues to increase. COVID-19 has already revealed serious types of social, organizational, logistical, economic, and political problems, though its real effect has yet to be seen. Country after country came to the decision to impose intermittent lockdowns, whether regional or national, based on the available scientific data in relation to the spread of the virus. In most European countries, the importance of human life and keeping the number of casualties low was the ultimate priority. However, there is a consensus among economists, politicians, and policy-makers that COVID-19 is likely to cause a world recession that has not been experienced since World War II (EBLIDA, 2020).

In this extraordinary situation, most information organizations have either closed their premises or operated with social distancing and contactless communication, coping with significant and ongoing changes to services, spaces, and other professional aspects. Information organizations around the world have long ago advocated the development of digital information resources and services, with novel paths for dissemination of research information, notably institutional repositories and open access for scholarly communication.

Consequently, libraries have already provided digital services, access to specific platforms, online programmes, opportunities for research interaction, support to online learning, and development of robust search interfaces. They are therefore well positioned to continue and expand their provision introducing new services to their

Libraries, Digital Information, and COVID. https://doi.org/10.1016/B978-0-323-88493-8.00018-5

clientele during this health emergency. It is worth mentioning that public libraries reported an increase in online borrowing throughout lockdown. For example, three times more books were borrowed in UK libraries, and a remarkable 358% increase in the number of people borrowing e-books during the first 3 weeks of lockdown was recorded (Chandler, 2020). Furthermore, access to digital resources has increased also in academic and research libraries, but to a less marked extent since academic communities were using electronic resources long before the crisis (EBLIDA, 2020). At this point, it should be mentioned that many electronic resource database vendors and publishers provided free access to COVID-19-related resources. Publishers unlocked their content and made possible resource sharing to support online learning and facilitate open research. This chapter aims to identify the range of services information organizations provide in response to COVID-19 pandemic; highlight the issues that arise in the effort to provide trusted information; and outline the challenges they face in this global health emergency.

2 Libraries' responses to the pandemic

Few studies have examined how different types of libraries responded, among other disasters, to the 2003 SARS outbreak, the 2005 H5N1, and the 2009 HIN1 virus crises (Featherstone et al., 2008, 2012; McGuire, 2007; Zach, 2011). The roles identified for librarians during such health emergencies have included disaster planning of operations at library and institutional level; protecting collections throughout the disaster and thus continuing to provide access; disseminating reliable information to clients, institutions, and the wider public; developing documents to improve their daily operation; supporting the community by providing emotional engagement; preparing reports, seminars, and training on the use of information tools; providing emergency reference service; evaluating information considered crucial for administrative decision-making; using educational technology; and developing new learning tools for e-learning in higher education (Featherstone et al., 2008, 2012; McGuire, 2007). However, Zach (2011), who investigated the responses of public libraries during the HIN1 emergency, found that although a number of libraries successfully provided risk-related information to their patrons, less than one-third of the participating libraries supplied information related to HIN1 or links to the appropriate resources. He stated that libraries provide mainly information about themselves and their events, and concluded that librarians in times of emergency need to play a more central role as providers of trusted information.

Most libraries' responses and roles identified in the SARS-, H5N1-, and HIN1-related literature might be similar to those identified during the present outbreak. However, the emphasis is different because of the novel characteristics of COVID-19, the changes in the information environment, the use of new health tools, the availability of digital health resources, the widespread use of social media, and the need for assistance in identifying trusted information. In particular, a number of studies have examined the way libraries have responded to the pandemic, focusing on digital health literacy, the provision of reliable health information, and digital divides

(Gann, 2020; Morgan-Daniel et al., 2020; Wang and Lund, 2020). Morgan-Daniel et al. (2020) underlined the important role information professionals play to prevent the negative impact of misinformation, the digital divide, and low level of health literacy. Similarly, Gann (2020) stressed not only the role of digital information and technologies in facilitating the needs of general public but also the threat of excluding people who need additional support, such as older people and those from deprived groups. This is a big threat, given that a large amount of information and resources are disseminated digitally. In addition, he emphasized the need for the provision of accurate information through reliable sources, stating that people with low digital health literacy can be exposed to inaccurate information. He underlined the importance of creating a mechanism that will bridge the digital divide and reduce digital inequality. In the same way, Harnett (2020) stated that individuals refer to the Internet and social media for information, support, and community, highlighting the need for health literacy. Finally, she stressed that the marginalized and populations at risk are most likely to have low health literacy access, suggesting that targeted communication methods should be adopted to alleviate fear and anxiety and enable active participation.

With reference to academic libraries, Ali and Gatiti (2020) identified the roles that libraries can undertake in this difficult environment: increasing public health awareness with the dissemination of information related to the pandemic; particular support to medical staff, academics, and researchers while offering general services to users. Guo et al. (2020) explored, through website investigation, social media access, and direct correspondence, the way Chinese academic libraries responded to the pandemic. They found that the majority of the participating libraries provided access to electronic resources, virtual references available 24/7, and online research support. Ninety-four percent released COVID-19 information on their websites, 93% published information on the WeChat official account as well as relevant education and training services, while 23% released COVID-19 information in their official micro-blogs.

Wang and Lund (2020) have investigated how public libraries responded to the pandemic through content analysis of online announcements about COVID-19. They found that 85% of participating libraries provided information about remote library resources, 69% provided links to health resources, 53% guidance on finding reliable information, 50% information about the virus, but only 16% information about virtual programmes offered. The findings indicate that libraries could play a vital role in the provision of reliable COVID-19 information to communities in contrast with the findings of the study conducted by Zach (2011) in which libraries' response to the need for H1N1-related information was low.

Increases in inequality of learning opportunities during the pandemic have also been identified. Jaeger and Blaabaek (2020) analyzed information about online borrowing in the inventories of all public libraries in Denmark during lockdown, focusing on families' daily takeout of digital books for children. They found that inequality in learning opportunities that existed before the lockdown has increased during the pandemic, as families with high socioeconomic status were more successful at using libraries, borrowing more digital books than families with low socioeconomic status.

The way specific libraries responded to the pandemic was also investigated: the virtual delivery of services; the reorganization of websites; the offering of webinars, web conferences, online reading groups, and storytelling activities through online teleconference tools; faculty support of online course development and research; the adjustment of remote learning environment-relevant services (virtual WEBEX reference, synchronous instruction sessions); initiatives adopted in the provision of digital services; the efforts made to counteract misinformation to health content; the provision of social services for vulnerable groups (e.g., EBLIDA, 2020; MacDonald, 2020; Mehta and Wang, 2020).

Overall, it appears that libraries reacted quickly to COVID-19. Along with digital information services and their promotion, librarians have reflected on the key issues raised during the crisis: misinformation; the need for trusted information available through a range of communications; the requirement for health and e-health literacy; the diminishing of inequality in learning and accessing reliable information.

3 Challenges for information organizations

Epidemiologists around the world agree that COVID-19 is here to stay and until we gather sufficient data, there will be great uncertainty. It is anticipated that the virus will affect every aspect of human activity. The closing of libraries or the restrictions imposed on their operation have significant implications for the communities which they serve. In global health emergencies, there is not necessarily a lack of information; rather, there is an abundance of conflicting information, making the need for access to reliable information more relevant than ever before. Libraries are not the only organizations responsible for information dissemination at times like these; however, their adoption of technological advances, active involvement in the learning and research process, and engagement with their communities place them in the front line.

The provision and promotion of libraries' electronic services and digital content, as well as training and support for access, has resulted in an increase in the number of library e-resources and website visits alongside growing numbers of users. It is encouraging that this is the case and libraries need to maintain this success when the situation is normalized. The promotion of digital information services and e-resources through libraries' websites, social media accounts, e-learning platforms, and community forums should be actively and continuously carried out, though promotional content should be more explicit, addressing the skills and competencies of wider user groups, ages and languages, adopting the approaches of media such as Instagram and TikTok.

Libraries should also engage in archiving and storing digital information activities produced across different channels. Archiving information in an organized, searchable, retrievable way in institutional repositories could further assist research of any type (health, political, historical, anthropological) now and in the future: an initiative that is likely to prove useful in the prevention of future health crises. Copyright issues will need to be considered and addressed.

It has become apparent, now more than ever before, that there is a need for digital information skills and competences (how to connect, share content and screen, adjust video-audio, fix basic connection issues, use VPN connections, and so on) as well as for customized interpersonal and communication rules and skills (discuss in turn, prepare an agenda, respect the time, moderate the call and participants, and so on). Increased use of digital health resources is likely to lead to a shift to online tools and information resources. Consequently, information organizations need to develop health literacy, e-health literacy, and media health literacy programmes to enable users to distinguish between genuine information and mere expression of opinion; differentiating between fact and rumor, misinformation and disinformation is a major problem. Individuals must be equipped with the necessary skills to identify, evaluate, and use health-related content. Libraries need to provide reliable and trusted information to relieve users' stress, anxiety, and fear of the unknown. Collaboration with health professionals and health educators will be particularly useful when promoting health resources in their areas of responsibility.

Information organizations could undertake digital inclusion initiatives such as the development of digital skills or provision of digital devices. These measures could minimize or eliminate the increase of inequality that has been widely observed during the present pandemic, especially for the marginalized and other people at risk. Collaboration with governmental agencies, profit and nonprofit organizations, and community forums is likely to be the necessary next step.

Libraries as community organizations have to find ways to become fully digital, strengthening community engagement and support in a digital setting. Given that there is an increased focus on our families and our local environment as exemplified by translating the numbers of COVID-19 patients and deaths into potential risks for our loved ones (Low and Smart, 2020), libraries could provide services to lower COVID-19-related anxiety and isolation. Social media could help in this direction, given that such platforms constitute the main fora for information sharing, communication, and community gathering.

The future economic fallout of COVID-19 will severely affect areas such as libraries' budgets, staff recruitment, development of electronic resources, provision of online access to content, operations, and required services. Libraries, as always, ought to make the most of the experiences gained and lessons learned during this health crisis and turn the difficulties into opportunities.

4 Conclusion

Undoubtedly, COVID-19 is one of the most serious health emergencies the world has been faced with in the last century. The rapidly evolving nature of pandemic caused information organizations, like all other types of institution, to respond quickly by providing COVID-19-related information and promoting innovative solutions to cope with the "new normal." Librarians must obtain all the necessary knowledge and the essential skills to provide information and digital services to their communities and to work successfully to address issues such as misinformation, fake news, and digital divides. But then, librarians have all the necessary means to turn the current health crisis into opportunities for development, helping to offer solutions to the many problems emerging from this extraordinary situation.

References

Ali, M.Y., Gatiti, P., 2020. The COVID-19 (Coronavirus) pandemic: reflections on the roles of librarians and information professionals. Health Inf. Libr. J. 37 (2), 158–162.

Chandler, M., 2020. Lockdown surge for library membership and e-book loans. Bookseller. 5 May https://www.thebookseller.com/news/member-surge-and-205-e-book-lockdown-lending-rise-change-libraries-long-term-1201874.

EBLIDA, 2020. A European Library Agenda for Post COVID-19 Era. http://www.eblida.org/Documents/EBLIDA-Preparing-a-European-library-agenda-for-the-post-Covid-19-age.pdf. (Accessed 17 November 2020).

Featherstone, R.M., Lyon, B.G., Ruffin, A.B., 2008. Library roles in disaster response: an oral history project by the National Library of Medicine. J. Med. Libr. Assoc 96 (4), 343–359.

Featherstone, R.M., Bolt, R.G., Torabi, N., Konrad, S.L., 2012. Provision of pandemic disease information by health sciences librarians: a multisite comparative case series. J. Med. Libr. Assoc. 100 (2), 4–112.

Gann, B., 2020. Combating digital health inequality in the time of coronavirus. J. Consum. Health Internet 24 (3), 278–284.

Guo, Y., Yang, Z., Yang, Z., Liu, Y.Q., Bielefield, A., Tharp, G., 2020. The provision of patron services in Chinese academic libraries responding to the COVID-19 pandemic. Library Hi Tech, https://doi.org/10.1108/LHT-04-2020-0098.

Harnett, S., 2020. Health literacy, social media and pandemic planning. J. Consum. Health Internet 24 (2), 157–162.

Jaeger, M.M., Blaabaek, E.H., 2020. Inequality in learning opportunities during COVID-19: evidence from library takeout. Res. Soc. Stratif. Mobil. 68.

Low, S., Smart, A., 2020. Thoughts about public space during COVID-19 pandemic. City Soc. 32 (1).

MacDonald, A.T., 2020. Library experiences during COVID-19: from crisis and uncertainty to moving forward in the new normal. Codex: J. Louisiana Chap. ACRL 5 (4), 70–81.

McGuire, L., 2007. Planning for a pandemic influenza outbreak: roles for librarian liaisons in emergency delivery of educational programs. Med. Ref. Serv. Q. 26 (4), 1–13.

Mehta, D., Wang, X., 2020. COVID-19 and digital library services—a case study of a university library. Digit. Libr. Perspect. 36 (4).

Morgan-Daniel, J., Ansell, M., Adkins, L., 2020. COVID-19 patient education and consumer health information resources and services. J. Consum. Health Internet 24 (3), 302–313.

Wang, T., Lund, B., 2020. Announcements information provided by United States' public libraries during the 2020 COVID-19 pandemic. Public Libr. Q. 39 (4), 283–294.

Zach, L., 2011. What do I do in an emergency? The role of public libraries in providing information during times of crisis. Sci. Technol. Libr. 30 (4), 404–413.

The role of research libraries in promoting open-access resources and maintaining online community

Jane Winters
University of London, London, United Kingdom

1   Introduction

Across the world in 2020, the COVID-19 crisis led to the closure of the physical spaces where people engage in and with Humanities research. University buildings, libraries, museums, and archives were shuttered for more than a third of the year in the United Kingdom, and have only gradually been able to welcome back staff, students, and visitors. During periods of lockdown, university libraries continued to provide services for their users, including enhanced online reference desks, new chat services, remote cataloguing, and so on. They were a vital source of support for researchers and students, who found themselves abruptly cut off both from their workspaces and some of the vital tools of their trade.

The value of digital collections under these circumstances was immediately and sharply brought into focus. For anyone with an Internet connection and membership of a well-resourced university library, it was still possible to access significant quantities of secondary literature online. The version of record for most journal articles is now a digital one, and even where a library does not have the necessary subscription, the proliferation of open-access preprints can offer at least temporary solutions to many a research dilemma.

2   The central importance of books in the Humanities

For researchers in many Humanities disciplines, books retain central importance. The growing availability of e-books undoubtedly reduced the impact of library building closures, but there are substantial gaps in provision and/or access. These may result from the problematic pricing and delivery practices which the pandemic has helped to expose. In an open letter to the UK government which has attracted 3600 signatures at the time of writing and significant media attention, the Campaign to Investigate the Academic ebook Market (2020) makes the case that "Ebooks are becoming increasingly unaffordable, unsustainable and inaccessible for academic libraries to purchase." Gaps in provision may also result from the limitations for some libraries of Non-Print Legal Deposit, which prevents off-site access to e-books acquired under that legislative framework. It remains the case, however, that significant numbers of books are

Libraries, Digital Information, and COVID. https://doi.org/10.1016/B978-0-323-88493-8.00007-0

simply not available in a digital format, particularly those published by small specialist presses. Many such titles fill the shelves of the research libraries of the School of Advanced Study (SAS), University of London: the Library of the Institute of Advanced Legal Studies, the Library of the Institute of Classical Studies and Joint Library of the Hellenic and Roman Societies, the Warburg Institute Library, and the Wohl Library of the Institute of Historical Research (there are also School research collections for Modern Languages, Commonwealth Studies, and Latin American Studies hosted within the University of London's Senate House Library). It is the nature of research libraries that they will hold rare or unique printed materials, often alongside special collections. These became immediately inaccessible when the SAS libraries closed on March 19, 2020, just ahead of the first national lockdown in the United Kingdom.

3   The challenge of maintaining business as usual

The reaction to library closures across the sector was a welcome indication of the value of libraries, and librarians, to students and researchers. Loss of access to physical buildings, reading rooms, and physical books was keenly felt. Access to books, at least, became possible as library buildings slowly reopened, and staff worked hard to develop new forms of click-and-collect service. This did not, however, solve the problem for research libraries with substantial nonlending and special collection holdings. These collections only became accessible again once people were able to book study slots, albeit at a much-reduced level than before the pandemic.

The challenge for the SAS Libraries was not just to keep as much "business as usual" going as possible, but to think imaginatively about how to help their readers find the research materials they needed. And this readership, in keeping with the School's remit to facilitate and promote postgraduate research in the Humanities at the national level, extends far beyond staff and students based in the University of London to encompass researchers throughout the United Kingdom, and indeed internationally.

4   British History Online (BHO) and the removal of paywalls

In the first instance, helping readers meant taking the decision to remove subscription fees from a major digital resource hosted by the Institute of Historical Research. British History Online (BHO) publishes "nearly 1,300 volumes of primary and secondary content relating to British and Irish history, and histories of empire and the British world," all of which have been double-rekeyed for accuracy of presentation and searching. It also makes available around 40,000 image scans and 10,000 historical map tiles (see https://www.british-history.ac.uk). The bulk of the material is freely accessible, but this open-access provision is sustained in large part with income derived from "BHO Premium." The premium service includes around 200 volumes of what is described as "prime research content." A blog post published on March 30, 2020, that is, less than 2 weeks after the closure of the SAS buildings, announced that with immediate effect the paywall for premium content would be lifted. Initially, this widening of access was scheduled to continue until July 31, 2020 (see https://update.lib.berkeley.edu/2020/03/30/free-access-to-british-history-online-bho-digital-collection-through-july-31-2020/), but it was subsequently extended to 30 September, in order to "cover the period when most MA students are engaged in dissertation research" (see https://blog.history.ac.uk/2020/03/british-history-online-makes-all-research-content-free-to-individual-users/).

This temporary removal of paywalls was far from unique. Publishers, libraries, and archives around the world began to suspend subscription charges, and in some cases develop bespoke solutions to make the newly free digitized content more accessible. A notable example is the work undertaken by the digital team at The National Archives (TNA) of the United Kingdom, not just to make digital records freely available, but to expose them via its Discovery service (see https://www.nationalarchives.gov.uk/about/news/digital-downloads/). Readers no longer needed to know in advance if something had been digitized but could locate open-access content by searching TNA's catalogue. The effort and ingenuity involved in an exercise like this while all staff were working from home, with almost no notice, should not be underestimated.

5 Discoverability

The question of discoverability was central to the next phase of service development within the SAS Libraries and the School of Advanced Study as a whole. This was a twofold problem: First, there was a need to surface and promote existing open-access resources; and second, while the open availability of previously paywalled content was enormously valuable for researchers, the plethora of different announcements and the variety of proposed arrangements were almost impossible for any one individual to keep up with. The challenge of uniting students and researchers with the content they needed was widely recognized. Individuals, organizations, and institutions quickly began to produce spreadsheets and lists of the publishers and content providers who were temporarily widening access to their resources, whether in whole or in part. One such list was set up and maintained by Jisc (see https://docs.google.com/spreadsheets/d/1zP 4OxreSGaf7Mb0WZB3k78tqrsaKaq13JodiZsv59zc/edit#gid=0). The Public Books Database similarly set out to catalogue all of the books which had been made open access by university presses, predominantly, although not entirely, in the United States (see https://www.publicbooks.org/public-books-database/). Even if a researcher knew of the existence of such lists, perhaps through their library, they would be confronted by an almost overwhelming amount of data, and often presented at a very high level (e.g., by publisher or collection rather than by subject).

6 Maximizing awareness

There are some striking examples of ingenuity in addressing the problem of how to maximize researcher awareness of new open content or special access arrangements. For example, the publisher Adam Matthew Digital partnered with the Royal Historical

Society to award 200 twelve-month subscriptions for early career researchers to its digitized collections. The subscriptions were allocated in three separate tranches in May, June, and July, with the aim of reaching the widest number of eligible researchers as rapidly as possible. No doubt Adam Matthew could have acted independently and still managed to reach researchers in need, but collaboration with a learned society permitted it to target its resources effectively, while also allowing the Society to provide assistance to members of its community at a very difficult time.

The solution adopted by the specialist research libraries of the School of Advanced Study was to compile lists, within their own subject fields, of open-access publications and other research resources, which could then be combined in a central directory of "Open access research resources for the Humanities" (see https://www. sas.ac.uk/support-research/libraries/open-access-research-resources-humanities). Working together, they could provide a valuable service for their specific subject communities, while also offering a macro-level view of the open research landscape for the Humanities. With additional input from academic staff in the School as necessary, lists were compiled for "Classics," "History," "Law," "Modern Languages," and "Renaissance Studies and the History of the Classical Tradition." Additional recommendations for resources and publications to be included were crowdsourced from readers and online users of the resource. The majority of tools, databases, and publications listed are permanent open-access resources, but material temporarily made open during the early months of the pandemic was also included.

Taking the "History" collection as an example, the first thing the user sees is an introduction from the Director of the Institute of Historical Research, Professor Jo Fox, acknowledging the challenges facing all historians, but particularly Master's students completing dissertations and those with fixed PhD or research project deadlines (see https://www.history.ac.uk/library/collections/online-resources/open-access-resources). A very specific research context is foregrounded and a framing established that would be recognizable to the vast majority of intended users of the resource. The lists are organized variously by type, period, geographical area, and even format (e.g., audio-visual or 3D and augmented reality). The broad section on secondary sources is divided into material held in "Your own institution's library" and "Books, journals, theses and institutional repositories." The national remit of all the SAS Libraries is reflected in the first of these subdivisions: The resource is not primarily concerned with directing readers to the holdings of the Wohl Library, but rather with making it as easy as possible for historians to locate what they need wherever they can find it. In keeping with this agenda, links are provided not just to open-access resources but to other useful tools, for example plugins like Unpaywall and Open Access Button which are designed to help researchers find open versions of articles in which they are interested (see https://unpaywall.org/; and https://openaccessbutton.org/). Readers are reassured that the lists of resources have been curated by IHR librarians, drawing on their subject expertise and understanding of historians' needs, as well as academic colleagues in the Institute. They are also, however, encouraged to contribute to the resource themselves, through an "online suggestions box." This is a co-created resource, launched and hosted by a research library with a keen understanding of its postgraduate constituency and the lifecycle of Humanities research.

7 Specialist libraries

The specialist nature of these research libraries is evident from the differences in emphasis and organization across the open-access directories. They have not been forced into a template, but reflect the expertise of the librarians and the shape of the individual disciplines represented. The resource for Classics, for example, has a section on "Digital Classics," open-access "Teaching tools," and "Podcasts, lecture series, blogs, and other distractions," while the Warburg Institute Library's directory is organized under the broad headings of "Image," "Word," "Orientation," and "Action," mirroring its unique cataloguing system. The role of these libraries in the national research infrastructure, and their close ties with their subject communities, ensured that the individual listings quickly became well known, effectively breaking through the sometimes overwhelming volume of help guides and spreadsheets that began to emerge in the spring of 2020.

8 Community building

The libraries of the School of Advanced Study, like other research libraries around the world, are not just concerned with the provision of information; they are also concerned with the building of community. Students and researchers work in libraries, but it is also where they socialize and build communities of shared interest. This is particularly true for specialist libraries, where conversations struck up over coffee can suggest new avenues of investigation or generate a longstanding collaboration. They are often host to seminars, workshops, and other events which showcase research that is deeply connected to their collections. They are places for formal and informal exchange. One thing that the events of 2020 have shown us is that some kinds of formal exchange can be relatively easily reproduced online, and even opened up to previously excluded audiences. The more casual, but no less important, interactions that occur in library spaces are more challenging to deliver digitally.

9 Virtual communities

In order to address this question, a number of virtual communities were developed alongside the directories of open-access resources. As noted on the pages of the Warburg Institute, "we have created a space to highlight the online events and resources available from the Warburg as well as other academic and cultural organizations, making them more easily accessible for everyone whilst at home." These virtual communities are the digital version of the library common room or resource centre. The English Studies virtual community developed a light-hearted and popular set of activities and resources focusing on "Literature in lockdown." It included Twitter votes for, among others, readers' favorite Dickens novel or fictional detective, and a regular Friday evening #CanterburyCocktails ("drinks with a literary twist"). Notable cocktails included the "Gin Eyre" and "For Whom the Bellini Tolls." The creativity with which research libraries and other cultural heritage organizations have used social media both to support their communities and to open up their collections for new audiences has been extraordinary, and it has helped to cement their centrality not just for research but for social and cultural life in the United Kingdom more generally.

10   Conclusion

The directory of "Open-access research resources for the Humanities" initiated by the libraries of the School of Advanced Study was put together with remarkable speed and ingenuity, something which was in evidence across the sector from mid-March 2020. It helped students to complete dissertations and researchers to meet at least some of their deadlines; it raised awareness not only about newly open-access publications but also about fully and permanently open-access resources of all kinds; it involved researchers in the co-creation of a knowledge base that will last well beyond the current pandemic; and it helped to sustain community at a time when many were isolated from their professional and social networks. It was a practical solution to an unprecedented global challenge, which relied on the insights and knowledge of subject librarians based in specialist research libraries.

Reference

Campaign to Investigate the Academic ebook Market, 2020. Open letter to the UK government. https://academicebookinvestigation.org/. (Accessed 16 February 2021).

Project and programme delivery in a pandemic setting

Scott Henderson
Imover Consultancy Ltd, Hebden Bridge, United Kingdom

1 Childhood chapters

When I was asked to help with this project, it took me back to the early 1970s and my regular trips as a young boy to Penwortham Library in the North West of the United Kingdom. Admittedly, there were no Nintendos, Xboxes or similar and certainly no social media back then, but I considered those trips as a real treat. The memories are vivid, and I can clearly recall the wonderful "booky" odour of the library and the sense of excitement of getting hold of a weighty tome to help feed my junior addiction to dinosaurs, my obsession with long ago battles or anything that would hold the interest of a sub 10-year-old boy.

That library closed in September 2016, part of a controversial cost-cutting exercise by County Hall, but like a sleepy phoenix the old library has recently re-opened its doors to host community events. Turning the clock forward a number of years, a library was in fact the first place I ever used the Internet, something which has gone on to play a large part in my career choice as an IT and Business Transformation Consultant. That early "surfing" took place in Preston's Harris Museum, Art Gallery and Library, an ornate and wonderful Victorian building at the administrative heart of Lancashire. The "Harris," as it is known by locals, was a gift to the town by a local lawyer in 1877 in memory of his father, the Reverend Robert Harris. Given this building has served the community for approaching 150 years, the old man would feel the "Harris" has been a suitably significant way of marking his 64 years of service of the town as vicar of the close-by St. George's church.

2 COVID challenge

As the years have gone by, I fear that I have concentrated a little too much on my career. Reading and especially using libraries have regrettably taken a back seat. Most recently, my work has taken me to the Midlands where I have worked with a number of local government authorities, implementing large-scale software projects for their HR and finance departments. Saying 2020 has been a challenging year is clearly an understatement, and the implementation of accounting and payroll systems in the public sector was impacted alongside everything else by COVID. However, what has been clear, covered in this chapter, is that this impact could have been much more significant; the situation has played out very differently from how some might have anticipated.

Libraries, Digital Information, and COVID. https://doi.org/10.1016/B978-0-323-88493-8.00012-4

If I think back to the announcement of lockdown, the initial reaction within my local government client base leaned towards concerns that project and programme delivery in this environment would be highly problematic, given all colleagues had overnight begun to work remotely. These concerns were not unfounded, in that the methodology being employed to facilitate a quality and timely delivery was a workshop-based approach with my delivery team and the client colleagues working together in the local council offices to deliver the desired outcomes. Reliance on the infrastructure that would support wholesale remote working at previously untested levels drew quizzical looks from all corners. There were even mumbled conversations where it was suggested that a high percentage of colleagues would use the lack of direct oversight from their leadership teams as the perfect opportunity to take it easy while working from home!

3   Opportunities on offer

How did this work out and what has been the outcome and the lessons learned? The answer to that can be viewed from a number of different perspectives: the individual, the delivery, the organizations, and globally.

Looking at the individual, we should consider the impact on mental health; isolation, loneliness, and fear have all played a part. These emotions, totally understandable given the nature and extent of the pandemic and the associated coverage in the media, have been of universal concern. What is interesting though, possibly due to an improved appreciation by employers of employees' mental health, is that sickness absences directly attributable to mental health conditions may have actually reduced, with evidence suggesting that this could be approaching a 10% reduction between 2019 and 2020. While absences due to poor mental health may have reduced, anxiety and depression, particularly around the first lockdown in Spring 2020, doubled among the UK population.

Resilience is clearly not in short supply, however, and spending more time with close family members, being and working in your own home, and having to spend far less time commuting, while still delivering in your work role, have been a major factor for large parts of the workforce. And as for the assertion that colleagues would use the lack of direct oversight as an invitation to "take things easy," my experience is the opposite. Living out our business lives online has actually increased our visibility and availability, such are the tools (instant messaging, video calls, and so forth) at our collective disposal. The consideration here might actually be whether this "always online" availability is a good thing in the longer term. Individuals will need discipline in the future to avoid working overly long days, driven by this heightened availability.

Of particular interest to me as a project and programme delivery professional with over 30 years' experience are the learnings to be taken for future delivery. The adaptability and flexibility of the human race is key here. Organizationally, entire new ways of working were adopted overnight and, as an individual who makes his living delivering software and large programmes, assimilating this fact is critical if we are to take positives from these difficult times. To bring this to life, any organization planning such a significant transition in working practices as moving an entire workforce to wholesale remote working would, prepandemic, have required a project or programme of at least 12 months to "guarantee" successfully landing the change. There would be planning, numerous strategies, proofs of concept, testing, training, and finally, assuming things go well, and this is sanctioned by the organization's leadership, implementation. These activities would be supported by an ample programme team, no doubt with well-rewarded consultants, ensuring a significant cost for the business involved. Compare that to what was achieved in late March 2020, with the delivery mechanisms changing completely overnight to a remote workforce showing the historic approach to be glacial. This is something that we should challenge going forward, embracing what can be achieved within a short period of time if you really need to. I will certainly consider this next time a client asks for an estimate of how long a particular piece of work could take!

Organizations have learnt much in the last year. Dealing with the implications of a pandemic on a local authority in the United Kingdom places huge demands on the organization; the pressure is felt keenly at senior levels. Dealing with life-or-death situations needs a laser focus from the authority leadership teams; managing this had to be the priority as we entered the pandemic. But what was to be of the projects and programmes that historically would have needed their direction? Again, the reality as to how this played out is interesting with an almost organic transfer of responsibility and accountability being observed.

How this happened is not clear! I was certainly not aware of downward communication that gave the direction required to ensure this accountability; what was observed was empowerment by osmosis, an illustration of human beings choosing the right path to deliver for the greater benefit of the organization, and in this case, the community they serve.

Wider organizational learnings included a greater appreciation of the genuine business benefit derived from positively managing the mental health of the workforce. What I have witnessed here has also been impressive, working with a large Indian-based technology company, observing the way in which this was managed. The process started with simple communications, reminding colleagues of good practice, such as taking a break during the working day, keeping a tidy work place, and so on. This soon evolved into online mindfulness sessions, prayer meetings, and even Zumba and Pilates classes. Even more impressively, these activities have continued and even increase in intensity over time, becoming part of the fabric of the way the organization does business, showing that this was not simply a box-ticking exercise.

More traditional benefits have emerged, with businesses completely overhauling their strategies around the need for sizeable city-based locations, favouring instead a gradual transition to fewer, smaller, and therefore less expensive, office premises. This change will not be realized overnight but the way in which organizations look at their estate requirements has been significantly disrupted and, in all likelihood, changed forever.

What can we embrace globally as a positive from this awful pandemic? The most apparent element results from the reduction in commuting and industrial activity and its incredible and positive impact on the planet in such a short time. Air pollution has been reduced almost universally since the lockdown commenced with some recorded levels showing startling reductions in harmful pollutant particle matter (see Table 9.1). The

Table 9.1 Reduction in particulate matter.

City	Average particulate matter 2020 ($\mu g/m^3$)	Reduction compared with 2019 (%)
Delhi, India	32.8	−60
London, United Kingdom	16.2	−9
Los Angeles, United States	5.5	−31
Madrid, Spain	6.4	−11
Mumbai, India	28.8	−34
New York, United States	4.4	−25
Rome, Italy	16.7	30
Sao Paolo, Brazil	10.1	−30
Seoul, South Korea	24.1	−54
Wuhan, China	35.1	−44

From COVID Air Quality Report. https://www2.iqair.com/sites/default/files/documents/REPORT-COVID-19-Impact-on-Air-Quality-in-10-Major-Cities_V6.pdf.

lowering is significant: United Kingdom shows 9% less particle matter when compared with 2019, whereas South Korea (54%) and India (60%) show a seismic reduction.

A final illustration of the improvements that have been observed is the fact that in the Northern Indian state of Punjab people can now see the Himalayan mountain range from more than 100 miles away for the first time in nearly 30 years!

4　Leveraging learnings

So, in summary, what can we learn from these experiences?

It is abundantly clear that the human spirit is indomitable and our ability to adapt, as demonstrated amply over the last few months, is strong; our collective capacity to accommodate even the most extreme of pressures is significant. What is key for me is how we embrace this adaptability and the changes we have made in working practices to build a working model that is a positive evolution of the past. Big tech companies have taken the lead here with Google, Facebook, and Microsoft all moving to a much more remote-working model. Financial benefits (as, for example, increased productivity, reduced real estate costs over the long term) have played a part, but we must not be overly cynical as colleague welfare has been a key consideration in these decisions. Other companies will follow suit. I strongly suspect that remote working on a scale unheard of prepandemic is here to stay. What I am certain about is that should we collectively find ourselves going back to the prelockdown grind, commuting up and down motorways and rail networks, slavishly attending the physical office as it once again becomes the expected way of doing business, then we will have failed. On a very personal level, I fully intend to embrace the positives, aiming to be an exemplar in this space. What is more I have made a promise to myself to re-engage with the wonderful libraries available to us in the United Kingdom. There will have been a number of books written on dinosaurs and battles since my last visit …

Part Two

Analysis and opportunities for new behaviours

Section A

How we learn?

Acceleration of digital learning and what it means for libraries

Sam Brenton[a] and Sandra Tury[b]

[a]University of London, London, United Kingdom, [b]University of London Worldwide, London, United Kingdom

1 The times they are a-changin'

Higher Education in the UK is changing, and we may be at a liminal point between two eras.

With hindsight, we can see as one project the period that began with the Robbins Report and the doubling of the number of universities in the 1960s, that saw the conversion of polytechnics into universities in the early 1990s, those elements of the 1997 Dearing report which provided the foundation for a mass higher education system, the target set in 1999 (BBC News, 1999) for 50% of young adults to experience higher education, and then the steady increase of participation in higher education by people under 30%–50.2% in 2017/18 (United Kingdom Department for Education, 2019). The project ran over six decades and was an attempt to move the UK from an elitist to a mass higher education system, with universities as the suppliers of ever greater equality of opportunity.

It is always difficult to judge when one era ends and another begins—the join is never neat, applying historical perspectives to the present is a risky business, and ideological shade can obscure clear sight of the real intents and effects of present changes. Nevertheless, when the Education Secretary withdrew the 50% target in July 2020, it felt like the end of a long period of broad consensus and common direction.

What does the next era hold for UK HE? None of us can know, though some of the signals are clear, and indeed, some of the seeds of the coming era were planted in the last: a greater range of alternative providers; flexible funding to drive change in behaviour on the demand and the supply side; disaggregation of monolithic degree awards; an increasingly utilitarian view of education as a feeder for a postindustrial economy (and a further waning of liberal humanist ideals); fiercer, metric-driven regulation; and ultimately, one senses, the breaking of the near-monopoly hold that universities have over their students once they are enrolled; and a growing recognition—a generation since we started doing it—that web-enabled technologies mean that high-quality learning and teaching can take place whether or not the learners and teachers are occupying the same physical space.

If we raise our eyes and look around the globe, we see that the massification of higher education is on the march, and though with a long way to go yet, there is great opportunity for expansion, and billions of lives to be transformed. The global demand

Libraries, Digital Information, and COVID. https://doi.org/10.1016/B978-0-323-88493-8.00014-8

for higher education has been growing for decades, driven by economic shifts and demographic changes. Global enrolments rose from 33 million in 1970, to 68 million in 1990, to 224 million in 2018 (UNESCO, 2020). There are predicted to be 377 million global enrollments in higher education by 2030 and 597 million by 2040 (Calderon, 2018). Growth is expected to be strongest in East Asia and the Pacific, South and West Asia and Latin America and the Caribbean (Calderon, 2018). Some of this growth will be met by bricks and mortar universities in-country, but the logic of sheer volume dictates that much of it will be online, or at least partially online.

We have learned, if we had not before, during the pandemic, that teaching online in this way is viable, but it requires the right technology. Digital poverty and the digital divide are real; you are unlikely to succeed if you just replicate face-to-face teaching online, and we have realized just how important effective learning design is when you are looking to move online.

What is the role and identity of the library in this new world? Is a library a building, or a virtual extension of a building? Is it its books and resources? Is it the people who use it? If the University of Yesteryear was a citadel, the library occupied the central tower of the citadel. What becomes of the central tower when the walls of the citadel have dissolved into a porous, networked, shapeshifting organism, one site of knowledge and learning connected to many others? And how does a library serve a student population who are used to roving across the network, magpie-like, to find and take knowledge when they need it and where they can find it?

The University of London has been offering distance learning since the mid-nineteenth century, and today provides high-quality, flexible, affordable online learning to some 48,000 students in 190 countries all over the world. That means we have practical experience in providing library services in a digital, dispersed world. Our online library is not a tower in a citadel; it is a row of computers in an open plan workspace. During the pandemic, of course, it has actually been a series of laptops in the studies, kitchens and living rooms of our talented online Librarians.

In this chapter, we offer a series of practical insights about the role and function of an effective digital library, based on long experience.

2   COVID and a paradigm shift in library services

The fundamental role played by academic libraries in support of learning, teaching and research is undisputed. According to the Society of College, National and University Libraries (SCONUL), "investing in the teaching and support services offered by the *library* can increase the employability of a university's graduates," can help to attract and retain graduates, and that "the quality of the library was found to be more important even than teaching contact time for prospective students" (SCONUL, 2019). This vital student service is now facing serious and unprecedented challenges, possibly a paradigm shift, and a "new normal" following the onslaught of the COVID-19 pandemic which forced academic institutions to close their doors in order to protect the safety of their students and staff and to accelerate the move to online services and to studying from home.

The transition to digital or online library provision is far from straightforward at the best of times but is hugely challenging when an institution has been given a few weeks to prepare. While in many institutions and libraries, discussions about re-opening campuses and physical libraries are taking place, it is clear that things may never be the same again, that studying as well as accessing libraries remotely is often necessary or even preferred. How can libraries leverage this crisis to create new and innovative digital libraries which meet the learning, teaching and research needs of the university they serve?

3 What is a digital library?

The University of London has long experience of providing digital library services to students at a distance, but what does a "digital library" mean? The term has been used in a variety of ways and has many "definitions and views" (Bawden and Rowlands, 1999, p. 181), and there is a lack of consensus regarding its use (Brophy, 1999). In this chapter, the term "digital library" is used to emphasize the nonphysical nature of the collections and access mechanisms where a user does not have to be physically present. Recent developments in digital communication and mobile technologies have made the provision of library services which are completely online possible.

The University of London's Online Library (OLL) was created in 2001. The decision to provide a wholly digital library service was informed by the need to provide an equitable library service to its large, diverse, and geographically distributed distance learners and faculty. While one could argue that providing a digital library service can result in an environment of the "digital rich" and "digital poor" among the communities it serves, experience at the University of London has shown that the barriers to digital provision are far fewer than those encountered when supplying physical learning materials to students based all over the world. The University of London Online Library provides access to over 100 million electronic items comprising e-journal articles, e-books, law reports, legislation, dissertations, conference proceedings, newspaper articles, and other materials, and offers an e-reference service via email, telephone, and online live chat which is run by a team of professional librarians.

4 The successful digital library

Creating a successful digital library which meets the learning, teaching, and research needs of any academic institution is not a simple transference of physical library collections and practices to an online version. It is much more complex, requiring careful planning, substantial investment, and a thorough understanding of the information needs and "information-seeking behaviour" of the users it serves, as well as the institution's teaching and research needs.

4.1   Institutional support

Support from senior management is essential for a digital library. The digital library strategy should be closely aligned with the parent institution's digital strategy and should be properly resourced. The central role played by the library in improving academic grades, development of information skills and in student recruitment and retention must be well understood. Unfortunately, in campus-based environments, support for distance learners can often be seen as supplementary to main on-campus activities. For digital libraries to make a real difference, universities must put the service at the heart of teaching and learning. The collapse of the Dawsonera platform in July 2020, which forced UK HE libraries to find new e-book platforms overnight, showed the urgent need for proper resourcing, contingency planning, and institutional support when running a wholly digital library.

4.2   Understanding your users

Understanding learners' needs seems very obvious, and academic libraries often undertake regular library satisfaction surveys in order to understand their users' needs. However, understanding distance learners' information and learning needs is much more complex and challenging because it requires libraries to look beyond the campus environment and services they and the university provide. It calls for a thorough understanding of the distance learners' individual learning needs, the information environment in which they work, the barriers to accessing and using the library and other information sources which stem from the students' specific and local environments, such as those imposed by time, distance, and instructional approaches (pedagogy) as well as ease of access to required information sources. Understanding the learner's personal characteristics, including their educational background and information literacy skills level, is also vital, in other words, their information-seeking behaviour (ISB). ISB is a purposive seeking of information as a consequence of a need to satisfy some goal (Wilson, 2000).

Research studies in the ISB of distance learners (Brooke et al., 2013; Byrne and Bates, 2009; Oliveira and Greenidge, 2020; Thórsteinsdóttir, 2005; Tury, 2014; Van de Vord, 2010) have all established that distance learners' needs and behaviour are different from those of on-campus students and that one size does not fit all. Tury's study, which investigated the information-seeking behaviour of 649 distance learning students registered with the University of London's distance learning programmes, made a series of recommendations for designing effective distance online/digital library services. These included consideration of the role of electronic provision versus other forms of provision; design for ease of access and ease of use; the need for access to physical libraries; the need for technical support; the need for student support in the broadest sense; the responsibility of the institution for full provision of information resources and the provision of information literacy skills; the design of distance learning programmes with integral information design rather than merely a translation of on-campus programmes; the need for communications and institution-wide information literacy strategy.

Following the recommendations of this study, the University of London Online Library has made several significant improvements to enhance the students' learning experience. These include the implementation of the resource discovery tool "Summon," which cross-searches the entire Online Library collections and returns a relevance-ranked set of results in a single search box; the Open Athens Single Sign-On authentication system which enables students to access all their learning materials, whether in Virtual Learning Environments (VLEs), the Student Portal, or the Online Library, with one single username and password. Additionally, information literacy skills tutorials have been into embedded into the curricula of several programmes, starting with postgraduate programmes. The implementation of the "Ask-A-Librarian Live" chat service has enabled students to chat in real time with reference librarians without incurring the costs of long-distance telephone calls. The tagging system within the "Ask-A-Librarian" system enables the Online Library to obtain meaningful feedback and statistics which are required to further improve the service. The delivery of a successful distance learning library service, therefore, requires a thorough understanding of the information and learning needs of distance learners and their information-seeking behaviour and designing services around the identified needs.

4.3   Quality assurance and benchmarking

A successful digital library responds to feedback but proactively seeks and responds to evidence of the impact of its services by a range of means. Digital library services must also be routinely benchmarked against other libraries, just like physical libraries, in order to ensure that standards of provision are kept and are in line with not only with user needs but also with the requirements of the accrediting and quality assurance bodies.

5   Digital infrastructure

Successful digital libraries must have a robust digital infrastructure to host all its digital collections, provide tools to support the efficient retrieval, access and use of all the resources, as well as provide extensive student support services.

5.1   What do distance learners want?

- Unlimited access to all the resources they need to complete their degree programme tasks
- Easy access to all the learning resources (including library resources), uncomplicated procedure, simple steps, preferably a one-stop-shop
- Flexible access anytime, anywhere, on any device
- Timely access to meet coursework and dissertation deadlines
- Seamless access (where the resource is from is not their concern; whether a library book, course handbook on VLE or interlibrary loan scan)
- One login (don't want to remember multiple passwords)
- Robust access method (failsafe, works every time)
- Consistent (same process every time)

- Personalized (can access resources that are relevant to their specific needs)
- Secure, cannot be hacked into (multiple passwords can lead to password loss).

Digital libraries for distance learners/researchers must adapt and be able to support their learners' needs wherever they are. For this to happen, a robust digital infrastructure which supports 24/7 access via a variety of digital devices, and seamless, easy, and secure access to all materials through a single point of entry, a one-stop-shop is fundamental.

5.2   Ease of access

Tury (2014, p. 441) established that distance learners will use resources which are easy to access at the expense of quality and reliability, and many exhibit the Principle of Least Effort (PLE). In fact, some students were found to go as far as consulting family and friends because they deemed it quicker than using the Online Library's academic collections. Since this study, the University of London has implemented the Open Athens Single Sign-on authentication system, to simplify the students' journey when accessing the library's resources. Not surprisingly, the Online Library satisfaction rates which were reported in the University-wide "Student Experience" survey went through the roof. Another benefit was that the number of basic enquiries which often related to access/login problems fell by over 50%. This demonstrates that a good authentication system, which provides seamless access to all the learning resources including those which are not held or owned by the library, is fundamental and has immense benefits for both learners and the library/university.

5.3   Dedicated and mobile compliant website

The library's website should be seen as the "front door" to the library. This means that it must be designed for ease of use and ease of access and must be hosted on a robust, secure, and mirrored server 24/7, providing access to all library collections and tools to support users. At the most basic level, it must be user-friendly, customizable, responsive and must meet WCAG 2.1 AA standards which are specified in the recent *Public Sector Bodies (Websites and Mobile Applications) Accessibility Regulations* (United Kingdom, 2018). The content management system should be easy to use, requiring little or no technical expertise to edit or add library content. The University of London Online Library website or gateway runs on "Drupal" a free and open-source web content management, which provides simple editing tools for all library staff. The website has also been personalized in order to meet the individual needs of each programme. This saves students valuable time by putting all the resources they need in one place, as well as enabling the limiting of e-resource licenses to specific programmes to help contain e-resource costs.

5.4   Discoverability

As mentioned above, distance learners' information-seeking behaviour shows a clear preference for resources which are easy to access, use, and are in one place—a one-stop-shop; therefore, a good resource discovery tool is essential. The University of

London implemented the "Summon" resource discovery tool in 2010. Before the implementation, distance learners were presented with a long list of subject-specific and multidisciplinary databases from which they had to choose. Students had to search a myriad of databases, often with meaningless titles, e.g., ABI Inform, JSTOR until they found one with content relevant to their research topic. All the individual databases had different user interfaces and often required unique syntax to be searched effectively. More often than not, this resulted in students resorting to freely available, unverified, and poor-quality internet sources.

The implementation of Summon was a game changer. One of the most important benefits of using a research discovery tool is the ability to meet student expectations of a single point of entry, a uniform search interface, and aggregated relevance-ranked search results in a single search box. Students can now search the entire library collection at a single stroke. It also provides an easy way for students to manage, export, and format references, and to contact a librarian (context-sensitive support). Its language features allow students to translate searches into their indigenous languages. For the first time, the Online Library was as easy to use as Google, but much better, because Summon only retrieves credible, academic, and authoritative content.

This implementation hugely enhanced students' library experience by simplifying use. It also enabled library staff to focus on fewer tools and a single interface when planning and delivering information skills sessions. Usage statistics which include geographical location of the users are also invaluable and enable the library to reshape its services in line with student needs. These solutions are not cheap, and many are not perfect, but they deliver considerable benefits for learners and help to meet their expectation of a library "which is as easy to use as Google."

6 Collection development

6.1 Digital collection development policy

One of the major challenges brought about by the COVID-19 pandemic is the unavailability of print collections and the increased demand for electronic resources. This change in user needs and behaviour requires academic libraries to change their collection development policies and prioritize digital resources over print. Until recently, academic libraries have adopted the "just-in-case" approach and have continued to heavily rely on print collection, even when this required offsite storage and large storage space costs. Further mass digitization must be undertaken to make library collections, including rare and unique special collections, more accessible.

Despite the obvious benefits, building a robust digital infrastructure, and digitizing content to an acceptable standard, is hugely challenging especially given the precarious financial situation in which many universities and their libraries find themselves. It will also require the resolution of copyright and licensing issues. Libraries will need to develop new strategies for negotiating with publishers and to lobby for greater and more affordable access to streaming media and e-books as well as collaborate with large digitization organizations.

6.2 Building online library collections

Building a robust digital collection which meets students' learning and other information needs, as well as curriculum and research requirements, must be informed by a thorough understanding of the learners' information-seeking behaviour, the digital information landscape, the taught curriculum and the research requirements of the individual course programmes, and close co-operation between the library, course developers and faculty, and a good working relationship with publishers and aggregators.

At the University of London, the Online Library is involved from the start of the programme design and development process. This enables the library team to check and acquire all the essential materials without which it would be impossible to meet learning or research outcomes. Not all core textbooks are available in e-format, and even where available, they may be prohibitively expensive. When this happens, it is vital for faculty and library to work together to find alternatives. Digital resources are expensive, and if costs are unchecked, they can quickly get out of hand. While this approach is complex and time-consuming, and may even require a programme to be redesigned, it ensures that students are well supported and resource licensing costs are kept at reasonable levels. As an example, one long-standing programme, the Bachelor of Business Administration, was redesigned and all essential and further readings provided. As a result, Online Library resource usage for this programme went up 580%, and the satisfaction with library services in the university-wide student experience survey (SES) went up by 33%.

In order to meet the needs of all its users, digital libraries must be aware of the tensions which exist between supporting the taught curriculum at undergraduate level and supporting researchers whose needs cannot be so clearly defined in advance, but in many cases have to be anticipated. In distance learning, programmes of study (discipline) and level of study (undergraduate versus postgraduate) have a significant impact on learners' information-seeking behaviour (Tury, 2014, pp. 361–363). Decisions based on the requirements of individual programmes can hugely reduce e-book license fees and can make stretched library budgets go further. Increasingly, libraries will no longer have the luxury of purchasing big deal bundles on the basis of everything available for everyone, unless there is a demonstrable need.

6.3 Licensing e-resources

Building a robust and relevant digital collection requires extensive knowledge of licensing, contract law, and copyright law, in addition to all the other collection development skills required in order to build a balanced collection such as a good knowledge of the information landscape and the taught curriculum. Print collections are governed by copyright, while digital resources are governed by contract law and although still subject to copyright law, in many cases the terms of the publisher license will supersede the copyright allowances. Resources are normally licensed on an annual basis, but sometimes publishers/aggregators will give a small discount if an institution signs up to a multiyear contract. Resource licenses contain details regarding "authorized users," i.e., who can access them, where they can be accessed from (on-campus/off-campus, UK/overseas), how much can be downloaded, whether they can be used for teaching purposes (in course packs) etc. It is therefore important for a digital library to ensure that all its learners' needs will be covered by the specific license before signing on the dotted line.

Infringements can result in suspension of the service and even fines, and inadequate access can have an adverse effect on the learners' experience. To complicate things further, license terms and annual price increases of digital resources vary from publisher to publisher, and often from institution to institution. This makes budgeting difficult compared with working with the fixed pricing of print materials. Consortia or sector-wide organizations such as JISC and NESLI negotiate licenses on behalf of UK higher and further education institutions but such deals are not necessarily cheaper and can be tied to commitments as long as 5 years.

Having robust usage data and a knowledge of where your users are based, their usage pattern and time zones can help to keep the number of copies, provision for simultaneous users, and licenses to a minimum. Recently, a number of publishers have moved from unlimited and credit-based e-book license models to simultaneous user models. This is a backward step and similar to a physical book being out on loan and therefore being unavailable to everyone else. This approach has made the buying of required and essential items prohibitively expensive and especially for programmes with large student numbers. It makes the sharing of e-books impossible. Moreover, set limits on download periods mean that a book could take much longer to circulate, unless a huge number of copies are purchased. Recently, one of our Discrete Mathematics titles, which cost £35.83 per copy for 400 unlimited credits, has been moved to a simultaneous user model costing £455 per single user on one of our programmes which has 1500 students. In response, in partnership with faculty, we have found two suitable alternatives, including one which is freely available. Good use of the copyright license for scanning and interlibrary loans can also be used to supplement stock deficiencies and contain e-license costs. Again, this works well when the curriculum needs are well defined such as at an undergraduate level.

7 Supporting library users (e-reference service)

Providing an efficient e-reference service is crucial in distance learning and particularly important for students who study independently and often in isolation. However, providing a reference service to remote users is more challenging than supporting on-campus students. When students are working from home, queries are often more urgent and less clearly defined, and often technical problems cannot be replicated from within the university network. Supporting a diverse number of learners with varying levels of information and digital literacy skills, and those whose first language is not English, can be a huge challenge.

An efficient reference service must therefore be staffed by professional and qualified librarians with good technical and IT trouble-shooting skills, team-working skills, as well as all-round knowledge of services and the curriculum. The key is to ensure that learners get timely resolutions to problems, because many are often juggling work with study and missing critical deadlines can set them back and even cause them to defer their modules or withdraw from the programme of study. Learners must be given options for accessing library support, including telephone, email, and live chat services which provide instant access to specialist librarians without incurring the cost of long-distance telephone calls. Supporting the development of Information literacy skills will also help to make learners more resourceful and will reduce the strain on the reference service team.

8 Information literacy

8.1 An embedded or fully integrated information literacy skills programme

Information literacy skills are fundamental to distance learning because they enable the students to fully exploit the resources provided by the library and carefully evaluate those they find elsewhere, as well as equip students with those core information skills which are vital for successful independent learning, lifelong learning, for the world of work and to thrive in a global information society. Information literacy has also been found to contribute to higher grades and student completion rates/retention.

Extensive studies by Tury (2014) and Tang and Tseng (2013) found that a significant proportion of distance learning students did not have the necessary information literacy skills to successfully access and use e-resources provided by modern online libraries. Students also exhibited the principle of least effort and tended to follow a path of least resistance, often using poor and unverified internet sources and even consulted family and friends rather than using the Online Library. This calls for an information literacy training programme, which is compulsory and fully integrated into the curriculum. A qualitative examination of the benefits of embedding information skills into one of the University of London postgraduate programmes: The "MA Global Diplomacy" revealed that it significantly increased library use, as well as changing the nature of enquiries from this group of students. In October 2013, 83% of all the enquiries from "Global Diplomacy" students were basic, and 17% were advanced; however, by June 2014, 34% were basic and 66% were advanced. This suggests that over the course of only 6 months—the passage of one of their four modules—students had acquired a meaningful level of information literacy skills. These core competencies and information literacy skills enhance critical thinking, academic success, and lifelong learning. It's therefore vital that libraries work closely with faculty to embed these skills into the curriculum, and to get the support of senior management in order to develop and promote a university-wide information literacy policy.

9 Conclusion

Learning in higher education is changing across the globe, driven by demographic and economic shifts which combine to create an unprecedented increase in demand for access to high-quality, flexible, and at least partially online provision. This trend has only been accelerated by the COVID-19 pandemic.

In that shifting landscape, libraries also have to adapt. In this chapter, we have drawn on our experience at the University of London of running a digital library for large cohorts of distance learners all over the globe, and have provided detailed, practical information about the nuts and bolts of running such a service, in the hope that this may be useful as a comparator, benchmark, or guide rope for the interested reader.

References

Bawden, D., Rowlands, I., 1999. Digital libraries: assumptions and concepts. LIBRI-COPENHAGEN 49 (4), 181–191. http://citeseerx.ist.psu.edu/viewdoc/download?doi=10.1.1.110.6580&rep=rep1&type=pdf.

BBC, 1999. UK Politics: Tony Blair's speech in full. http://news.bbc.co.uk/1/hi/uk_politics/460009.stm. (Accessed 14 December 2020).

Brooke, C., McKinney, P., Donoghue, A., 2013. Provision of distance learner support services at UK universities: identification of best practice and institutional case study. Libr. Trends 61 (3), 613–635. https://doi.org/10.1353/lib.2013.0003.

Brophy, P., Digital libraries in Europe: an educational perspective, http://eprints.rclis.org/9764/1/8psab012.pdf, 1999, (Accessed December 2020).

Byrne, S., Bates, J., 2009. Use of the university library, eLibrary, VLE, and other information sources by distance learning students in University College Dublin: implications for academic librarianship. New Rev. Acad. Librariansh. 15 (1), 120–141. http://eprints.teachingandlearning.ie/1911/1/Byrne%20and%20Bates%202009.pdf.

Calderon, A.J., 2018. Massification of Higher Education Revisited. RMIT University, Melbourne.

Oliveira, S.M. and Greenidge, N., Information seeking behavior of distance learners: what has changed in twenty years?, J. Libr. Inf. Serv. Dist. Learn., 14(1), 2020, 2–27, doi:https://doi.org/10.1080/1533290X.2020.1791301 (Accessed December 2020).

SCONUL, 2019. The Value of Academic Libraries. https://www.sconul.ac.uk/page/the-value-of-academic-libraries. (Accessed December 2020).

Tang, Y., Tseng, H., 2013. Distance learners' self-efficacy and information literacy skills. J. Acad. Librariansh. 39, 517–521. https://doi.org/10.1016/j.acalib.2013.08.008.

Thórsteinsdóttir, G., 2005. The information seeking behaviour of distance students: a study of twenty Swedish library and information science students. [Doctoral Dissertation], Valfrid, Borås.

Tury, S., 2014. The Information-seeking behaviour of distance learners: a case study of the University of London International Programmes. [Doctoral Thesis] City University of London https://openaccess.city.ac.uk/id/eprint/19613.

UNESCO, 2020. UIS Statistics. http://data.uis.unesco.org/. (Accessed December 2020).

United Kingdom, 2018. Public Sector Bodies (Websites and Mobile Applications) Accessibility Regulations. https://www.legislation.gov.uk/uksi/2018/952/made. (Accessed December 2020).

United Kingdom Department for Education, 2019. Participation Rates in Higher Education: Academic Years 2006/2007–2017/2018 (Provisional). https://assets.publishing.service.gov.uk/government/uploads/system/uploads/attachment_data/file/843542/Publication_HEIPR1718.pdf. (Accessed December 2020).

Van de Vord, R., 2010. Distance students and online research: promoting information literacy through media literacy. Internet High. Educ. 13 (3), 170–175. https://www.sciencedirect.com/science/article/abs/pii/S1096751610000266.

Wilson, T.D., 2000. Human information behavior. Inform. Sci. 3 (2), 49–56. https://www.researchgate.net/publication/270960171_Human_Information_Behavior.

Further reading

Asher, A.D., Duke, L.M., Wilson, S., 2013. Paths of discovery: comparing the search effectiveness of EBSCO discovery service, summon, google scholar, and conventional library resources. C&RL 74 (5), 464–488. https://crl.acrl.org/index.php/crl/article/view/16327.

Association of College & Research Libraries (ACRL), 2016. The 2016 guidelines for distance learning. http://www.ala.org/acrl/standards/guidelinesdistancelearning. (Accessed December 2020).

Bengtson, J.A., Coleman, J., 2019. Taking the long way around: improving the display of Hathi trust records in primo. Inf. Technol. Libr. 38 (1), 27–39. https://doi.org/10.6017/ital.v38i1.10574.

Goodsett, M., 2014. Discovery search tools: a comparative study. Ref. Rev. 28 (6), 2–8. https://doi.org/10.1108/RR-12-2013-0312.

Guardian, 2012. Harvard University says that it can't afford journal publishers' prices. www.theguardian.com/science/2012/apr/24/harvard-university-journal-publishers-prices. (Accessed December 2020).

Neary, L., 2019. You May Have to Wait to Borrow a New e-Book from the Library. Macmillan e-book embargo. https://www.npr.org/2019/11/01/775150979/you-may-have-to-wait-to-borrow-a-new-e-book-from-the-library?t=1607086622964. (Accessed December 2020).

Quality Assurance Agency (QAA), 2019. Subject benchmark statements for law. Accessible from https://www.qaa.ac.uk/docs/qaa/subject-benchmark-statements/subject-benchmark-statement-law.pdf. (Accessed December 2020).

Rowland, F., Rubbert, I., 2001. An evaluation of the information needs and practices of part-time and distance-learning students in the context of educational and social change through lifelong learning. J. Doc. 57 (6), 741–762. https://doi.org/10.1108/EUM0000000007105.

Sewell, C., Kingsley, D., 2017. Developing the 21st century academic librarian: the research support ambassador Programme. New Rev. Acad. Librariansh. 23 (2–3), 148–158. https://doi.org/10.1080/13614533.2017.1323766.

Society of Legal Scholars, 2009. A library for the modern law school: a statement of standards for university law library provision in the UK—2009 revision. http://www.legalscholars.ac.uk/documents/SLS-Library-for-a-Modern-Law-School-Statement-2009.pdf. (Accessed December 2020).

Stitz, T., Blundell, S., 2018. Evaluating the accessibility of online library guides at an academic library. J. Access. Des. All 8 (1), 33–79. https://doi.org/10.17411/jacces.v8i1.145.

Tait, A., 2000. Planning student support for open and distance learning. Open Learning 15 (3), 287–299. https://doi.org/10.1080/713688410.

Thompson, H., 2002. The library's role in distance education: survey results from ACRL's 2000 Academic Library Trends and Statistics. Coll. Res. Libr. News 63 (5), 338–340. https://doi.org/10.5860/crln.63.5.338.

Tury, S., Baume, D., 2020. Academic Library Services in Strange Times. https://london.ac.uk/news-and-opinion/centre-distance-education/academic-library-services-strange-times. (Accessed December 2020).

Tury, S., Robinson, L., Bawden, D., 2015. The information seeking behaviour of distance learners: a case study of the University of London International Programmes. J. Acad. Librariansh. 41 (3), 312–321. https://doi.org/10.1016/j.acalib.2015.03.008.

Walters, W.H., 2012. Patron-driven acquisition and the educational mission of the academic library. Libr. Resour. Tech. Serv. 56 (3). https://journals.ala.org/index.php/lrts/article/view/5528/6796.

Libraries, learning, and porous boundaries: Reimagining the library landscape and its inhabitants

Ellen Buck and Anna Nunn
University of Suffolk, Ipswich, United Kingdom

1 Introduction

The impact of COVID-19 on the accessibility of education across all sectors cannot be underestimated. The pandemic has brought disruption to early years education, milestone assessment periods, further and higher education, preventing many from continuing, completing, and engaging with both formal and wider social learning opportunities and resources. With the closure of schools, colleges, universities, and libraries, education professionals needed to respond quickly and creatively. Families were asked to homeschool their children, and, during the last quarter of the academic year, as the UK lockdown had seen much teaching completed, universities moved teaching online and adapted assessment methods and regulations to provide flexibility, while ensuring that subject benchmarks, learning outcomes, and quality standards were as robust as ever (Quality Assurance Agency, 2020).

The closure of educational institutions and the move to online delivery surfaced issues of digital poverty and the digital divide across the country. In response, the UK Government provided technology funding for primary and secondary providers (Department for Education, 2020) while universities looked internally to access and participation-driven bursaries (Office for Students, 2020a). However, while at least partially resolving access to technology, this response does little to address other challenges faced by higher education students. These include the ability to access and establish safe and productive learning environments and practice and to develop the skills to access well-curated and authoritative information sources, a need highlighted by the COVID infodemic (Okike Benedict, 2020; Salman Bin and Bhatti, 2020); all while juggling complex lives made worse by the COVID lockdown.

For many, the university library is the place in which they access information in a range of flexible learning environments (Bryant et al., 2009). The role of the librarian is to facilitate access to these environments and resources, while supporting the development of information literacy skills in their broadest sense. It has never been more important for students to be able to manage, share, and create new knowledge, in and across local, regional, and global networks; networks which stretch beyond the university and the communities it serves.

Libraries, Digital Information, and COVID. https://doi.org/10.1016/B978-0-323-88493-8.00008-2

This chapter considers the role of the library as a learning environment, in a world which has been rapidly, and perhaps permanently, impacted by a global event previously unexperienced by its inhabitants. Looking at the evolution of library usage and provision, with specific reference to one UK Higher Education Institution (HEI), the University of Suffolk, the chapter will explore the role of the professional librarian and qualifying librarian as educator and enabler within the porous learning environments established in response to the COVID-19 pandemic.

The chapter begins by presenting the COVID-19 response by the UK University at the heart of this chapter.

2   Learning through the pandemic: Creating the porous learning environment at the University of Suffolk

The University of Suffolk (UOS) is a "new kind of university, custom built for the modern world" (University of Suffolk, 2020b). As a university at the heart of its community, it also sits, as Johnston et al. (2018) suggest, at the intersection of a digital divide, one that manifests itself geographically, financially, and in levels of digital literacy. For UOS, like other UK HEIs, digital has become embedded into learning and teaching and wider service delivery, supporting the widening of opportunities for participation, responding to a demand for increased flexibility in higher education provision (Barnett, 2014) and resulting in the wide adoption of blended pedagogies (AdvanceHE, 2020).

The COVID-19 pandemic, and the immediate response of a "lift and shift" of learning experience from the physical to the virtual classroom, demonstrated the University's ability to respond with agility. It also provided the opportunity to re-ignite the institutional, academic conversation about what the University pedagogy could and should be, short and longer term; how would we engage learners across widespread geographic and rural contexts, creating and sustaining learning across disrupted and disconnected learning spaces?

The importance of revisiting space and place is recognized by the AdvanceHE *Creating Socially Distanced Campuses and Education Project* with the distinction made between the "pragmatic and practical" considerations of space and the "emotive concepts such as belonging and community" of place (Brown and Parkin, 2020, p. 6). The concept of belonging and the impact of relationships are recognized in literature and presented in conceptual frameworks of engagement (Fredricks et al., 2004; Furlong and Christenson, 2008; Lawson and Lawson, 2013) alongside the role of positive emotions and self-confidence in achievement (Bandura et al., 1996; Fredrickson, 2001). The impact of the pandemic on student engagement and sense of belonging, emotional investment and connection with institution, peers and lecturer, the enabling of social presence in a "climate that supports and encourages probing questions, scepticism and the contribution of more explanatory ideas" (Garrison and Anderson, 2003, p. 50) needed to drive response.

2.1   From online delivery to online pedagogy and the digital divide

The criticality of instructionally designed content in supporting learning was evidenced in earlier work completed by the University in the design of blended degree apprenticeships, with nursing students needing to connect theory and practice across physically disconnected learning environments: the University and the hospital (Phippen et al., 2020). This work became the foundation of the blended approach at Suffolk and informed the development of academic staff training (University of Suffolk, 2020a). Course teams were asked to complete this training and implement standards developed for the online learning environment to support the negotiation of learning, construction of pathways, and bridges between content, resource, and experience and to encourage social presence.

However, for blended pedagogies to be successful, students must also have skills, confidence, and equipment to engage in an online environment and appropriate physical study environments from which to do so. The Office for Students (2020b) highlighted the impact of broadband speeds on learning post lockdown and a lack of spaces conducive to support learning. This experience was explicit in applications for extenuating circumstances at the University, but students were also citing a lack of access to the library and its physical resources.

While the evidence from earlier work at the University as cited above (Phippen et al., 2020) seemed to indicate an increase in engagement through well-designed blended learning—measured as time spent *in* learning content, this was achieved pre-COVID and the impact of barriers it created to learning. Yet, what this appears to have shown is that "presence" in learning does not have to rely on presence in the classroom. In the "during-COVID" learning landscape, students could not rely on physical social learning networks, physical resources, or physically ask for help with technology in the University's physical learning environments. The ability to bring students together physically in the formative weeks of their joining the University or progressing into higher levels of their courses was not possible, but as noted, the importance of creating a sense of belonging, of togetherness and connection with each other, their course teams and their wider services support teams needed to be managed and enabled in alternative ways. These findings are congruent with the work of Redmond et al. (2018) that focussing on online engagement through lenses of emotional, social, collaborative, cognitive, and behavioural characteristics of the learning and activities developed could have more impact.

2.2   Reaching beyond the curriculum: Normalizing digital

With blended learning established as the learning experience for returning and new students to the University for academic year 2020–21 and beyond, steps were taken to manage expectations and perception of online learning to mitigate the impact of digital poverty, support students in transitioning into University, and prepare them for an experience which would be very different from the one they anticipated when first making the choice to join. Tai et al. (2019) highlight the perception that for some, online learning is a poor substitute for physical on-campus learning and that online learning is itself a barrier to engagement, supporting those who argue the concept of the digital native is a myth (Bennett and Maton, 2010; Helsper and Eynon, 2010; Margaryan et al., 2011).

The University's response was to create an online induction module, replicated in part as a module for reengaging returning students. Situated in the University's online learning environment, new students gained access on acceptance of offer and from mid-summer began a programme of instructionally designed activities, introducing self-management, health, and well-being, unpacking what it means to be a University of Suffolk student, and critically, online or digital safety and behaviours and expectations for online and blended learning. This was supported through the use of discussion boards and live streamed events, with the express intention of normalizing the digital experience before academic delivery began. It was also an opportunity to promote a new bursary created to support those needing to purchase new IT equipment.

In front loading introductions to academic and information literacy skills, the approach brought blended delivery to the professional services teams responsible for these areas and, specifically, Library and Learning Services staff. Rather than delivering a number of on-campus *Get Ahead: Preparing to study at University* sessions, the teams were challenged to think about how they could deliver content and opportunities through the online learning environment. The opportunity for them to engage with the same training as academic colleagues was provided, but it proved challenging to move past the default "lift and shift" approach, turning face to face workshops into online workshops delivered through the virtual classroom or through scheduled online drop-in activities. The team needed to be thinking not about how to replicate face to face online, but how to recreate the individual experiences, opportunities for collaborative exploration and immersion in academic environments, including the library in innovative and flexible ways.

3 Recreating the university library as space and place in the blended HE environment

The library as "space and place" continues to exist at the heart of the university, both geographically and philosophically. Traditionally viewed as the institutional provider of study space and, importantly, collections to support learning and teaching and research, research literature now explores the future of the academic library and academic librarian in light of the evolving demands of the modern library user, strategic leader, increases in transnational education, and changes in the pedagogies of higher education (Bower et al., 2017; Collins and Garcia, 2020; Delaney and Bates, 2014; Gwyer, 2018). The role and shape of the library continues to evolve, driven not least by the nexus, as identified by Pinfield et al. (2017) in their report for SCONUL *Mapping the future of academic libraries*.

In parallel with the adoption of blended pedagogies in the academic classroom, university libraries have seen increased demand for digital over print. While this has not necessarily resulted in decreased demand for use of the physical library space (SCONUL, 2015, 2018), research from around the world is now reporting the impact of COVID on the lived experience of students, in terms of a [perceived] lack of resources and appropriate study spaces (Bao, 2020; Pokorná et al., 2020) underlining the need for institutions to be cognizant of this when managing their response to the pandemic and associated anxieties (Izumi et al., 2020). The lack of collections and study spaces, perceived, or real, clearly links to the library's function as space, but it also speaks to the more philosophical conceptualization of the library as a space in which students can be together, work collectively, and feel embedded in the university ecosystem.

3.1 Information literacy: A strategic positioning for social change

For leaders of university libraries, alignment of the library to the "values, mission and goals of the institution of which it is a part" (Freeman, 2005, p. 2) is critical if they are to evidence ongoing purpose in an increasingly marketized, information-driven world. Positioning the library as an ecosystem where environment and inhabitants directly contribute to student achievement, and engagement through skills development in information, digital and employability-driven literacies, "makes it clear that libraries and librarians have a major role to play in learning and teaching" (Corrall and Jolly, 2019, p. 113).

Information literacy has long been an essential element of the work of the Learning and Teaching Librarian, and, as such, the pandemic provides an opportunity for librarians and libraries to put themselves at the heart of an institutional response. The pandemic, however, should be viewed simply as a driver, or an enabler, for both immediate and longer term strategic action. In disconnecting learning communities and social communities, COVID-19 has created a pathway for real social innovation. Corrall and Jolly (2019) highlight this, looking to The Young Foundation (2012, p. 18) definition of social innovations as "new solutions…that simultaneously meet a social need…and lead to new or improved capabilities…and better use of assets and resources."

This definition of social innovation is echoed in the conceptualization of information literacy from the Library and Information Association (CILIP, 2018, p. 4) as a skillset which

allows individuals to acquire and develop their understanding of the world around them; to reach informed views; where appropriate to challenge, credibly and in an informed way assumptions or orthodoxies (including one's own), and even authority; to recognise bias and misinformation; and thereby to be engaged citizens, able to play a full part in democratic life and society. Information literacy helps to address social exclusion, by providing disadvantaged groups with the means of making sense of the world around them and participating in society

It is reasonable to suggest then that at the confluence of social innovation and the sustaining of communities and participation is the need for safe and reliable and authoritative information, accessible by all through porous boundaries of collaboration. This has been highlighted again through the pandemic, with information positively used to research and develop responses and negatively used to create and spread misinformation. As the world grappled with the onset of COVID, World Health Organization Director-General, Tedros Adhanom Ghebreyesus said "we're not just fighting an epidemic; we're fighting an infodemic" (World Health Organization, 2020); the way to fight an infodemic is to ensure that everyone has access to the right information, in the right way, as and when they need it.

In an increasingly digital world where the quickest and easiest way to find an answer is to "Google it," an assumption could be made that participants are already capable of finding and reusing information. To an extent this is true, but in a posttruth era, the ability to see beyond the printed word, and "fake news," the ability to know when to look for information, how to test, and then apply information in a live environment suggests information literacy training needs to stretch to include online media literacy and knowledge management. These skills must be, and increasingly are, tested through curriculum and assessment, looking beyond the content of bibliographies to the ability to locate, test, and apply information in context under pressure, shifting the knowledge premium from recall to application.

4   The role and professional identity of the librarian as gatekeeper to information

CILIP (2020) describes academic and research librarian roles as those who facilitate access to information and support skills development in relation to information literacy, referencing, searching, and copyright, and this description readily conforms to traditional conceptualizations of the librarian. Recent literature exploring the professional identity of the librarian suggests that the identity of the librarian is, and has always been, "fluent, dynamic, and responsive to user needs" (Klein and Lenart, 2020, p. 22). For the professional—and professionalizing—librarian, contextual variables, the renegotiation of social perceptions and personal experience result in a librarian professional identity continuum (Pierson Cameron et al., 2019). Personal identity is relational and iterative, a developing social construct, creating and created by a community and cultural identity underpinned by shared symbols, language, aspirations (Dewey, 1916; Hall and Du Gay, 2013; Mead, 1934).

Nichols Hess (2020b) has explored the differentials in influencers on identity and self-identification between library professional teaching in predominantly on-campus or blended—online modalities, as well as impact of institution type and time spent in role (Nichols Hess, 2020a). These are interesting areas for consideration, especially when conceptualizing librarianship as a community of practice, the transition or development from "newcomer" to "old timer" (Lave and Wenger, 1991), along the librarian professional identity continuum. The impact of the pandemic on the community in which the librarian is located, and the shift from on-campus to blended or online delivery has considerable potential to disrupt these understandings and behaviours; and asks librarians to look beyond the walls of the library, past the role of information literacy instructor, collection manager, and even beyond the role of educator. Instead, as the findings of the initial online learning pilot indicated, in repositioning themselves as online or digital librarians, there is a need for librarians to also consider the elements for engagement in an online environment, creating a duality of relational identity formation and presence for learner and "teacher."

Initial data from the University online preentry programme demonstrated that in the same way that instructionally designed content increased in-content learning from an academic and subject-based perspective, so too it could result in increased participation in ongoing support. There is a need for ongoing review of this data, and how the development of introductory relationships on this space may continue to influence engagement with information literacy through the remainder of the disconnected academic year and beyond. This too may see a need for librarians to continue to establish their professional selves in a digital learning landscape.

4.1 The professionalizing librarian: A case study

The University of Suffolk established a graduate trainee librarian role to provide an opportunity to grow librarian talent and, critically, to provide opportunity for longer-serving librarians to be exposed to new approaches to librarianship and enable conversations which would broaden thinking about information literacy sessions with a fundamental understanding of pedagogical theories and application (Jacobs, 2008).

The following statements are extracts from the trainee in post on assumptions made in relation to the profession after a number of years of prequalificatory experience in public and academic libraries:

I made a series of assumptions about the Library and Information Science (LIS)
profession, which I have also seen reflected in others. For example:

- *the title of librarian is typically given to whoever has a clear role within the service (i.e. helpdesk staff) and not necessarily to those with a LIS qualification;*
- *the librarian's role is not always considered a nuanced one; - definitions of the role typically include customer service, acquisitions, and collections management but may not include management or data analytics;*
- *because there is limited understanding about what the role can entail (potentially because it is so various) the idea of a LIS master's qualification can come as a surprise to some.*

Does this limited understanding of the profession lead to exclusivity of the LIS
profession? Does it perpetuate stagnation/lacking innovation within the profession? Is
there a librarian stereotype and, if there is, how does this contribute to the exclusivity
of the profession? Does the Librarian need to be 'reworked' to open the profession to
innovation, new ideas, new perspectives?

And the decision-making process for entering the profession:

My eventual decision to enter the LIS profession was less to do with 'The Library'
(the space, construct, books etc.) and more to do with information – how we retrieve,
understand and use it; how inequalities in information access and literacy can perpetuate
a range of social and economic issues. That said, I am in a privileged position when it
comes to LIS. I have over five years of experience in public and academic libraries. I have

a rounded knowledge about the various and shifting shapes LIS professions can take and have used this to inform my professional interests.

When researching accredited LIS courses in the UK, I felt what was available could be divided into two types: Library-centric and Information-centric. Library-centric courses tended to focus, unsurprisingly, on traditional library staples: classification, cataloguing, information organization etc. Information-centric programmes were more general in focus, with a broader alignment to LIS rather than 'The Library' as a concept.

Ultimately, I decided upon a course with a broader scope and information alignment (Information Science), which would be studied through a more specific, library-orientated lens (Library Management).

Is it the responsibility of CILIP to ensure that all accredited courses express a general LIS alignment? Is there a place for the traditional library school as it once was? Can we/ should we continue to call it Library school at all?

These reflections and observations, while noted prepandemic, are congruent with the notion that librarianship can and perhaps should look beyond the needs of the library to the needs of the institution in which it resides (Fraser-Arnott, 2019).

For the University of Suffolk, and the librarians within it, this means looking to institutional strategy and agenda for widening participation, as part of a community-impact institution. As the University moves to online and blended in response to the pandemic, new opportunities for transnational education and distance learning break down the walls of the institution, and the library, extending the community on which it aspires to have positive impact. For Learning and Teaching Librarians, online learning necessitates a need to move from live, hands-on delivery of skills development to online asynchronous and instructionally designed learning. Collections must be curated to enable at point of need access, with those accessing them equipped to "mix and match" these collections with the limitless of authoritative and "fake" information sources available.

5 Conclusion

This chapter has presented the work of the University of Suffolk in responding to the impact the COVID-19 pandemic has had on the delivery of learning and teaching and traditional library services to all within its community. It has also reflected on what this has meant for the library as place and the role of the librarians within it.

Librarians are asked to rise to the challenge of an at least partial reinvention of self, their role, and identity in a digital landscape. This process has begun through the provision of preentry skills, which in itself surfaced the need for established librarians to be challenged to think beyond live synchronous learning to the development of scaffolded and constructively aligned learning; of ways to engage with, access, and critically evaluate information to support new assessment demands of information retrieval and application. The reflections of the professionalizing librarian reveal this understanding of information, and its role in social justice and innovation is central to the decision-making process for profession entry.

For others, outside of the library profession, the need to understand the academic librarian as the professional in the subject of information will be achieved through the strategic repositioning of the library and librarian as critical in the post-pandemic world, where learning, collections, and information extend beyond institutional walls through porous boundaries and across extended communities.

References

AdvanceHE, 2020. Blended Learning. [Online]. Available: https://www.advance-he.ac.uk/knowledge-hub/blended-learning-0#:~:text=Blended%20asynchronous%20learning%20introduces%20more,spaces%20in%20which%20they%20learn. (Accessed 31 October 2020).

Bandura, A., Barbaranelli, C., Caprara, G.V., Pastorelli, C., 1996. Multifaceted impact of self-efficacy beliefs on academic functioning. Child Dev. 67, 1206–1222.

Bao, W., 2020. COVID-19 and online teaching in higher education: a case study of Peking University. Hum. Behav. Emerg. Technol. 2, 113–115.

Barnett, R., 2014. Conditions of Flexibility: Securing a more Responsive Higher Education System. HEA. [Online]. Available: https://s3.eu-west-2.amazonaws.com/assets.creode.advancehe-document-manager/documents/hea/private/resources/fp_conditions_of_flexibility_0_1568036618.pdf. (Accessed 31 October 2020).

Bennett, S., Maton, K., 2010. Beyond the 'digital natives' debate: towards a more nuanced understanding of students' technology experiences. J. Comput. Assist. Learn. 26, 321–331.

Bower, K., Sheppard, N., Bayjoo, J., Pease, A., 2017. Establishing the role and impact of academic librarians in supporting open research: a case study at Leeds Beckett University, UK. New Rev. Acad. Librariansh. 23, 233–244.

Brown, G., Parkin, D., 2020. Space and Place—Creating Socially Distanced Campuses and Education Project. AdvanceHE. [Online]. Available: https://s3.eu-west-2.amazonaws.com/assets.creode.advancehe-document-manager/documents/advance-he/SDCE%20Project%20-%20Leadership%20Intelligence%20Report%20-%20Space%20and%20Place%20FINAL_1591362872.pdf?X-Amz-Content-Sha256=UNSIGNED-PAY-LOADandX-Amz-Algorithm=AWS4-HMAC-SHA256andX-Amz-Credential=AKIATYAYEYO3HUY745WI%2F20201107%2Feu-west-2%2Fs3%2Faws4_requestandX-Amz-Date=20201107T120300ZandX-Amz-SignedHeaders=hostandX-Amz-Expires=604800andX-Amz-Signature=859c1249ab8f19c70bc3d92f162755429c5be02-2bb3e1fa8bd54e4efd62fd782. (Accessed 31 October 2020).

Bryant, J., Matthews, G., Walton, G., 2009. Academic libraries and social and learning space: a case study of Loughborough University Library, UK. J. Libr. Inf. Sci. 41, 7–18.

CILIP, 2018. CILIP Definition of Information Literacy 2018. [Online]. Available: https://infolit.org.uk/ILdefinitionCILIP2018.pdf. (Accessed 31 October 2020).

CILIP, 2020. Academic and Research Librarians. [Online]. Available: https://www.cilip.org.uk/page/AcademicResearchLibrarians. (Accessed 31 October 2020).

Collins, I.S., Garcia, I.B., 2020. UK university libraries supporting transnational education (TNE) partnerships. Insights UKSG J. 33, 1–6.

Corrall, S., Jolly, L., 2019. Innovations in learning and teaching in academic libraries: alignment, collaboration, and the social turn. New Rev. Acad. Librariansh. 25, 113–128.

Delaney, G., Bates, J., 2014. Envisioning the academic library: a reflection on roles, relevancy and relationships. New Rev. Acad. Librariansh. 21, 30–51.

Department for Education, 2020. Get Help With Technology During Coronavirus (COVID-19). [Online]. Available: https://www.gov.uk/guidance/get-help-with-technology-for-remote-education-during-coronavirus-covid-19. (Accessed 28 October 2020).

Dewey, J., 1916. Democracy and Education. Macmillan, New York.

Fraser-Arnott, M., 2019. Personalizing professionalism: the professional identity experiences of LIS graduates in non-library roles. J. Librariansh. Inf. Sci. 51, 431–439.

Fredricks, J.A., Blumenfeld, P.C., Paris, A.H., 2004. School engagement: potential of the concept, state of the evidence. Rev. Educ. Res. 74, 59–109.

Fredrickson, B.L., 2001. The role of positive emotions in positive psychology: the broaden-and-build theory of positive emotions. Am. Psychol. 56, 218–226.

Freeman, G.T., 2005. The library as place: changes in learning patterns, collections, technology and use. In: Council on Library and Information Resources (Ed.), Library as Place: Rethinking Roles, Rethinking Space. Council on Library and Information Resources, Washington, DC.

Furlong, M.J., Christenson, S.L., 2008. Engaging students at school and with learning: a relevant construct for all students. Psychol. Sch. 45, 365–368.

Garrison, D.R., Anderson, T., 2003. E-learning in the 21st Century; A Framework for Research and Practice. Routledge Falmer, London.

Gwyer, R., 2018. "This is an opportunity for librarians to reinvent themselves, but it is about moving out of their areas": new roles for library leaders? New Rev. Acad. Librariansh. 24 (3–4), 428–441.

Hall, S., Du Gay, P., 2013. Questions of Cultural Identity. Sage Publications, London.

Helsper, E.J., Eynon, R., 2010. Digital natives: where is the evidence? Br. Educ. Res. J. 36, 503–520.

Izumi, T., Sukhwani, V., Surjan, A., Shaw, R., 2020. Managing and responding to pandemics in higher educational institutions: initial learning from COVID-19. Int. J. Disaster Resil. Built Environ. 12 (1), 51–66. ahead-of-print.

Jacobs, H.L.M., 2008. Information literacy and reflective pedagogical praxis. J. Acad. Librariansh. 34, 256–262.

Johnston, B., Macneill, S., Smyth, K., 2018. Conceptualising the Digital University: The Intersection of Policy, Pedagogy and Practice. Palgrave Macmillan, Cham.

Klein, S., Lenart, B., 2020. In search of shifting and emergent librarian identities. Partnership 15 (1), 1–27.

Lave, J., Wenger, E., 1991. Situated Learning: Legitimate Peripheral Participation. Cambridge University Press, Cambridge.

Lawson, M.A., Lawson, H.A., 2013. New conceptual frameworks for student engagement research, policy, and practice. Rev. Educ. Res. 83, 432–479.

Margaryan, A., Littlejohn, A., Vojt, G., 2011. Are digital natives a myth or reality? University students' use of digital technologies. Comput. Educ. 56, 429–440.

Mead, G.H., 1934. Mind, Self and Society. University of Chicago Press, Chicago.

Nichols Hess, A., 2020a. Academic librarians' teaching identities and work experiences: exploring relationships to support perspective transformation in information literacy instruction. J. Libr. Adm. 60, 1–23.

Nichols Hess, A., 2020b. Instructional modalities and perspective transformation: how academic librarians' experiences in face-to-face, blended/hybrid, and online instruction influence their teaching identities. J. Libr. Inf. Serv. Dist. Learn. 13, 1–16.

Office for Students, 2020a. Access and Participation Plans. [Online]. Available: https://www.officeforstudents.org.uk/advice-and-guidance/promoting-equal-opportunities/access-and-participation-plans/. (Accessed 31 October 2020).

Office for Students, 2020b. 'Digital Poverty' Risks Leaving Students Behind. [Online]. Available: https://www.officeforstudents.org.uk/news-blog-and-events/press-and-media/digital-poverty-risks-leaving-students-behind/. (Accessed 31 October 2020).

Okike Benedict, I., 2020. Information dissemination in an era of a pandemic (COVID-19): librarians' role. Library Hi Tech News 37, 1–4.

Phippen, A., Bond, E., Buck, E., 2020. Effective strategies for information literacy education: combatting 'fake news' and empowering critical thinking. In: Baker, D., Ellis, L. (Eds.), Future Directions in Digital Information. Chandos Publishing, Kidlington.

Pierson Cameron, M., Goulding, A., Campbell-Meier, 2019. An integrated understanding of librarian professional identity. Glob. Knowl. Mem. Commun. 68, 413–430.

Pinfield, S., Cox, A., Rutter, S., 2017. Mapping the Future of Academic Libraries: A Report for SCONUL. [Online]. Available: https://www.sconul.ac.uk/sites/default/files/documents/Mapping%20the%20Future%20of%20Academic%20Libraries%20Final%20proof_0.pdf. (Accessed 31 October 2020).

Pokorná, L., Indrák, M., Grman, M., Stepanovsky, F., Smetánková, M., 2020. Silver lining of the COVID-19 crisis for digital libraries in terms of remote access. Digit. Libr. Perspect. 36 (4), 389–401. ahead-of-print.

Quality Assurance Agency, 2020. COVID-19 Support and Guidance. [Online]. Available: https://www.qaa.ac.uk/news-events/support-and-guidance-covid-19. (Accessed 31 October 2020).

Redmond, P., Heffernan, A., Abawi, L., Brown, A., Henderson, R., 2018. An online engagement framework for higher education. Online Learn. 22 (1), 183–204.

Salman Bin, N., Bhatti, R., 2020. The Covid-19 'infodemic': a new front for information professionals. Health Inf. Libr. J. 37, 233–239.

SCONUL, 2015. Changing Trends in Loans, Visits and the Use of E-books. SCONUL. [Online]. Available: https://www.sconul.ac.uk/sites/default/files/documents/Analysis%20_Loans%20ebooks%20visits%20June%202015.pdf. (Accessed 31 October 2020).

SCONUL, 2018. The Continuing Evolution of UK Academic Libraries. SCONUL. [Online]. Available: https://www.sconul.ac.uk/sites/default/files/documents/The_continuing_evolution_of_UK_academic_libraries.pdf. (Accessed 31 October 2020).

Tai, J.H.-M., Bellingham, R., Lang, J., Dawson, P., 2019. Student perspectives of engagement in learning in contemporary and digital contexts. High. Educ. Res. Dev. 38, 1075–1089.

The Young Foundation, 2012. Social Innovation Overview: A Deliverable of the Project: "The Theoretical, Empirical and Policy Foundations for Building Social Innovation in Europe" (TEPSIE), European Commission—7th Framework Programme. Brussels.

University of Suffolk, 2020a. Brightspace Guidance and Development Resources: Digipaths. University of Suffolk. [Online]. Available: https://libguides.uos.ac.uk/celt/brightspace/digipath. (Accessed 31st October 2020).

University of Suffolk, 2020b. Never Stand Still. [Online]. Available: https://www.uos.ac.uk/NeverStandStill. (Accessed 31 October 2020).

World Health Organization, 2020. Munich Security Conference: Director-General Tedros Adhanom Ghebreyesus. [Online]. Available: https://www.who.int/dg/speeches/detail/munich-security-conference. (Accessed 9 November 2020).

Digital-first approaches and the library brand in a post-pandemic world

Richard Maidment-Otlet
EdTech and Marketing Consultant, Bristol, United Kingdom

1 Introduction

The COVID-19 pandemic has accelerated the move toward an Education 4.0 vision where learning, teaching, and research are primarily delivered online, fully exploiting the potential of the latest digital technologies such as artificial intelligence (AI) and blockchain. In this chapter, it is argued that while the library provides core essential services that support this movement, the library brand is not visible and therefore may not be seen as relevant today to end users. By looking back at some of the core affordances of information technologies and changing social and economic structures through the ages up to the present time, it is demonstrated that the library function is now more important than ever. Many of the structures we have in place are still largely those created to support the printing press. The library is uniquely positioned to provide many of the supporting structures that are critical to the success of more hybrid models of teaching, learning, and research online.

The chapter opens by considering information technology tools and changes over time, including the increased movement to online and the information issues that these changes have raised. Looking to the role of the library in a post-pandemic world, in line with the increased movement to online, a digital-first approach is considered and what this might mean for libraries. Finally, it is argued that there is a tension between whether the library should be a passive service provider or should adopt a more active approach, forging a strong global brand in the process.

2 Mediating frameworks and a digital information environment

There is a close relationship between changing technologies and changes in the way we consume, access, organize, and use information and knowledge. The library has long played a key role in supporting users and helping them in their quest for knowledge and learning. Wherever there have been changes in technologies through time, the issues associated with those technologies and our use of information and knowledge have changed too. Examining these key changes and issues reveals that there are common threads that run through them that are centered on information and our use

Libraries, Digital Information, and COVID. https://doi.org/10.1016/B978-0-323-88493-8.00016-1

of it. Three key characteristics of information, when mediated by technology, can be identified: its fixity, fluidity or movement, and mutability—the ease with which it can be changed. The underlying constant is that information itself is highly unstable. This is depicted in Fig. 12.1.

This visually demonstrates the extremes of the characteristics. For example, an information tool may display elements of all the characteristics but may often have propensity toward one in particular. The specific characteristics are not isolated from each other and are impacted by the context of the activity and human agency, whether collective or individual, and the mediating frameworks of tools. This is depicted in the outer circle. For example, a highly mutable tool such as a web page may be stabilized by employing other tools such as critical appraisal and the cross-checking of multiple sources of information.

One of the first major information technology developments that brought about a key change was writing. Writing is closely related to power and stabilizing information because of its ability to "fix" information easily. However, writing is also by its very nature highly mutable and easy to change. A second development and change can be identified in the codex or book. The familiar book is an organized grouping of "fixed" writing. The concept of a collection or portfolio of information is still fundamental to the way we organize information today. Books also have great longevity in an

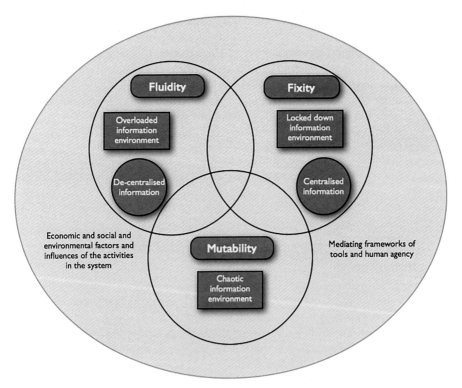

Fig. 12.1 Information tensions.
Author's own artwork.

unchanged "fixed" form, as opposed to digital, which is highly "mutable." However, while the information in a book appears "fixed," the development of book catalogs, classifications, page numbers, and reference sections also gives the text itself more "fluidity," as it allows the reader greater access more quickly. The third development was the printing press. Printing vastly increased both "fixity," as many copies could be made more easily, and "fluidity" at the same time as the information in the book could be widely disseminated to many more people than previously.

The fourth development has been the provision of online information over the Internet and available on the web. This has resulted in near direct access for users to increasing amounts of information, presented in various formats and on various platforms. Critically, the Internet is not bound to a physical space as earlier technologies—such as a book to a library—were. Other information tools soon appeared too, such as hypertext, which in turn led to new behaviors, as it facilitated the ability to "jump" between web pages and "surf the Internet." These behaviours sit in opposition to the concept of a hierarchy of information, as found in textbooks, or information that is presented in a linear fashion or builds from explanatory to complex. Combined with the rapid rise in mobile technologies, it has facilitated much greater "fluidity" and global reach. It has also had the effect of decentralizing information from one particular grouping to many that are linked in space and time. The huge increase in fluidity has had a destabilizing effect. These factors have worked to dilute the traditional concept of an "information authority." This notion of speed, fluidity, and the reduction in distance, combined with the movement beyond physical limitations, has synergies with Borges (1999, p. 216) concept of the "total library." He describes this as a "vast, contradictory library, whose vertical wilderness of books run the incessant risk of changing into others that affirm, deny, and confuse everything like a delirious god." Without some stabilizing support structures in place, it is hard for us to access and use information effectively. Just a few current-day examples include issues of information overload, misinformation, and fake news. However, online information technologies also offer many greater positive opportunities, such as increased accessibility, mobility, and equality. The most recent movement online of learning, teaching, and research in a short space of time caused by COVID-19 has highlighted the opportunities and also the issues outlined above as well as the gaps in provision and support.

3 Frameworks

Organizing and mediating frameworks of tools can be identified. These have emerged and evolved over time. For over two millennia, we have elevated the format of the book as the "truth-bearing" information source. Whole institutions and information systems—such as the publishing industry—have built up around it. However, online information technologies, and the processes and systems surrounding them, have had little time to evolve and embed. A further problem is that many of the structures we have in place today are still largely those based upon, and created to support, the printing press, such as the scholarly communications model and bibliographic circle depicted below (Fig. 12.2). While the academic publishing model is changing and

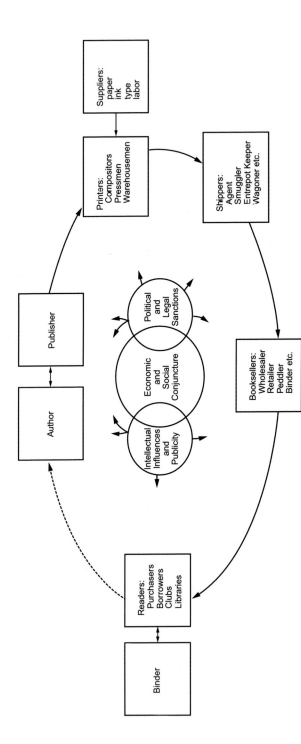

Fig. 12.2 The bibliographic circle (Darnton, 2009, pp. 179–182).

evolving quickly, this state of flux has left the library struggling to maintain both high-quality book collections and to pay large bills to publishers for digital resources emanating and massively benefiting, essentially from the old system. There is also a question to ask about whether we would be better to seek out new approaches, rather than modifying the old systems.

The library is a core information technology tool and an organizing and stabilizing framework. While the name "library" is intrinsically bound to the book deriving from the Latin word for "libr," the services and functions that the library provides are critical to access to information and knowledge, whether online or physical. Typically, these services are divided into backend services, focused on selecting, collecting, organizing, conserving, and preserving, and frontend services such as providing access and resource discovery on behalf of a defined community of users (Borgman, 2000, p. 38). However, the movement of information online has rendered the most visible and physical elements of the library less visible to end users, who may not look beyond their Google search engine for access and even consider Google to be their library.

As Lis Parcell (2019) highlights, libraries' role in digital capability is often misunderstood. Libraries have a strong culture of collaboration, cooperation, and innovation and have often played a driving force in the introduction of new technologies: "libraries have embraced digital practice for over three decades." She attributes this misunderstanding to outdated images of libraries in the popular imagination and highlights that where they have introduced new and innovative technologies and improvements, it has always been in a seamless way, minimizing disruption for students and staff. It is not surprising that library functions remain largely invisible to the end user. However, the role of the library is becoming increasingly important. As already highlighted above, the move to learning and teaching online almost overnight caused by the pandemic has been highly disruptive. Unsurprisingly, it has also revealed many issues, however what has been achieved so far in such a relatively short space of time by institutions across the world is a huge achievement.

4 Key issues

The literature is understandably limited at the present time, but key areas that need addressing can be identified:

- Greater investment in the "less visible" campus digital infrastructure
- Equality of access to learning technology
- Support in using technology tools
- Access online resources that are easy to find and search
- Internet bandwidth beyond city limits at the extremes of networks
- Increased flexibility in the teaching and learning models
- Hybrid online models that mix online and campus-based learning, teaching, and research
- Digital resources available in multiple formats, allowing greater accessibility for all

Many of these relate directly to the role and functions of the library. While the disintermediation of traditional information access methods and the increasing independence of the information user are an inevitable part of the changing information environment, the visibility of the library is a serious issue. If users are not aware of library services and functions, they will not necessarily look to the library for support. This threatens to undermine and further marginalize the essential services and functions that the library provides.

How the library might reposition its services and brand in the post-pandemic world is considered next.

5 Digital-first approaches, increasing visibility, and developing a global brand

As highlighted above, the library function is already supporting many users with information skills and access to resources, as well as providing critical backend services. These services and functions are needed now more than ever as online learning and teaching models continue to adapt and change. It has been argued that these services are unique to the library in a time when the core element—information itself—is in a state of great instability. These services are still typically bound to the specific institutional community of learners, academics, and researchers. However, this author believes that the reach and visibility of these services could be further extended and on a global scale: first, by adopting a digital-first strategic approach to all services and functions, and second by developing a strong and relevant global brand.

5.1 Digital first

One of the key tenets of a digital-first approach is to consider every function of the library, as well as any new opportunities, or problems to be solved, with the assumption that the solution should be as digital as possible. This involves doing two things: first, adopting the user's viewpoint and imagining that every touchpoint that they have with the library is digital first rather than physical; second, moving as much of the service provision as possible to digital platforms using automation, powered by AI and blockchain. This could include targeting new customers, automating backend functions—and some of frontend ones too—such as help desks, as well as developing smart analytics to track performance and user behaviors and responding to needs as they are identified.

Three key strands need to be coordinated to achieve this: first, identifying and implementing the appropriate new technologies; behind the scenes, enabling the digital technology to take care of the everyday business of the library; second, reviewing and amending existing business models or developing new ones, and another element is looking for new revenue streams where possible to offset the additional investment costs; and third, and probably the hardest, is changing human and cultural behaviours. This is a system-wide change and slow and incremental changes are unlikely to be successful or significantly innovative. Everyone needs to adopt a digital-first mindset if it is to be successful. Inevitably job roles will change. However, with the technology working in the background to do the "heavy lifting," staff time is freed up to spend in the foreground, as for example, managing customer issues not catered for by the system or developing and adapting online resources.

Adopting a digital-first approach does not mean that library spaces are no longer important or needed. Looking beyond the pandemic, the library space is still at the heart of the campus both virtual and physical, and this is unlikely to change. If anything, freed from the need to store books on often expensive real estate, this feature can be given to designing spaces that foster collaboration and act as a center for cultivating ideas and innovation. The library space is also an important cultural reminder and symbol, with a rich heritage that makes it a critical part of the library and institutional brand image.

5.2 The library brand as global information specialist

The library has an enviable brand value proposition, as David Pescovitz highlights: "at their core, libraries in the information age provide a public means of accessing knowledge and that's what people crave" (2016, para 4).

As discussed above, libraries are good at collaborating, providing seamless experiences and anticipating end user and customer needs. Whether a conscious approach or not, this approach displays a passive branding strategy relying on the end user and customer finding their services, as well as the library having a deep understanding of the customer. On the other hand, an active branding strategy involves putting effort, time, and resources into actively promoting your brand. Neither option is easy. It requires a great deal of skill if you are to gain attention. The benefit of active branding is that you have control over the interactions with consumers. It is a good way to establish who you are and what you can do for the customer as well as introduce new products and services. Positioning the library as a core global information specialist and provider will take a good amount of active branding, certainly initially. In reality, both approaches are needed. Passive branding has to be built on an extensive established online presence or quite simply no one will know that you are there, let alone what you can do for them. Once established, it requires constant monitoring: tracking user behaviors and trends and ensuring your offer remain relevant to their needs. Much of this work can be automated. An established strong brand is recognizable at basic levels in terms of exactly what a user or new customer can expect by engaging with that brand.

6 Conclusion

By developing a strong brand built on a digital-first approach, the locus of attention will be on the library, a trusted leading-edge online global information specialist and knowledge provider, offering world class customer service. Once the brand is established, users will want to engage with this brand and seek it out. Google in this new context is more of a partner, working as an access point. Once a strong brand is established, it will also open up new partnerships and alternative revenue streams to the library.

To understand how libraries will change by the mid-21st century, people need to understand what function they currently serve.

(Pescovitz, 2016)

The evidence suggests that the role of the library is as important now as it has ever been if we are to make sense of today's online information environment and enable greater equality of access to information and knowledge. The core services that libraries provide are already well established and built on a rich trusted heritage and tradition. The disruption caused by COVID-19 to traditional learning, teaching, and research structures has accelerated the move toward online and this provides an opportunity for libraries to firmly establish their role on a global scale in ways that would have taken years prepandemic. The move to online has also brought the weaknesses and gaps in online learning support structures into sharp relief, with many complaining about poor user experience and universities being unprepared. Hybrid models certainly look to be a solution, as the evidence shows that users want both; it is probably a model that is here to stay. Many commercial information resource and platform providers have rushed to exploit this expanded marketplace. The opportunity and need for academic libraries to occupy this space is now.

References

Borges, J.L., 1999. The Total library Jorge Luis Borges: The Total Library. Penguin, London.

Borgman, C.L., 2000. From Gutenberg to the Global Information Infrastructure: Access to Information in a Networked World. MIT Press, Cambridge, MA.

Darnton, R., 2009. The Case for Books: Past, Present, and Future. Public Affairs, New York.

Parcell, L., 2019. Creating the Library of the Future. https://www.jisc.ac.uk/blog/creating-the-library-of-the-future-03-may-2019. (Accessed 18 January 2021).

Pescovitz, D., 2016. Libraries of the Future are Going to Change in Some Unexpected Ways. https://www.businessinsider.com/libraries-of-the-future-2016-8?r=US&IR=T. (Accessed 20 January 2021).

During COVID-19: Emerging themes in higher education

Sayeda Zain
Mont Rose College of Management & Science, London, United Kingdom

1 Introduction

COVID-19 has caused unprecedented disruption to the education sector all over the world. Since the start of the pandemic, HE leaders are collaborating to find ways of handling this challenging and uncertain situation. The decisions taken now are critical, as they will change the future educational landscape. Communication strategies and priorities are shifting; institutions are trying to find new ways to reach faculty, staff, and students. Remote working and online engagement are becoming the norm.

2 Educational disparity

People face emotional, physical, and economic difficulties through to illness or unemployment. The future is uncertain for the millions of students who have graduated this year as they face a world crippled economically by the pandemic. According to UNESCO, over 1.5 billion students in 165 countries are out of school because of COVID, forcing academics to explore new ways of teaching and learning (Academic Impact, 2020). Anticipated changes relate to continuity of teaching and learning, maintaining student employability, developing new educational resources, regulating and facilitating quality HE and affordability (Academic Impact, 2020). Innovative cross-border and cross-sectoral collaborations are needed to face the challenges posed by the current crisis. For example, UNESCO's Global Education Coalition aims to facilitate inclusive learning opportunities for children and young people; more such partnerships are needed to provide and promote open, flexible learning systems (Academic Impact, 2020).

The current crisis could lead to a range of scenarios that could affect industries differently. For example, conventional sectors and industries may experience significant changes in consumer behavior. Students may be reluctant to return to traditional models after experiencing remote and online education models at a lower cost than traditional provision. Furthermore, changes in job markets may lead people to use their transferable skills to enter a different industry.

We could see changes in both curriculum and delivery models in HE.

Libraries, Digital Information, and COVID. https://doi.org/10.1016/B978-0-323-88493-8.00022-7

3 Social and emotional needs

COVID-19 has changed the social and emotional needs of staff. According to the Collaborative for Social, Emotional, and Academic Learning (CASEL), Social and Emotional Learning (SEL) is defined as "the process through which children and adults understand and manage emotions, set and achieve positive goals, feel and show empathy for others, establish and maintain positive relationships, and make responsible decisions." Emotions are essential for learning; the social brain is the leading force in cognition (NCSL, 2020).

Other challenges relate to the identification and management of the stress and trauma that students and school personnel have experienced during closure of buildings and provision and also as they reopen. Educational institutions require a coherent strategy to remove anxiety about academic performance, prioritize healing, and strengthen communication that will improve academic learning and make staff and students feel connected to the educational community (NCSL, 2020).

Educational institutions can develop a three-tier system for the support of students.

Tier 1—**Support for all students**—will require the development of welfare and healing programmes for the whole institution, encompassing welfare advisories, peer circles, groups, community models, and more.

Tier 2—**Targeted interventions**—will require changes to how institutions manage referrals to counseling and support services.

Tier 3—**External support**—will need a focus on how to manage referrals to community health and mental health services.

Educational institutions can offer online and interactive courses for teachers and managers on topics such as assessing and addressing stress and trauma among students and colleagues; establishing healthy learning environments infused with supportive relationships and with separate courses for early childhood, elementary, and secondary students and settings; embedding healing practices into the daily routines of schools and classes; integrating academically rigorous content and social/emotional supports (The Aspen Institute, 2020).

Educational institutions also need to develop a three-tier system of staff support.

Tier 1—**Support for all staff**—All staff should receive support for trauma, social and emotional skills, stress management and reduction, along with self-assessments and self-care and wellness programmes.

Tier 2—**Targeted interventions**—Some staff may need more targeted support such as group coaching, therapy, or support groups, or help from mental health providers.

Tier 3—**External support**—A few staff may need more intensive, individualized support measures put in place through employee assistance programmes, including referrals to community-based mental health providers (The Aspen Institute, 2020).

Educators need to develop ways to track student engagement during online teaching and learning, such as log-ins, class participation, teacher contact, coursework submissions. These data should not be collected or used for punitive purposes. The reason behind the tracking of student engagement is to identify promising practices to study and share, to identify challenges, and to allocate resources accordingly. Student surveys can be used to gather information about experiences during online learning; this will be useful for future planning and evaluation (The Aspen Institute, 2020).

In an unprecedented situation like that of today, planning for the future is more vital than ever, especially as the likely impacts are still evolving and the full economic impact is unclear. However, it is evident how effectively many institutions have been at continuing to serve not only their students but also their communities (sgENGAGE, 2020).

4 Students with special needs

The present COVID pandemic may have intensified issues faced by students with disabilities, such as:

(1) The assistance some students receive from notetakers and sign-language interpreters may be less readily available.
(2) Hearing or visually impaired students may struggle to access lectures and webinars as teaching and learning move online.
(3) Some students may be self-isolating because of underlying health conditions and be unsure how to access the support they need.
(4) Students with mental health conditions may find their impairments intensified by the lockdown.

Some disabled students may belong to groups vulnerable to the pandemic, such as black, Asian, or minority ethnic students, or those who do not have family support will be facing more issues. Some students are worried that their attainment will be affected by modified assessment processes that may not take full account of their needs (Office for Students, 2020) (Fig. 13.1).

Some students who find it difficult to attend lectures in person have benefited from receiving teaching and learning support at home. However, attention must still be paid to digital accessibility to ensure that all students can use resources. But for many disabled students, difficulties remain, encompassing the nonavailability of the right hardware and software to access lectures, webinars, and tutorials and the completion of coursework. Some may struggle with looking at screens for extended periods. Neurodiverse students have reported concerns with online conferencing because of the need for multitasking and the array of features on offer (Office for Students, 2020).

Universities and colleges are adapting their strategies to assist disabled students, though more challenges and issues will emerge as the pandemic continues. In the United Kingdom, the Office for Students (OfS) is working with different HE sector bodies and disability charities to identify emerging practice. Universities, colleges, and students' unions are also sharing practice and resources. This will help to develop services for these students (Office for Students, 2020).

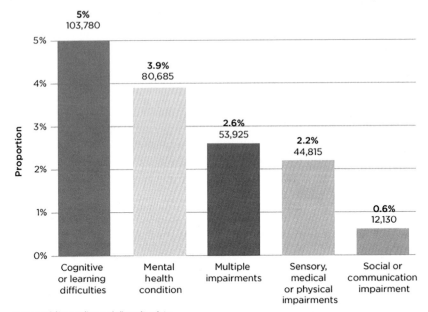

Source: OfS equality and diversity data.
Note: 85.7 per cent of students do not declare a disability.

Fig. 13.1 Proportion of students studying in England who declared a disability by impairment, 2018–19.
Information and graph courtesy of the Office for Students under the terms of the Open Government Licence.

5   Digital learning platforms

Educational institutions have moved toward online learning, resulting in an unprecedented push to adopt digital platforms whose design might not always be driven by best pedagogical practices. Business-driven development of digital learning technologies and platforms may not be aimed primarily at improving learning and teaching but at making a profit.

This is dangerous in a COVID pandemic, where educational institutions need to act quickly to ensure continuity of teaching and learning, helping to maintain the operation of society generally. Universities and colleges do not have time for detailed comparisons of digital learning platforms or to ponder broader and deeper social and educational visions of their uses. This provides opportunities for digital learning industries to make a profit in a seller's market. These technological choices will impact microlevel teaching and learning experiences and mesolevel organizational relations to create broader and unpredicted macrolevel societal impacts (Teräs et al., 2020).

> *The post-COVID-19 world demands creative, explorative learning implemented in open access peer-to-peer platforms where people are able to meet around a problem chosen and defined by their own initiative (…) peers currently puzzled about the same terms and problems.*
>
> *(Illich, 1971, p. 19)*

Teräs et al. (2020) state that "Academics should avoid the temptation to overcome the COVID crisis with ready-made, top-down solutions and the ed-tech industry's pedagogical colonialism… It is imperative to actively engage people, networks, projects, research, and public discussions to promote critically and reflectively informed praxis." Moreover, a wider societal dialog is required about the kind of education society wants to develop in the COVID-19 world.

According to Mpungose (2020), students prefer social media sites like Facebook and WhatsApp for communication, which are not officially adopted by universities for e-learning. Students who are digital natives and are techno-savvy enjoy the use of Web 2.0 applications. The digital platforms should be used as a depository and should be customized to be linked to social media sites like WhatsApp/Facebook, lecture-recording software (CamStudio), video and audio conferencing (Zoom, YouTube live, Skype, Microsoft Teams), and other learning resources in order to provide interactive lectures, both synchronous and asynchronous (Mpungose, 2020). As a result, Hamidi and Chavoshi (2018) further argue that if students can use social media successfully, universities should consider using them for e-learning.

6 Effective remote teaching

COVIDEd Tech Hub with the UK's Department for Education conducted research which highlights key themes and recommendations on pedagogies developed in response to the move to remote teaching during the pandemic. These include:

(1) In remote teaching, innovation in pedagogical performance depends on teachers' levels of digital skills. They need to plan well-structured lessons to meet individual needs.
(2) Teachers can make students aware of their presence by using different platforms and activities like dialog, interactive sessions, whether this is online or through centralized radio or TV broadcasting.
(3) Remote learning is a challenge for vulnerable and disadvantaged students. They are at risk of disrupted learning continuity and other potential harms while out of institutions. Regular teacher engagement and contact with these students will therefore be critically important.
(4) Effective remote learning should maximize students' engagement and promote metacognitive strategies.
(5) The creation of remote learning resources will be a significant burden for teachers; providing centralized guidance and open educational resources will be valuable.
(6) Remote teaching activities can be further enhanced with the use of both online learning and offline media such as TV and radio broadcasting. (Education Development Trust, 2020a).

7 Professional development strategies

Leaders have to prepare teachers for educational technology use within significant time constraints.

> *Some countries succeeded in setting up support for teachers; in the case of Korea, the Ministry of Education facilitated the creation of a support network of digitally savvy teachers who volunteered to mentor their peers and help them use digital tools before the academic year started again online.*
> *(Ministry of Education, Korea, 2020)*

Mexico built on existing platforms online (aprende en casa) and on television (Capacita TV) to help teachers develop their capacity to teach remotely and plan their lessons. Teachers are encouraged to take Massive Open Online Courses (MOOCs) and attend online conferences on digital tools and teaching online and to watch pedagogical programmes on educational TV channels to update their lesson plans.

(OECD, 2020)

In Hungary, as teaching shifted online, the government observed "remarkable dynamism" from schools, as they designed their own solution in a significant bottom-up approach across the country (OECD, 2020).

These progressive developments have demonstrated the innovation and change capacity of schools that can be fostered in the future.

Educational systems can emerge from this crisis with a renewed, confident, highly-skilled, and autonomous teaching profession that exerts its agency collaboratively. School principals can be key to promote and shape the culture of change and innovation … to adapt to the external context by involving teachers and other stakeholders more in decision making, and reviewing … organisational structures in favour of more organic models that can adapt quickly to an ever-changing environment. This emergence of a 'new normal' in Education will precede the development of a 21st century model of school.

(OECD, 2019)

Given current experiences and experiments, it is evident that institutions have to adopt a multipartner approach to delivery, including partnerships with the private sector for ICT infrastructure. Multilevel and cross-sectoral partnerships are critical to a successful and rapid rollout of remote learning. In general, the focus of such partnerships to date has been on improving communications infrastructure, providing students with ed-tech equipment, subsidizing the cost of Internet access or mobile data, developing educational content, or making existing content freely available, and developing new educational platforms (Education Development Trust, 2020b).

8 Conclusion

The COVID-19 pandemic has disrupted education all over the world. Institutions have been forced to move teaching and learning services online without having enough time to develop and test new online pedagogies and digital platforms to satisfy diverse student needs. During this transition, many new themes have emerged, which will completely change the education sector's landscape. However, because of digital poverty, many students are still unable to continue their studies, and new graduates are facing a crippled economy; the external environment is uncertain.

The pandemic has affected the emotional and social needs of staff and students adversely. Institutions need to develop a coherent strategy to manage anxiety and trauma, finding ways to make people feel connected to their communities.

The difficulties of students with special needs have escalated. Organizations and regulators are working with cross-sector bodies, charities, student unions, and others to share practices and resources to provide better services to these students.

Institutions using digital learning platforms for teaching and learning have realized that they should link them to social media sites like Facebook, YouTube, WhatsApp, Zoom, and M/S Teams, to develop and offer more interactive and inclusive teaching. Remote teaching resources, activities, and pedagogies need more enhancement, and teachers are required to develop better IT skills to improve their online teaching methodologies.

Countries worldwide have adopted different approaches to mitigate the effects of the pandemic and build a better future. It is an opportunity for policymakers to cooperate and learn from each other to improve their services.

References

Academic Impact, 2020. COVID-19 and Higher Education: Learning to Unlearn to Create Education for the Future. UN Academic Impact. Available from: https://academicimpact.un.org/content/COVID-19-and-higher-education-learning-unlearn-create-education-future.

Education Development Trust, 2020a. An Overview of Emerging Country-Level Responses to Providing Educational Continuity Under COVID-19: What's Working? What Isn't? Education Development Trust. Available from: https://edtechhub.org/wp-content/uploads/2020/05/whats-working-whats-not.pdf.

Education Development Trust, 2020b. Providing Educational Continuity Under COVID-19: Best Practice in Pedagogy for Remote Teaching. Education Development Trust. Available from: https://www.educationdevelopmenttrust.com/our-research-and-insights/commentary/providing-educational-continuity-under-COVID-19-be.

Hamidi, H., Chavoshi, A., 2018. Analysis of the essential factors for the adoption of mobile learning in higher education: a case study of students of the University of Technology. Telemat. Inform. 35 (4), 1053–1070. https://doi.org/10.1016/j.tele.2017.09.016.

Illich, I., 1971. Deschooling Society. Harper & Row, New York.

Ministry of Education, Korea, 2020. Press Release, All Schools Postpone the New School Year. Ministry of Education, Korea. Available from: http://english.moe.go.kr/boardCnts/view.do?boardID=265&boardSeq=80295&lev=0&searchType=null&statusYN=W&page=1&s=english&m=0301&opType=N.

Mpungose, B.C., 2020. Emergent transition from face-to-face to online learning in a South African University in the context of the Coronavirus pandemic. Humanit. Soc. Sci. Commun. 7 (13). https://doi.org/10.1057/s41599-020-00603-x. Available from.

NCSL, 2020. Addressing Social and Emotional Needs During COVID-19: Emerging Themes in School Reopening Guides. NCSL. Available from https://www.ncsl.org/research/education/COVID-19-addressing-social-and-emotional-needs-for-reopening-schools.aspx.

OECD, 2019. TALIS 2018 Results (Volume I): Teachers and School Leaders as Lifelong Learners., https://doi.org/10.1787/1d0bc92a-en. TALIS, OECD Publishing. Available from.

OECD, 2020. A Framework to Guide an Education Response to the COVID-19 Pandemic of 2020. OECD. Available from: https://globaled.gse.harvard.edu/files/geii/files/framework_guide_v2.pdf.

Office for Students, 2020. Disabled Students. Office for Students. Available from: https://www.officeforstudents.org.uk/publications/coronavirus-briefing-note-disabled-students/.

sgENGAGE, 2020. 3 Higher Ed Themes Emerging During COVID-19. sgENGAGE. Available from: https://npengage.com/higher-education/higher-education-trends-COVID19/.

Teräs, M., et al., 2020. Post-COVID-19 education and education technology 'solutionism': a seller's market. Postdigit. Sci. Educ. 2, 863–878. Available from https://doi.org/10.1007/s42438-020-00164-x.

The Aspen Institute, 2020. State Actions to Support Social, Emotional, and Academic Development: Fostering Connectedness in The Pandemic Era. The Aspen Institute. Available from: https://assets.aspeninstitute.org/content/uploads/2020/05/AESP-State-SEAD-Actions-for-COVID-19.pdf?_ga=2.65068460.381308074.1591918195-130589232.1590623480.

Further reading

The World Bank, 2020. Remote Learning, EdTech & COVID-19. The World Bank. Available from: https://www.worldbank.org/en/topic/edutech/brief/edtech-COVID-19.

World Bank Blogs, 2020. Managing the Impact of COVID-19 on Education Systems Around the World: How Countries are Preparing, Coping, and Planning for Recovery. World Bank Blogs. Available from: https://blogs.worldbank.org/education/managing-impact-COVID-19-education-systems-around-world-how-countries-are-preparing.

Student satisfaction with library resources in the COVID-19 era: A case study of Portuguese academic libraries

14

Maria Luz Antunes[a,b], Carlos Lopes[b,c], and Tatiana Sanches[b,d]
[a]ESTeSL (Instituto Politécnico de Lisboa), Lisboa, Portugal, [b]APPsyCI—Applied Psychology Research Center Capabilities and Inclusion, Lisboa, Portugal, [c]ISPA—Instituto Universitário, Lisboa, Portugal, [d]UIDEF, Instituto da Educação, Universidade de Lisboa, Lisboa, Portugal

1 Introduction

Academic libraries aim to provide access to information to students, teachers, and researchers, ensuring their satisfaction with their needs. The behaviour of the students in relation to this information is determined by their needs, generated from the methodological requirements of the activities to be carried out, the existing conditions for their performance, and the sociopsychological characteristics of each one. According to Núñez-Paula and Zayas-Caballero (2013), the need for information (while learning) generates a behaviour that translates into beliefs, motivation, enthusiasm, skills and knowledge, but also an adaptability to circumstances to successfully achieve the answers to the original problem. Students, being one of the groups circulating in the academic community, do not have a linear or unique behavioural pattern. Even if integrated into the same context and under the same conditions, they are carriers of their own and unique experiences, generating performances that are also their very own and unique. To understand the behavioural pattern of students who attend libraries, it is necessary to know their motivations and their perceptions and their levels of satisfaction with the service provided (Rapchak et al., 2018).

Libraries have a mission to satisfy all those who use their space and services; a satisfied user will pass on a positive opinion to others, but a dissatisfied user will pass on a negative opinion to many more. Hernon and Altman (1996) state that "many libraries consider customers poor judges of the quality of information services… what the customer thinks about both the process and the outcome of the service is the important issue in customer's perceptions" (p. 7). In the context of academic libraries, students may express a favourable or unfavourable opinion about the services provided by a library; this opinion will prevail as a determinant of the quality of the service, regardless of the beliefs of the organization. It means that if students are satisfied with the service provided and with the response obtained, "satisfaction is a sense of contentment that arises from an actual experience in relation to an expected experience" (Hernon and

Libraries, Digital Information, and COVID. https://doi.org/10.1016/B978-0-323-88493-8.00017-3

Whitman, 2001, p. 32). According to Lopes (2006), the most important thing in the future for libraries will not be the possession of books or access to sophisticated information technologies but having the largest number of regular users who are highly satisfied with the products and services made available. In this context, the intention of the user satisfaction studies that have been developed in academic libraries is to identify areas of scrutiny and measure the usability of services by the academic community. Lopes considers that this is an evaluation process, which encompasses the users' view, underlying a strategy of orientation on the part of the library, in the search to serve users and to gain users' satisfaction (Lopes, 2006).

In the current context of great transformations and human and social adaptation, it is important to know the work developed by academic libraries to respond effectively to their first and final clients: the students. It has never made so much sense to understand the perception and needs of users and potential users so that organizations, respecting their mission, can fulfill what people expect from them and which gives them a reason to exist, understanding if the information passes in time and without noise, and identifying who is doing this work in the institutions.

In this scenario, COVID-19 closed academic libraries in early March 2020 for an indefinite period (IFLA, 2020). With no time to plan, libraries were physically shut down to protect the security of the entire academic community and turned into online services to allow remote working. All the work done over the years curating digital content, building robust formative strategies with students, making them aware of electronic resources, defining typologies and suitability, providing information literacy skills has seemingly been a successful project, reassuring librarians and libraries.

Faced with COVID-19 and social isolation, academic students were suddenly confined to distance learning. Academic institutions reinvented themselves, finding ways of providing their services remotely.

In this context, the three academic institutions under analysis (a public college, a public polytechnic institute, and a private university institute), located in Lisbon (Portugal), with a total population of 15,399 undergraduate and master's degree students from diversified fields of knowledge (Arts, Health Sciences, Business Sciences, Communication, Education, Engineering, and Psychology), reinvented themselves and adapted to the pandemic scenario. Integrating the practice of teaching that underpins the formation of the individual, promoting citizenship, and encouraging the active participation of students in the institution and the community, in the field of services, research, development, culture, and artistic creation, never has the mission of these three institutions of higher education made so much sense.

It is therefore important to determine student satisfaction for the institutions and in particular for their libraries: whether or not their information needs are satisfied; whether they know what the reliable sources of information are; if they feel their information needs are satisfied; if they feel supported in the information evaluation process; if they consider that the reference interview, carried out remotely, is satisfactory and meets their demands. The restrictions on physical access to the campuses of the three institutions and their ten libraries, and specifically to face-to-face services, have created challenges for the management of the organization and the functioning of its services, especially to students.

Thus, the objectives of this study were as follows:

1. To perceive the satisfaction of academic students over libraries' responses to their information needs, whether at the level of services or through electronic resources.
2. To assess whether academic students consider themselves prepared to search, assess, and manage the retrieved information now that they work autonomously and depend exclusively on digital content.

These goals are intended to answer the question: will academic students be satisfied with the distance services offered by their libraries during the current pandemic? The answer will allow us to identify the expectations and difficulties perceived by students and help to identify ways of improving the delivery of face-to-face and distance services of academic libraries.

2 Methods

In this section, we will include details of the questionnaire as well as data collection and analysis.

2.1 Participants

The sample is nonprobabilistic and consists of 434 students from the three institutions (Table 14.1).

Table 14.1 Descriptive characteristics of analysis sample (*N*=434).

Variable	Summary value		
Gender		Freq.	%
Female		341	(78.6%)
Male		91	(21%)
Other/Prefer not to say		2	(0.4%)
Age			
Mean age (SD), years	(Range 17–77)	23.81	8.597
Cycle of study			
Undergraduate students	1st year	188	(54.7%)
	2nd year	44	(12.8%)
	3rd year	94	(27.3%)
	4th year	18	(5.2%)
Master students	1st year	67	(74.5%)
	2nd year	23	(25.5%)
Institutions			
Inst. Politécn. Lisboa	Polytechnic institute	198	(45.6%)
ISPA – Instituto Universitário	Private university institute	201	(46.3%)
Inst. Educação	Public college	35	(8.1%)

2.2 Instrument

A student evaluation questionnaire was designed on Office forms (see the question-naire in supplementary material). The questionnaire was circulated in the three insti-tutions, through institutional email, first in the second half of May 2020, a period that covered the beginning of social confinement in Portugal, but in which teaching activ-ities continued remotely and libraries continued to provide services at a distance. The questionnaire was circulated again in October 2020, at the beginning of the academic year, when students adopted new learning practices marked by the division of classes and by physical attendance alternate weeks.

The questionnaire identified the objectives of the study and stated the ethical ap-proach regarding anonymity and confidentiality of data. It was structured in four sections: (1) the satisfaction of libraries' responses to information needs; (2) the sat-isfaction over electronic resources made available by libraries; (3) the self-perceived assessment of students' information skills; and (4) sociodemographic data.

2.2.1. The aim of the **libraries' response to information needs** was to assess student satisfac-tion regarding access to electronic resources from home, information obtained through library websites, how to retrieve information (catalogs, databases), the digital resources made available, and, in general, the support provided by library teams. To express re-spondents' degrees of satisfaction, a Likert scale was used: 1. Completely unsatisfied; 2. A little unsatisfied; 3. Reasonably satisfied; 4. Very satisfied; 5. Completely satisfied.

2.2.2. In view of the **electronic resources made available by the libraries**, the aim was to assess the degree of student satisfaction with digital resources such as library catalogs, B-ON (a Portuguese consortium that ensures access to a vast number of scientific jour-nals and electronic services to the national academic and scientific community—see www.b-on.pt), PubMed, Scopus, Web of Science, *E*-books Academic Collection, RCAAP (a portal which aims to collect, aggregate, and index open access scientific contents from Portuguese institutional repositories—see https://www.rcaap.pt/). It constitutes a single-entry point for searching, discovery, and recall of thousands of scientific and scholarly publications, namely journal articles, conference papers, thesis, and dissertations, distrib-uted by several Portuguese repositories, SciELO, and others. To express their degree of satisfaction, students used the same Likert scale. It should be noted that the term "library catalogue" has been changed to "library database," as the term "catalogue" has, for the academic community, a different connotation.

2.2.3. Because **students access the libraries' electronic resources in a remote, independent way**, their level of satisfaction with the stages of the search, assess, and retrieve infor-mation and their information skills were evaluated using a Likert scale (1. I completely disagree, 2. I disagree, 3. I neither agree nor disagree, 4. I agree, 5. I completely agree).

2.2.4. The sociodemographic **data** collected age, gender, the cycle of studies, and course year data.

3 Results

Overall, 88% of students are reasonably, very, or completely satisfied with access to electronic resources from home. This figure drops a little (83.6%) over the degree of satisfaction with the information obtained from the library website (Table 14.2).

Table 14.2 The libraries' response to information needs by study cycles.

Your satisfaction with the library's response to your information needs (%)	Undergraduate students/Master students				
	1	2	3	4	5
1. Your satisfaction in accessing electronic resources from home	4.65/5.55	8.43/2.22	32.27/16.67	**35.46/45.56**	19.19/30.00
2. Your satisfaction with the information obtained through the library website	3.49/5.55	13.66/7.78	**37.50/18.90**	31.10/**53.33**	14.25/14.44
3. Your satisfaction with the way to recover information (catalogs, databases) and to use it	3.20/5.56	8.43/4.44	**44.48/34.44**	30.23/**37.78**	13.66/17.78
4. I am satisfied with the digital resources made available by the Library because they helped me with my information needs	5.81/6.67	12.80/4.44	30.81/22.22	**33.43/45.56**	17.15/21.11
5. I am satisfied with the support provided by the library team	3.78/4.44	7.27/5.55	**34.01/20.00**	29.36/**38.90**	25.58/31.11

Note: Likert scale: 1. Completely unsatisfied; 2. A little unsatisfied; 3. Reasonably satisfied; 4. Very satisfied; 5. Completely satisfied.

Of the total responses, 88.7% were positive about how to retrieve information through databases and 53.9% are very or completely satisfied with the digital resources made available, because they feel they have helped them respond to their information needs.

Regarding the support provided by the library team during the pandemic period, 88.9% of the undergraduate students and 90% of the master students express satisfaction.

Most libraries develop training sessions on the resources made available, in the library space, but also in a classroom context, in a culture of close collaboration with teachers. The contents are varied, as well as their duration. This study highlights the percentage of students who are unaware of the existence of some databases (Table 14.3), and because they are unaware, they do not answer the question. Undergraduate students are unaware of access to Scopus with 58.14%, RCAAP with 54.94%, PubMed with 51.46%, Web of Science with 50.87%, e-books database with 50.29%, and B-ON with 43.31%. More than half of the master students do not know that they have access to Scopus (52.22%), PubMed (44.45%), and the Web of Science (38.89%), exactly the three most important databases for the rationale of their research work. The library database is also unknown to 29.5% of students; it is also the database with the highest percentage of dissatisfaction among the total number of students.

Of the electronic resources subscribed, B-ON is the best-known resource and with which master students feel most satisfied (30%). As far as open access resources are concerned, 56.6% of undergraduate students, who know and use them, are reasonable, very, or completely satisfied with SciELO, 43.6% with PubMed, and 39.24% with RCAAP. Master students who know and use open access resources show reasonable or complete satisfaction with SciELO (71.1%), RCAAP (62.2%), and PubMed (47.7%).

Regarding the difficulties experienced, undergraduate students highlight the library database (10.7%) and B-ON (9.5%), while master students also refer to the library database (8.8%) and then B-ON, PubMed, Web of Science, and RCAAP (resources presenting the same percentage of difficulty: 7.7%).

Undergraduate students who know the electronic resources presented are reasonably, very, or completely satisfied with the library database (66.5%), SciELO (56.68%), other electronic resources made available (54.94%), B-ON (47.09%), Web of Science (44.76%), E-books Academic Collection (43.89%), PubMed (43.6%), RCAAP (39.24%), and Scopus (37.2%). Regarding master students, they are reasonably, very, or completely satisfied with the library database (77.7%), other electronic resources (72.2%), SciELO (71.1%), B-ON (63.3%), RCAAP (62.2%), E-books Academic Collection (55.5%), Web of Science (53.3%), PubMed (47.7%), and Scopus (42.2%).

Analyzing the degree of student satisfaction with their information skills, by accessing electronic resources in a remote, autonomous way, students express agreement and an absolute agreement about their abilities to perform information searches (91.24%), the master students being the ones who demonstrate the highest security (94.4%) (Table 14.4).

Table 14.3 Assessment of student satisfaction with the electronic resources made available by libraries.

| | Your satisfaction with the electronic resources made available by libraries (%) | | | | | |
| | Undergraduate students/Master students | | | | | |
	1	2	3	4	5	NS/NR
Library database	2.91/5.56	7.85/3.33	**29.65**/18.89	27.33/**38.89**	9.59/20.00	22.67/13.33
B-ON	2.62/4.44	6.98/3.33	20.93/15.56	20.06/**30.00**	6.10/17.78	**43.31**/28.89
PubMed	2.03/6.67	2.91/1.11	18.02/12.22	17.73/22.22	7.85/13.33	**51.46**/**44.45**
Scopus	2.03/4.44	2.62/1.11	17.73/13.33	14.54/18.90	4.94/10.00	**58.14**/**52.22**
Web of Science	2.03/5.56	2.33/2.22	20.06/13.33	17.15/23.33	7.56/16.67	**50.87**/**38.89**
E-books Academic Collection	2.32/3.33	3.49/3.33	21.22/14.45	15.99/27.78	6.69/13.33	**50.29**/**37.78**
RCAAP	2.32/3.33	3.49/4.44	16.57/10.00	14.83/25.56	7.85/26.67	**54.94**/**30.00**
SciELO	3.20/4.45	3.20/2.22	20.64/13.33	21.22/**32.22**	14.82/25.56	36.92/22.22
Other electronic resources	2.62/2.22	3.78/2.22	20.35/17.78	22.38/**30.00**	12.21/24.45	38.66/23.33

Note: Likert scale: 1. Completely unsatisfied; 2. A little unsatisfied; 3. Reasonably satisfied; 4. Very satisfied; 5. Completely satisfied. The option "Does not know/Does not answer (NS/NR)" was also included.

Table 14.4 Level of student satisfaction with their information skills.

How do you feel about your information skills? (%)	Undergraduate students/Master students				
	1	2	3	4	5
I feel comfortable doing information searches	2.32/1.11	7.27/4.44	21.51/6.67	**48.55/61.11**	20.35/26.67
I know how to recognize reliable information for my field of study	2.03/1.11	4.94/3.33	23.84/14.45	**54.07/57.78**	15.12/23.33
I can assess the importance of different information resources	1.45/0.00	6.11/2.22	18.31/7.78	**57.27/52.22**	16.86/37.78
I recognize the importance of correctly and adequately citing the work of others	0.58/0.00	2.62/0.00	10.47/1.11	42.73/43.33	**43.60/55.56**
I try to refer correctly and properly with the requested referencing style	1.16/0.00	2.04/1.11	9.88/2.22	45.35/40.00	41.57/**56.67**

Note: Likert scale: 1. I completely disagree; 2. I disagree; 3. I neither agree nor disagree; 4. I agree; 5. I completely agree.

Regarding the recognition of reliable scientific literature for their field of study, 71.6% of students show agreement or an absolute agreement. Also, in this parameter, the master students, most of whom are already professionals, reveal 81.1% of certainty in their response.

Of the group of students, 77.4% agree and agree absolutely in the assessment of the importance of the different information resources, but the master students answer with 90%, revealing to be able to distinguish and assess the importance of an article, book, chapter, or thesis for their different works. They are also those who, in an almost absolute way (98.8%), recognize the importance of correctly and adequately citing the work of others.

In general, the average information skills shown are positive: close to level 4 in most parameters and for all students and clearly above level 4 in the parameters of citation and bibliographical reference for master's degrees. Nevertheless, in the assessment of students' self-perception of their skills, and on a scale of 0 to 10 points, the average is 7.0 with master students slightly higher (7.3) (Fig. 14.1).

At the end of the questionnaire, the students were asked about the greatest difficulties that had been experienced in searching and retrieving information, the answer being intentionally left open. The analysis of the answers allowed listing a set of concerns described in Table 14.5.

It should be noted that only 30.1% of students responded that they had not experienced any difficulties in researching and retrieving information; of these, 24.4% were undergraduate students and 5.7% were master students.

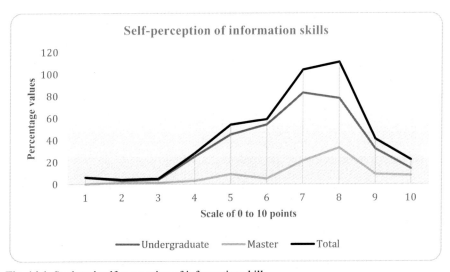

Fig. 14.1 Students' self-perception of information skills.

Table 14.5 The students' concerns regarding search and information retrieval.

Students' concerns regarding search and information retrieval
• How to locate Portuguese scientific information.
• Do not know where to search.
• How to work with so much information.
• How to select the best one from so many databases and frame it in the subject under study.
• How to define the most appropriate keywords.
• How to build a search equation.
• The time spent in the search.
• How to find resources that are reliable and of quality.
• Understanding the relationship between keywords and resources.
• How to extract the results.
• There are so few electronic books.
• How to access articles and books that are blocked. And why are they blocked?
• The dispersed and user-friendly access to scientific works and with much access/consultation restrictions.
• B-ON does not give access to all full texts.
• Unable to access B-ON.
• The location of references available only in printed books.
• Do not know that one could remotely access the contents.
• Do not know how to safeguard the data of a search and migrate them to Mendeley.
• Do not have a priori materials, tutorials, and other kinds of help.
• Ignorance of the existence of VPNs.
• How to work with the VPN.
• Lack of time.
• Lack of disclosure.
• Training is necessary!

4 Discussion

Academic institutions, libraries, and their students are being affected not only by the COVID-19 pandemic and social confinement but also by progressive and adaptable deconfinement. But this is the opportunity for libraries to demonstrate that, even behind closed doors, they continue to provide essential services to ensure access to reliable sources of information for the academic community and to provide information skills, even remotely; this is the opportunity to rethink access to information, which is not free from doubts, technological difficulties, and asymmetry of knowledge (Tanus and Sánchez-Tarragó, 2020).

The use of electronic resources has exploded in all academic libraries. However, the results regarding their use are not favorable to the student community, because they reveal ignorance of their existence. The percentage is high, which is worrying. These figures must be carefully analyzed as they imply the planning of a formative and pedagogical intervention that will guarantee the resolution of this problem. Electronic resources are subscribed in a global way in the three institutions with the objective of supporting the study and research of the entire academic community. The data in the present chapter point to a concern resulting from the students' ignorance of the resources made available by the institutions; it means that dissemination actions are not effective in reaching all interested parties, a problem that needs addressing urgently.

It seems logical that PubMed, a biomedical database, is used mainly by students of Health Sciences, Dance, Biomedical Engineering, and Psychology. It is not surprising, therefore, that such a high percentage of ignorance of its existence is recorded. On the other hand, such a significant lack of awareness of Scopus on the students' side, a database to which everyone has had access in recent years, is worrying and shows that the work of dissemination and training should be rethought.

In addition to the databases subscribed to by libraries and open access resources, students were also questioned about other electronic resources. The aim was to find out what other resources (other than printed resources) students consulted at home, focusing on the digital content that was made available during the pandemic via open access or a virtual private network.

In the same context, and analyzing qualitatively the answers to the open question, students reported having many difficulties searching for information, organizing their stages, defining the most appropriate and representative keywords, building a search equation, knowing what is most appropriate, determining which information is most reliable, understanding why there is open and closed content, safeguarding search results in a reference manager, and installing and using a VPN. This scenario identifies the lack of dissemination, the lack of knowledge, and the lack of training of students. It is therefore necessary and urgent to define an intervention strategy in information literacy skills.

As far as the libraries' website is concerned, it will strategically have to be viewed as a gateway into virtual space. Over the years, this issue has not received the prominence it deserves, but libraries must take an interventionist role and rethink their websites now that they represent one of the main paths of interaction with students in distance learning. Following the principles of usability, libraries' websites should become easier to use.

Libraries have, over the last decade, developed an alternative but secure way of disseminating research through their institutional repository, also supporting open access publishing. This is the time to strengthen the dissemination of these utilities to the academic community. As an aggregating portal, RCAAP is, because of the results obtained, still unknown to most students; it is imperative to make it known, stimulating the research of academic products and the increase of research skills.

In the coming years, higher education will have to consider greater investment in the development of electronic content, which may be a challenge in the face of decreasing budgets. More than ever, libraries need not only the support of a network of libraries, librarians, and content publishers but also organizational leaders to plan and manage their response and ensure continued access to information for students, wherever they are. Responding positively to the students' information needs has been the planning strategy of libraries in higher education over the years. In future, greater access to streaming media and electronic books, which are abundant and relatively negotiable with publishers, should be considered.

Placing librarians in the flow of the teaching–learning process has also been a trend for years in academic institutions. However, not all academics recognize this performance and not all librarians have access to the classroom, limiting themselves to the reference meeting in the library space. Providing information literacy skills, leading students to look at information resources more critically, stimulating reflective analysis of results, evaluating them, quoting them, and referencing them in an ethical, legal, and responsible manner are skills and behaviours that need to be inculcated in students (García-López et al., 2019). This guarantees a safer way of being, especially when, in times of confinement, it is necessary to work individually and remotely.

If classes are kept at a distance, deeper integration of both library resources and librarians into undergraduate and master's course management systems is essential to ensure the acquisition of information literacy skills by students. Although there has already been online training in this subject, librarians can create and improve a more effective collaboration culture with teachers, sharing strategies for exploiting digital content in research, retrieval, assessment, and use of information by students (Downie, 2007). The leaders of the organization will be responsible for recognizing and formalizing this intervention.

5 Conclusion

The perception of academic students concerning their libraries' response to COVID-19 is satisfactory, recognizing support received as being positive. However, the use of available electronic resources has not been as expected; most students are unaware of the availability of reference databases on campus and the possibility of using them remotely. As for information literacy skills, students manifest a positive self-perception of their knowledge and skills regarding research, retrieval, citation, and referencing of information. But, when expanding their responses through the open answers, numerous difficulties and asymmetries were identified.

To mitigate some of these problems immediately, strategies were created to allow dialog with students and improve their online interactions with available resources:

- At the polytechnic institute, for each information resource, a reference librarian and a unique email were identified. The resources and their emails were disseminated by the community, enabling each student to contact the appropriate professional to answer their questions and problems. Distance training (via Zoom, Teams, and Skype) and real-time training on each database, both in a class context and in customized meetings with each working group, were also prioritized.
- The public college directed all enrollments and reference questions to the email service, with a personalized answer for each student who had questions. There was also a greater concern in providing access to the e-books acquired, highlighting one of them each month with a brief review; the objective was to disseminate the collection of electronic books and generate curiosity, stimulating usage.
- In the private university institute, the OpenAthens platform was used for remote access to resources, and tutorials were created orientation toward learning how to use them. Personalized service was reinforced through several channels: email, Zoom, and microsite. A green way

to digitalize teaching and learning and research support documents was created. Also, the weekly meetings of the library team provided an adjustment of strategies in response to the needs of the community.

In addition to these interventions, this study aims to create deeper impacts in the medium and long term through the definition of formative and pedagogical strategies in information literacy skills among undergraduate and master students. It is, therefore, necessary to define the contents to be taught, the length of sessions, and the identification of the most appropriate time for delivery within the academic year. It is also imperative that this strategy be extended and normalized, involving the various administrative units, all librarians and libraries, and all study cycles. To this end, it will be necessary to raise the awareness of the leaders of the organizations and to formally implement the proposals through institutional policies.

This study had some limitations: (1) the strictly descriptive approach of the results, through the calculation of percentages; (2) the period in which it was developed, in which students received many dozens of emails daily, from teachers, colleagues, and their institution, requiring extra attention so as not to lose information—the study email may have been lost; (3) students clearly prefer their personal email and only sporadically access institutional email.

For future development, it is intended to carry out the design and formal implementation of an information literacy programme for undergraduate and master students, analyzing *a posteriori* its results. As this is an exploratory study, it is intended in future studies to analyze and validate the metric elements of the questionnaire using data analysis through descriptive and inferential statistics.

In the era of COVID-19, the role of academic libraries is essentially the same as nine months ago: to support the academic community. However, the challenge is to determine the form and content to be adopted in meeting this goal to best effect. More attention must be paid to digital resources and user education for their full access and use, in order to benefit students and contribute to their academic success.

A Appendix

Student satisfaction with library in the COVID-19 era.
Faced with COVID-19 and social isolation, academic students were suddenly confined to distance learning and to use scientific and educational resources made available by academic libraries.

The aim of this questionnaire is to perceive the satisfaction of academic students over the response of libraries' responses to their information needs, whether at the level of services or through electronic resources, and to assess whether academic students consider themselves prepared to search, assess, and manage the retrieved information.

It consists of nine questions and only one answer is expected.

The answer to the questionnaire will not take more than five minutes.

The study is confidential and guarantees the anonymity of the participants.

Thank you for your collaboration!

Table A.1

The satisfaction of libraries' responses to information needs

1. Your satisfaction regarding access to electronic resources from home.[a] 2. Your satisfaction with the information retrieved through library website.[a] 3. Your satisfaction with how to retrieve information (catalogs, databases) and the way to use it.[a] 4. I am satisfied with the electronic resources available in the library because they help me to answer my information needs.[a] 5. I am satisfied with the support provided by library team.[a]	○ Completely unsatisfied ○ A little unsatisfied ○ Reasonably satisfied ○ Very satisfied ○ Completely satisfied

The satisfaction over electronic resources made available by libraries during the pandemic

6. Electronic resources: Library website[a] B-ON[a] PubMed/MEDLINE[a] Scopus[a] Web of Science[a] *E*-books Academic Collection[a] Institutional repository[a] RCAAP[a] SciELO[a] Other electronic resources[a] 7. Satisfaction, in general, with the electronic resources made available.[a]	○ Completely unsatisfied ○ A little unsatisfied ○ Reasonably satisfied ○ Very satisfied ○ Completely satisfied

Self-perceived assessment of students' information skills

8. How do you assess your information skills? I feel comfortable doing information searches.[a] I know how to recognize reliable information for my field of study.[a] I can assess the importance of different information resources.[a] I recognize the importance of correctly and adequately citing the work of others.[a] I seek to correctly and adequately refer according to the requested referral standard.[a]	○ I completely disagree ○ I disagree ○ I neither agree or disagree ○ I agree ○ I completely agree
9. What were the greatest difficulties experienced in search and information retrieval?[a]	Open question

Sociodemographic data

10. Age	A number between 17 and 70
11. Sex	Do select: M/F/Other
12. Cycle of study	Do select: Undergraduate/Master
13. Course year	Do select: 1/2/3/4

[a] Required answer.

References

Downie, J.A., 2007. Instruction design collaborations with government information specialists. Ref. Serv. Rev. 35 (1), 123–136. https://doi.org/10.1108/00907320710729418.

García-López, F., Martínez-Cardama, S., Pacios, A.R., 2019. Professor—librarian team-teaching: online lifelong training in the university. J. Libr. Inf. Serv. Dist. Learn. 13 (3), 294–306. https://doi.org/10.1080/1533290X.2018.1536014.

Hernon, P., Altman, E., 1996. Quality in Academic Library. Ablex, Norwood.

Hernon, P., Whitman, J.R., 2001. Delivering Satisfaction and Service Quality: A Customer-Based Approach for Libraries. American Library Association, Chicago.

IFLA, 2020. COVID-19 and the global library field. https://www.ifla.org/covid-19-and-libraries. (Accessed 10 July 2020).

Lopes, C.A., 2006. Qualidade de serviço em bibliotecas universitárias: desenvolvimento e validação de um instrumento de avaliação. Facultad de Traducción y Documentación, Universidad de Salamanca, Salamanca.

Núñez-Paula, I.A., Zayas-Caballero, I., 2013. Perspectiva histórica y metodológica del sistema conceptual relativo al comportamiento informacional. Bibliotecas Anal. Invest. 8–9, 50–75.

Rapchak, M.E., Nolfi, D.A., Turk, M.T., Marra, L., O'Neil, C.K., 2018. Implementing an inter-professional information literacy course: impact on student abilities and attitudes. J. Med. Libr. Assoc. 106 (4), 464–470. https://doi.org/10.5195/jmla.2018.455.

Tanus, G.F., Sánchez-Tarragó, N., 2020. Atuação e desafios das bibliotecas universitárias brasileiras durante a pandemia de COVID-19. Rev. Cub. Inform. Cien. Salud 31 (3), e1615.

No one left behind

15

Rob May
ABE Global, London, United Kingdom

1 Introduction

The world is facing a human capital catastrophe. The shutdown of education systems in 2020 is likely to create a global skills deficit which depresses income earning potential, slows national economic recovery, and subtracts from the overall welfare of society for many years to come, possibly for the remainder of this century. Alongside, the total impact on millions of children who may remain permanently excluded from education is incalculable. When the COVID-19 pandemic struck in early 2020, worldwide school closures forced 1.5 billion students, or 87% of the world's learning population, out of their classrooms (Strauss, 2020). There is little doubt that COVID-19 was an unprecedented public health emergency which required urgent focus on the obvious logistical challenge of reducing the viral transmission to save lives. But as school and college closures continued throughout 2020, considerable evidence started to emerge of unrecoverable learning losses. School and exam systems the world over either froze or delayed assessments.

Why did this happen? After all, business continuity planning is supposedly a cornerstone of public governance and regulation in most developed countries. Education providers and awarding organizations are subjected to accountability frameworks where, among other continuity commitments, they must demonstrate exam contingency plans so as to ensure an uninterrupted flow of students into higher education and into the labor market. Private and public organizations drill for responses to terrorist incidents, financial shocks, technological shutdowns, cyberattacks, and natural disasters. Yet, according to the UNESCO Global Education Coalition, 58 out of 84 surveyed countries postponed or rescheduled exams during the 2020 summer session, only 23 (27%) successfully introduced alternative assessment methods such as online or home-based testing, and only 22 maintained public exams, while in 11 countries they were completely canceled (UNESCO, 2020).

The pandemic exposed the weaknesses of conventional continuity planning, assessment methods, and the limits of regulatory oversight but also highlighted the determination of learning communities across the global south, which were often quick to improvise, in some cases exploding the myth around the third world's lack of resilience. The pandemic has also challenged the idea that learning technology is being effectively integrated into state schooling systems or that it has had a "game changing" effect. That is not to diminish the gains made in recent years through learning technologies which have helped to engage marginalized young people in some of the world's poorest communities—see https://www.abeuk.com/global-skills-projects/capacity-building/abe-works-unesco-read-and-earn-federation-economic-capacity.

Libraries, Digital Information, and COVID. https://doi.org/10.1016/B978-0-323-88493-8.00035-5

Innovative technologies, practices, and ideas abound across the educational landscape. Learning technology provides the tantalizing capability to "jailbreak" the existing architecture of the way schools teach and test, which is currently based almost exclusively around standardization. Student-centric technologies enable modular customization, which is ideal for supporting learners who are forced to work away from the physical school setting. Over the past decade, the learning technology market has exploded at a dizzying pace. The value of the e-learning market, which is just one component of the remote learning ecosystem, had surpassed $200 billion in 2019 and was anticipated to grow at over 8% annually between 2020 and 2026 (Wadhwani and Gankar, 2020). A post-pandemic surge in learning technology spending is now likely.

Despite the swell in learning technology and the concomitant promise to transcend geographies, progressive technology-based pedagogy has remained largely experimental and fragmented in the public education mainstream. Spreading and codifying teaching and learning practices has not occurred at the level to provide seamless learning experiences through a major crisis. Going into the pandemic, access to technology and hardware remained concentrated in rich western countries, but even in these locations, access is still subject to a "digital divide" between economies. The OECD average for children having access to a computer and home Internet connection is 89%, but this falls to 60% in Japan and as low as 23.5% in Indonesia.[a]

In low-income countries, 3.8 billion people still have no access to the Internet,[b] yet despite this unequal distribution of resources, COVID-19 has in one sense had a leveling effect, as access to technology, money, and resources was unable to guarantee consistency and quality in education provision, whether the student was living in Surrey or Suriname. The "quality" of provision offered during the pandemic is difficult to measure, but anecdotal evidence is emerging that students in well-equipped western education systems found that they were presented with hastily "onlineified" learning materials. Different levels of technological skills and competencies in individual teachers also accounted for disparities in the distance learning experience.

This chapter begins by exploring the scale of lost learning. It then sketches some reasons why, despite having access to learning technology for more than a decade, it was ultimately of only limited value in most national learning estates. Contrastingly to many expectations, schools in low- and middle-income countries were able to maintain teaching and exams and even increase engagement through utilizing a range of "lowtech" media. To illustrate this, the discussion takes up the case of ABE, a multinational NGO providing education and assessment services in business and entrepreneurship skills across emerging and frontier economies. Like many not-for-profit organizations, the pandemic created an existential financial crisis for ABE and its partner schools,

---

[a] Data available from OECD. Internet access is defined as the percentage of households which reported that they had access to the Internet. In almost all cases this access is via a personal computer either using a dial-up, ADSL or cable broadband access. This indicator is measured in percentage of all households. https://data.oecd.org/ict/internet-access.htm.

[b] At Davos on January 23, 2018, the United Nations Broadband Commission set a global broadband target to bring online the world's 3.8 billion not connected to the Internet by 2025, in a policy package called "Connecting the Other Half" https://www.broadbandcommission.org/newsroom/Pages/all-pressreleases.aspx.

but the organization focused on the potential humanitarian crisis and set out to work with an array of stakeholders to implement new ways of delivering education in fragile environments. ABE invoked a social mission that would act as a steering concept for every organizational decision: "No One Left Behind." Finally, this chapter offers a perspective on measures which must be undertaken to prevent spiraling losses from further Corona-related lockdowns.

2 The scale of the learning losses

In the throes of the global public health crisis, short-term responses focused on imposing restrictions designed to reduce the spread of the virus. The long-term economic consequences of lost learning were largely sidelined and are still subject to controversial debate. This is because it is difficult to reliably measure the full impact of school closures, particularly as exit strategies vary considerably between substate regions and countries. We can, however, extrapolate the potential economic losses based on an analysis of data from the OECD's Survey of Adult Skills (PIAAC), which surveyed numeracy and literacy skills of a representative sample of the population aged between 16 and 65 across 32 countries between 2011 and 2015, and which correlated assessment scores with longitudinal labor market income information to estimate the impact of skills differences on earning potential over a lifetime. Hanushek and Woessmann (2020) have modeled these data to reveal that a loss of one-third of a school year represents a loss of potential income of between 2.5% and 4% over the student's adult working life. These figures assume that schools normalize quickly and that protracted closures are avoided. If not, a full year of lost learning could affect individual income over a lifetime from 7.7% (pooled average) to as much as 16.7% (the survey's highest projected loss was in Singapore). Placed in context, in 2018 the average lifetime earnings of men in the UK were £643,000, and for women, average lifetime earnings were £380,000. At present values, a loss of 4% equates to £25,720 for men and £15,200 for women—see https://www.ons.gov.uk/releases/humancapitalestimatesuk2004to2018.

Of course, these figures fail to account for creative destruction in the labor market due to automation, job substitution, and new job creation, but at a national level, it is obvious that the current trajectory of lost earnings will depress future GDP significantly as today's cohort of students will make up around 25%–30% of the workforce in 10-15 years' time. With record amounts of public debt piling up and a post-pandemic imperative to reimagine the technological processes that underpin the production and supply of goods and services, a less skilled and less wealthy workforce indicates a major downstream crisis.

The OECD data relate mainly to developed countries and therefore only tell part of the story. School closures could turn back the clock on gains made in reducing global poverty and promoting gender equality. Reported gains in poverty reduction are subjective to begin with. According to the World Bank, over the last 15 years, 802 million people have been lifted out of absolute poverty (Barnes and Wadhwa, 2019). The World Bank defines the international poverty line (IPL) as living on less than $1.90 per day. But the IPL is explicitly designed to reflect a staggeringly low standard of living, well below any reasonable conception of life with dignity (Alston, 2020). Deeper analysis of World Bank statistics shows that 77% of the world's population are still financially insecure, existing on less than $10 per day (adjusting for purchasing power parity) meaning that they struggle to access food, housing, and other essentials of human security. This chilling statistic has remained largely static for three decades (Edward and Sumner, 2013).

For many households across the global south, lockdowns have seen incomes and savings decimated overnight. In most developing countries, public school is not free; the costs are borne by the students' families. Households which struggled to afford school and college fees no longer can, and where they find they can keep going, it is highly likely that boys' education will be prioritized. Research from the Malala Fund (2020) suggests that the pandemic will have a long-lasting impact for marginalized girls, estimating that more than 20 million secondary school-age girls could be left behind and find themselves permanently out of school after the lockdowns have passed. Although predictions on the social impact of lost learning are problematic, we can look at the effect of isolated closures connected to previous epidemics. UNESCO reported an increase in adolescent pregnancies by up to 65% in Sierra Leone during the 2014 Ebola epidemic—see https://en.unesco.org/news/covid-19-school-closures-around-world-will-hit-girls-hardest. Most girls attributed this directly to being outside the protective environment provided by schools. The United Nations Population Fund (UNPF) suggested in April 2020 that as many as 13 million more child marriages could occur over the next 10 years (UNPF, 2020). As the pandemic has worsened poverty and food insecurity, many girls are again prioritizing marriage over education.

Educating girls is vitally important for breaking the cycle of gender exploitation, including the eradication of sexual and physical abuse, child marriages, and a lifetime of domestic servitude. The World Bank estimates that ending child marriage and early childbearing could dramatically reduce unsustainable population growth. Concerted efforts by governments and civil society organizations had reduced the number of out-of-school primary school-age girls from 65 million globally in 1996 to 31.6 million in 2014. Before COVID-19, global efforts in this direction suggested gains in well-being for populations could reach more than $500 billion annually by 2030. The public spending benefits of lower under-five mortality rates and malnutrition were estimated to reach more than $90 billion annually—see https://www.worldbank.org/en/topic/girlseducation. Educated girls are safer, healthier, more financially secure, marry later, have fewer children, and are more likely to be involved in democratic processes, values which are then transmitted to subsequent generations. The socioeconomic impact of lost learning presents a worrying second-order consequence of school closures. Fortunately, political leaders in most countries have recognized this and have prioritized restarting public education over reopening other parts of the economy. The protective, pastoral environment of schools is important for the social and psychological development of young people. Nonetheless, returning to classrooms was nonnegotiable as it emerged that the only effective way to ensure complete continuity of education and engagement has been to send children back into bricks and mortar settings, where they and their teachers are more likely to become vectors for a deadly virus. We have to ask, in a world with a $6.5 trillion global education market, which has had access to leading edge learning technology for more than a decade, why has remote education proved so ineffectual?

3   Disparity in the adoption of online teaching and learning

We must first consider the obvious barriers to the ubiquitous adoption of learning technology. The macrolevel "heavyweight" organizational design of the school system is geared against customized, individual learning. Overall, the school system does not teach to mastery levels or multiple intelligences but to timescales, processing batches of students in a system where everything from the layout of buildings to the streaming of students is designed around standardization. At the same time, there is a microlevel functional problem of "lightweight teams," that is, a low level of coordination between different departments and actors within a school. Changes to the way that faculty members set, deliver, and assess routine coursework are controlled within subschool departments (Christensen, 2008). In the UK, this was shown to be the case during COVID-19, when many parents and children had to grapple with different digital learning platforms beamed out from the same school. Combined, these macro- and microlevel conditions create a sclerotic environment, disenabling progressive change.

Different levels of tutor confidence in using online platforms may also have accounted for disparities in learning quality and engagement. In Germany, a study found that time spent on schoolwork was halved during COVID-19 from 7.4 h per day to only 3.6 h, with time spent watching television, gaming, and using social media increasing to 5.2 h per day—see https://www.ifo.de/en/research/ifo-center-for-the-economics-of-education. This points to the fact that technology was clearly available, and it was just poorly coopted for educational purposes. In the UK, University College London's Institute of Education estimates that children spent an average of 2.5 h per day on schoolwork during lockdowns, with 71% of state school children receiving no more than one online lesson per day—see https://www.ucl.ac.uk/ioe/research. While the technology exists to transition lessons online, it appears that maintaining engagement, mentoring, and momentum has been a real and significant challenge.

Technology also offers the opportunity for the "massification" of content and delivery. State school systems are funded and controlled by the government. Schools teach to a national curriculum and awarding organizations set a core syllabus as the basis for lesson planning. Despite other state incursions in society, it is curious that the logistical coordination of delivering national provision was neglected. This cannot be attributed simply to the complexity of organizing a digital response to school closures or to the argument that cohorts may be at different levels as most students fell behind anyway due to substantial reductions in learning time. Responses from other parts of the world demonstrate how a central government mandate could rapidly mobilize free-to-access online learning platforms in order to engage larger audiences. In February 2020, the Chinese government instructed a quarter of a billion full-time students to continue studying through online methods such as Tencent Classroom (Kaur, 2020), resulting in the largest online movement in the history of education—see https://www.weforum.org/agenda/2020/04/ coronavirus-education-global-covid19-online-digital-learning/. Alongside academic content, China also mandated online provision of psychosocial support.

There remains the issue of a significant accessibility gap between students from privileged and disadvantaged backgrounds depending on income brackets. To overcome this, traditional "low-tech" media modes have been coopted in some regions of the world. Across sub-Saharan Africa, radio broadcasting was used extensively to transmit lessons. Some school districts formed local media partnerships to offer local educational broadcasts, with separate television channels used to broadcast content for different ages. The Government of Rwanda began a home learning initiative which supported children by coordinating a range of experts and partners in the basic education subsector to design scripts, content, and interactive sessions for radio broadcast lessons, providing an inclusive and accessible model circumventing the need for smartphones and Internet access, and leveraging the 98% radio penetration in the country. Across Jordan (Bilal et al., 2020), Lebanon, Morocco, and Bahrain, governments coordinated content development sprints to move as much learning and exam preparation as possible onto television channels (Milks and McIlwane, 2020).

In Argentina, the Ministry of Education was proactive in curating digital resources. One programme "Seguimos Educando" was developed by the Ministry of Education and the Secretariat of Media and Public Communication and began broadcasting 14 of educational content per day from April 1, 2020, in addition to the large-scale dissemination of teaching materials and student workbooks—see https://www.educ.ar/noticias/etiqueta/seguimos-educando. In Cambodia, the Ministry of Education, Youth and Sport partnered with the Japan International Cooperation Agency (JICA) to provide free online lessons to young students alongside TV programming and materials made available on the Ministry's Facebook pages—see https://www.jica.go.jp/english/news/ field/2020/20200617_01.html).

Where connectivity was less of an issue, education technology companies were quick to ramp up global server infrastructure in order to offer free services, sensing the long-run marketing potential of getting users "hooked" on their platforms. BYJU, a Bangalore-based online teaching platform, has risen to become the world's most highly valued EdTech firm. During COVID-19, BYJU announced free live classes on its Think and Learn app, resulting in a 200% increase in the number of new students— see https://www.thebusinessresearchcompany.com/report/online-tutoring-global-market-report-2020-30-covid-19-growth-and-change. Lark, a Singapore-based platform, offered teachers and students unlimited video conferencing time and autotranslation capabilities—see https://www.larksuite.com/news/Lark-Makes-Its-Next-Generation-Digital-Collaboration-Platform-Available-for-Free. Across the developed world, capacity expansion was rapid and reliable, so why was actual online teaching and learning so patchy?

In many developed countries, including the UK, the COVID-19 experience points to a lack of government ambition in providing an enabling structure for innovation. Funding is only a small part of the equation; cramming classrooms with computers is of no use in an emergency. While some governments have dished out free digital equipment to students, many schools were unable to adapt to new teaching practices despite availability of the latest tools. The ontology of functions and relationships within the education "industry" has changed little in 300 years. Disruptive change is occurring heroically and tangentially rather than systematically, largely because the short-term nature of political administrations is not equipped to steward the long-term radical changes needed to confront the demand for standardization, high-stakes assessment events, and the regulatory and funding disincentives to change—such as national league tables. Going into COVID-19 lockdowns, insufficient tutor training, low integration of technologies at a macrolevel (system) and microlevel (school), and little preparation resulted in a lottery of learning experiences.

There are major infrastructure challenges to overcome in poorer parts of the world. Millions of students remain without Internet access and are excluded from online learning strategies. How did education institutions in developing countries implement their own education strategies and policies to achieve education continuity? The UK-based NGO, ABE, offers an interesting lens into developing world educational challenges. Since 1977, it has operated as an examinations board providing services to a network of hundreds of partner schools across Africa, South America, the Caribbean, and Southeast Asia.

4 The impact of school closures on developing countries

Moses Mkwichi is Principal of an ABE partner college, the K&M School in Malawi's capital, Lilongwe. According to the International Monetary Fund, Malawi is one of the poorest countries in the world with 25% of the total population living in extreme poverty. Malawi displays many of the characteristics of a fragile state, particularly in terms of the way that its governance institutions function. With the support of international civil society, Malawi had started to make steady and positive gains in providing access to education. Between 2004 and 2013, the proportion of households with school-age children attending school increased to 63% (IMF, 2017). For Moses, the impact of COVID-19 has been devastating:

> *"As a college that is wholly funded and run by tuition fees, we were almost left for dead. Students who used to have face to face lessons could not attend tuition because of the government ban of gatherings. We have lost all of our expected revenue and tutors were not paid for the entire period leaving us with a massive liability to settle. No government agency came to our rescue. This resulted in the abject poverty of staff members. Students lost so much learning which resulted in delayed completion of diplomas and hence lost future income for Malawi."*

South Africa is in the grip of an energy crisis which began in 2007 and which continued throughout 2020 with supply frequently falling behind demand and destabilizing the national grid. An ongoing cycle of widespread rolling blackouts or "load shedding" created additional problems for learners ordered to stay at home. While students were encouraged to access lessons online, this presented an obvious challenge for poor students due to lack of Internet and data coupled with erratic electricity supply. Teachers adapted quickly to virtual learning, utilizing free platforms such as Zoom, Google, and WhatsApp, but they also had to rearrange their timetables to accommodate both the students who could engage during class time and those who could not, monitoring power flows as well as trying to teach. Ernest Mahlaule, CEO of Destiny Village Education, an ABE partner in Johannesburg, reflects:

> *"Mainly students from well off households were better placed to maximize on the new normal until a universal solution could be found including free data and devices for poorer students. Since digital learning is not going anywhere, the least that should happen now is an increased focus on a blended approach."*

Other schools across the global south reported a more positive response, despite facing similar deprivation challenges. In Trinidad and Tobago, more than 20% of citizens currently live below the IPL (UNDP, 2019), but many schools and colleges demonstrated surprisingly seamless transitions to online delivery. SITAL College communicated changes with all students within one day, with all classes going fully online within a fortnight. Ann-Marina White, Principal, explains the process SITAL went through:

> *"At first, we used Zoom mainly and subsequently a virtual learning platform. We used a variety of communication tools such as WhatsApp, FB Messenger and email to contact students. We worked closely with lecturers to follow-up with students who appeared to be off the radar and provided best practice guides and training for online teaching, which included strategies to keep students engaged. Overall school enrolment actually began to increase because of the convenience of online learning and a reduction in fees. On the downside, physical interaction and the dynamics that contribute to softer skills such as collaboration and emotional connections were compromised. New [online teaching] skills must be developed and incorporated into the curriculum as well as building the discipline necessary in students for online learning, such as independent study, taking ownership and communicating more effectively."*

At CTS College in Port of Spain, initially 8% of students dropped out of full-time education due to parents' job losses and uncertainty over continuing their studies online. But as the stay-at-home order continued, CTS noticed a gradual increase in engagement as the school adapted to using technology. Nine months after the initial lockdown order, schools remained closed with all learning taking place via online classes, but at CTS, student numbers have increased far beyond enrollments prior to COVID-19 as online learning has removed many of the physical and financial barriers to accessing learning. School autonomy has had both positive and negative effects in developed countries and in developing countries, depending on the level of resilience and creativity within the school's leadership, the agency to rapidly implement ideas and strategies on the ground, and the stability of local economic conditions.

In many of the above examples, governments introduced few, if any, social relief measures, and the focus of these measures was not on education but on ensuring access to basic necessities, healthcare, and food supplies. The Universal Declaration of Human Rights affirms that education is a fundamental and indispensable human right for everyone and is one of the most powerful tools in lifting children and adults out of poverty, and yet operational responses to continuous education were in the main left to be driven by the private sector, NGOs, and the creativity of individuals, with mixed results. Policymakers should also be aware that education does not just affirm human rights and dignity and deliver personal economic advantages, but good education is also a matter of national security. In 1958, the US legislated the National Defense Education Act primarily in response to the Soviet Union launching Sputnik. The Act prioritized the continuity and improvement of not only Science but also of History, Languages, and Political Science under the principle of national interest. In a world where geopolitical and economic power is being redistributed, and where an uncertain future means that medical breakthroughs, entrepreneurship, and frictionless trade will become ultimately important, the former US National Security Advisor, General H.R. McMaster believes that "lawmakers should approach education reform with similar urgency today… [because]… improvement in education may be the most important initiative to ensuring that future generations are able to innovate and create opportunities for their children and grandchildren" (McMaster, 2020).

ABE recognized the humanitarian and economic disasters that would arise from "kicking the problem down the road" and worked with schools and colleges to introduce open-book exams which could be taken at home without reliance on power supplies and technology. Some populations were skeptical about the validity of open-book assessments assuming that the format would encourage collusion and plagiarism. ABE found that this was not the case. ABE utilized a "blended AI" solution combining powerful antiplagiarism software with vigilant marking by human examiners. During COVID-19, the instances of failure through detected malpractice actually declined from 19% globally to 9%—see https://www.abeuk.com/white-paper-adapting-assessments-vicky-mose.

Where online classes were an appropriate response, ABE created more online content to supplement local distance learning. They introduced microcredentials in critical skills to keep students motivated with achievements that were immediately visible, and they also adjusted the format of school-based programmes to create remote learning versions. ABE avoided focusing too much on the technology, as large local disparities prevented a universal solution. Instead, ABE invoked a social mission "No One Left Behind" and used a range of touchpoints and feedback loops to capture data and coordinate different responses for different regions. The main drive was to act fast, as freezing or delaying educational services would quickly accumulate into excluded learners and multiply the economic losses, as well as hasten the insolvency of hundreds of learning institutions. The deeper integration that ABE and other NGOs have deployed during COVID-19 elucidated many of the barriers to widespread adoption of online teaching and learning. Some of these were obvious beforehand: the cost of devices is a barrier, but that can be overcome through redistributive fiscal policy; access to power and connectivity remains difficult in many parts of the world, but that is also being addressed. The agility and power of platforms was also not an issue. In fact, virtual learning environments improved during COVID-19. Open-book exams and remote proctoring software meant that exams could take place securely and reliably, from anywhere. The deeper barriers are harder to overcome, but quickly addressing these systemic weaknesses is essential to ensure that online and blended learning modes can entice more young people back to education.

5 Conclusion

The COVID-19 crisis exposed significant weaknesses in education systems around the world. Reform is partly about widespread incorporation of new technologies, but technology is only part of the solution. More broadly, reforms must be guided by a genuine long-range political process which embraces a multitude of changes. The extent to which innovation occurs and the extent to which it is amplified are subject to political choices, but there is a growing problem of "asymmetric information" wherein policymakers are disconnected from the realities of education delivery or the pace of learning technology. There is also a problem of "policy amnesia" wherein new administrations rehash old ideas under the banner of "reform," only to repeat the failures of previous ministries ad infinitum, compounding the dominant logic that chokes the life out of real reform programmes.

The ability to innovate in a school setting has been decentralized, and that has produced some promising initiatives, but now officials must reaggregate these gains into a collective change programme and an operational plan to deal with future national school closures. The ability to execute and scale up change depends on both the quality and technical knowledge of public servants and the courage and commitment of elected officials. The responses of governments in performing a coordinating role have varied considerably across countries. COVID-19 exposed a lack of bureaucratic quality and capacity across many different countries but most surprisingly perhaps in major developed economies. As a result, these governments and regulatory watchdogs now face a credibility deficit.

In reimagining the structure of education and assessment, and developing bold public policy choices, supranational institutions, think tanks, and NGOs must be invited to perform a path-finding role. The work, vision, and reach of NGOs transcend the myopic political priorities and timescales of government. Throughout COVID-19, it was NGOs and supranational agencies such as the UNESCO Global Education Coalition for COVID-19 Response, UNICEF, Global Partnership for Education, Education Cannot Wait, Education Development Trust and ABE, and many more that worked alongside education providers on executing technical responses. Ultimately, the structure of national education systems resides within the political constraints and possibilities of sovereign states, yet the labor market and the higher education sector are ever more globalized. NGOs are best placed to observe and filter best practice from around the world and to work with governments to set a common, far-reaching agenda. The World Bank's policy platform launched in December 2020 is a welcome manifesto. The World Bank will offer targeted financial support to remove demand-side constraints such as eliminating school fees and supporting initiatives which challenge social norms regarding gender-based schooling—see http·//pub-docs.worldbank.org/en/764111606876730284/TheFutureOfLearning-dic1-2.pdf?cid=ECR_E_NewsletterWeekly_EN_EXT&deliveryName=DM86830.

This is helpful, but more work is needed to challenge the status-quo bias that pervades national systems. First of all, exemplars of best practice emerging from COVID-19 must be "lifted and shifted" across the whole learning sector, a process which must be overseen with urgency by education ministries. The private sector can "bubble up" innovation, but within state-controlled systems, the state must coordinate and "massify" best practice. During the pandemic, ABE responded to an increase in disintermediation as students demanded access to materials and assessments directly from the awarding body, circumventing the cost of face-to-face college tuition. The growing range of massive open online learning platforms which combine high-quality tuition with accreditation within sophisticated, cost-effective platforms certainly raises questions about the future architecture of post-16 education and suggests that many markets are now reaching an inflection point, which may be accelerated post-COVID-19. The pandemic has also prompted questions over summative, high-stakes exams. Britain, France, and Ireland were among the countries which quickly canceled their exams, bringing to a grinding halt the educational supply chain that feeds universities and companies and resulting in a subsequent muddle to try to calculate (guess) how individuals would have fared in one of the most important events of their lives. During one of the most distressing episodes in contemporary human history, the lack of a credible national contingency caused devastating anxiety for millions of young people.

Awarding organizations also need to take responsibility for exam reforms. According to a November 2020 "barometer of trade" survey of 21 UK technical exam boards, less than 13% of units could be taught online and less than 16% of units offered could be assessed online (Gordon Associates, 2020). Countries have been talking endlessly about revising exam systems but deemphasizing high-stakes exams is not the same as trashing assessments altogether. Society still needs a reliable indicator of an individual's strengths and competencies, and qualifications or more widely "credentials" form an indispensable social contract between education systems and labor markets.

During COVID-19, access to technology was not the most important indicator of consistent learning, but multimedia did play an important role. Moreover, a "total capabilities approach" is needed to ensure that in the future no learner is left behind. This should start with rapid sprints to codify the best practice globally that emerged from global COVID-19 responses, involving panels of technical experts from the learning coalface; it should include plans to centralize and coordinate a national response in times of future emergencies, not relying on the private sector or the abilities of autonomous schools to pivot to distance learning. The UK has a distinguished heritage of distance learning providers and some of the world's best digital delivery software and artificial intelligence developers which must be consulted. Schools must seek to consolidate platforms and practices at the microlevel, with more funded capacity geared toward the training needed to deliver blended and remote learning. Finally, energy and resolve are needed to guide a transformation in serious structural reform. Technology can allow for more customization in teaching and therefore more effective instruction, which in the pandemic would have enabled more continuity in personal learning journeys and promoted social equity (Moe and Chubb, 2009). Gathering students together in large halls for memory recall tests is now looking more like an outdated concept and barely resembles the way that problems are solved in the information-rich real world of work. Of course, this chapter shows that local conditions will often dictate appropriate responses, but it also demonstrates that with enough political will and determined ingenuity, education can still get through. COVID-19 has been a vehicle for creative disruption in the education sector. Now all of us must learn the lessons.

References

Alston, P., The Parlous State of Poverty Eradication: Report of the Special Rapporteur on Extreme Poverty and Human Rights, United Nations Human Rights Council, June 2020. https://www.ohchr.org/EN/Issues/Poverty/Pages/parlous.aspx.

Barnes, D., Wadhwa, D., 2019. Year in Review: 2019 in 14 charts. The World Bank. https://www.worldbank.org/en/news/feature/2019/12/20/year-in-review-2019-in-charts.

Bilal, A., Blom, A., Goldin, N. and Nusrat, M., Jordan's education response to COVID-19: speed, support, and sustainability, World Bank Blogs, September 24th 2020. https://blogs.worldbank.org/arabvoices/jordans-education-response-covid-19-speed-support-and-sustainability.

Christensen, C.M., 2008. Disrupting Class: How Disruptive Innovation will Change the Way the World Learns. McGraw-Hill, New York, pp. 35–39.

Edward, P., Sumner, A., 2013. The geography of inequality: where and by how much has income distribution changed since 1990? Centre for Global Development. Working paper no. 341, September https://www.cgdev.org/publication/geography-inequality-where-and-how-much-has-income-distribution-changed-1990-working.

Gordon Associates, December 2020. Awarding Organisation Barometer of Trade survey, UK.

Hanushek, E.A. and Woessmann, L., The economic impacts of coronavirus: Covid-19 learning losses, 2020, OECD, September. http://www.oecd.org/education/The-economic-impacts-of-coronavirus-covid-19-learning-losses.pdf.

International Monetary Fund, July 2017. Country Report: Malawi Economic Development, No. 17/184. 17file:///C:/Users/robm/Downloads/cr17184%20(5).pdf.

Kaur, D., October 2020. E-Learning is on the Rise in APAC. Techwire. https://techwireasia.com/2020/10/e-learning-is-on-the-rise-in-apac-and-its-going-mobile/.

Malala Fund special report, 2020. COVID-19 and Girls' Education. https://downloads.ctfassets.net/0oan5gk9rgbh/6TMYLYAcUpjhQpXLDgmdIa/3e1c12d8d827985ef-2b4e815a3a6da1f/COVID19_GirlsEducation_corrected_071420.pdf.

McMaster, H.R., 2020. Battlegrounds: The Fight to Defend the Free World. William Collins, London, pp. 424–439.

Milks, J., McIlwane, J., 2020. Keeping the world's children learning through COVID-19. UNESCO. https://www.unicef.org/coronavirus/keeping-worlds-children-learning-through-covid-19.

Moe, T., Chubb, J.E., 2009. Liberating Learning. Wiley & Sons, San Francisco, pp. 172–183.

Strauss, V., 1.5 Billion children around globe affected by school closure. What countries are doing to keep kids learning during pandemic, 2020, The Washington Post, March 27th. https://www.washingtonpost.com/education/2020/03/26/nearly-14-billion-children-around-globe-are-out-school-heres-what-countries-are-doing-keep-kids-learning-during-pandemic/.

UNDP Human Development Report, 2019. Inequalities in Human Development in the 21st Century Briefing note for countries on the 2019 Human Development Report. Trinidad and Tobago. http://hdr.undp.org/sites/all/themes/hdr_theme/country-notes/TTO.pdf.

UNESCO, April 2020. Exams and Assessments during the Covid-19 Crisis: Fairness at the Centre. https://en.unesco.org/news/exams-and-assessments-covid-19-crisis-fairness-centre.

United Nations Population Fund (UNPF), April 2020. Millions more cases of violence, child marriage, female genital mutilation, unintended pregnancy expected due to the COVID-19 pandemic. https://www.unfpa.org/news/millions-more-cases-violence-child-marriage-female-genital-mutilation-unintended-pregnancies.

Wadhwani, P. and Gankar, S., E-Learning Market Trends 2020–2026, Global research Report, Global Market Insights, May 2020. https://www.gminsights.com/industry-analysis/elearning-market-size.

COVID-19 and the digital divide in higher education: A Commonwealth perspective

Lucy Shackleton* and Rosanna Mann*
Independent Consultant, ACU, London, United Kingdom

1 The Association of Commonwealth Universities

Accredited by the United Nations and the Commonwealth, the Association of Commonwealth Universities (ACU) is an international organization dedicated to building a better world through higher education. With over 500 member universities across 50 countries, the ACU's international network spans more than 10 million students and over a million academic and professional staff.

2 Context

Higher education (HE) makes a vital contribution to society and is integral to delivering across all 17 of the United Nations' Sustainable Development Goals (ACU, 2019). The COVID-19 pandemic has illustrated the importance of the sector, with universities at the forefront of scientific responses to the virus, and countless examples of students and institutions providing direct support to their communities.

It has also resulted in unprecedented upheaval. In April 2020, universities and other tertiary education institutions were closed in 175 countries and communities. It is estimated that over 220 million postsecondary students had their studies stopped or significantly disrupted due to the pandemic (World Bank, 2020).

Many universities migrated education, research, and administration activities online to ensure continuity in teaching and learning, research, and innovation. However, given disparities in Internet access and connectivity, this transition poses both immediate and longer-term challenges for access, equity, and inclusion.

Prior research demonstrates a persistent "digital divide," defined by the OECD as "the gap between individuals, households, businesses and geographic areas at different socio-economic levels with regard to both their opportunities to access information and communication technologies (ICTs) and to their use of the Internet for a wide variety of activities" (OECD, 2001). This is particularly relevant in a Commonwealth context, where only 18% of people living in low-income Commonwealth countries

---

* On behalf of the Association of Commonwealth Universities.

Libraries, Digital Information, and COVID. https://doi.org/10.1016/B978-0-323-88493-8.00015-X

have Internet access, compared to 85% in high-income countries (Commonwealth Secretariat, 2020).

Digital disparities, both between and within countries and institutions, risk compounding existing educational inequalities, compromising the pipeline of skilled graduates and undermining HE's potential to drive an inclusive post-COVID recovery.

At the same time, the pandemic provides a window of opportunity for universities, governments, and policy-makers to accelerate digital transformation, enhance institutional resilience, and ensure the lessons of the pandemic inform the drive for inclusive and equitable access to HE by 2030.

3 Survey design and methodology

In this context, the ACU conducted a digital engagement survey designed to better understand the short-term impacts of COVID-19 on staff, students, and university leaders across the Commonwealth in May 2020. The survey elicited 258 responses from 33 countries, with 66% from Africa, 21% from Asia, 4% from Europe, 4% from the Pacific, and 4% from the Americas and the Caribbean. 44% of respondents were academics, 25% were professional services staff, 17% were students, and 10% were senior leaders (deans or above).

As a self-selected online survey about digital engagement, there is inherent bias in the sample and caution should be taken in interpreting and extrapolating results. Given the survey design, tests for statistical significance were not undertaken and all findings are based on descriptive statistics.[a] Findings presented in this chapter are a subset of the full results which can be found online (see here: https://www.acu.ac.uk/media/2345/acu-digital-engagement-survey-detailed-results.pdf).

4 The "great pivot online"

The ACU's digital engagement survey confirmed the transformative impact of the pandemic across the Commonwealth, illustrating "the great pivot online" across education, research, and administration. The vast majority of respondents reported that campuses had been fully (52%) or partially (45%) closed as a result of COVID-19. Institutions moved swiftly to ensure continuity of education, with four-fifths (81%) of respondents reporting that some (24%), most (24%), or all (33%) teaching and learning had moved online. 69% of respondents said they had been able to undertake research activities online.

However, closer analysis revealed a more nuanced picture, demonstrating the extent to which the impact of COVID-19 has differed across diverse contexts. For example, the degree to which teaching and learning were reported to have moved online

---

[a] Given small sample sizes in some segments, differences are only reported when the percentage difference is more than 10% points or where a clear trend is apparent. Response percentages may not add up to 100% due to rounding.

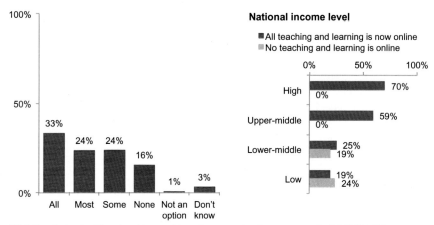

Q24. *To what extent has teaching and learning moved online as a result of COVID-19?*

Fig. 16.1 Extent teaching and learning moved online as a result of COVID-19.

as a result of the virus correlated closely with national income level (see Fig. 16.1 below).[b] 70% of respondents from higher-income countries said all teaching and learning had moved online, compared to 59% of upper-middle, 25% lower-middle and 19% low-income respondents. Conversely, 19% of respondents from lower-middle-income countries and 24% of respondents from low-income countries said that no teaching and learning had moved online. This was not the case for any respondents from high-income and upper-middle-income countries.

Encouragingly, disparities relating to the impact of COVID-19 on research activities were less apparent by national income level. However, the pandemic appeared to have had a variable impact by discipline: 79% of academics in the Arts, Social Sciences and Humanities said they have been able to undertake research activities online, compared to 67% of academics in the Natural, Environmental and Earth sciences and 69% in Applied Sciences and the professions.

4.1 Differentiated digital access

Survey results also highlighted the diversity of individual experiences among respondents, in particular in relation to access to digital infrastructure and connectivity. For example, while the vast majority (98%) reported Internet access for remote working, only 45% of respondents reported access to broadband, compared to 79% reporting access to 3G/4G/LTE mobile data.

Respondents' connection quality varied depending on national income level and professional status. 83% of respondents from high-income countries had access to broadband. By contrast, this figure was 63% for respondents from upper-middle-income

---

[b] Countries have been classified according to the World Bank Country and Lending Groups for the 2021 fiscal year, available online here: https://datahelpdesk.worldbank.org/knowledgebase/articles/906519.

countries, 38% for respondents from lower-middle-income countries, and only 19% for respondents from low-income countries.

Likewise, individuals' digital access also varied according to their professional status. Within universities, senior leaders were most likely to have access to broadband (74%), followed by professional services (52%), academics (38%), and students (30%). Furthermore, there is some indication that this disparity matters: Respondents with only mobile data or telephone dial-up were, for example, more likely to agree that the pandemic has affected their ability to undertake research (43% compared to 33% of those with a broadband connection).

5 Opportunities and challenges

5.1 Remote working

While there was widespread recognition of the potential benefits of remote working, from enhanced resilience in the face of other emergencies (such as torrential rains or flash floods) to reducing carbon emissions, a lack of infrastructure and capacity among staff and students was frequently cited as a barrier to success. The most frequently cited challenges associated with remote working across all respondents were Internet speed (69%), data costs (61%), Internet reliability (56%), and the difficulties of contending with time zones (38%).

Unsurprisingly, individuals from low-income countries were more likely to identify infrastructure-related challenges than their counterparts in high-income countries (see Fig. 16.2). Where respondents from low-income countries cited data costs (86%), Internet speed (81%), and Internet reliability (62%) as their main challenges, respondents from high-income countries were less likely to cite challenges overall and the top-cited challenge among respondents in this category was working across time zones (53%). Senior leaders were also less likely than academics to cite data costs (48% compared to 68%) and Internet speed (63% compared to 74%) as challenges.

Responses indicated that institutional support for remote working is available, across a range of regional contexts. Over half of respondents (57%) received some form of support from their employers, with the most common being a contribution towards data costs (37%) and the provision of devices (31%). In addition, support by universities towards staff or students' data or devices also correlates with a higher likelihood of broadband access (57% of those who receive support have broadband access, compared to 28% who do not).

However, access to support for remote working varied by both national income level and professional status, suggesting that those facing the most challenging circumstances are the least likely to have access to the necessary support. Respondents from high-income countries were most likely to receive support (87%), followed by upper-middle-income countries (70%). Respondents from lower-middle-income countries (51%) and low-income countries (52%) received similar levels of support. Within institutions, senior leaders (81%) and professional services staff (82%) were

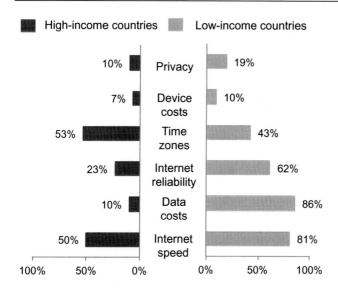

High-income countries   Low-income countries

10%	Privacy	19%
7%	Device costs	10%
53%	Time zones	43%
23%	Internet reliability	62%
10%	Data costs	86%
50%	Internet speed	81%

100% 50% 0%   0% 50% 100%

Q21. What challenges do you face in participating remotely in online activities such as video calls and webinars? [tick all that apply]

Fig. 16.2 Challenges of participating remotely in online activities.

more likely than students (45%) and academics (40%) to report institutional contributions towards devices or data.

5.2   Online educational delivery

The most frequently cited perceived challenges associated with the online delivery of teaching and learning were student accessibility (81%), staff training and confidence (79%), connectivity costs (76%), and student engagement (71%). Connectivity costs were the most frequently reported challenges for respondents from low-income countries (86% compared to 27% for respondents from high-income countries). Respondents from high-income countries, with high levels of connectivity, were more likely to cite challenges relating to student perceptions of quality (57%) and professional body discouragement (33%) (for full results, see Fig. 16.3). More specifically, qualitative responses referenced concerns regarding data costs, Internet connectivity, equipment, and reliable power supplies and others focussed more on perceived pedagogical disadvantages, such as the absence of a relationship between teacher and student in online contexts.

Yet there was also a striking recognition that if delivered successfully, online teaching and learning had the potential to play a transformative role in driving access and inclusion. The greater flexibility afforded by online teaching and learning was also viewed by some as a pedagogical advantage, with a number of staff and students citing students' ability to access content at their discretion; the active role students can play in their own learning; and the additional care and attention given by teachers to the preparation of online versus in-person teaching material.

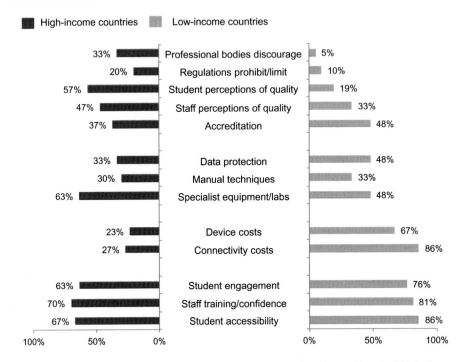

Q26. What do you feel are the challenges for developing online teaching and learning? [tick all that apply]

Fig. 16.3 Challenges for online teaching and learning.

5.3 Research activity

Finally, qualitative responses from research active staff suggested that they encountered fewer challenges in migrating their activities online. Respondents reported having pivoted to online activities, such as online data collection and analysis, grant applications, and write-ups, in the short term. Some students and staff also highlighted the advantages in online working, for greater collaboration. However, respondents shared concerns about the impact of the pandemic on research activities in the medium term. This concern was particularly pronounced among those requiring access to specialist facilities, or reliant on field research.

6 A lasting legacy for the pandemic?

Survey results indicate some confidence that the "online experiment" precipitated by the pandemic will cement online working practices, enhance digital capacity, and increase online educational delivery activities in the long term.

6.1 New ways of working

Just under half (45%) of respondents said they worked online (virtual meetings, working from home, online training, or CPD) all the time or frequently (weekly) before the pandemic, and 14% said they never did. By contrast, 84% of respondents predicted working online all of the time or weekly after the pandemic and only 1% predicted never working online. This notable shift online is driven by a large increase in the proportion of respondents saying they would work online weekly (from 26% before to 65% after the pandemic) as there was no change in the proportion of respondents saying they would work online all of the time (see Fig. 16.4).

The degree to which respondents anticipated they would work online after the pandemic correlated with national income level, with respondents from high-income countries most likely to say they expected to work online all of the time or weekly (90%) and respondents from low-income countries least likely to say this (76%). Higher expectations for future online working after the pandemic were apparent among senior leaders (93% all of the time/weekly) with students showing the lowest

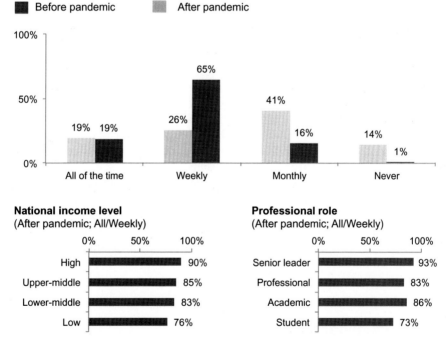

Q11. How frequently did you work online at your university before the pandemic (virtual meetings, working from home, online training or CPD)?
Q15. How frequently do you foresee yourself working online at your university after the pandemic?

Fig. 16.4 Frequency of working online before and after the pandemic.

expectations (73%). Respondents receiving institutional support for data and devices were also more likely to foresee high levels of online working (87% compared to 69% of respondents who received no support) (see Fig. 16.4).

6.2 The future of online education

Just over half (53%) of respondents agreed that online teaching and learning are more susceptible to "corruption" than face-to-face learning, and there was a clear preference for blended learning over degrees studied solely online. 90% of respondents agreed that a blended degree, involving a combination of online and face-to-face learning, was equivalent to a degree earned only through face-to-face learning. By contrast, 47% felt a degree studied solely online was equivalent. However, COVID-19 has resulted in a clear improvement in perceptions of the quality of online and blended learning, with 81% of respondents agreeing that it had improved during the March–May 2020 period.

These changing attitudes are also arguably represented in respondents' predictions for future institutional priorities. While a fifth (20%) of respondents reported that online teaching and learning occurred at all or most of their institutions' departments before the pandemic, over half (53%) said they anticipated online teaching and learning to take place as part of blended programmes in all or most departments after the pandemic. As per Fig. 16.5, this view was particularly held by respondents from high-income countries (77%) and senior leaders (85%) (see Fig. 16.5). It also correlated with levels of prior digital engagement: 88% of respondents who reported that online teaching and learning occurred across *all or most* departments *prior* to the pandemic thought *all or most* departments would offer this as part of blended programmes *after* the pandemic. Only 26% of respondents who reported that none of their departments delivered online teaching and learning prior to the pandemic were confident that all or most departments would offer blended programmes after it.

More widely, the vast majority (89%) of respondents agreed that their institutions have the *will* to develop high-quality online teaching and learning, while 82% of respondents agreed that their institution had the *capacity* to develop high-quality online teaching and learning. Respondents from high-income countries, senior leaders, and professional services were most likely to say their institution had the capacity and will, indicating a potential gap between strategy and implementation (see Fig. 16.6).

7 Recommendations

The results of the ACU's digital engagement survey highlight a stubborn digital divide, apparent in universities' capacity to adapt to the pandemic. As well as a clear digital divide between countries of differing national income levels, there is a divergence in resources, attitudes, and behaviours within institutions, across students, academics, professional services staff, and senior leaders, suggesting a "double digital divide."

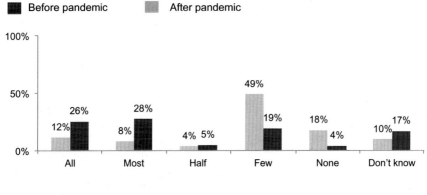

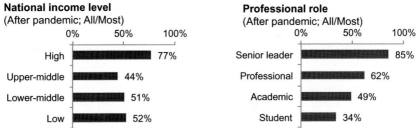

Q23. How much online teaching and learning occurred at your university before the pandemic?
Q25. How much online teaching and learning do you anticipate will continue to take place in your university, as part of blended programmes, after the pandemic?

Fig. 16.5 Prevalence of online teaching and learning across university departments before and after the pandemic.

	Will	Capacity
All respondents	89%	82%
National income level		
High	100%	93%
Upper-middle	93%	85%
Lower-middle	87%	79%
Low	86%	86%
Professional role		
Senior leader	100%	93%
Professional services	98%	92%
Academic	82%	74%
Student	84%	80%

Q29. To what extent do you agree/disagree with the following statements: My institution has the will to develop high-quality online teaching and learning; My institution has the capacity to develop high-quality online teaching and learning

Fig. 16.6 Perceptions of institutional will and capacity.

Despite these challenges, however, survey results indicated some confidence that the "online experiment" precipitated by COVID-19 will lead to lasting change. In particular, digital transformation in response to the pandemic presents an impetus to address capacity issues and a window of opportunity for widening access to HE through online and blended delivery.

However, the challenges highlighted by the survey show that decisive action to ensure no one is left behind in the shift online is required if this opportunity is to be grasped. In this context, the ACU has called on governments, policy-makers, and universities across the Commonwealth and worldwide to help create the conditions for successful digitalization in HE.

Recommendations presented to Commonwealth Education Ministers, and circulated prior to the UNESCO Extraordinary Session of the Global Education Meeting in October 2020, urged governments to:

- Prioritize funding for higher education, in recognition of its vital contribution to society and to post-COVID recovery worldwide
- Invest in tackling the digital divide in higher education through funding, financing, and public-private partnerships
- Widen access to higher education and lifelong learning by supporting digital transformation initiatives in universities
- Bring university leaders, telecommunications companies, global employers, and students together to develop a common agenda for the future of digital higher education
- Provide a platform for institutions to share knowledge at different stages of their digital transformation journeys and to discuss common challenges

and universities to:

- Provide financial and technical support to improve access to data, devices, and broadband
- Identify and develop targeted policies to address the digital divides within universities to ensure no one is left behind
- Mainstream digital transformation across every element of institutional strategy and planning
- Recognize that the ability to move research activities online varies considerably according to discipline, putting research in particular areas at risk

References

Association of Commonwealth Universities, 2019. Higher Education's Essential Contribution to the SDGs. https://www.acu.ac.uk/news/higher-education-s-essential-contribution-to-the-sdgs/. (Accessed 25 January 2021).

Commonwealth Secretariat, 2020. The State of the Digital Economy in the Commonwealth. https://thecommonwealth.org/sites/default/files/inline/Digital%20Connectivity%20 Report_low%20res_.pdf. (Accessed 12 December 2020).

OECD, 2001. Understanding the Digital Divide. OECD Publishing, Paris, https://doi. org/10.1787/236405667766. OECD Digital Economy Papers, No. 49. (Accessed 12 December 2020).

World Bank, 2020. The Covid-19 Crisis Response: Supporting Tertiary Education for Continuity, Adaptivity and Innovation. http://documents1.worldbank.org/curated/en/621991586463915490/ The-COVID-19-Crisis-Response-Supporting-Tertiary-Education-for-Continuity-Adaptation- and-Innovation.pdf. (Accessed 12 December 2020).

Section B

Supply of information

The use of data in publishing and library acquisition strategies

17

Melissa Fulkerson
Elsevier, Cambridge, MA, United States

1 Introduction

Academic publishers play many roles in the supply chain of research content. Publishers of academic books in Science, Technology, Engineering and Medicine (STEM) disciplines endeavour to supply foundational content to support the evolving needs of the research community, by enabling deep learning of scientific concepts. The demand for this content is signalled either through patron requests for specific titles, through usage behaviour, or through analysis of market trends.

Publishers can use data gleaned from the usage of content in different disciplines or across different content types (such as books and journals together) to gain a deeper understanding of how researchers and students use scientific content and how to make prudent decisions for the future. The uncertainty of what a post-COVID world will look like from a social and economic standpoint makes data all the more useful for both publishers and libraries to make decisions that are in the best interest of their strategy and the needs and desired outcomes of those they serve.

Using data to make collection decisions is not a new concept; libraries have used circulation data as a metric to help make decisions on how to weed print collections for many years. However, as content platforms have become more sophisticated and publishers and vendors shift more towards electronic delivery, the options available to both publishers and libraries for data points to aid in decision-making have become more sophisticated as well.

It should be noted that the author of this work has her basis of experience in STEM book publishing. The publishing process for books moves at a slower pace than that of scientific journals; the planning and writing processes both tend to take longer, and the content often has a longer shelf life. Therefore, it is important for book publishers to read signals early in order to make informed decisions. This chapter is intended to discuss issues and impacts related to the STEM book publishing and acquisition workflow.

2 Data and its role in publishing strategy

Journals (primary literature) and books (foundational content) are the main content categories for academic publishing. However, when content providers in STEM publish books, they must further refine their goals for publishing in a particular manner

Libraries, Digital Information, and COVID. https://doi.org/10.1016/B978-0-323-88493-8.00004-5

or for a particular use case. There are many unique content types that exist within a books portfolio:

- **Major Reference Works**: comprehensive, foundational introduction to a discipline. Can be encyclopaedias or other multivolume works.
- **Textbooks**: pedagogical examination or didactic presentation of key subject area concepts and methods.
- **Monographs**: compendiums of information or data sets or techniques for the field, providing quick answers on the job. Also can be complete, advanced, and detailed descriptions providing depth in a given subject area. Can be broad or very niche.
- **Book Series/Serials**: in-depth explorations of recent developments and methods in a field. A periodical model for current reference content that bridges the space between primary research and established knowledge.

Each of these content types serves a unique purpose, and thus, understanding how and why each is used can help publishers build strategies for the future. A publishing strategy that leverages a combination of said book types ensures a thorough and complementary coverage in a given discipline, with the breadth and depth the subject matter demands.

In a customer-centric business, decisions should always include the viewpoint of what customers (buyers and users, who may have different priorities and goals) need or what problem the new product is solving, and content strategy is no different. Robust data in conjunction with real-world input can help give direction to a publisher trying to decide between two projects in different disciplines. The content strategist of tomorrow will use a mix of quantitative and qualitative data to ensure they are making decisions to the benefit of their strategic goals and their customers' needs.

The work of publishers used to be as much about the technology of publishing— typesetting, printing, and binding—as the core editorial processes. As the industry has evolved, publishers now "outsource most of the work that once was done within the publishing house: design and layout, printing, binding and distribution" (Jelušić and Stričević, 2011). Consequently, there has been growing emphasis on the developmental functions of publishers. Perhaps among the most important of these is the commissioning of projects within the editorial unit. This is a function that can be supported by many forms of data to ensure that what a publisher chooses to release is the right topic, developed by the right subject matter expert(s). The following example illustrates how Elsevier's content acquisitions team in the STEM segment uses data to create strong portfolios.

Publishers rely heavily on the use of data to drive their strategies forward and ensure they are publishing the right content for the markets they serve. This process often begins with the research itself. They use tools such as Scopus, an abstract and citation database, and SciVal, a research assessment tool for institutions, to figure out the direction research is going in their respective disciplines. There are several metrics publishers can use to learn about the landscape in a particular discipline. These can include but are not limited to:

- **Article growth:** measured by subject or geography
- **Field-Weighted Citation Impact**: the ratio of the total citations received by the denominator's output, and the total citations that would be expected based on the average of the field (Colledge, 2014)

- **Usage**: the measure of downloads of literature published in a given field
- **Funding:** research grants, applications, and awards by governments or funding bodies
- **Use case and intended level:** research or education; lower or upper undergraduate, graduate, and professional
- **Nontraditional or altmetrics**: social media views, discussions, or recommendations

Some of these factors are considered as part of the Snowball Metrics Landscape which are "designed to facilitate cross-institutional benchmarking" (Colledge, 2014) and, when taken together, help to paint a picture of where science is now and where it will be going in the future. This view helps a publisher consider how many books and what types of books they should publish on a given topic. In a broad and growing segment, it would not be uncommon to publish a mix of textbooks, monographs, serials, and major reference works to ensure the topic is covered in the appropriate level of depth for the various users for whom it is intended. Conversely, in a niche subject area it may be suitable to have a small or narrow output and still cover the topic appropriately. In addition to citation and usage metrics on primary literature, publishers consider market signals such as size or maturity of a given subject, segment, or technology.

There is also an element of qualitative data to the portfolio-building process. Publishers spend time speaking with customers—researchers, authors, and faculty— in a given discipline, to ensure there is a human element to the strategy as well. The feedback received from field interviews helps to ensure the portfolio is balanced and is not simply chasing only the most novel technologies due to a prevalence of primary literature being published at the time. Compiling all of this quantitative and qualitative data creates a complementary relationship between the foundational and the cutting-edge research and ensures the portfolio has few gaps. It should also be noted that using data allows publishers to ensure they are reflecting the needs of an increasingly global and diverse community through their output. Considering factors such as country and institution of author affiliation, collaboration across countries or across industry and academia, and demographic information such as gender and race can help ensure a diverse and representative author base.

Lastly, data around quality play a role and require a more human touch beyond the binary metrics. "Quality" is a term that is hard to define and can have different meaning depending on the context. In this context, editorial staff review content and send proposals out for peer review to identify the quality of a project in nascency at proposal stage and also in output. Accuracy, fitness-for-purpose, timeliness, authority, and market need are all reviewed to ensure the right author is sharing their expertise on the right topic at the right time. Publishers can use metrics like H-index (which measures a scientist's productivity and citation impact) to find new authors, though it is only one of many sources used to determine the most appropriate voices in a given field.

In short, content acquisitions teams are using data to determine what the needs of the portfolio are based on where research is now and where they think it is going in the future, to ensure the output is what customers will need. This impacts the size of annual subject collections and over time can shape the depth and breadth in which a subject is covered in the overall portfolio. It allows the publisher to be predictive in identifying trends and having foundational content ready to publish early in the growth of some emerging fields.

Because there is internal alignment in books and journals content strategy, one of the natural outcomes is that the two content types complement each other on ScienceDirect, the publisher platform which hosts book and journal content together. The impact of this is "co-usage," which Elsevier defines as an instance of use in which a patron accesses both books and journals in the same session. Users often vacillate between the two while using the platform, which demonstrates the strength of ScienceDirect in supplying the right content based on a user's need, but also the strength of the content itself to continue to provide a seamless breadth of knowledge.

Elsevier's internal technologists have developed an analysis tool that helps individual institutions understand the co-usage patterns at their library, in order to use that data to help make acquisition decisions. Libraries can see not only which books are being used, but also how frequently books and journals are used together, and with this information, they can better understand how well their holdings align with the education or research goals of the institution (Fig. 17.1).

As the usage analysis tool has evolved and the measurement of co-usage has become more prevalent, several things have become clear. First is that there is very diverse usage across disciplines, which content teams can use to ensure they have a clear view of what disciplines in science are being used together. The tool has helped to illustrate how interdisciplinary science has become and how broad any individual

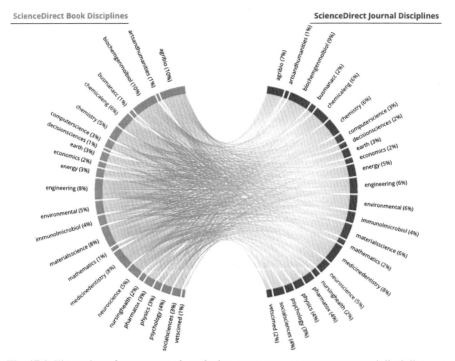

Fig. 17.1 Illustration of co-usage tool, analysing usage across content types and disciplines on ScienceDirect.
Image © Elsevier, 2019.

researcher needs to be in their own knowledge or their access to content to aid in learning new concepts. Publishers can add this information to the suite of metrics used to help inform the types of books published and the breadth and depth authors might need to cover in their individual projects.

Another key finding is that there is evidence to demonstrate that access to books is not only driving books usage, but that it is driving journals usage as well. An internal study conducted by Elsevier in 2019 demonstrated that institutions with full access to the ScienceDirect e-book offering saw increased usage of available journals, when compared to institutions without access to books (Elsevier, 2019). This gives weight to the assertion that foundational book content plays a significant role in the overall research landscape.

And perhaps the best illustration of how this all comes together is the use and pervasiveness of ScienceDirect Topics, which use artificial intelligence and machine learning to create comprehensive reviews on specific topics. ScienceDirect Topics pages are created using book content and are intended to help users get up to speed quickly on a new topic and then determine how to take their research forward. Data gleaned from the usage of Topics can help determine what content is having an impact at a particular institution, which again can help librarians make decisions about how to use their acquisitions budgets in the best way by acquiring content that has demonstrated value to patrons.

Since their launch in 2017, ScienceDirect Topics have grown rapidly and are now the second highest driver of traffic on ScienceDirect, driving more than 13 million uses per month globally across over 350,000 unique pages. These pages are highly discoverable on the open web as well as being deeply linked in journal articles and have had a notable impact in raising discoverability and demand for books in libraries.

All of these examples illustrate the point that the more publishers can learn about the evolving needs of the markets they serve, the more they can use that knowledge and partner with libraries to ensure a better outcome for researchers and students.

3 Data and its role in library acquisition strategy

As mentioned previously, this same data can be used by librarians or other buyers, to ensure their budgets—which are constantly under pressure—are used in the most effective manner. Because libraries work with dozens and even hundreds of vendors, it may be daunting to receive and attempt to analyse many disparate data points and make decisions across multiple platforms without having a clear picture of the broader landscape. Publisher platforms will often have the deepest available view, but this level of data is not available from all publishers. In these scenarios, library aggregators and other vendors that help manage library systems can play a great role in collating and helping guide decision-making for content providers without their own platforms. These vendors will often be able to provide a view on print resources as well.

One of the main uses of data that librarians report is to run a cost-per-title or cost-per-use analysis. This is a long-standing and generally accepted method of determining the value of an e-book investment. This method, while effective at creating an easy comparison metric across publishers or disciplines, ignores a few qualitative factors:

- What is the library's mission and how does that impact collection choices?
- What are the research goals of the institution?
- What is the library's educational mandate, particularly in COVID environments with a significant amount of remote work? Is acquiring textbooks for classroom use critical to student support?
- What are the quality metrics of the various sources of content being compared? Does volume alone help the library achieve its mission, or are there other factors needed to determine the true value of one portfolio compared to another?

These qualitative measures can help paint a picture about what the library really values and what role it plays in serving its community. Budget challenges often require parties to come back to cost, so conversations tend to naturally revolve around "cost per..." metrics. But it is a decision each library has to make for itself, to consider what purpose the content serves and what the library values about the access, and therefore what importance the content has.

For a library that values supporting the research community through things like reducing friction in access to content or ensuring highly interdisciplinary collections, large-scale subscriptions may be a more valuable option than title-by-title purchasing. However, for a library that values having the most focussed collections for its core research areas, more targeted options may be relevant. More detailed analysis on usage, turnaways, citations, and other value metrics can help better illustrate the value that the book or the collection will bring. These decisions all live outside of the "cost per..." metrics but help to give colour and ensure the investments are in support of the library's mission. Usage is an important measure of demand and should not be ignored, but rather should be one of the factors in a comprehensive analysis.

One aspect of the library's content holdings that came into spotlight during the campus shutdowns in the early stages of the COVID-19 pandemic was course materials. Global libraries have been at different stages of a journey into acquiring e-materials for classroom use, and libraries had been used to buying several copies of print textbooks for course reserves. The sudden need to provide remote access for students while simultaneously removing access to print materials forced many libraries to make quick decisions on how to acquire e-resources to support classroom use, while at the same time managing all of the other professional and personal challenges the pandemic has visited upon communities. Faculty had to learn how to teach online (many for the first time), students had to learn how to manage online classes for the first time, and the stress of the global health crisis loomed over all of it. This raised the profile of challenges that exist in the textbook model within academic libraries; there is inconsistency in availability and access of course materials across publishers, and there is no one true solution that allows academic libraries to provide campus-wide access to all the materials students will need for their courses.

The use of data can aid in this heightened challenge by broadening the concept of what learning materials can be. Many libraries already have a wealth of content available campus-wide through various vendors. Within STEM disciplines, faculty and students may benefit from creating course packs that use a wider base of various types of content, including traditional textbook materials, other types of book and journal content, and open educational resources. Because the library is the repository for the majority of this nontraditional educational content, there may be an additional opportunity for the library to utilize these materials to support a broad and fruitful learning experience for students. There are indeed challenges to be sorted out in the industry with how classroom materials can be provided through the library, but a wider view of how e-resources can be used may provide a bridge to a new way of learning.

When considering how print materials may continue to play a role in the post-COVID library, these same qualitative measures of value can help guide libraries in how to use their budgets and best meet patron needs. It is currently unclear what campuses will look like after the pandemic subsides and students return to consistent in-person learning to some degree. It is likely that on many campuses, a combination of print and digital collections will remain the norm, though a preference towards electronic and away from print will allow libraries to offer the most flexibility to their more diverse user bases.

There are operational benefits to moving towards electronic as well. Electronic offerings allow more flexibility and the ability to generate more granular data and analyse things like usage and turnaways in a much higher level of detail than print circulation. For that reason, electronic offerings give librarians more control over their budgets and determining where they choose to invest. Conversely, it can be difficult to manage costs when libraries are maintaining both print and electronic holdings. For example, duplication is more likely across print and electronic when large subscription packages are chosen, but the labour required to manually manage collections at the title level can be untenable and the trade-off may be worth it. Librarians who have a trusted partner relationship with their vendors can use the available data to ensure their budgets are used in the most prudent way possible.

An informal poll of librarians at a recent webinar hosted by Elsevier showed that for 46% of librarians polled, greater than 60% of their collections are already available digitally (Elsevier, 2020). Many librarians know that going forward, collections will be more heavily weighted towards digital assets, but individual libraries will need to find the balance that makes sense for their unique circumstances, and the myriad sources of data available aim to assist in making those hard choices.

4 Value chain implications of going digital

Publishers and libraries have been "going digital" for many years, but the urgency of the COVID-19 pandemic and the subsequent move to remote learning have accelerated this shift. This has introduced an almost limitless number of challenges for most institutions in all points of the supply chain, but it also provides a great opportunity to learn about what is really working and calibrate strategies along the way. As mentioned, the availability of different types of data helps ensure that both suppliers and customers are making the most efficient decisions possible.

Understanding the usage and demand patterns can help publishers release better content and can help libraries decide what to acquire. Getting to that level of understanding is much easier to do in a digital environment once we collectively move past print circulation or "cost per..." metrics as the defining benchmark of value.

There is work to be done on measuring the quantifiable impact of books on research, and what role foundational content plays in improving outcomes in scientific research. Questions like this take all parties even further along in the quest to use data to make sure the right content is being published and libraries are acquiring what makes the most sense for them. This is only something that can truly be measured once the global publishing and library communities are in a digital environment with access to the data in a more robust way.

Disclosure statement

The author of this chapter is employed by Elsevier Ltd., the publisher of this work. The author received no compensation for her contribution.

References

Colledge, L., 2014. Snowball Metrics Recipe Book. https://www.snowballmetrics.com/wp-content/uploads/snowball-metrics-recipe-book-upd.pdf. (Accessed 15 November 2020).

Elsevier, 2019. Elsevier Internal User Study. Elsevier, London.

Elsevier, 27.10.2020. Elsevier Ebook Webinar. Elsevier, Singapore. https://www.brighttalk.com/webcast/18191/450635/apac-ebook-forum-2020-covid-19-the-future-of-digital-information-for-libraries.

Jelušić, S., Stričević, I., 2011. A Librarian's Guide on How to Publish. Chandos, Oxford.

Trustworthy or not? Research data on COVID-19 in data repositories

18

Otmane Azeroual[a] and Joachim Schöpfel[b]
[a]German Centre for Higher Education Research and Science Studies (DZHW), Berlin, Germany, [b]GERiiCO Laboratory, University of Lille, Lille, France

1 Acceleration, quality, and trust

The first case of the COVID-19 (or coronavirus) pandemic was identified in Wuhan, China, in December 2019. Ten months later, when starting to write this chapter (October 22, 2020), the World Health Organization (WHO) dashboard announces 41,104,946 confirmed cases and 1,128,325 deaths. The pandemic has become a major economic, social, and health policy priority in many countries, and the research is soon expected to provide insights and results relating to the development and innovation of new treatment protocols, drugs, and vaccines. Referenced by Google Scholar, about 108,000 papers have already been published on COVID-19, and likely 10 times more on related topics. The US COVID-19 Open Research Dataset (CORD-19), created by the Allen Institute for AI in partnership with Microsoft, IBM, the National Library of Medicine, and others, in coordination with The White House Office of Science and Technology Policy, contains over 100,000 research papers with full text about COVID-19, SARS-CoV-2, and related coronaviruses, provided to the global research community to apply recent advances in natural language processing and other AI techniques to generate new insights.

Most of the papers on COVID-19 are open access (Aristovnik et al., 2020; Arrizabalaga et al., 2020). Additionally, an important number of preprints—preliminary reports that have not been peer-reviewed—have been posted on preprint servers such as medRxiv, with nearly 8000 articles, and bioRxiv, with more than 2000 articles (Fig. 18.1). Acceleration, speeding up research and innovation, is one purpose of open science (Haider, 2018). The Budapest Open Access Initiative declared in 2001 that "removing access barriers to [peer-reviewed journal literature] will accelerate research… make this literature as useful as it can be and lay the foundation for uniting humanity in a common intellectual conversation and quest for knowledge" (BOAI, 2001).

The trouble with acceleration is selection and quality. After noting that the server is receiving many new papers on coronavirus SARS-CoV-2, bioRxiv reminds (and warns) that these preprints "should not be regarded as conclusive, guide clinical practice/health-related behaviour, or be reported in news media as established information" (BioRxiv, 2020). Bypassing the "lengthy process" of peer-reviewing and the "reduction of quality control can lead to the spreading of misinformation creating

Libraries, Digital Information, and COVID. https://doi.org/10.1016/B978-0-323-88493-8.00027-6

COVID-19 preprints (cumulative)
(up until 2020-11-01)

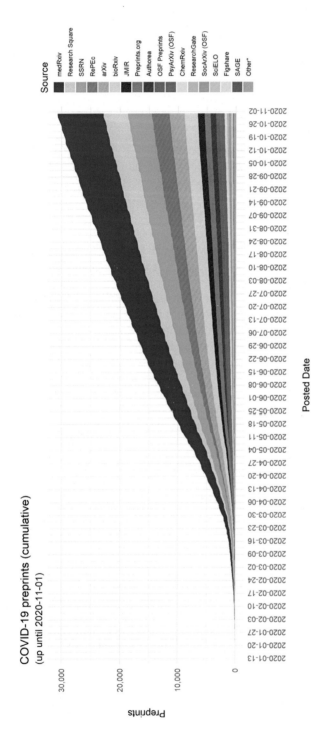

Source

Fig. 18.1 COVID-19 preprints (cumulative).

Source: Nicholas Fraser, COVID-19 preprints https://github.com/nicholasmfraser/covid19_preprints.

additional problems that could originally be addressed during the peer-reviewing procedure" (Rios et al., 2020). The issue is, as mentioned above, the absence of peer review or some other form of quality control and selection.

The same observation can be made regarding the second pillar of open science: the open access to research data, "defined as factual records (numerical scores, textual records, images and sounds) used as primary sources for scientific research, and that are commonly accepted in the scientific community as necessary to validate research findings" (OECD, 2007). Since the start of the coronavirus pandemic, a growing number of data is shared on different kinds of platforms. The COVID-19 data repository hosted by Figshare contains 2109 items, with 877 datasets. Elsevier's Mendeley Data search engine retrieves 11,314 resources on COVID-19 in data repositories, like Zenodo (2141), Mendeley Data repository (323), Harvard Dataverse (191), Apollo Cambridge (178), or the Robert Koch Institut repository at the Humboldt University, Berlin (69). The real number of COVID-19 datasets is hard to estimate; among the retrieved items are software, posters, and other research materials, and much data are not available on data repository because the research is still in progress or because of legal, industrial, or other reasons.

The problem with research data sharing is that data repositories most often do a superficial check of deposits; they try to ensure that the content is research data and not "rubbish" but do not provide a deeper assessment and moderation of the intrinsic, scientific quality and value of the data. The case of the controversy over hydroxychloroquine (HCQ) and the Surgisphere papers (Piller, 2020) shows that uncontrolled sharing of unreliable, early, and nonvalidated findings is not only an academic problem but also, at least potentially, a societal issue and a matter of passionate and engaged debate in the media and by politicians. Belief in misinformation about COVID-19 poses a potential risk to public health; therefore, scientists play a key role as disseminators of factual and reliable information (Roozenbeek et al., 2020).

Yet, on the other hand, Besançon et al. (2020) highlight that the lack of data sharing or third-party reviewing has led to the retraction of four major papers and had a direct impact on the study design and conduct of international trials. A review of 689 clinical trials regrets a lack of quality, coordination, and research synergies and, moreover, the lack of systematic sharing of trial data for the generation of evidence and metaanalyses (Janiaud et al., 2020). The issue is not too much data versus not enough data. The underlying question is about trust: How to ensure the quality of freely available research results? What is or could be done to increase the data's trustworthiness?

2 Control and assessment of data deposits

The quality of datasets is generally addressed using the dimensions of accuracy, currency, completeness, and consistency (Batini et al., 2009). These dimensions are not specific for research data. What is specific and special with research data has been described as their "contextual quality" (Stausberg et al., 2019, following Wang and Strong, 1996), because of the particular and often dynamic nature of datasets in given discipline environments, communities, and infrastructures; especially in research fields that produce unstructured and semistructured data, manual data quality checks are considered an important safeguard against fraud (Konkiel, 2020).

Research data infrastructures and, in particular, research data repositories play an essential role in this issue, insofar as their main function is preservation and dissemination. In the context of open science, data repositories are a key element in the deposit and sharing of datasets. Today, there are many and very different data repositories, disciplinary, institutional, governmental, and other platforms, some covering a large spectrum of research fields, while others focused on a particular topic, community, equipment, or material. According to international directory re3data, 1438 research data repositories provide some kind of quality management—about 55% of all registered platforms. But only 79 repositories (3%) declare certified procedures to ensure data quality.

Often, as mentioned above, ingestion control is light. Mendeley Data, for instance, provides manual checking for all posted datasets to ensure the content constitutes research data (raw or processed experimental or observational data), is scientific in nature, and does not only contain a previously published research article. Spam or nonresearch data are rejected but there is no validation or curation of the contents of valid research datasets (Haak et al., n.d., forthcoming). Another example is the Inter-university Consortium for Political and Social Research repository (ICPSR) which performs manual data and documentation (metadata) quality checks as part of the data deposit process, rejecting deposits with inadequate documentation and/or of poor quality.

Academic journals have the potential to contribute to the quality check of datasets. At *Cell Press*, for instance, the peer review process includes looking at the data. If an author publishes an article in *Cell Press*, the associated data are then also asked for, and the editors and reviewers look at the data and check for the data quality. The journal *Cell* has published hundreds of papers on the COVID-19, one part of them (like Schulte-Schrepping et al., 2020) along with reviewed and validated datasets.

This seems to be an exception, however. Following the "Transparency and Openness Promotion" initiative of the Center for Open Science, less than 5% of the already evaluated and registered journals mention peer-reviewing of deposited datasets. An editorial of the *International Journal of Cardiovascular Sciences* states that "most of the time, reviewers do not examine the raw data of the studies they review," adding that "one of the multiple benefits of Open Science is that research data can be checked by anyone who accesses the data repository, thereby reducing the likelihood of scientific misconduct" (Mesquita, 2020). In other words, academic journals, at least, should ask for (if not require) the deposit of datasets.

Data journals and, more generally, data papers are a new way to publish data and information about data and to ensure a certain level of peer review of deposited and shared data. Quality control of data papers—some kind of peer review—always implies an evaluation of the datasets themselves and their respective repositories. But for the moment, this new way of academic publishing represents a very small and marginal part of the overall research output (Schöpfel et al., 2019).

3 What makes data trustworthy?

The purpose of data sharing is reuse. Reuse requires some kind of guarantee of the data's integrity, authenticity, and quality. When this guarantee is missing, in the absence of evaluation and quality control, how does one trust research data? What makes research data trustworthy?

The crucial but not the only variable of trustworthiness is the quality of infrastructure, the data repository; the two other variables are the quality of the underlying research and, of course, of the data itself (Fig. 18.2).

The quality of the underlying research process can be described in terms of research ethics, as "doing good science in a good manner" (DuBois and Antes, 2018). Good science means research conducted according to common standards of excellence, while good manners include, among others, appropriate data storage, management of conflicts of interest, protection of human participants and animal subjects, honest reporting of findings, and proper citation of sources. In the field of COVID-19, the suspicion of conflict of interest is one of the major concerns in the debate concerning the credibility and trustworthiness of research outcomes. Other studies mention a large variety of ethical principles applying to scientific values, such as honesty, objectivity, integrity, carefulness, openness, trust, accountability, respect for colleagues and for intellectual property, confidentiality, fairness, efficiency, human subject protection, animal care, and so forth.

Scientific integrity has been described in terms of individual behaviour, covering scientific misconduct such as falsifying research data, ignoring or circumventing major aspects of human-subject requirements, not properly disclosing conflict of interest, changing the design, methodology or results of a study in response to pressure from a funding source, inappropriately assigning authorship credit, and so on (Martinson et al., 2005). The reputation of the research team, of the individual author and of the affiliated institutions, will contribute to the perceived quality of research, without being a guarantee. The application of open science principles like transparency and openness is designed to foster the "doing good science in a good manner."

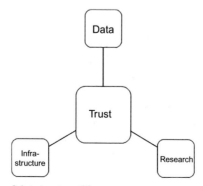

Fig. 18.2 Three variables of data trustworthiness.

With respect to data repositories, two types of use should be distinguished: the use of repositories to store, preserve, and share research data (deposit); and the use of repositories to verify published results, merge datasets, perform reanalyses, and so on (reuse). In the first case, the focus will be on the device, the reliability and security of the system, the promise of service (e.g., long-term preservation), the ease of deposit, the number of deposits by other researchers, and so on. In the second case, trustworthiness is also, and above all, conditioned by the content, the resources stored, and this will involve quality variables (the quality of the data and the quality and richness of the metadata), the right to reuse (licences), and interoperability with other operating systems.

This relationship between user confidence in preservation devices and confidence in the digital content of those devices has been modeled for digital archives in general (Donaldson, 2019) and formalized as an ISO standard (Open Archival Information System, ISO 14721:2012). Empirical studies, such as those by Yakel et al. (2013) or Yoon (2014), have led to a better understanding of some of the key factors of trust or mistrust in data repositories. Among these factors, three appear to be particularly important: the transparency of the system, the guarantee (promise) of long-term preservation (sustainability), and the reputation of the institution that manages and/or hosts the system. In addition to these factors, there are other criteria, such as the perception and experience of the functionalities and services and the quality of the data and the measures implemented to control, guarantee, and improve this quality, in terms of data sources and selection upstream and cleansing further downstream. Section 4 will deal with some of these issues.

The institution plays a separate role. Part of the trust placed in a platform of this type is linked to the characteristics of the institution responsible for and in charge of the platform. What is its reputation? Is it a reference in this field? What is its field of activity, does it have authority in this field? Who does it work with? What are its own references?

Recently, Science Europe presented a list of minimum criteria for a trustworthy repository, organized around four major themes: the assignment of unique and durable identifiers, the use of traceable and community-based metadata (standards), data access and licensing, and preservation, including the guarantee of data integrity and authenticity (Science Europe, 2019). Lin et al. (2020) summarized five principles under the acronym "TRUST"—that make data repositories trustworthy:

- **Transparency**: The repository must provide transparent, honest, and verifiable evidence of practices and procedures to convince users that it is able to guarantee the integrity, authenticity, accuracy, reliability, and accessibility of data over a long period of time. Transparency also means providing accurate information about the scope, target user community, mission and policy, and technical capabilities of the repository (including conditions of use).
- **Responsibility**: Repositories should take responsibility for managing their data holdings and serving the user community, through adherence to the designated community's metadata and preservation standards and the management of the deposited datasets, such as technical validation, documentation, quality control, protection of authenticity, long-term preservation, IP management, protection of sensitive information assets, and the security of the system and its content.

- **User focus**: Data repositories must provide services that correspond to the practices and needs of the target user community, which may vary from one community to another; they should be integrated into the data management practices of the target user communities and can therefore respond to the evolving needs of the community.
- **Sustainability**: Repositories must guarantee uninterrupted access to data, through risk management and a sustainable governance and business model.
- **Technology**: Repositories should have reliable, high-performance technology, i.e., appropriate software, hardware, and technical services that are up to the challenge, including compliance with standards and the implementation of measures to ensure the security of the system and data.

Regular audits and certification is one way to go there and to show compliance with standards, principles, and quality criteria. In the field of research data repositories, a couple of certificates have been developed, including the World Data System (WDS) certificate supported by the International Council for Science (ICSU) and the Data Seal of Approval (DSA) developed by the Dutch organization DANS from 2008. In 2018, the two procedures converged into the CoreTrustSeal (CTS), which today is the most recognized international certificate. The CTS certificate contains 16 themes with specific requirements for the organizational infrastructure, for the digital object management and for the repositories' technology. If the compliance with all requirements is needed for certification and to ensure the repositories' trustworthiness, four themes in particular address research data quality (CTS 2019):

(1) **Confidentiality/ethics (CTS requirement 4)**: *The repository ensures, to the extent possible, that data are created, curated, accessed, and used in compliance with disciplinary and ethical norms.* The main concern is disclosure risk, the risk that an individual who participated in a survey can be identified or that the precise location of an endangered species can be pinpointed. Expected good practice includes special guidance and procedures and the request of confirmation that data collection or creation was carried out in accordance with legal and ethical criteria.

(2) **Data integrity and authenticity (CTS requirement 7)**: *The repository guarantees the integrity and authenticity of the data.* This requirement covers the whole data lifecycle within the repository; good practice includes checks to verify that a digital object has not been altered or corrupted, documentation of the completeness of the data and metadata, a version control strategy, a strategy for data changes, maintaining provenance data and related audit trails, and maintaining links to metadata and to other datasets.

(3) **Appraisal (CTS requirement 8)**: *The repository accepts data and metadata based on defined criteria to ensure relevance and understandability for data users.* Which are the criteria of data acquisition and metadata? How do repositories control and validate the deposit of data? Good practice includes a collection development policy to guide the selection of data for archiving, procedures to determine that the metadata required to interpret and use the data are provided, automated assessment of metadata adherence to relevant schemas, and a list of preferred formats and checks to ensure that data producers adhere to the preferred formats.

(4) **Data quality (CTS requirement 11)**: *The repository has appropriate expertise to address technical data and metadata quality and ensures that sufficient information is available for end users to make quality-related evaluations.* Repositories must be able to evaluate completeness and quality of the data and metadata, and they must ensure there is sufficient information about the data for the designated community to assess the quality of the data.

Good practice includes quality control checks to ensure the completeness and understandability of data deposited, the ability of the scientists to comment on, and/or rate data and metadata, and the provision of citations to related works or links to citation indices.

Together, these recommended good practices of data management contribute to the quality and trustworthiness of research data repositories, as much for the deposit as for the reuse of data. But certification requires a considerable effort of self-assessment and, subsequently, of a long-term action, monitoring, maintenance, and constant improvement. At the time of writing, about 100 data repositories have obtained the CoreTrustSeal certificate—less than 5% of all registered data repositories. With respect to COVID-19, 51 research data repositories are registered in the re3data directory, mainly from the United States and the European Union; only one, the WHO's International Clinical Trials Registry Platform (ICTRP), has been certified.

A last approach to make research data repositories trustworthy has been presented as FAIR guiding principles for scientific data management and stewardship (Wilkinson et al., 2016). Their objective is to improve the infrastructures that support the reuse of research data, by making data findable, accessible, interoperable, and reusable, with a focus on improving the ability of machines to automatically find and use data, as a complement to reuse by researchers. The "FAIRization" of data repositories relies to a great extent on the standardization of metadata and protocols. It is important to keep in mind the vision of this approach, which aims to foster the coherent development of the global Internet of FAIR data and services, particularly within the framework of the European Research Area and the European Open Science Cloud (EOSC) infrastructures. While inclusion in a FAIR and/or certified repository can be thought of as an indicator of quality, on its own, the FAIR principles do not aim to this day to ensure the quality of research data itself.

4   How to improve data quality

One major problem with research data is the ever-increasing volume; another is the large variety of format, typology, structuration, size, description, context, origin, and more. The standards, recommendations, and certifications require action to assure data quality, such as quality checks and data cleansing procedures. We mentioned above the need for appraisal, for some basic validation and for selection based on "good research practice." What can and should data repositories do to ensure data quality of accepted datasets, beyond fast checking, quick reviewing, and request of confirmation that data collection or creation was carried out in accordance with legal and ethical criteria?

Authorities, business and research communities expect scientific institutions and infrastructures to have the quality of their research data under control. A high data quality is therefore essential for an organization to become or remain trustworthy with its target groups of users (Budianto, 2019). But quality needs to be measured and improved continuously, because of constant changes, quality deterioration, obsolescence, and so on (Mahanti, 2019). According to recent studies, many institutions are dissatisfied with the quality of the research data collected and processed, and rate it as low or rather low (Cai and Zhu, 2015; Logan et al., 2020). Often, they only improve their data quality occasionally, or do not take any action at all.

If institutions want to ensure consistently high quality, they should set up an ongoing data quality initiative. This does not have to be an all-or-nothing project, but can initially be carried out on a departmental basis and gradually expanded. Libraries, which of course rely on high-quality data, are particularly useful in this regard. The overriding goal of such an initiative should be that the research data in the respective area are uniform, complete, and up-to-date. Inconsistent and incorrect research data lead to wrong decisions, loss of trust, failure of projects, employee dissatisfaction, and more. For this reason, the following questions always arise, especially with exponentially increasing amounts of data: How can insufficient research data in institutions be identified? How can the quality of the data be improved?

In Computer Science, many papers have discussed methods for the data quality management in information systems from different domains, such as the first-time-right principle, the closed-loop principle, data catalogue, data profiling (Azeroual et al., 2018b), data cleansing (Azeroual et al., 2018a), data wrangling (Azeroual, 2020), data monitoring, data lakes (Mathis, 2017), data text mining (Azeroual, 2019), and machine learning (Duka and Hribar, 2010; Maali et al., 2010); these papers have also shown how the methods can be used in practice to ensure data quality. The methods of data cleaning and monitoring range from fully automated to mostly manual operations, which is closely related to the amount of knowledge required for each operation. However, before these methods can be used, a number of steps must be performed.

First of all, the importance of high data quality must be anchored in the awareness of employees. Only when management is aware that data repositories are not functioning properly without clean data can the strategic goal of clean data storage be successfully transferred to libraries. In order to make employees aware of the potential of a clean data repository, it helps to formulate specific goals. These can then be tracked with data quality management, for example, by improving transparency and decision-making in facilities or stabilizing customer relationships. The starting point for data cleansing is knowing the actual quality of the research data. Today, effective analysis tools and methods are available to record and map the current situation. Quality problems with manageable effort can be identified, and the error frequency can be given in an order of magnitude. Usually redundant author data, incomplete datasets, and incorrectly recorded data, as well as contradictions between different databases, occur. Before the actual data cleansing can begin, rules should be worked out that define clear standards for which data are relevant and what a clean dataset should look like. For example, is the author's metadata required or optional? Or is a dataset with affiliations of the author already considered complete? Based on these characteristics, it is possible to evaluate the data repository and determine what to do with incorrect data.

The data records can be cleaned up as soon as they are recorded in institutions or transferred to a data repository. With the systematic initial cleaning of incorrect data, a solid basis for a permanent data maintenance strategy can be created. It is important to determine which level of quality is to be achieved over what time period by a first cleanup run. However, data quality assurance must not remain a one-off problem. Keeping it clean is the key to long-term success. In order to guarantee perfect data quality in the long term, processes for regular quality control and data cleansing should be set up. The following steps of data cleansing of a data repository can be used here and can also be reused as continuous mechanisms for monitoring data integrity (Azeroual et al., 2018a):

(1) **Parsing** is the first critical component of data cleansing and helps the user understand and transform the attributes. Individual data elements are referenced according to the metadata. This process locates, identifies, and isolates individual data elements, as, for example, for names, addresses, zip code, and city. The parser profiler analyzes the attributes and generates a list of tokens from them, and with these tokens, the input data can be analyzed to create application-specific rules. The biggest problem here is different field formats, which must be recognized.

(2) **Correction and standardization** is necessary to check the parsed data for correctness, then to subsequently standardize it. Standardization is the prerequisite for successful matching, and there is no way around using a second reliable data source. For address data, a postal validation is recommended.

(3) **Enhancement** is the process that expands existing data with data from other sources. Here, additional data are added to close existing information gaps. Typical enrichment values are demographic, geographic, or address information.

(4) **Matching** There are different types of matching: for reduplicating, matching to different datasets, consolidating, or grouping. The adaptation enables the recognition of the same data. For example, redundancies can be detected and condensed for further information.

(5) **Consolidation (Merging)** Matching data items with contexts are recognized by bringing them together.

Many errors can be avoided by doing these data cleansing steps directly when entering data. According to Azeroual et al. (2018a), all of these steps are important in order to achieve and maintain maximum data quality in a database or information system. Quality errors in the acquisition and integration of several data sources in one system are eliminated by data cleansing. The manual effort for data cleansing can be minimized through a high degree of automation. During data cleansing, duplicates are eliminated, data types corrected, or incomplete data records completed. Finally, data monitoring checks the quality of the available data at regular intervals. If the data quality changes, the monitoring system provides information and enables new analysis or corrective measures to be initiated. Only if the data quality is continuously monitored and the results are communicated, can the quality of the data stocks be maintained over longer periods of time. If there is no monitoring, the quality level achieved will continuously decrease over time. The change in quality levels can be tracked via trend reports and alarms from data monitoring.

For a consistent and redundancy-free data repository, not only those who are responsible for the data quality in the specialist departments, but also for the entire facility should be named. Clear responsibilities—for data entry and error correction—avoid distributed responsibilities and specific data storage in parallel data repositories, which would have to be continuously synchronized and checked for redundancies. At the same time, those responsible for data maintenance need freedom of action and access to management in order to initiate and implement improvements. Even if employees are actively involved in data quality management, they should be trained regularly. Data quality remains present in day-to-day business; factors that cannot be regulated via automatic mechanisms should be consistently observed. There are numerous applications on the market to minimize the manual effort in facilities to ensure high data quality. They automate data analysis, data cleansing, and data monitoring processes using intelligent algorithms. The huge amounts of data in the big data environment can only be kept at a high-quality level with such supporting software.

Achieving and maintaining high data quality are in the best interests of any institution that wants to derive added value from its research data, but this costs money. However, poor data quality can cost even more in the medium term. For example, in addition to a multitude of challenges (such as many data sources, different data formats, and different updates) which make efforts to improve data quality more difficult, the research on COVID-19 is changing in front of our eyes and is more open, transparent, and collaborative within a few months or weeks become. Many relevant research data and publications on COVID-19 are currently freely accessible; many of the publications enable direct access to the original data on which they are based. Many scientific papers also appear as a so-called preprint at the moment of completion, without delay due to a peer review process and other adversities of the commercial publication process. This transparency is by no means a guarantee that the majority of COVID-19 studies are of high quality and of a high ethical standard. It is therefore necessary to identify and correct these problematic studies early on before storing this publication data in data repositories. If quality is taken into account during data acquisition, many metadata errors can be eliminated from the outset. This is more effective than laboriously looking for mistakes afterward. Problems with poor data quality should be addressed before the data is used—right at its place of origin. Since the real costs of incorrect, incomplete, and redundant data are difficult to quantify, many scientific institutions delay investments in targeted data quality management. Investing in data quality cannot be combined with a return on investment. However, this can be a prerequisite for the successful further development of the business model. Institutions should therefore make data quality a strategic goal. Looking at future developments, with the increasing networking inside and outside of institutions, it becomes clear that topics such as data repositories can only be successfully implemented if the challenge of managing the flood of data professionally is accepted at the same time. It is to be expected that the use of data repositories will increase significantly in the coming years and their application can only succeed if a clean amount of data is available.

5 Conclusion

On November 13, 2020, the WHO dashboard gave 51,848,261 confirmed cases and 1,180,868 deaths due to COVID-19. The pandemic is far from over. In the meanwhile, about 10,000 new papers have been published, and Mendeley Data indexes 7121 more datasets, an increase of 63%. More and more information of all kinds, volume, velocity, and variety: This is part of what can be called the academic big data. So, what about the fourth V: veracity?

Given the fact that not all published results are reliable and trustworthy, this chapter has provided insights into the control of data deposits, the factors that make data trustworthy, and the methods and procedures to improve quality of deposited data. Data repositories and their hosting institutions play a key role; essential requirements to ensure a minimal level of data quality and reliability have been listed and described.

When the European Union member states prepared their action plan for open science (Amsterdam Call for Action, 2016), the political concern focused on Ebola and Zika. The 2020 COVID-19 pandemic for the first time demonstrated the potential of open science, but also the issues, especially with early and nonvalidated results. The pandemic has triggered many open science initiatives (see Uribe-Tirado et al., 2020) and many calls for opening research to make research results available for everyone, as soon and as open as possible. The severity of the pandemic has increased academic scientists' willingness to share data and results, even if other factors like corporate ownership of data and increased competition can also generate obstacles "since disclosing crucial data and information can improve competitors' positions and reduce one's chances to succeed" (Younes et al., 2020). It is too early to assess if and how open science contributes not only to acceleration of research but also to innovation; if and how, for instance, the very short delay for the development of new vaccines (Pfizer, BioNTech) was at least partly conditioned by open and seamless access to research results or not. Data sharing has advantages and disadvantages, as well for the individual scientist as for the community and the scientific development as a whole (Rios et al., 2020). Other issues have been raised, in particular potential data misuse and abuse of published virus genome sequences; "traceability should be a key function for guaranteeing socially responsible and robust policies. Full access to the available data and the ability to trace it back to its origins assure data quality and processing legitimacy" (Minari et al., 2020).

Yet, if open science is partly the cause of some of the issues associated with data quality, it also provides the solution, through increased accessibility, transparency, and integrity of research data and the whole process. Open science is not the problem; the problem is inappropriate adoption of open science principles (Besançon et al., 2020). Not less but more open science is the way forward, with preregistered analyses, registered reports, open reviews of methodologies and data, data sharing by default via dedicated platforms, and so on. If data are open, it can be assessed, by usual peer-reviewing but also by "crowd-reviewing." Another perspective is artificial intelligence. Elsevier is looking into automated machine learning detection of scientific fraud; together with Humboldt University in Germany, they are working on mechanisms to check the integrity of the articles, the images, and the data (HEADT Centre). The next years will show if and how this AI approach will contribute to the quality, integrity, and trustworthiness of research data. Probably (hopefully), this will be after the COVID-19 pandemic.

References

Amsterdam Call for Action, 2016. Amsterdam Call for Action on Open Science, Amsterdam, April 4–5. https://www.government.nl/topics/science/documents/reports/2016/04/04/amsterdam-call-for-action-on-open-science.

Aristovnik, A., Ravšelj, D., Umek, L., 2020. A bibliometric analysis of COVID-19 across science and social science research landscape. Sustainability 12 (21), 9132. https://doi. org/10.3390/su12219132.

Arrizabalaga, O., et al., 2020. Open access of COVID-19-related publications in the first quarter of 2020: a preliminary study based in PubMed. F1000Research 9, 649. https://doi. org/10.12688/f1000research.24136.2.

Azeroual, O., 2019. Text and data quality mining in CRIS. Information 10, 374. https://doi. org/10.3390/info10120374.

Azeroual, O., 2020. Data wrangling in database systems: purging of dirty data. Data 5, 50. https://doi.org/10.3390/data5020050.

Azeroual, O., Saake, G., Abuosba, M., 2018a. Data quality measures and data cleansing for research information systems. J. Digit. Inf. Manag. 16 (1), 12–21. https://arxiv.org/abs/1901.06208.

Azeroual, O., Saake, G., Schallehn, E., 2018b. Analyzing data quality issues in research information systems via data profiling. Int. J. Inf. Manag. 41, 50–56. https://doi.org/10.1016/j. ijinfomgt.2018.02.007.

Batini, C., et al., 2009. Methodologies for data quality assessment and improvement. ACM Comput. Surv. 41 (3), 1–52. https://doi.org/10.1145/1541880.1541883.

Besançon, L., et al., 2020. Open science saves lives: lessons from the COVID-19 pandemic. BioRxiv. https://doi.org/10.1101/2020.08.13.249847. 2020.08.13.249847.

BioRxiv, 2020. COVID-19 SARS-CoV-2 Preprints from medRxiv and bioRxiv. https://connect. biorxiv.org/relate/content/181.

BOAI, 2001. Budapest Open Access Initiative. https://www.budapestopenaccessinitiative.org/ read.

Budianto, A., 2019. Customer loyalty: quality of service. J. Manag. Rev. 3 (1), 299–305. https:// doi.org/10.25157/jmr.v3i1.1808.

Cai, L., Zhu, Y., 2015. The challenges of data quality and data quality assessment in the big data era. Data Sci. J. 14, 2. https://doi.org/10.5334/dsj-2015-002.

CoreTrustSeal Standards and Certification Board, 2019. CoreTrustSeal Trustworthy Data Repositories Requirements 2020–2022., https://doi.org/10.5281/ZENODO.3638211.

Donaldson, D.R., 2019. Trust in archives—trust in digital archival content framework. Archivaria 88 (Fall), 50–83. https://muse.jhu.edu/article/740193/summary.

DuBois, J.M., Antes, A.L., 2018. Five dimensions of research ethics: a stakeholder framework for creating a climate of research integrity. Acad. Med. 93 (4), 550–555. https://doi. org/10.1097/ACM.0000000000001966.

Duka, D., Hribar, L., 2010. Implementation of first time right practice in software development process. In: The 33rd International Convention MIPRO, Opatija, pp. 382–387.

Haak W. et al., Mendeley data. In Schöpfel J. and Rebouillat V. (Eds.), Les entrepôts de données de recherche, Forthcoming, ISTE Editions, London.

Haider, J., 2018. Openness as tool for acceleration and measurement: reflections on problem representations underpinning open access and open science. In: Herb, U., Schöpfel, J. (Eds.), Open Divide? Critical Studies on Open Access. 17–28, Litwin, Sacramento CA https://lup.lub.lu.se/search/publication/070c067e-5675-455e-a4b2-81f82b6c75a7.

Janiaud, P., et al., 2020. The worldwide clinical trial research response to the COVID-19 pandemic—the first 100 days. F1000Research 9, 1193. https://doi.org/10.12688/ f1000research.26707.2.

Konkiel, S., 2020. Assessing the impact and quality of research data using Altmetrics and other indicators. Scholarly Assess. Rep. 2 (1). https://doi.org/10.29024/sar.13.

Lin, D., Crabtree, J., Dillo, I., et al., 2020. The TRUST Principles for digital repositories. Scientific Data 7 (1), 144. https://doi.org/10.1038/s41597-020-0486-7.

Logan, C., et al., 2020. Improving data quality in face-to-face survey research. PS: Polit. Sci. Polit. 53 (1), 46–50. https://doi.org/10.1017/S1049096519001161.

Maali, F., Cyganiak, R., Peristeras, V., 2010. Enabling interoperability of government data catalogues. In: Wimmer, M.A., Chappelet, J.L., Janssen, M., Scholl, H.J. (Eds.), Electronic Government. EGOV 2010. Lecture Notes in Computer Science, vol. 6228. Springer, Berlin, Heidelberg, https://doi.org/10.1007/978-3-642-14799-9_29.

Mahanti, R., 2019. Data Quality: Dimensions, Measurement, Strategy, Management, and Governance. ASQ Quality Press, Milwaukee, WI.

Martinson, B.C., Anderson, M.S., De Vries, R., 2005. Scientists behaving badly. Nature 435 (7043), 737–738. https://doi.org/10.1038/435737a.

Mathis, C., 2017. Data lakes. Datenbank Spektrum 17, 289–293. https://doi.org/10.1007/s13222-017-0272-7.

Mesquita, C.T., 2020. Open science and the role of cardiology journals in the COVID-19 pandemic. Int. J. Cardiovasc. Sci. 33 (4), 305–306. https://doi.org/10.36660/ijcs.20200191.

Minari, J., Yoshizawa, G., Shinomiya, N., 2020. COVID-19 and the boundaries of open science and innovation. EMBO Rep. 21 (11). https://doi.org/10.15252/embr.202051773.

OECD, 2007. OECD Principles and Guidelines for Access to Research Data from Public Funding, Report. Paris https://www.oecd.org/sti/inno/38500813.pdf.

Piller, C., 2020. Who's to blame? These three scientists are at the heart of the Surgisphere COVID-19 scandal. Science, 20. https://doi.org/10.1126/science.abd2252. June 8.

Rios, R.S., Zheng, K.I., Zheng, M.H., 2020. Data sharing during COVID-19 pandemic: what to take away. Expert Rev. Gastroenterol. Hepatol. 14 (12), 1125–1130. https://doi.org/10.1080/17474124.2020.1815533.

Roozenbeek, J., et al., 2020. Susceptibility to misinformation about COVID-19 around the world. R. Soc. Open Sci. 7 (10), 201199. https://doi.org/10.1098/rsos.201199.

Schöpfel, J., et al., 2019. Data papers as a new form of knowledge organization in the field of research data. Knowl. Organ. 46 (8), 622–638. https://doi.org/10.5771/0943-7444-2019-8-622.

Schulte-Schrepping, J., et al., 2020. Severe COVID-19 is marked by a dysregulated myeloid cell compartment. Cell 182 (6), 1419–1440.e23. https://doi.org/10.1016/j.cell.2020.08.001.

Science Europe, 2019. Practical Guide to the International Alignment of Research Data Management. Science Europe Working Group on Research Data, Brussels. https://www.scienceeurope.org/media/jezkhnoo/se_rdm_practical_guide_final.pdf.

Stausberg, J., et al., 2019. Indicators of data quality: review and requirements from the perspective of networked medical research. GMS Medizinische Informatik, Biometrie und Epidemiologie 15 (1). https://doi.org/10.3205/mibe000199. Doc05.

Uribe-Tirado, A., et al., 2020. Open science since COVID-19: open access + open data. SSRN Electron. J. https://doi.org/10.2139/ssrn.3621047. June 3.

Wang, R., Strong, D., 1996. Beyond accuracy: what data quality means to data consumers. J. Manag. Inf. Syst. 12 (4), 5–33. https://doi.org/10.1080/07421222.1996.11518099.

Wilkinson, M.D., et al., 2016. The FAIR guiding principles for scientific data management and stewardship. Sci. Data 3 (1), 160018. https://doi.org/10.1038/sdata.2016.18.

Yakel, E., et al., 2013. Trust in digital repositories. Int. J. Digit. Curation 8 (1), 143–156. https://doi.org/10.2218/ijdc.v8i1.251.

Yoon, A., 2014. End users' trust in data repositories: definition and influences on trust development. Arch. Sci. 14 (1), 17–34. https://doi.org/10.1007/s10502-013-9207-8.

Younes, G.A., et al., 2020. COVID-19: Insights from innovation economists. Sci. Public Policy. https://doi.org/10.1093/scipol/scaa028. paaa036.

Impact of the COVID-19 pandemic on scientific production

19

Juan D. Machin-Mastromatteo, Javier Tarango, and José Refugio Romo-González
Autonomous University of Chihuahua, Chihuahua, Mexico

1 Introduction

In recent years, a major concern of countries planning for social and economic growth has related to the development of multiple indicators and their resulting positioning and ranking, particularly those related to scientific production. One of the goals of such development, especially for countries with underdeveloped or peripheral economies, involves achieving autonomy in the generation of knowledge to avoid scientific dependence.

Each country's advances in scientific production are commonly represented using quantitative indicators, which are usually linked to the number of publications and the impact of the journals where researchers are publishing. Other levels of impact analysis are not necessarily applied, such as social, individual, disciplinary, institutional, regional, or national (Abramo and D'Angelo, 2014). These conditions are regularly impersonal, they represent a metrification of scientific production, and such quantitative indicators are increasingly generating more doubts, criticisms, and even rejection by researchers, a paradoxical outcome being the lack of recognition by scientists themselves (Mattedi and Spiess, 2017).

Countries' rankings and impact levels in terms of science, technology, and innovation (STI) have regularly been manifested through the development of public policies that seek to promote STI, influencing aspects such as (a) innovation, economic growth, and human development; (b) strengthening and promoting education and research; and (c) management processes and the role of the state in regulating and developing STI, both in the public and private sectors (Rincón, 2013). The desire of countries to integrate mechanisms for regulating and measuring STI has resulted in the generation of structural models that define scientific production patterns in three main areas: (a) defining regulations and public policies to govern STI development; (b) identifying the role of researchers for achieving scientific purposes; and (c) establishing the types of scientific products to be generated as priorities, which in turn become the quantitative parameters used to measure the desired behaviours (Delgado et al., 2020).

The creation of management structures for scientific production is typically built through processes of planned change, with the implementation of measurement projects and the generation of formal structures and policies. The COVID-19 pandemic has disrupted all aspects of productive life, including such STI structures and

Libraries, Digital Information, and COVID. https://doi.org/10.1016/B978-0-323-88493-8.00020-3

work modes, generating, almost spontaneously, a new set of behavioural patterns in scientific production and its dissemination and dissemination processes, including both good and bad practices.

2 The challenges of scientific production during the pandemic

The changes that are currently being experienced show both disruption and tragedy without recent precedent, but the scientific community is experiencing a fundamental and hopeful transformation (Taraborelli, 2020). The challenges to scientific production in terms of these unplanned transitions involve numerous actors, among which we can highlight researchers, librarians, citizens, teachers, and students, that is, both producers and consumers of knowledge (Heathers, 2020). According to our review of the literature, it is possible to identify nine challenges that scientific production has experienced due to the pandemic, which are grouped into three areas: (a) editorial system; (b) promotion and dissemination mechanisms; and (c) complementary services (see Fig. 19.1), which we detail in this chapter.

2.1 Corruption in the editorial models and processes

Some of the challenges of scientific production are not new. However, it is possible that they have been accentuated recently, as with the case of the corruption of science for political and economic purposes, perhaps a characteristic of our time, where scientific findings and economies are manipulated to advance political agendas (Chossudovsky, 2020). This situation has occurred in the pharmaceutical industry, which exerts pressure on the publication of strategic topics and even attempts to block other companies. Larivière et al. (2020) consider that major crises have often revealed the (not always)

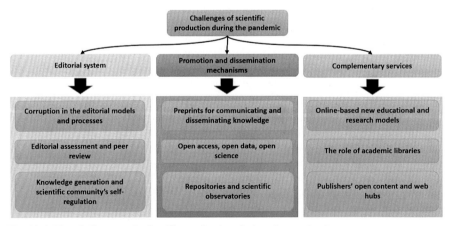

Fig. 19.1 The challenges of scientific production during the pandemic.

explicit rules and practices of scientific communication, which turns out is not really satisfying the needs of science and society.

Heathers (2020) presents another example of corruption in science through the case of *The Lancet*, one of the oldest and most respected medical journals, where an article that was offering strong conclusions and whose results were considered authoritative was published. However, the use of the proposed drugs turned out to be dangerous to COVID-19 patients. This article was promptly retracted, which is considered an important process in modern publishing history, since, given researchers' rush to publish (derived from the "mantra" "publish or perish" and its related behaviours and systems), the peer review process might fail in some cases, and hence, it will not detect anomalous data or findings. By January 26, 2021, Retraction Watch (2021) counted 66 retractions of documents related to COVID-19 and published in 2020, of which 19 were preprints published in medRxiv, bioRxiv, and on the Social Science Resource Network (SSRN). One corresponded to a conference presentation, and 46 were retractions of journal articles, of which perhaps the most scandalous cases were three articles retracted from *The Lancet*, two from the *Journal of the American Pharmacists Association*, two from *Cureus,* one from the *New England Journal of Medicine*, and one from *PLOS ONE*. Five articles are related to the use of hydroxychloroquine and two deal with ivermectin, while one associated 5G technology to the induction of COVID-19 in cells. Soltani and Patini (2020) present a brief evaluation of 26 of these retracted articles, and, according to their results, the reasons behind these retractions included doubts or errors in the data, results, or conclusions. The presence of corruptive elements in science, in the context of COVID-19, and according to Aspesi et al. (2020), causes a series of uncertainties in the following areas:

- Scientific, including issues related to the infection itself.
- Political and social, related to social and political unrest, changes in cultural attitudes and public opinion toward science, as well as cooperation and open societies.
- Economic, due to the deterioration of the financial conditions for the publishing systems to function properly.
- Specific to higher education, since the question remains as to what will happen to budgets, students, and classes.
- Industrial, which involves responses from commercial providers.
- Regulatory, such as mandates and support systems to provide immediate open access to publications corresponding to research financed with public funds.

2.2   Editorial assessment and peer review

The pandemic has shed light on how the scientific community can self-regulate and make the criticisms and evaluations of new results more scalable. Taraborelli (2020) comments that changes could occur to the traditional peer review process, which is opaque and errors that may escape it might take months or years (if ever) to be identified and then cause the article to be retracted. Rather, the cited author points out that the peer review process requires the defects of a manuscript to be identified more quickly, which could include aspects such as (a) detecting defective results and methods that are reused for similar manuscripts or incomplete documents; and (b) enabling the revision and improvement through collective comments that may even generate new research questions, as well as expanding manuscripts' results and usefulness. Recent trends such as open peer review and preprints present opportunities to do the above, while also opening research findings to a broader scientific community and seeking greater rigour in verifying the quality of manuscripts, including plagiarism detection.

Radical changes in the dynamics of scientific publishing have led to the generation of a new form of accelerated scientific production, with new studies appearing at a frenetic pace, positively offering results in real time, but without taking the validation time and steps that science requires and deserves, which is the negative side of the issue (Flamarique, 2020). This causes an excess of preprints that not only increase information overload but also may allow the ability to disseminate scientific information quickly, especially during emergencies such as the current one (Grados, 2020). According to Taraborelli (2020) and UCM (2020), preprints:

- Are scientific manuscripts that are available before being peer-reviewed and formally published.
- Unlike the traditional publication process, which can take months or years to complete, researchers can publish a preprint immediately.
- Although scientific journals are often found behind paywalls, preprints are completely freely accessible to both the interested public.
- Preprint defendants have called for the creation of places of rapid response for its review.

The role of peer reviewers can be considered to be at stake, when new review models begin to emerge. In this context, Rabin (2020) highlights some emerging concerns:

- Questioning whether the peer review process is broken.
- Scientists around the world fear that the rush to make COVID-19 research results available has overwhelmed the peer review process, and hence, it is not working properly.
- The credibility of medical journals may be particularly questioned when they are most necessary (especially in times of a pandemic), since it is a generally accepted fact that peer review allows ensuring and maintaining the quality of research, because it requires the evaluation of a manuscript by at least two experts in the field.

The peer review process produces evaluations on a manuscript, which may require authors to develop revisions, corrections, or they can even recommend the rejection of the document because of important flaws.

Accelerated publication processes, characterized by the abundance of research on COVID-19, have also reshaped peer review in scientific journals to ensure rapid dissemination, but there is a risk of approving poor-quality manuscripts, with critical flaws, or erroneous results, which ends up being very harmful for any discipline (Know, 2020; Segura, 2020; Soltani and Patini, 2020). Chossudovsky (2020) considers that harmful dynamics in publications include actions such as (a) manipulation of images and alteration of data that cannot be verified, and (b) publication of false scientific studies and use of suspicious data in important scientific studies, which may be published and then retracted even in leading scientific journals. However, according to

Taraborelli (2020), by sparking an uncontrolled race to increase knowledge, COVID-19 has somehow accelerated open access and open science. Jarvis (2020) specifies that the main challenges faced by journals and peer review, which have worsened during the pandemic, include the following:

- Journals have received an overwhelming number of articles on the subject that are awaiting to be reviewed, hoping that it will be conducted as fast, if not faster than usual, which is why scientific journals have tried to speed up the editorial review and peer review processes.
- Wide interest of scientists and health professionals to share their findings on the subject, even by professionals who were not previously dedicated to topics related to health emergencies, particularly those from the social sciences and humanities.
- Given the overabundant need for more peer reviewers, people with less experience or no experience have been approached to conduct them, which can lead to the dissemination of inaccurate results, although many manuscripts are rejected by editors due to the lack of expert reviewers.

Additionally, Soltani and Patini (2020) point out that the context of the pandemic and the retraction of articles related to COVID-19 (a problem that we discussed in the previous section) has promoted and strengthened postpublication reviews; some researchers have even been encouraged to review their own published work.

The two most popular systems for disseminating preprints on COVID-19 are the bioRxiv and medRxiv repositories; as of December 2, 2020, there were 11,101 preprints, 8702 at medRxiv and 2399 at bioRxiv (bioRxiv, 2020). Most of these studies have the following characteristics: (a) They try to identify speculative articles, while others are based on computational models, or on conspiracy theories, and (b) 75% publicly provided information on their clinical selection procedures and 32% involved researchers to apply assessment criteria on their content (Know, 2020; Porter and Hook, 2020; Simba Publishing, 2020). Traffic to these servers has also increased substantially: medRxiv pageviews have soared to 15 million per month, compared to 1 million per month before the pandemic began (Taraborelli, 2020). In the first 2 weeks of May, the rate at which new documents on COVID-19 were added increased to an average of 650 preprint articles per day. In addition, preprints have been strongly positioned in the research ecosystem of this topic, as by May they represented a quarter of the documents produced (Porter and Hook, 2020).

There are other concerns related to information overload, since the excess of publications and data make it difficult to take advantage of them (Flamarique, 2020). It is also important to note that scientific articles tend to show special care in the expression of their metadata (specifically title, abstract, and keywords), though it seems that during the pandemic there has not been less control over the correct use of specialized terminology in metadata, as some terms that correspond to different dimensions have been used indiscriminately or as synonyms, such as COVID-19, SARS-COV-2, Novel Coronavirus, Coronaviruses, Systemic Inflammatory Response Syndrome, Coronavirus Disease, Severe Acute Respiratory Syndrome Coronavirus 2, or nCov-2019 (Grados, 2020).

2.3   Knowledge generation and the scientific community's self-regulation

According to Aspesi et al. (2020), recent changes in knowledge generation schemes, especially within the context of the pandemic, could affect institutions in the following ways:

- The current and ensuing financial crises will exacerbate the problem of radically reallocating the available funds almost exclusively to those institutions with high volumes of scientific publication, given the required budgetary adjustments.
- Research funding may well affect open access publication, and on one side, it might be favourable to repositories and institutional journals, while on the other side it might seriously prevent some researchers from publishing in important open access journals with article processing charges (APC).
- The introduction of new medical research programmes or the expansion of existing ones (specifically those on the SARS-CoV-2 virus) could partially offset the possible decrease in funding for research and limit the negative impact represented by the growth in the volume of articles.
- There may be an additional negative impact on the ability of academic libraries to sustain their acquisitions and keep their subscriptions.

The current challenges of scientific publications include at least the following tensions, which have been accentuated in the research related to COVID-19: (a) closed science and publications as opposed to open ones, which are gaining more ground; (b) the dominance of certain countries or regions; (c) the explosion in the number of publications in a very short time makes it difficult to be up to date on the subject; and (d) those who publish in high-impact sources, have high indicators, and enjoy appropriate funding will be the most recognized and successful researchers (Porter and Hook, 2020); hence, the usual divides among researchers are kept, if not aggravated. Moreover, Porter and Hook (2020) discuss the following risks regarding research in universities:

- A decrease in research funding, as governments are under pressure to manage national debts and health system expenditures.
- Universities' income from international students will affect many institutions in economies that have diversified their business models and educational institutions to cater to such markets.
- Perhaps government policy will once again drive institutions to produce more applied research, which will directly benefit the economy in the short term.

COVID-19 has posed more immediate challenges for researchers around the world, who have rapidly reoriented their studies to meet public health needs, as well as researchers from other disciplines, who have addressed the challenges of the pandemic from their own approaches. These changes in customary research practices have led to an exceptionally large volume of work being generated in a short time, even from fields of knowledge with slower growth.

As of December 2, LitCovid, which according to its authors is the most exhaustive resource of COVID-19 research, counted 76,534 articles indexed in PubMed on the topic (Chen et al., 2020). Moreover, to illustrate the volume of COVID-19-related indexed documents that were published during 2020 (until January 26, 2021) and in various disciplines, we applied in Scopus the search query used by LitCovid ("coronavirus"

OR "ncov" OR "cov" OR "2019-nCoV" OR "COVID-19" OR "SARS-CoV-2"). This resulted in 98,154 documents published in sources indexed in Scopus, of which only five are marked to be retracted; obviously, Medicine is the discipline with most publications (46.9%), followed by Biochemistry, Genetics and Molecular Biology (7.37%), Social Sciences (7.10%), Immunology and Microbiology (4.68%), Pharmacology, Toxicology and Pharmaceutics (2.91%), Nursing (2.88%), Environmental Science (2.62%), Computer Science (2.52%), Engineering (2.29%), and Psychology (2.08%). Although information professionals have been active publishing research related to responses to the pandemic, it is difficult to provide a precise percentage for the field of Library and Information Science without a much deeper analysis, because Scopus classifies some of our journals in the Social Sciences and others in Computer Science. Table 19.1 presents all the disciplines and their percentage of documents, based on the total of 98,154 indexed in Scopus. The total number of articles between LitCovid and

Table 19.1 Percentage of COVID-19-related documents indexed in Scopus per discipline.

Discipline	% of documents published
Medicine	46.90%
Biochemistry, Genetics and Molecular Biology	7.37%
Social Sciences	7.10%
Immunology and Microbiology	4.68%
Pharmacology, Toxicology and Pharmaceutics	2.91%
Nursing	2.88%
Environmental Science	2.62%
Computer Science	2.52%
Engineering	2.29%
Psychology	2.08%
Neuroscience	1.92%
Multidisciplinary	1.79%
Agricultural and Biological Sciences	1.67%
Business, Management and Accounting	1.60%
Arts and Humanities	1.37%
Health Professions	1.36%
Economics, Econometrics and Finance	1.22%
Mathematics	1.19%
Chemistry	1.07%
Physics and Astronomy	0.99%
Chemical Engineering	0.76%
Energy	0.73%
Dentistry	0.70%
Materials Science	0.69%
Decision Sciences	0.54%
Veterinary	0.53%
Earth and Planetary Sciences	0.48%
Undefined	0.03%

Data from Scopus (2020).

Scopus differs, because the former uses PubMed, which indexes sources from health disciplines, while Scopus is multidisciplinary.

Larivière et al. (2020) draw attention to the fact that not all articles on COVID-19 are open access. This contradicts a worldwide agreement, to which many commercial publishers are signatories. The Statement on data sharing in Public Health Emergencies (Wellcome, 2020) was first established in 2016, within the context of the Zika virus outbreak. Signatories of this agreement commit to provide the World Health Organization (WHO) and the general public with access ("as rapidly and openly as possible") to the results of medical research whenever a worldwide public health emergency arises, which can be achieved by making all contents about the topic open access or by providing free access for the duration of the outbreak. It is strange, therefore, that not all the content published by the publishers that signed the agreement are openly available. This is verifiable by accessing commercial publishers' COVID-19 content hubs that, although a very good initiative, are incomplete, as they do not offer access to all COVID-19-related research (many articles behind paywalls are even from health disciplines; hence, it is odd to find some of them unavailable in databases from publishers that signed the Wellcome agreement). Many of them are difficult to navigate, and some even lack proper searching functionality, which is needed in every information system with a large volume of documents.

Online or virtual education might seem as an aspect outside of knowledge generation and consumption, but it is another aspect that has particularly been challenged and impacted by the pandemic, as it has been more than a viable alternative for educational institutions; it has been the only option to continue providing educational programmes at all levels of instruction. Aspesi et al. (2020) consider two fundamental aspects: (a) A significant number of students may be willing to switch to online courses and even online degrees, but it is not clear how many universities are appropriately equipped to run programmes of this nature; (b) some publishers have experience and resources to offer courses and even programmes and may harness such an opportunity. Perhaps the biggest issue with education, particularly in "old-fashioned" universities, and others perhaps more modern, is that the pandemic caught many institutions by surprise, so the staff were not prepared enough to face the challenges ahead. Hence, under the pandemic, universities have to compete in the same arena with other educational providers that use online tools as a matter of routine, while universities had to adopt them immediately.

2.4   Open access, open data, and open science

According to the Complutense University of Madrid (UCM, 2020), open science is the ideal mechanism to respond to situations such as this pandemic. One of the ways that open science manifests itself is through preprints, and their growing popularity may allow for a more solid model of open science to be developed, promoting greater collaboration, accelerating scientific progress, and allowing the full force of scientific research to be available to scientists and nonscientists (Taraborelli, 2020). Le Guillou (2020) claims that preprints also promote two fundamental conditions:

- The need to share information and research results quickly.
- The promotion of open science, as well as open data.

Both conditions have changed the ways in which scientific discourse is experienced and have been strengthened in these times of the pandemic. Although the most critical views of preprints present them as a less polished, even rushed, or hasty version of a scientific manuscript, nevertheless, preprints are a different scientific product and one that may be laying the foundation for a new model of scientific communication. They have become the most important large-scale collaborative experiment in modern science; the speed at which they allow research results to be available reflects the way systems are adapting in the research community to ensure that knowledge spreads as quickly as possible, as well as ensuring that more actors can make judgments about the contents (Porter and Hook, 2020). The usual processes of exclusive publication in scientific journals have been changing. Preprints have allowed researchers to make their results public once their research is completed, but these are unreviewed manuscripts (Flamarique, 2020).

According to Know (2020), repositories are rapidly disseminating science about the pandemic and are rigorously evaluating their content to protect themselves from poor-quality work, and to avoid receiving documents that make predictions about treatments. For Taraborelli (2020), this development has strong similarities with the trajectory of collaborative knowledge production systems (such as Wikipedia), while open repositories imitate the nonlinear and iterative structure of scientific discourse.

Society's access to research results is limited by journals' open access policies and the interests of commercial publishers, which gives rise to other interests that seek to change scientific policies to guarantee a generalized, rapid, and effective access to science by society in general (UCM, 2020). An increase in openness has not necessarily represented lax editorial boards; on the contrary, they have become a source of power and responsibility over publication, in addition to representing a greater academic governance on journals, with more ethical and responsible editorial cultures (Grove, 2020).

Scientific openness is breaking disciplinary barriers, fostering collaboration, accelerating dissemination, and drastically expanding the audience of scientists who can review, criticize, or corroborate the findings of a study, in addition to increasing the speed of all these processes (Taraborelli, 2020). Open access gains more strength when its objectives are to advance science and serve society, in addition to removing the barriers of access to content (through legal mechanisms), while open science ensures that all research, including its data, documents and processes are immediately available without restrictions and to all interested stakeholders (Larivière et al., 2020). The pandemic has revealed the benefits of open data for collaboration and a faster development of medical research. Open science will promote a greater exchange of data and research compared to the past, since there are multiple exchange tools available online (Le Guillou, 2020), which will continue to multiply.

There have been many initiatives to gather and provide open access to COVID-19 research and data. The WHO (2020) has established a content hub with a database by the Latin American and Caribbean Centre on Health Sciences Information (BIREME) that has been updated daily and can be either searched or downloaded. At the time of writing, the database has 102,633 full texts and 13,370 preprints. Since the beginning of 2020, Google Scholar's homepage has been including a section with direct links to websites with COVID-19-related research from some journals, publishers, and preprint servers (CDC, NEJM, JAMA, Lancet, Cell, BMJ, Nature, Science, Elsevier, Oxford, Wiley, and medRxiv).

Individual researchers have also prepared compilations of resources, for instance, Uribe-Tirado (2020) compiled open science resources, which facilitates access to data sources and open access documents about COVID-19, which the author claims that shows the benefits of scientific openness models. Governmental bodies have also offered new services in the context of the pandemic. For instance, in Latin America, the Brazilian Ministry of Science, Technology and Innovation (2020) and the Mexican National Council of Science and Technology (2020) have each developed portals with open access to documents and data related to the pandemic.

Scholars in charge of library and information science journals or guest editors had the initiative of making calls for papers to publish special issues dedicated to COVID-19, all of them to appear in Emerald-published journals:

- *Information and Learning Sciences* published a two-part special issue "Evidence-based and Pragmatic Online Teaching and Learning Approaches: A Response to Emergency Transitions to Remote Online Education in K-12, Higher Education, and Librarianship" (available in open access for the first 6 months) (Reynolds and Chu, 2020).
- *Digital Library Perspectives* is publishing two special issues: "Digital libraries and COVID-19: responding to a global emergency," appearing in 2020, and "Digital libraries and COVID-19: the new normal" to be published in 2021 (Tammaro and Machin-Mastromatteo, 2020).
- *Library Hi Tech* will be publishing in 2021 "COVID-19 Pandemic and Health Informatics" (So et al., 2020).
- *Information Discovery and Delivery* is going to publish "Using Data Science to Understand the Coronavirus Pandemic," also in 2021 (Tian et al., 2020).

In the world of open data, we have the case of Figshare (2020), a data repository mainly used by researchers to make their research data freely accessible. In this case, a COVID-19 hub has been set up to upload directly the data from research related to the virus and the pandemic, guaranteeing at the same time a more direct access to data about this topic.

Many commercial publishers including the major six in size have also opened specialized web hubs with access to scientific information, full texts, and scientific dissemination information, as well as health, psychological, and educational recommendations, resources, and support materials (Elsevier, 2020; Emerald Publishing, 2020a; Springer Nature, 2020; SAGE, 2020; Taylor & Francis, 2020; Wiley, 2020a). For instance, these offer advice to set up online meetings and courses, as well as tutorials for making sure library users know about enabling remote access to the major databases, especially because physical access to the campus is restricted. The following paragraphs summarize some of the available initiatives, although this is not an exhaustive selection.

Major publishers who are also signatories of the Wellcome agreement have opened access to most of their publications on the pandemic. Emerald Publishing (2020b) also offered a fund to finance the APCs for publishing articles on the pandemic in their journals, regardless of the field. Wiley (2020b) has also created a portal with information related to online education resources, which includes information to find online resources for various disciplines and for facilitating online courses, covering aspects such as rubrics, evaluation, feedback, video production, and among other topics that may aid teaching.

Springer made a small collection of around 500 books free to download during the first semester of 2020. Elsevier has made available a tool for conducting data mining on the COVID-19 publications that they have published, something that is widely known that commercial publishers are usually very reluctant to do; this publisher is also providing special resources for researchers, students, and professors in health disciplines, as well as medics, librarians, and journalists. Frontiers (2020), a publisher of gold open access journals, is offering a website that gathers information about funding opportunities for COVID-19-related research. Finally, the Association of University Presses (2020), a group of around 80 university presses around the world, including Oxford, Cambridge, MIT, Cornell, Harvard, and Uniandes, has also provided free downloads of parts of their collections.

One of the most relevant trends, driven by COVID-19, is that many of the largest publishers signed the Wellcome agreement and have mostly followed it, while offering other types of resources during the pandemic. Other publishers' responses were mixed, with some quickly providing full open access to their articles, while others provided temporary access and custom licences; yet others did not provide content at all (Aspesi et al., 2020). In promoting open access, Aspesi et al. (2020) highlight that publishers have concerns regarding income and profitability:

- In the short term, they seem to believe that the income they obtain from academic library subscriptions will be seriously reduced, which will turn into a long-term problem.
- Many academic libraries will face reduced budgets, and maybe, they will be discontinuing other services first, rather than interrupting payments for their existing subscriptions, which will then be seriously reassessed.
- In the future, academic libraries will likely demand more favourable conditions when they renew their contracts and sign new, transformative, and complex agreements, though this could take longer to materialize than expected.

A significant reduction in subscriptions will likely occur globally and may force publishers to offer better terms, because even before the pandemic, increases in subscriptions and APCs were no longer sustainable or even reasonable, especially in developing countries. An intriguing development is that Springer Nature announced that, from 2021, it will start charging APCs of €9500 per article to publish them in Nature and other 32 journals of this publisher, under a gold open access model (Else, 2020); this is to our understanding the highest price that any publisher has ever considered, and it will be next to impossible for developing countries' institutions to even consider paying it, as they struggle with APCs from US$ 500 to 1000.

Another effective form of scientific dissemination has been conducted by scientific observatories. In addition to LitCovid (Chen et al., 2020), which we mentioned earlier, the Ibero-American Observatory of Science, Technology and Society offers information on worldwide COVID-19-related scientific publications by using PubMed, including the number of publications by country, comparisons between the production of countries and collaboration data among researchers (Organization of Ibero-American States, 2020).

2.5   The role of academic libraries

Libraries in general, and medical libraries in particular, have assumed a leading role in the promotion of scientific information in the context of the pandemic, by: (a) identifying the information skills required by medical librarians and their users, beyond information search, retrieval, access, and use; (b) appropriately using evidence-based medicine to identify the suitability of scientific information for making appropriate medical decisions; and (c) fighting against unscientific assumptions and beliefs (Grados, 2020).

The actions of medical libraries are characterized by: (a) promoting public health awareness through preventive measures; (b) avoiding fake news and alternative facts; and (c) avoiding the proliferation of misinformation and conspiracy theories, thus preventing infodemic (excessive amount of information) and misinformation, which makes it difficult for people to find reliable sources (Organização Pan-Americana da Saúde and Organização Mundial da Saúde, 2020; Research Information, 2020). According to the sources cited above, these challenges offer the possibility of supporting research teams by providing access to the most recent and reliable information and publications, in addition to facilitating support in the writing of scientific articles and providing filters to face information overload.

Based on the new behavioural patterns of information use, two aspects related to academic libraries are of concern: Their reopening for post-pandemic operation (or the so-called new normal) and their new modus operandi for using available resources might be of no interest to users and become unused resources. In the case of the reopening processes of academic libraries, anticipating such a possibility, there have been proposals for adopting biosafety protocols in order to reopening in a safer and more effective way, and at various stages, without affecting the stability of the physical collection and including aspects such as disinfecting buildings, office equipment, and collections (Ramírez et al., 2020).

The closing, opening, and closing processes in libraries have obviously been impacting face-to-face services; in addition, such processes require interrupting and restarting of work and operations, which imply financial and other costs. Adapting to new changes also requires resources; if face-to-face services are to be provided again, it is necessary to "re-ignite the engines," and if libraries do not return to their regular operations, new online services must be created, while existing ones are strengthened. Such restarting and suspension of activities create difficulties and concerns, at least in terms of sustainability. A group of experts who participated in a webcast organized by Research Information (2020) concluded that it will be necessary to:

- Generate online services.
- Develop content selection processes.
- Define controls for accessing and using physical information resources.
- Seek mechanisms to continue supporting research.
- Generate digitization processes of available information resources.
- Integrate openness models to promote publication.
- Generate digital literacy programmes with a focus on online education and publishing.

3 Conclusion

The quality conditions required to publish manuscripts, to evaluate them with transparency and strong scrutiny, have always been accepted as necessary. The pandemic has strengthened this position and drawn further attention to their flaws. The abundance of publications without quality control mechanisms causes issues of information overload, but they have strengthened interesting scientific production dynamics and highlighted the importance of open models and products, as well as to the need for maintaining quality in scientific communication. Teachers, researchers, librarians, and information users must adapt to these new challenges of scientific production, first within the period of the pandemic and then considering the emerging changes after it, when it will be time to define new guidelines and set firmer positions regarding new products and workflows related to research, editorial evaluation, peer review, content generation, and forming the new information services that will be demanded.

References

Abramo, G., D'Angelo, A., 2014. How do you define and measure research productivity? Scientometrics 101, 1129–1144. https://doi.org/10.1007/s11192-014-1269-8.

Aspesi, C., Allen, N., Crown, R., Joseph, H., McArthur, J., Schockey, N., 2020. 2020 UPDATE. SPARC landscape analysis and roadmap for action. SPARC, s.l. 10.31229/osf.io/2pwft.

Association of University Presses, 2020. Open up. https://covid19.up.hcommons.org/open-up. (Accessed 2 December 2020).

bioRxiv, 2020. COVID-19 SARS-CoV-2 preprints from medRxiv and bioRxiv. https://connect. biorxiv.org/relate/content/181?page=3. (Accessed 2 December 2020).

Chen, Q., Allot, A., Lu, Z., 2020. LitCovid. https://www.ncbi.nlm.nih.gov/research/coronavirus. (Accessed 2 December 2020).

Chossudovsky, M., 2020. Who Was Behind It? Anthony Fauci's Intent to Block HCQ on Behalf of Big Pharma. Global Research: Centre for Research and Globalization. https:// www.globalresearch.ca/the-corruption-of-science-the-hydroxychloroquine-lancet-study-scandal-who-was-behind-it-anthony-faucis-intent-to-block-hcq-on-behalf-of-big-pharma/5715568. (Accessed 2 December 2020.

Delgado, R., Tarango, J., Machin-Mastromatteo, J., 2020. Scientific evaluation models in Latin America and the criteria for assessing researchers. Inf. Dev. 36 (3), 457–467. https://doi. org/10.1177/0266666920943966.

Else, H., 2020. Nature journals reveal terms of landmark open-access option. Nature 588, 19–20. https://doi.org/10.1038/d41586-020-03324-y.

Elsevier, 2020. Novel Coronavirus Information Center. https://www.elsevier.com/connect/coronavirus-information-center. (Accessed 2 December 2020).

Emerald Publishing, 2020a. Coronavirus, the management of epidemics & the broader impact on society. https://www.emeraldgrouppublishing.com/topics/coronavirus. (Accessed 2 December 2020).

Emerald Publishing, 2020b. New publishing fund to help researchers rapidly share their findings related to COVID-19. https://www.emeraldpublishing.com/coronavirus. (Accessed 2 December 2020).

Figshare, 2020. COVID-19 open research data. https://COVID19.figshare.com. (Accessed 2 December 2020).

Flamarique, L., 2020. Cómo el Coronavirus ha afectado a las publicaciones científicas. https://www.lavanguardia.com/ciencia/20200720/482344667309/como-coronavirus-afectado-publicaciones-cientificas-articulos.html. (Accessed 2 December 2020).

Frontiers, 2020. Coronavirus funding monitor. https://coronavirus.frontiersin.org/covid-19-research-funding-monitor. (Accessed 2 December 2020).

Grados, R., 2020. Testimonio sobre una biblioteca médica durante la pandemia. Otlet: Revista para Profesionales de la Información (10). http://www.revistaotlet.com/perspectivas-linda-grados-testimonio-biblioteca-medica-pandemia. (Accessed 2 December 2020).

Grove, J., 2020. Open-access publishing and the coronavirus. https://www.insidehighered.com/news/2020/05/15/coronavirus-may-be-encouraging-publishers-pursue-open-access. (Accessed 2 December 2020).

Heathers, J., 2020. The Lancet has made one of the biggest retractions in modern history. How could this happen? https://www.theguardian.com/commentisfree/2020/jun/05/lancet-had-to-do-one-of-the-biggest-retractions-in-modern-history-how-could-this-happen. (Accessed 2 December 2020).

Jarvis, C., 2020. Journals, peer reviewers cope with surge in COVID-19 publications. https://www.the-scientist.com/news-opinion/journals-peer-reviewers-cope-with-surge-in-COVID-19-publications-67,279. (Accessed 2 December 2020).

Know, D., 2020. How swamped preprint servers are blocking bad Coronavirus research. Nature 581, 130–131. https://doi.org/10.1038/d41586-020-01394-6.

Larivière, V., Shu, F., Sugimoto, C., 2020. The Coronavirus (COVID-19) outbreak highlights serious deficiencies in scholarly communication. https://blogs.lse.ac.uk/impactofsocialsciences/2020/03/05/the-coronavirus-COVID-19-outbreak-highlights-serious-deficiencies-in-scholarly-communication. (Accessed 2 December 2020).

Le Guillou, I., 2020. COVID-19: How unprecedented data sharing has led to faster-than-ever outbreak research. https://horizon-magazine.eu/article/COVID-19-how-unprecedented-data-sharing-has-led-faster-ever-outbreak-research.html. (Accessed 2 December 2020).

Mattedi, M., Spiess, M., 2017. The evaluation of scientific productivity. Hist. Ciênc. Saúde Manguinhos 24 (3), 1–19. https://doi.org/10.1590/s0104-59,702,017,000,300,005.

Ministry of Science, Technology and Innovation, 2020. La ciencia abierta es la vida: Directorio de fuentes de información científica que se puede acceder libremente sobre Coronavirus. http://diretoriodefontes.ibict.br/coronavirus. (Accessed 2 December 2020).

National Council of Science and Technology, 2020. Bienvenidos al Repositorio CONACYT COVID-19. https://covid-19.conacyt.mx/jspui. (Accessed 2 December 2020).

Organização Pan-Americana da Saúde, Organização Mundial da Saúde, 2020. Webinar Informação científica sobre COVID-19: O papel dos preprints. https://youtube/BRPssxFrY4c. (Accessed 2 December 2020).

Organization of Ibero-American States, 2020. Seguimiento en tiempo real de las publicaciones científicas sobre COVID-19. https://observatoriocts.oei.org.ar/2020/03/25/el-radar-del-observatoriocts-seguimiento-en-vivo-del-COVID-19. (Accessed 2 December 2020).

Porter, S., Hook, D., 2020. How COVID-19 is Changing Research Culture. Landscape Trends and Cultural Changes in the Global Research System. Digital Science, London, https://doi.org/10.6084/m9.figshare.12383267.

Rabin, R., 2020. The pandemic claims new victims: prestigious medical journals. https://www.nytimes.com/2020/06/14/health/virus-journals.html. (Accessed 2 December 2020).

Ramírez, E., Soria, V., Paquini, R., 2020. Protocolo de bioseguridad para la reapertura de las bibliotecas del Sistema Bibliotecario y de Información de la UNAM, posterior al confinamiento precautorio ante la pandemia ocasionada por SARS-COV-2. Universidad Nacional Autónoma de México, Mexico City. http://dgb.unam.mx/extras/pdf/protocolo/protocolo-Bioseguridad-Reapertura-SIBIUNAM.pdf. (Accessed 2 December 2020).

Research Information, 2020. Webcast: COVID-19 and the future of the academic library. https://event.webcasts.com/viewer/event.jsp?ei=1330655&tp_key=ab6912a48c. (Accessed 2 December 2020).

Retraction Watch, 2021. Retracted coronavirus (COVID-19) papers. https://retractionwatch.com/retracted-coronavirus-covid-19-papers. (Accessed 26 January 2021).

Reynolds, R., Chu, S., 2020. Guest editorial. Inf. Learn. Sci. 121 (5/6), 233–239. https://doi.org/10.1108/ILS-05-2020-144.

Rincón, I., 2013. Ciencia y tecnología: Política pública para el crecimiento económico y desarrollo humano. Enl@ce: Revista Venezolana de Información, Tecnología y Conocimiento 10 (2), 91–102. https://www.redalyc.org/pdf/823/82328320007.pdf. (Accessed 2 December 2020).

SAGE, 2020. Coronavirus (COVID-19) research. https://journals.sagepub.com/coronavirus. (Accessed 2 December 2020).

Segura, C. 2020. El nivel de los artículos científicos sobre la COVID-19 ha sido decepcionante. https://elpais.com/ciencia/2020-06-05/el-nivel-de-los-articulos-cientificos-sobre-la-COVID-19-ha-sido-decepcionante.html. (Accessed 2 December 2020).

Simba Publishing, 2020. COVID-19 to accelerate transition to open access publishing. https://www.simbainformation.com/about/release.asp?id=4605. (Accessed 2 December 2020).

So, S., Paulino, Y., Huang, P., 2020. Using data science to understand the coronavirus pandemic. https://www.emeraldgrouppublishing.com/journal/idd/using-data-science-understand-coronavirus-pandemic. (Accessed 2 December 2020).

Soltani, P., Patini, R., 2020. Retracted COVID-19 articles: a side-effect of the hot race to publication. Scientometrics 125, 819–822. https://doi.org/10.1007/s11192-020-03661-9.

Springer Nature, 2020. Coronavirus (COVID-19) research highlights. https://www.springernature.com/gp/researchers/campaigns/coronavirus. (Accessed 2 December 2020).

Tammaro, A., Machin-Mastromatteo, J., 2020. Editorial: Digital libraries and COVID-19: responding to a global emergency. Digit. Libr. Perspect. 36 (4), 333–335. https://doi.org/10.1108/DLP-11-2020-096.

Taraborelli, D., 2020. How the COVID-19 crisis has prompted a revolution in scientific publishing. https://www.fastcompany.com/90537072/how-the-COVID-19-crisis-has-prompted-a-revolution-in-scientific-publishing?s=09,2020. (Accessed 2 December 2020).

Taylor & Francis, 2020. COVID-19: novel Coronavirus content: Free to access. https://taylorandfrancis.com/coronavirus. (Accessed 2 December 2020).

Tian, X., Xing, Y., He, W., 2020. Using data science to understand the coronavirus pandemic. https://www.emeraldgrouppublishing.com/journal/idd/using-data-science-understand-coronavirus-pandemic. (Accessed 2 December 2020).

Universidad Complutense de Madrid, 2020. La ciencia en abierto aumenta al 90% en la crisis del Coronavirus, con EE. UU. y China a la cabeza. https://www.ucm.es/otri/noticias-la-ciencia-en-abierto-aumenta-al-90-en-la-crisis-del-coronavirus-con-eeuu-y-china-a-la-cabeza. (Accessed 2 December 2020).

Uribe-Tirado, A., 2020. Recopilación sobre ciencia abierta desde el COVID-19: Acceso abierto + datos abiertos. http://eprints.rclis.org/39864. (Accessed 2 December 2020).

Wellcome, 2020. Statement on data sharing in public health emergencies. https://wellcome.ac.uk/press-release/statement-data-sharing-public-health-emergencies. (Accessed 2 December 2020).

Wiley, 2020a. Covid-19: Novel Coronavirus outbreak. https://novel-coronavirus.onlinelibrary. wiley.com. (Accessed 2 December 2020).

Wiley, 2020b. Online teaching resources. https://www.wiley.com/network/instructors-students/ covid-19-online-teaching-resources-1. (Accessed 2 December 2020).

World Health Organization, 2020. Global research on coronavirus disease (COVID-19). https:// www.who.int/emergencies/diseases/novel-coronavirus-2019/global-research-on-novel- coronavirus-2019-ncov. (Accessed 2 December 2020).

Section C

Psychological effects—Adjustment or radical alteration?

Something old, something new

20

Rick Rylance
University of London, London, United Kingdom

The frontispiece to Alberto Manguel's *The Library at Night* (2006), a rich and various celebration of libraries, books, and reading, is a photo of an epigraphic stone which is all that remains of an ancient Athenian library (Manguel, 2006). The stone says that opening times last "from the first to the sixth hour" and "it is forbidden to take works out of the library." The motifs of restriction and exclusion are familiar.

Raymond Williams's brilliant 1958 essay "Culture is Ordinary" is a meditation on the significance of the locked library in Hereford Cathedral (Williams, 1989). The library now is a replica and welcomes visitors, but its original locks and chains dangle like cobwebs in a temperature-controlled, heritage environment (Fig. 20.1). Back in 1958, having secured access to the library with difficulty, and while waiting for a bus outside the cloisters, Williams reflected on his life's journey from a working-class home in the Welsh borders to Cambridge University. He considers writing he encountered which interprets culture in ways that restrict access or constrain valuation. Reading Clive Bell's Bloomsbury-ite *Civilisation* (1928), for instance, he writes: "I experience not so much disagreement as stupor. What kind of life can it be, I wonder, to produce this extraordinary fussiness, this extraordinary decision to call certain things culture and separate them, as with a park wall, from ordinary people and ordinary work?" Essential to Williams's thinking are two not incompatible but often rivalrous meanings of the idea of *learning*. Learning is both an activity—continuous, open, participatory, developmental—a verb in fact, and also a gerund, a noun form, a body of defined and approved materials and artefacts to which access is, either explicitly or inexplicitly, controlled: a world of locks and walls (Fig. 20.2).

Issues of value and access have always been central to libraries. What should be stored? Who should see it? The offer of digital open access is to circumvent these questions and close the gap between the two meanings of learning in Williams's account. Large-scale, web-based access promises abundance delivered with convenience to your desk at nugatory cost as long as you have institutional backing, unconstrained as in ancient Athens by time ("from the first to the sixth hour"), or place ("it is forbidden to take works out of the library"). It is a break from history.

Many things have already changed. As I write in November 2020, during the second UK COVID-19 lockdown, my wife Hilary Fraser is sitting at her desk editing Walter Pater's *The Renaissance* (Pater, 2021), one of 10 volumes in the first comprehensive scholarly edition of his collected works. Pater's book was a path-breaking, enormously influential late-19th-century collection of interpretative criticism. It was enabled by his local access, as a don, to the closed if not chained libraries of Oxford University.

Libraries, Digital Information, and COVID. https://doi.org/10.1016/B978-0-323-88493-8.00034-3

Fig. 20.1 The chained library at Hereford Cathedral.

Fig. 20.2 Raymond Williams at Saffron Walden.

The publisher is Oxford University Press, but the general editors are Canadian and the team editing individual volumes is internationally scattered. The project is funded, generously, by the Social Sciences and Humanities Research Council (SSHRC) of Canada. It will appear in handsome, shelf-ready hardback, with the traditional, bushy OUP colophon on the spine, and in due course will have a zippy digital platform in the Oxford Scholarly Editions Online series. In other words, it is versatile, international, and collaborative (between both scholars and organizations) and thus in line with much in the nature of modern research.

We live in south Devon in the United Kingdom, well over a 100 miles from the nearest copyright library, and COVID travel and health restrictions fence us in. And yet the work thrives because of access to the web. This is not merely a matter of summoning-up the published sources behind Pater's references and allusions. Our shelves are populated by these. It is a matter of piecing together networks of intellectual connection which extend beyond the explicit. This is enabled by that enormous fingertip archive stored on the web.

In one sense, there is nothing new here. Gleaning the implied has always been done in the stacks, catalogues, and reading rooms of conventional libraries. So, what is the difference? It is one of access, of amplitude (not all libraries have as much as we would like), of convenience (no ties to opening hours, the uncertainties of borrowing, or the inconveniences of travel), and of pace. This work can all be done more quickly, all things considered, such as travel. It is also a matter of extent. If one of the purposes of Hilary's edition is to embed Pater's thinking in the connections of its paper-linked intellectual world, this can be accessed more extensively. The elucidation becomes more comprehensive, the connections more agile, the links more dexterous, the portrait fuller and more encompassing, and the stimulus greater.

It can be said that this is an adjustment not a radical alteration; that Internet-based access offers fast-tracking of well-established procedures. Further, enhanced search and access are only meaningful when understood as realizations of the many alterations that have changed scholarly work since Raymond Williams waited for his Hereford bus. Technological facility has moved in step with enlarged horizons of thought and increased investigative scope and zeal. In this case, for instance, considerations of work by 19th-century women (sometimes not well stored in conventional libraries), of international range (Pater's is above all a cosmopolitan book), and of political, religious, philosophical and ideological context. Does this constitute a revolution in method?

Consideration of technologies of analysis as well as access is relevant. Have comparable advances in method accompanied those in access? There is noticeably less affirmation here. Some have pointed to what might be called the innovations of bulk: the capacity of machine-based analysis to range further and wider to uncover, for instance, the evolutions of language and ideas over millions of texts and across centuries in ways beyond unaided human capacity. When Raymond Williams wrote his 1976 book *Keywords: A Vocabulary of Culture and Society* (Williams, 1976), his method of tracing cultural history through the evolution of words and concepts was based on one man's (enormous) reading and sense of pertinence and significance. What extra, one wonders, might be done in this way by machine-assisted research and data gathering?

But does increase in yield represent innovation in method? Voluminous quantity still requires sensitivities to the analysis of change, nuance, ambiguity, historical context, the difference between majority and minority usage, and so on, to be illuminating.

An answer to this question requires better expertise than I possess and some patience. But I observe that, even if the answer is that this is not an innovation in method, nonetheless increases in quantities of data, habits of teamwork and collaboration, pacier communications, and the relaxation of the restraints of place mark new and major trends in approach and working habits, especially in the humanities. Technology is changing the circumstances of research and its procedures, if not its analytical methods. The COVID experience of home confinement moves with the pre-COVID tide and strengthens it. It is likely to supercharge existing trajectories in a transitional phase.

An awful term "scraping" is often used about data gathering among techno-wonks and those who like its breezy, mechanistic lustre. It is a term to be wary of, suggesting as it does concern only with surface. But this opens another issue in this transitional phase. There is interdisciplinary research on the value and limitations of screen-reading (I survey this in Chapter 1 of my book *Literature and the Public Good* (Rylance, 2016)). In particular, there is an unresolved debate about the impact of reading format on cognition, and some tentative evidence that reading on screen encourages superficiality. When asked about their preferences, readers consistently favour paper for reading complex or long material, or (as in the case of literature for example) material that requires sustained absorption. There is a phenomenon known as "F-shaped reading" on screen, detected by eye-tracking equipment, where the reading eye at first reads across a "page" of screen text but quickly hastens down, reading only the beginnings of lines until, in a cautionary or guilty pause, it briefly reads across the lines again, before slipping down the front-ends to the bottom. The resulting shape is like a capital letter "F."

It is too soon to say how established this mode of reading is or will become, or what its consequences may be, including perhaps on the way people write as well as read. After all, we all "skim" read in different ways, or write for different readerships. It is a professional accomplishment, and there is (slightly disconcerting) evidence that correlates facility in "F-shaped reading" with academic career success especially in scientific areas. High-flyers read more, read faster, and move on. However, there is also a hypothesis that less material is retained in this way and for a shorter time. The brain holds less and has less to marshal when it considers complex questions. The processing capacities of the screen-developed brain may also be more limited. This is connected to a familiar everyday phenomenon known as "look-it-up memory" wherein the handiness of mobile phones means that the bit of information required is within easy reach to the impairment of overall memory function. As the significance of bodily location in a web-based world diminishes, knowledge of virtual locatedness increases. Knowing where to find something, and not what it is, becomes more crucial. If memory was once metaphorically a library (a familiar analogy), it might now seem more like a traffic system. In this, to return to my imaginary, 21st-century version of Raymond Williams's book *Keywords* based on a massive, digitally gathered corpus, the human skills of analysis and knowing where significance lies seem more, not less, important.

We live in transitional times indeed, and it would be silly to pronounce confidently on a destination. In coming to terms with the digital revolution, there are widely acknowledged uncertainties attaching to the technology, and the infrastructure that sustains it. Assurances about the durability of hardware and software are disputed, and the rapid obsolescence of ever-updating equipment is a worry in terms of long-term storage as well as continued access. Lumber rooms in universities are stuffed with dusty machines of yesterday's design, all useless, and my desk drawers have floppy disks of Amstrad vintage among their clutter. Single-source dependencies are worrisome and sometimes regrettable: ask someone with a broken reading device on holiday. And there is little evidence of clear or sustained planning over matters such as creating national, let alone international, protocols for long-term repository management, curation, accessibility, and archiving policy. Lurking behind all this looms the question of cost. Such things cost big-time—very big-time. If you think about it, this is visible in micro-matters: who pays for software licences? For library subscriptions to periodicals? For IT maintenance? Those institutionally employed tend to take meeting these costs for granted.

It is also obvious that while web-based materials facilitate access, they do not eliminate exclusion or restriction. The desire to monetize information for gain, and not merely to meet cost, leads pretty quickly to the creation of paywalls, of subscription or facilitation fees, and to protracted disputes about copyright with the imposing power of tech-company giants and media conglomerates. The British Library has been locked in dispute with Rupert Murdoch's News International about charging for access to *The Times* newspaper archive which News International now owns, although it did not spend a penny creating it. The BL acquired its copies for public access purposes by public access means. Similarly, a high-profile case in the US arose in 2011 in response to Google's offer to digitize the collections of the Library of Congress, a dauntingly expensive undertaking probably beyond public means (Darnton, 2011). This offered to create more versatile and extensive access, but was likely to reintroduce Hereford-style virtual chains of "access denied" messages as control is yielded to a profit-orientated entity. (The celebrated book historian Robert Darnton was a leading figure in opposition to the proposal.)

The public good issues here are considerable and sometimes connected to not-entirely groundless anxieties about surveillance. What is being read, by whom and for what purpose, has always featured in library policies (reserved collections, special access rooms, under-the-counter books, publications with razored-out passages) and folklore. The literary critic John Sutherland, in his autobiography *The Boy Who Loved Books* (2007), notes that it was widely believed that the reading room of the public library in Colchester, where he grew up, always had a plainclothes policeman keeping an eye on readers, especially of the *Daily Worker* (Sutherland, 2007). But the scrutiny of what one is reading virtually requires no on-site Mr. Plod (what a boring job that would anyway have been). Nor is it explicitly acknowledged who is observing and for what purposes (which may be commercial). COVID has revealed the hunger for population-wide data. It has also revealed the already considerable but expanding appetite for reading on screen.

All times are ones of transition. It cannot be otherwise. The ways in which research is conducted, the fresh institutional relationships negotiated, the revolution in library services, the new opportunities for access, the glut of material exposed and available, and the new functionalities rubbing along with old skills—all of these trends are decades-long. We do not know how long the current COVID emergency will last but its impacts in this respect, I suspect, are those of acceleration. Much has been said about the transition to screen-based teaching in higher education, but this is but one part of a long-term transitional sequence which may be among the most important events of our time. Meanwhile, the questions it poses are many and mainly unresolved, as history always is.

References

Darnton, R., 2011. Google's Loss: The Public's Gain. New York Review. 28 April.

Manguel, A., 2006. The Library at Night. Yale UP, London.

Pater, W., 2021. The renaissance: studies in art and poetry. In: Fraser, H. (Ed.), The Collected Works of Walter Pater, vol. 1. Oxford University Press, Oxford (forthcoming).

Rylance, R., 2016. Literature and the Public Good. Oxford University Press, Oxford.

Sutherland, J., 2007. The Boy Who Loved Books: A Memoir. John Murray, London.

Williams, R., 1976. Keywords: A Vocabulary of Culture and Society. Fontana, London.

Williams, R., 1989. Culture is ordinary. In: Gable, R. (Ed.), Resources of Hope: Culture, Democracy, Socialism. Verso, London.

Library space and COVID-19: Re-thinking of place and re-designing of digital space

21

Evgenia Vassilakaki[a] and Valentini Moniarou-Papaconstantinou[b]
[a]European Insurance and Occupational Pensions Authority (EIOPA), Frankfurt, Germany,
[b]Dept. Archives, Library and Information Studies, University of West Attica, Athens, Greece

1 Introduction

Libraries have long been collection-centred organizations. Services developed and offered aimed to fulfill the specific requirements of the different types of collections stored in the library building (Wilders, 2017). The physical space left for users was merely intended for requesting, consulting, and reading printed material. Technological advances and the development of new educational tools and learning approaches gradually shifted the focus. Libraries recognized the need to transition from collection to connection, promoting innovation, co-creation, and proactive learning among users (Jochumsen et al., 2015). User participation and involvement, alongside user-driven innovation and co-creation, soon became the library's core underpinning value in user-centred approaches. This trend led to changes in information services offered as well as the interior design of libraries. Innovative new library buildings were built, such as the Tianjin Binhai Library, Qatar National Library, the National Library of Greece at Stavros, Niarchos Foundation Cultural Center, and the Oodi Library in Finland.

Now more than ever, libraries serve a diverse clientele which seeks sanctuary, privacy, information, assistance, social opportunities, and more. Libraries need to reflect whether or not they continue to be a safe space, where users "can feel secure and free to express themselves, learn, and achieve without censure or harm" (Wexelbaum, 2016), providing services and resources for everyone, without favor, prejudice, or discrimination.

A user-centred approach was adopted across all functions of a library with an unconscious distinction between physical and digital space. Digital information services were developed and offered with the use of online resources and relevant digital technology. This occurred alongside the reorganization and redesign of physical space according to users' information, social-interaction and learning needs.

Libraries, like all other organizations, had to physically lockdown because of COVID-19, adhering to measures issued and enforced globally in order to prevent the spread of the virus, though they continued offering their preexisting online information services. But what about all that library space? All those square metres that were designed and fitted out to address users' needs? All that digital equipment and special

Libraries, Digital Information, and COVID. https://doi.org/10.1016/B978-0-323-88493-8.00038-0

rooms and social interaction corners? And what about all those needs not satisfied because COVID shut the buildings? Above all, do libraries provide information, learning, and social environments digitally instead of in physical environments? This chapter aims to address these questions.

2   From space to place: An evolution

Over the last decade, there were significant developments and discussions about library space related to the construction of new, modern, eco-friendly, large-scale buildings designed by major architectural offices around the globe, with the active participation of user and library communities. The inauguration of prestigious library buildings made the front pages of well-known online newspapers and digital press rooms. People came in their hundreds to explore and use the new information services, overcrowding reading rooms, and maker spaces.

Much emphasis and energy were placed on different methods and techniques to capture user information needs. Techniques, approaches, and methodologies deriving from various disciplines such as marketing, management, communication, spatial theory, literacy, social constructionism, and so on were adopted as innovative ways of addressing users' emerging information needs and offering innovative services in newly designed spaces.

In particular, space-time and cognitive mapping techniques were used to track users' actions in space and time using mental mapping to delve into users' perceptions of physical space (Choy and Goh, 2016; Given and Leckie, 2003). Re-envisioning library functions and conducting outcomes/programmatic assessment were another way for space planning (Hanson and Abresch, 2016), while a "four-space" model puts the emphasis on experience, involvement, empowerment, and innovation with a view to creating an inspiration space, a learning space, a meeting space, and a performative space (Jochumsen et al., 2012; Ellis and Goodyear, 2016).

Research into the cumulative effect of space aimed to explore how physical environments could create communities; facilitate interaction between users of various backgrounds and with differing information needs; and record the activities in which users engage while spending time in the library. The focus was placed on users' experiences, characteristics, and types of activity that create place (Hanson and Abresch, 2016).

This "creation library" approach is a model that facilitates a place where media conveying information, knowledge, art, and entertainment are created through the use of a range of equipment and facilities. Authors, editors, performers, and other visual creators are assisted in their efforts by developing creative works, performances, and accommodating personal and/or group use (American Library Association, 2011).

Using persona descriptions to inform the design of library space entails the use of both qualitative and quantitative methods with a view to identifying user patterns, which are then developed into meaningful descriptions validated across the initial personas created (Zaugg, 2016). These are some of the approaches, models, and methodologies used and developed to inform the design of library space to achieve user-centric missions, personal well-being, work productivity, and, most importantly, a sense of community among the various user groups.

Once experiences, information needs, interactions, and activities are recorded, these are then reflected in the architectural and interior design of library space. The architecture ought to be open and flexible and reflect concepts such as "library as place," "library as platform" (Andrews et al., 2016), facilitating e-learning, m-learning (mobile), u-learning (ubiquitous), and virtual learning (Hanson and Abresch, 2016) by providing the necessary equipment and dedicated space.

Modern libraries accommodate various spaces such as (a) reading rooms, (b) computer areas, (c) seminar rooms for offering different types of information literacy programme, (d) quiet areas for individual study (which may be overlooked or considered outdated), (e) collaborative space, (f) sanctuary space, (g) interaction space, (h) community space, (i) maker spaces, (j) conference rooms, (k) exhibition areas, (l) events areas, and (m) performative spaces (Jochumsen et al., 2015). The aforementioned list is not meant to be exhaustive but rather indicative of the variety of information needs these spaces aim to address. These are a series of interactive environments where users can express themselves, work collaboratively or individually, and fulfill their information, learning, and social needs. Such spaces need to be flexible and fluid in nature allowing users to shift "personas" depending on need. The library identity is hidden mainly within the clientele information needs and environment requirements (internal and external) they serve. Elements such as the technology used, hours/access, study areas, aesthetics, and amenities are especially important in addressing today's user information needs (Hirschbiel and Petzold, 2016; Ojennus and Watts, 2017). Andrews et al. (2016) elegantly pointed out that "the library has become a central location for users to connect with and learn from one another, create and remix with its resources and infrastructure, display and discuss their work, and capture and preserve community knowledge."

All these methodologies and techniques aimed to capture users' information needs in terms of specific space utilization. Attention was placed on accommodating various types of studying and learning processes (in large groups, in small groups, for individual study and so on) in order to increase users' productivity; facilitate student/teacher exchange outside the classroom; encourage lifelong learning; and keep a realistic ratio between quiet and collaborative study space. In the context of enriching users' educational experiences, libraries created space dedicated to performing art assignments (music, theatre, radio) and thus increasing social interaction, learning, productivity, and co-creation. In the era of social distancing and contactless communication, how can libraries transform their physical space into digital and address users' relevant information needs?

3 Library space and COVID-19: Place versus digital space

Social distancing and digital interaction are the "new normal": the new way of communicating, interacting, learning, doing business, and socializing in the era of COVID-19. Libraries need to realize this change: a change that is here to stay for a long time and thus alter the way we work, live, interact, learn, and socialize. As many challenges are posed regarding the opening of physical space (implementing additional hygiene and cleaning measures for space and collections, limiting the number of users in different areas, controlling entrance and exit, making appointment arrangements for visiting the premises, controlling the time spent in the library), libraries need to adjust to change.

Like other professionals, librarians reacted quickly, shifting to teleworking and promoting existing online information services through all available channels (website, social media accounts, e-learning platforms). These information services consisted of "traditional" digital services: providing access to e-journals, e-books, databases, and material from digital libraries and institutional repositories. In addition, libraries supported online requests for digitization and online distribution of material when copyright was not an obstacle. Content was used and promoted through digital platforms (Graff et al., 2019; EBLIDA, 2020).

Libraries developed and promoted additional online information literacy programmes and courses to address the growing digital information needs of their users. At the same time, there was a need to enhance the digital skills and competencies of users of all ages. Responding to the growing need for information on the new virus, its symptoms, treatments, vaccines, and concomitant lockdown measures, libraries put together and provided lists with information and e-resources concerning COVID-19 and recent developments. The library's role in providing information, instructions, and guidelines on how to identify fake news during the pandemic proved to be especially important. Libraries developed and distributed online quick checklists on how to identify, judge, and report fake news, as published and shared on social media.

When the first wave subsided and the number of new cases and casualties started to fall, libraries attempted to reopen their buildings. This proved challenging because space had to be reworked and rearranged to reduce the risk of creating crowds. This took a much effort but the solutions did not last long because soon the second wave of the pandemic followed and libraries had to close once more (EBLIDA, 2020).

What happens then to the thousands of square metres of space? The notion of library as "third place" becomes more relevant than ever. Arguments regarding the reasons why a user would visit a library, especially now, when all material and information needed is online become stronger than ever (Montgomery and Miller, 2011; Gray et al., 2018; Pierard et al., 2016). In an era of physical distancing and teleworking, of e-learning and e-socializing, libraries need to rethink their core objective of serving as a meeting place for collaborative learning and community interaction and engagement. This core value needs to transition to a digital space, with innovative features and characteristics that will foster interaction, engagement, and collaboration.

In this context, it is important for libraries to explore new ways of addressing online users' information needs as they previously related to the various physical spaces (social interaction, community engagement, performing activities) but in a digital context. The main challenge that users must overcome with social distancing and lockdown is missing your friends; it relates to real-life interaction: socializing, community building, and small talk engagement. Aspects of these activities and interactions were provided by the different physical spaces in the libraries. The element of group learning, social communication and interaction, and group engagement in social and educational events as well as networking are important and cannot be covered simply by offering digital available resources.

Libraries need to create "digital space" in the same way they provided "physical space." They have all the know-how, techniques, methodologies, and relevant tools for developing, promoting, and offering collaborative, interactive, and engaging digital spaces that will allow and facilitate: group reading and learning; interactive collaboration, communication, and engagement in performing and other social activities; networking and sharing information; and assisting creative activities through use of innovative services and tools.

The global digital gap is wide. Libraries need to collaborate with public authorities and private organizations and business on approaches to fostering access to necessary equipment (personal computers, tablets, smartphones) and Internet connections (Wifi to all households). There will also be a need for training in the use of these technologies and tools through the development of focused information literacy programmes to equip users across ages, ethnicities, and cultures with the necessary skills for the new digital era.

A few years ago, there was the notion of "second life." Technology was developed and tested but projects lost momentum because of the lack of the widespread adoption of relevant equipment and necessary digital skills. "Second life" included important elements of social interaction, community building, and user engagement in social and learning contexts, and, most importantly, it was built on a "digital space." Today, when there is a need for people to continue learning and interacting, despite social distancing, these technologies and others seem more relevant than ever.

So far, libraries have used digital space only for promoting their digital information services through social media and using conference platforms for hosting webinars. Digital library space now needs to embrace the notion of place, where a user can book a quiet room for studying, having at the same time access to all online resources; meet virtually with classmates to work on assignments and with teachers to ask for further guidance and assistance; ask the librarian; take part in online conferences and webinars; take part in performing activities; and socialize and interact with user groups.

Libraries should reflect on their existing methodologies and techniques, but now apply them to a virtual/digital environment. Basic elements in the design of physical space such as co-construction and user engagement in the design process are now more relevant than ever. Libraries ought to create a single digital point of entry to the digital space of all offered services and resources to their clientele.

4 Conclusion

Libraries are more relevant than ever in the time of COVID. The extent to which this is obvious to our users across borders and across countries, languages, and cultures is unclear; however, in a globalized world, are libraries perceived and valued the same way in different countries? Do the services now being offered reflect all relevant and necessary information needs?

We have the means, the knowledge, and the know-how to address and fulfill users' information needs; however, these must be applied in a virtual, digital environment, accommodating in an effective and efficient way users' social interactions and overall learning needs.

Only libraries that adjust to the likely new normal will maintain and increase their user base. In these challenging times, when libraries—as physical space—need to close down to prevent a further spread of the virus, they need to create and sustain their digital presence.

It is apparent that the role of digital space coordinator, information provider, IT specialist, or information literacy provider is more relevant than ever. New roles will replace traditional ones; additional digital skills and competences will be sought to help people respond to the challenges posed; and open and flexible management and staff professional development, and the re-organization of management structures to more agile models, are needed urgently. Librarians must become more familiar not only with planning, architecture, and interior design, but also with elements such as IT design and systems thinking, corporate change management, organizational strategic planning, risk assessment, and business continuity.

References

American Library Association, 2011. Confronting the Future: Strategic Visions for the 21st Century Public Library. American Library Association, Washington, DC.

Andrews, C., Downs, A., Morris-Knower, J., Pacion, K., Wright, S.E., 2016. From "library as place" to "library as platform": redesigning the 21st century academic library. In: The Future of Library Space. Advances in Library Administration and Organization, vol. 36, pp. 145–167.

Choy, F., Goh, S.N., 2016. A framework for planning academic library spaces. Libr. Manag. 37 (1/2).

EBLIDA, 2020. A European Library Agenda for Post COVID-19 Era. http://www.eblida.org/Documents/EBLIDA-Preparing-a-European-library-agenda-for-the-post-COVID-19-age.pdf. (Accessed 17 November 2020).

Ellis, R.A., Goodyear, P., 2016. Models of learning space: integrating research on space, place and learning in higher education. Rev. Educ. 4 (2), 149–191.

Given, L.M., Leckie, G.J., 2003. 'Sweeping' the library: mapping the social activity space of the public library. Libr. Inf. Sci. Res. 25 (4), 365–385. available at: https://doi.org/10.1016/S0740-8188(03)00049-5.

Graff, T.C., Ridge, R.D., Zaugg, H., 2019. A space for every student: assessing the utility of a family friendly study room in a university library. J. Libr. Admin. https://doi.org/10.1080/01930826.2019.1626650.

Gray, J.M., Burel, M., Graser, M., Gallacci, K., 2018. Applying Spatial Literacy to Transform Library Space: A Selected Literature Review. vol. 87 SIUE Faculty Research, Scholarship, and Creative Activity, pp. 1–19 (1) https://spark.siue.edu/siue_fac/87?utm_source=spark.siue.edu%2Fsiue_fac%2F87&utm_medium=PDF&utm_campaign=PDFCoverPages.

Hanson, A., Abresch, J., 2016. Socially constructing library as place and space. In: The Future of Library Space. Advances in Library Administration and Organization, vol. 36, pp. 103–129.

Hirschbiel, M.C., Petzold, J., 2016. A space for everyone and everyone in the space: re-designing existing library space to inspire collaboration. In: The Future of Library Space. Advances in Library Administration and Organization, vol. 36, pp. 253–283.

Jochumsen, H., Rasmussen, C.H., Skot-Hansen, D., 2012. The four spaces: a new model for the public library. New Libr. World 113 (11/12), 586597. https://doi.org/10.1108/03074801211282948.

Jochumsen, H., Skot-Hansen, D., Rasmussen, C.H., 2015. Towards culture 3.0—performative space in the public library. Int. J. Cult. Policy 23 (4). https://doi.org/10.1080/10286632.2015.1043291.

Montgomery, S., Miller, J., 2011. The Third Place: The Library as Collaborative and Community Space in a Time of Fiscal Restraint. Faculty Publications, p. 32. http://scholarship.rollins.edu/as_facpub/32.

Ojennus, P., Watts, K.A., 2017. User preferences and library space at Whitworth University Library. J. Librariansh. Inf. Sci. 49 (3), 320–334.

Pierard, C., Shoup, J., Clement, S.K., Emmons, M., Neely, T.Y., Wilkinson, F.C., 2016. Building back better libraries: improving planning amidst disasters. In: The Future of Library Space. Advances in Library Administration and Organization, vol. 36, pp. 307–333.

Wexelbaum, R., 2016. The library as safe space. In: The Future of Library Space. Advances in Library Administration and Organization, vol. 36. Emerald Group Publishing Limited.

Wilders, C., 2017. Predicting the role of library bookshelves in 2025. J. Acad. Librariansh. 43 (5), 384–391.

Zaugg, H., 2016. Using persona descriptions to inform library space design. In: The Future of Library Space. Advances in Library Administration and Organization, vol. 36, pp. 1–22.

Online misinformation, its influence on the student body, and institutional responsibilities

Andy Phippen[a] and Emma Bond[b]
[a]Bournemouth University, Bournemouth, United Kingdom, [b]University of Suffolk, Ipswich, United Kingdom

1 Introduction

At the time of writing, in the United Kingdom, the opposition party (BBC News, 2020a) has just made a call for social media platforms to prevent the spreading of "antivax" misinformation and the need to "stamp out" such information. They argued that emergency laws would hold platforms responsible should they fail to take down false stories about emerging COVID-19 vaccination programmes. Platforms, they stated, should be held financially and criminally liable if they fail in their *duty of care* to remove such information.

The COVID pandemic has accelerated concerns about the impact of misinformation on society, emerging from an era of "posttruth" and "fake news" where there is much concern about information with no basis in fact and the use of digital platforms to deliver it. And while the roots of both fake news and posttruth lie in politics and political rhetoric (Rochlin, 2017) (fake news, in particular, moving into the public consciousness as a result of its repeated use by politicians on both sides of the Atlantic), misinformation extends far beyond those worlds to impact on society as a whole. The COVID pandemic has rapidly increased concerns about misinformation because, frankly, misinformation about a pandemic can be incredibly dangerous. During the pandemic, many examples of misinformation that has surfaced via social media (Brennen et al., 2020). To look specifically at COVID-19 misinformation:

- COVID-19 is fake and being used by governments to control populations
- COVID-19 is being spread by the rollout of 5G networks
- Wearing masks to prevent the spread of COVID-19 reduces blood oxygen levels in the wearer
- COVID-19 vaccines will alter your DNA
- COVID-19 is being used to encourage vaccination programmes, and the vaccine contains a microchip developed by Bill Gates that will result in the mind control of the population so as to be controlled by the New World Order.

Arguably, the COVID-19 pandemic has been the perfect vehicle for an acceleration of misinformation due to the complexity and need for *hard* information to be able to understand it fully, resulting in a moral panic. Stanley Cohen's seminal work (Cohen, 2002) considered how media discourse can be used to fire up social concerns about

Libraries, Digital Information, and COVID. https://doi.org/10.1016/B978-0-323-88493-8.00029-X

things of which mainstream culture has little knowledge. We can consider the foundations of Cohen's exploration around how *traditional* media might create panic among a population based upon the complexity of the issues, and how digital platforms might accelerate these concerns. Cohen defined three core aspects of a representation of a moral panic. The panic must be:

1. *new* (alien to the population and difficult to recognize, "creeping up on the moral horizon"), but also *old* (relating to traditions and historical stories);
2. *damaging*, but also *warning signs* for real danger;
3. *transparent* (out in the open for everyone to see) but also *opaque*, requiring detailed explanation from experts to make people aware of the "real harm."

In examining the COVID pandemic, this is a perfect storm for a moral panic:

1. While the virus itself is new, we have a history of how to deal with pandemics in the past (e.g., the often quoted "Spanish flu") and the damage they cause;
2. The early reporting on COVID-19 clearly showed the harm in a very visual manner;
3. While there is a great visibility in the media, and social media, about the impact of COVID-19, to actually understand the pandemic, epidemiology, and vaccination requires detailed scientific knowledge that is complex.

As a result of the complexity, and need for criticality in understanding the information about the pandemic, there is undoubtedly a need for easy answers, which can be made available quickly and easily on social media. The pandemic has had an impact on everybody's everyday lives, and, arguably, if people need to find answers to justify these impacts, and the hard-scientific information is complex, difficult to understand and does not have easy answers, social media, and peer information, might provide these answers *we are looking for*, rather than the answers *we need to hear*. Often referred to as confirmation bias (Nickerson, 1998), we can observe that social media provides the means to access information from any perspective on a given topic. The lack of regulation of platforms means that, within legal boundaries, users are welcome to publish whatever they wish. Within the "echo chambers" (Flaxman et al., 2016) in which most social media users exist, they will be drawn to information, regardless of factual accuracy, that will align with personal belief systems. Therefore, it will confirm what they think, regardless of whether the information they are consuming has a basis in fact or evidence. A cursory examination of hashtags such as #kbf (Keep Britain Free) and, until recently, #Q (Zuckerman, 2019), illustrate these echo chambers in effect. #kbf, in particular, can be seen to emerge from the increasing restriction of civil liberties as a means to control the spread of COVID in the United Kingdom.

While there are some libertarian arguments for the allowing of posting anything online (within legal boundaries) (Bambauer and Bambauer, 2017) which are legitimate, and the infamous section 230 of the Communications Decency Act 1996 in the United States (Sheridan, 1997) absolves platforms of any responsibility for what is published on their platforms (and in doing so, limits the potential for any UK opposition party's attempts to make them criminally responsible for what is posted), the increasing evidence base around the impact of misinformation during the pandemic is clear to see. For example, during the pandemic, we have seen attacks on telecommunications engineers installing 5G masts (Hearn, 2020), shop workers spat on for asking people to wear masks in stores (Iqbal, 2020), and "antimask" protests where the violent demonstration took place (BBC News, 2020b). We have also observed through this pandemic that, to return to Cohen's formulae, transparent but opaque information is sometimes a challenge when the evidence presented is being used to justify a temporary removal of what a citizen might refer to as civil liberties. Why would someone attempt to unpick complex scientific data when it is being used to justify something you disagree with? Far better, it would seem, to find alternative sources of information that justify your refusal to engage with these requests.

As a result of the social disruption underpinned with misinformation, we have seen evidence of a challenge in itself to scientific data, mathematical modelling, and the use of evidence in policy forming. There are many examples of media reporting debunking the scientific methods (Hussain, 2020; Boyd and Robinson, 2020; Johnston, 2020) and being critical of the contradictory nature and complexity of academic enquiry— the view given from this narrative is that we need answers that are clear, we do not need scientists telling us the future is uncertain and models are predictive rather than accurate. If scientists cannot provide us with clear simple answers, we have no interest in looking at complex data.

Clearly, misinformation is a problem for society as a whole, and the UK Government's Online Harms agenda (UK Government, 2020a) lists misinformation (referred to as "disinformation" in the policy documentation) as a potential, and poorly defined online harm. We are seeing, particularly through recent COVID reports and the US election, social media platforms starting to tag misinformation to inform end users that what has been posted is factually inaccurate, disputed, or incorrect. In some cases, there is automated takedown, and reporting has also become more transparent and clearer that concerns will be dealt with. Certainly, there is a need for society as a whole to engage in "upskilling" in recognizing misinformation and its harms, and knowing how to respond to it. Nevertheless, in a volume about the impact of COVID-19 on libraries and digital information, we should pose the question—Is this something that should be of concern for institutions, and what can be done about it?

2   Higher education and misinformation

By way of illustration, we present a scenario experienced by one of the authors who recently delivered a class to students, entitled "Is Alexa Listening to You?" The opening premise implied that an Amazon Echo is a device that sits in your kitchen constantly listening to conversations, recording everything, sharing information with companies, and generally being a massive surveillance risk. We went on to ask for a show of hands regarding how many people in the room had spoken to a friend on the phone and then saw adverts in their social media feed related to the conversation (most in the room claimed to have experienced this). As the lecture progressed, the narrative actually explored students' propensity to buy into myth and rumour, without investigating on their own or exploring what is claimed. Taking things at face value, one can see that speaking to a friend on the phone, and then seeing an advert might imply a correlation. However, as we discussed, a topic of conversation with a friend related to a type of product might also suggest this was on the individual's mind and perhaps they also search from this type of product? Perhaps, it was proposed, it was more likely that the information sharing did not occur as a result of the algorithmic process of voice data, but by sharing search history, which the individual had consented to when signing up for their Google account?

Within the lecture, we explored online misinformation, with a focus on a number of themes such as the mocking of far-right protests in London that used photoshopped images to imply illiteracy and incontinence, the use of "fake news" narratives online by the 45th US President, and a detailed exploration of the @SouthLoneStar twitter account (Burgess, 2017), and its tweets during the Westminster Bridge terrorist attack in the United Kingdom in 2017. While the account is now well established as being one of a number of Russian troll accounts, the name and imagery in the account imply the user is what one might refer to as an "American patriot." The tweets that attracted the most public attention at the time centred on a photograph of an Islamic woman walking past a crowd treating someone who had been injured in the attack. A particular tweet that stated, alongside this image, "the main difference between Muslims and Christians #PrayForLondon #Parliament #Westminster" was used to show the type of discourse presented by the account. The question was posed "what is the nationality of the poster of these tweets?" to which most of the class, after some discussion, stated that they were clearly American. When asked why they thought this they claimed that the name of the account (Texas Lone Star), handle (@SouthLoneStar), and profile image (a male in a Stetson hat) all suggested this was an American, and the Christian discourse in the post would align with this belief. When they were told this was actually an account from a Russian troll farm this was generally met with surprise by the students, and prompted a discussion on why "bots" and troll farms exist, and that we should not always believe what is presented at face value online. We continued by exploring how we make judgements about online resources and their quality, and it was generally believed that if something is shared a lot by the like-minded individual, this in some way makes it higher quality than something with few likes or shares. However, with some examples of misinformation and how it manipulates these expectations, at the end of the session most were of the view that, regardless of rumours they had heard and things they had read online, it was unlikely that Alexa was listening to them.

However, at the end of the session, a student approached the author. "But it's true," said the student, "devices do listen to your conversations and share that data with online platforms." The student went on to explain something that happened to him last year regarding arranging a meeting with his academic mentor, whom he had never met and, he stated, had only ever conversed with on the phone. After arranging, on the phone, to meet the mentor, the student noticed that his mentor then appeared as a potential Facebook friend. This, he claimed, proved that his phone was listening to him, interpreting the voice data, and sharing said data with Facebook, who then made use of that data to send him a friend recommendation.

However, the question was asked whether he had ever emailed the mentor. "Oh yes, he replied, I did once." We then explored the fact that the University used a cloud-based US email provider whom, one might assume, would have data-sharing agreements with social media platforms, and the student was consented to this data sharing when signing up for the email account. This, perhaps, was a more logical reason for the friend recommendation than his phone listening to him. Nevertheless, here was a belief developed from *somewhere* that phones listen in to conversations, and this was clearly shared with his peers (given most of the class believed this was true).

With a dearth of education in the statutory sector around what we might refer to as critical digital literacy (see later), why would we expect students to be aware of this particularly digital phenomenon? In order to appreciate this scenario at a technical level, there is a need to understand what cloud-based systems are, understand how email systems work, and aggregate data and the data-sharing agreements that exist between "Internet giants" (and how we consent to them when we sign up to these platforms after clicking the "yes" box regarding agreeing to the terms and conditions we did not read).

There is much assumed knowledge when it comes to digital literacy, as though we make the prejudiced assumption that because people use digital technology to communicate, they know how it works. An analogy we frequently use is that of the motor car—while many people are capable of driving a car, far fewer are knowledgeable about the functioning of the internal combustion engine. However, the analogy tends to fail when we consider that in order to drive a car, the user must at least have their knowledge and capabilities tested. This is certainly not the case with digital technology, even though, as we have described earlier, irresponsible use of digital technology can certainly result in harm to others.

Moreover, there is much problematic discourse around the assumed knowledge of students prior to arriving at university (Phippen et al., 2020). Sometimes, unhelpfully referred to as "digital natives" (Prensky, 2001), a theory that because someone was born in an era where digital technology was ubiquitous, they had some innate ability to engage with it with capabilities that are missing from previous generations (again, generalized as "digital immigrants"). While this crude generalization is now widely debunked (e.g., Helsper and Eynon, 2010), its use still pervades in popular discourse and we have certainly been in attendance at seminars and workshops around students and digital literacy where senior speakers, from government and regulators, have spoken of this generation of students being natives capable of navigating the digital world without further support.

This assumption is further compounded with a belief that because there are statutory requirements from the school sector to deliver education around online safety and digital literacy, all students would have received instruction and learned about critical approaches to engaging with digital information. However, this is certainly not the case with evidence to show that both staff education, and online safety education, being delivered extremely inconsistently across the country (Phippen, 2016). Furthermore, statutory guidance (UK Government, 2020b) centres on the delivery of education to ensure young people are "safe" online, not learners who engage with information resources with an open mind and critical approach. This is unlikely to change in the immediate future—in the United Kingdom, the focus of policy remains on the prevention of online harms and an expectation that social media providers are technically capable of preventing these harms from manifesting (which, we might argue, demonstrates the technical knowledge and critical thinking capabilities of those who define policy). While mis(*dis*)information is defined in the policy white paper (and therefore legislative intention), the focus is on its elimination rather than how to address it at a critical level. There seems to be no legislative intention to strengthen compulsory curriculum to encompass critical digital literacy more wholly across UK schools.

We would argue that the rise in misinformation, its availability, and prevalence are potentially more harmful than those things we might propose as more direct online harms and it pervades across society as a whole and has the potential to cause civil disobedience and unrest. While online harms directed at the individual are clearly unacceptable and victims should have protection in law, there is less potential for social disruption as a result of something, like revenge pornography or cyberbullying than there is from a coordinated campaign of destabilization and misinformation.

This is not something that universities can ignore. We cannot assume that students will arrive at our institutions with inbuilt knowledge to be critical thinkers around digital information. We would argue that the academy has a responsibility to develop students to realize this goal—to be able to engage with information resources, then to judge them critically, to look for different viewpoints, and to provide evidence around the opinions that are forming. However, literature suggests that when it comes to the trust of information resources, particularly those online, the converse is true (e.g., Bråten et al., 2011; Hargittai et al., 2010). In Bråten et al. (2011), the authors propose that if a student is not already knowledgeable about a subject, they are more likely to trust less reliable information sources, and they will also rely on peers to understand a topic—an implied confirmation bias among peers to service the knowledge gap. This was reinforced by Leeder (2019) who researched how skilled students were at detecting "fake news" stories, and by McNeill (2018) who showed the reliance on the echo chamber in developing one's knowledge. There is certainly sufficient evidence in the literature to show that much work still needs to be done.

3 Misinformation and the academy

John Stuart Mill, frequently quoted about the role of higher education, is, perhaps, relevant here:

> *The object of universities is not to make skilful lawyers, physicians or engineers. It is to make capable and cultivated human beings.*

As an aside, amidst a discussion on misinformation, while this quotation is frequently referred to in both popular and academic publications, it is rarely correctly cited. The actual comment comes from his inaugural speech at St Andrews in 1867 (Mill, 1867), and the popular comment is misquoted. The full quote is actually more germane to our discussions:

The proper function of an University in national education is tolerably well understood. At least there is a tolerably general agreement about what an University is not. It is not a place of professional education. Universities are not intended to teach the knowledge required to fit men for some special mode of gaining their livelihood. Their object is not to make skilful lawyers, or physicians, or engineers, but capable and cultivated human beings.

The quote is frequently used to illustrate that universities should not merely take the arguably neoliberal perspective of return on investment and the value of the graduate to the economy (Olssen and Peters, 2005). There is arguably a current prevailing political view that universities are the lynchpin in the knowledge economy to produce workers who are capable of delivering the professions needed to realize fiscal value in the postindustrial world. We might argue that there has been, with some disciplines, a move to produce a skilled employee, rather than a critical thinker, and as a result perhaps lost sight of the value of the "capable and cultivated human being" in any industry.

We have certainly observed, in our calls for more effective critical digital literacy in university education, counterarguments that state this would have a detrimental impact on the "career-aligned" curriculum because "we would have to remove some subject content to put this in." This is, we would argue, failing to realize Mill's vision of higher education and render the academy little more than a training agency. In focusing too closely on employability metrics, do we risk missing the fact that effective critical thinking which, in the connected world, requires strong digital literacy skills, is now fundamental to any career, and, indeed, more generally for liberal society as a whole?

There is a necessity to extend the perception of digital literacy from early definitions that considered the essentials of how we might interact with emergent, interconnected, digital media (Gilster and Glister, 1997), toward what Buckingham (2010) referred to as cultural understanding within the digital space. Recently, considerable emphasis has been placed on developing students' digital skills. However, digital literacy is not merely expecting students to be capable of using the IT systems with which we provide them to deliver their education on the 21st-century campus, it is getting them to appreciate the role of digital technology in society and how to effectively assess information in order to be able to judge its worth and its evidential underpinnings, and, in the connected world, whether there is value or harm in the sharing of this information. Digital literacy is not simply limited to the need for technical knowledge by those who wish to work in Science, Technology, Engineering, and Mathematical (STEM) subjects.

Within higher education, we have a justified obsession with the peer-reviewed process and its rigour in determining whether information is worthy of publication. While there are some discussions regarding the fairness of the peer review (Jefferson et al., 2002) and its efficacy at preventing the publication of misinformation, it is generally viewed as the best approach we have at determining quality in information being published. Even in the open access publication drive that has occurred as a result, in part, to the online world, there is still a need for review, it is not free for all where any information is published and the quality will rise to the top.

We would argue that the peer-reviewed process is more important than ever. While printed publishing had hard limits in terms of the volume of information that could be produced, we no longer live in that world. Information storage is cheap, and information dissemination is immediate. In this world of infinite information, it is easy to find something that agrees with your viewpoint, but that does not necessarily make it a good thing. In an online world, where we are all able to be publishers, the need for critical review of information to benchmark quality is even more important.

Yet there is sometimes a disconnect between what we do as researchers and what we do as teachers. While the importance of peer review is crucial in the research process, it seems that sometimes the importance of this rigour is poorly articulated. If we are to consider critical thinking in digital literacy—be able to understand the nature of the information with which you have been presented, its sources, its implied biases, and its evidence base—this, surely, ties into the more established principles of accurate citation and referencing in order to provide evidence when making an argument in academic writing.

This is something we already encourage in the student body but perhaps fail in our duties in articulating effectively why this needs to be done. The penalties for plagiarism are high. It is disappointing that we have both experienced many conversations with students about the use of referencing which illustrates that they do not fully appreciate why they are doing it. With many comments like "all they taught me at university was to use Harvard referencing and write essays" perhaps highlights the failings of the sector to articulate the rationale for this. We have also spoken with many students who are anxious about getting referencing "right." But this generally focuses on whether they have formatted the reference, or in-text citation, correctly, and captioned a quotation effectively. Perhaps, again, we are assuming that students already know what this aspect of critical thinking is for, and therefore, we do not have to explain it to them. However, once an explanation is given about the use of different sources to underpin arguments, to not state opinion as fact, and to not take credit for someone else's work and the value of rigour in presenting evidence, they will generally more effectively engage with the critical debate, as they appreciate its nature. Using referencing effectively is not a pointless academic exercise; it is a practical embodiment of critical thinking. To return to Mill's speech:

> *What professional men should carry away with them from an University, is not professional knowledge, but that which should direct the use of their professional knowledge, and bring the light of general culture to illuminate the technicalities of a special pursuit. Men may be competent lawyers without general education, but it depends on general education to make them philosophic lawyers who demand, and are capable of apprehending, principles, instead of merely cramming their memory with details.*

What we are arguing here is that critical digital literacy, the sort of knowledge that allows critical inquiry with online information resources, is part of what Mill referred to, over 150 years ago, as the "general education" that is provided by universities.

The separation of critical digital literacy and critical argument in academic writing is a false one and falls, once again, into the trap of taking the view that because something is online, it needs to be treated differently—as if because the information lies online rather than in a printed tome, it does not require the same scrutiny. We are often faced with comments such as "well, it's different online," yet we fail to see what it should be. In our rush to defend the curriculum from attack by "irrelevant" key skills, we are failing to appreciate the broad and important nature of being able to use digital information critically.

As we have discussed in the previous work (Phippen et al., 2020), there are some essential questions that need to be posed for any information source:

- From where did you source the information?
- Who was the author?
- Is there any means to check the validity of their claims they make?
- Are you referring to it correctly?
- Are you presenting the information as fact or opinion?

We might add, in terms of making judgments on misinformation, further questions around who shared the information, how frequently it is shared, and whether the sharer actually is human or bot. As we have discussed previously related to the *SouthLoneStar* fake account, it is not just the authenticity of the information that should be judged, but also the legitimacy of the sharer themselves.

However, these additional steps are surely just a logical extension of general education—making general education fit into a connected world, where information sources are as likely to come from a peer than a credible media source and the need to appreciate how information is formed, disseminated, and consumed online are essential skills for any capable and cultivated citizen in the global, connected, society, not just those who wish to have STEM careers.

4 Conclusion

In a text that is considering how COVID has impacted on libraries and digital information, we would argue that COVID has become a moral panic that acted as a catalyst to accelerate an acceptance of fake news and misinformation as we locked down and became more reliant on digital connections and life online. While there is clear evidence that fake news and misinformation have existed for a long time prior to the pandemic, we have seen a focus on the impact of misinformation on both academic evidence and society as a whole. Put simply, misinformation can result in physical harm; it is not a concept where harm remains in the virtual world.

We have explored the nature of misinformation arising from the pandemic and also presented an empirical scenario to illustrate the unmatched expectations for critical thinking among the student body and how misinformation can underpin opinions that can be justified with lazy inquiry. Universities cannot assume that critical digital literacy will have been achieved prior to students arriving at the (physical and virtual) institutions and, moreover, one might argue that the development of critical thinking about digital information has a role in the general education that universities should provide.

If we are to do nothing, the rise of misinformation will continue. We have seen its impact during the COVID pandemic and the very real damage it can do to both society in general and also to the reputation of rigorous information and scientific inquiry. A UK politician, during the Brexit debates, was quoted as saying "people have had enough of experts" (Deacon, 2016). We would suggest that it is imperative that universities fight back against a mistrust of fact and produce graduates capable of being critical citizens and arguing from a basis of fact and evidence, not conjecture.

References

Bambauer, J.R., Bambauer, D.E., 2017. Information libertarianism. Calif. L. Rev. 105, 335.

BBC News, 2020a. Covid-19: stop anti-vaccination fake news online with new law says Labour. BBC News. 15 November https://www.bbc.co.uk/news/uk-politics-54947661.

BBC News, 2020b. Covid: London anti-lockdown protest leads to 104 arrests. BBC News. 5 November https://www.bbc.co.uk/news/uk-england-london-54827535.

Boyd, C., Robinson, M., 2020. 'SAGE was put on a pedestal... but their models clearly didn't reflect reality': Tory MP slams scientific advisers as damning documentary reveals they relied on WIKIPEDIA data and wrongly predicted virus would peak in June. Daily Mail. 19 November https://www.dailymail.co.uk/news/article-8961245/SAGE-used-dodgy-data-WIKIPEDIA-model-Covid-crisis-spring-BBC-documentary-reveals.html.

Bråten, I., Strømsø, H.I., Salmerón, L., 2011. Trust and mistrust when students read multiple information sources about climate change. Learn. Instr. 21 (2), 180–192.

Brennen, J.S., Simon, F., Howard, P.N., Nielsen, R.K., 2020. Types, Sources, and Claims of COVID-19 Misinformation. Reuters Institute, pp. 1–13. 7.

Buckingham, D., 2010. Defining digital literacy. In: Medienbildung in neuen Kulturräumen. VS Verlag für Sozialwissenschaften, pp. 59–71.

Burgess, M., 2017. Here's the first evidence Russia used Twitter to influence Brexit. Wired. 10 November https://www.wired.co.uk/article/brexit-russia-influence-twitter-bots-internet-research-agency.

Cohen, S., 2002. Folk Devils and Moral Panics: The Creation of the Mods and Rockers. Psychology Press.

Deacon, M., 2016. EU referendum: who needs experts when we've got Michael Gove? The Daily Telegraph. 6 June https://www.telegraph.co.uk/news/2016/06/06/eu-referendum-who-needs-experts-when-weve-got-michael-gove/.

Flaxman, S., Goel, S., Rao, J.M., 2016. Filter bubbles, echo chambers, and online news consumption. Public Opin. Q. 80 (S1), 298–320.

Gilster, P., Glister, P., 1997. Digital Literacy. Wiley Computer Pub., New York.

Hargittai, E., Fullerton, L., Menchen-Trevino, E., Thomas, K.Y., 2010. Trust online: young adults' evaluation of web content. Int. J. Commun. 4, 27.

Hearn, A., 2020. 5G conspiracy theories fuel attacks on telecoms workers. The Guardian. 7 May https://www.theguardian.com/business/2020/may/07/5g-conspiracy-theories-attacks-telecoms-covid.

Helsper, E.J., Eynon, R., 2010. Digital natives: where is the evidence? Br. Educ. Res. J. 36 (3), 503–520.

Hussain, D., 2020. Revealed: Chilling government graphs showing second wave deaths soaring above May's peak in weeks 'were WRONG' and were secretly toned down after being used to justify new lockdown. Daily Mail. 6 November https://www.dailymail.co.uk/news/article-8919913/Chilling-government-graphs-showing-second-wave-deaths-soaring-Mays-peak-WRONG.html.

Iqbal, N., 2020. Coughed on, spat at: UK shop workers fear asking customers to wear masks. The Guardian. 13 September https://www.theguardian.com/world/2020/sep/13/coughed-on-spat-at-uk-shop-workers-fear-asking-customers-to-wear-masks.

Jefferson, T., Alderson, P., Wager, E., Davidoff, F., 2002. Effects of editorial peer review: a systematic review. JAMA 287 (21), 2784–2786.

Johnston, L., 2020. UK lockdown was a 'monumental mistake' and must not happen again—Boris scientist says. Daily Express. 26 August https://www.express.co.uk/life-style/health/1320428/Coronavirus-news-lockdown-mistake-second-wave-Boris-Johnson.

Leeder, C., 2019. How college students evaluate and share 'fake news' stories. Libr. Inf. Sci. Res. 41 (3), 100967.

McNeill, L.S., 2018. 'My friend posted it and that's good enough for me!': source perception in online information sharing. J. Am. Folk. 131 (522), 493–499.

Mill, J.S., 1867. Inaugural Address: Delivered to the University of St. Andrews, Feb. 1st 1867. Longmans, Green, Reader, and Dyer.

Nickerson, R.S., 1998. Confirmation bias: a ubiquitous phenomenon in many guises. Rev. Gen. Psychol. 2 (2), 175–220.

Olssen, M., Peters, M.A., 2005. Neoliberalism, higher education and the knowledge economy: from the free market to knowledge capitalism. J. Educ. Policy 20 (3), 313–345.

Phippen, A., 2016. Children's Online Behaviour and Safety: Policy and Rights Challenges. Springer.

Phippen, A., Bond, E., Buck, E., 2020. Effective strategies for information literacy education: combatting 'fake news' and empowering critical thinking. In: Future Directions in Digital Information. Chandos Publishing, pp. 39–53.

Prensky, M., 2001. Digital natives, digital immigrants. On the Horizon 9 (5).

Rochlin, N., 2017. Fake news: belief in post-truth. Libr. Hi Tech 35 (3), 386–392.

Sheridan, D.R., 1997. Zeran v. AOL and the effect of Section 230 of the Communications Decency Act upon liability for defamation on the Internet. Alb. L. Rev. 61, 147.

UK Government, 2020a. Online Harms White Paper. https://www.gov.uk/government/consultations/online-harms-white-paper/online-harms-white-paper.

UK Government, 2020b. Keeping Children Safe in Education. https://www.gov.uk/government/publications/keeping-children-safe-in-education- -2.

Zuckerman, E., 2019. QAnon and the emergence of the unreal. J. Des. Sci. 6, 1–15.

Crowdsourcing COVID-19: A brief analysis of librarian posts on Reddit

Daniella Smith
University of North Texas, Denton, TX, United States

1 Introduction

At first, most of the world believed that coronavirus disease (COVID-19) would be a passing illness (O'Donnell, 2020). It was then learned that it spread globally and would wreak havoc for months (BBC, 2020). Among the repercussions of this pandemic were travel delays, misinformation in the news, and a realization that social distancing was needed to decrease the spread. As the world slowly shut down, essential workers (such as grocery store workers and government personnel) wondered if safety precautions would be taken to protect them.

Library workers are among those affected by the changes introduced by COVID-19 (International Federation of Library Associations and Institutions, 2020). Library workers must balance risks against offering vital information services needed by patrons to communicate and access essential data. Some people found the library superfluous before the pandemic (Denning, 2015). Then as the pandemic continued, the need for libraries has been highlighted (Kirchner, 2020). There are children out of school who need Internet access, and adults find that they can no longer support themselves because they have been laid off from work. They cannot afford entertainment or Internet access. Some homeless individuals need a place to go and rely on the library as a safe haven. Hence, libraries have again shown themselves to be pillars of society for their educational and social worth (Rosen, 2020).

2 Literature review

The corpus of research examining the COVID-19 response of libraries is growing. A few researchers have provided insight into library responses. Notably, Erich (2020) studied how libraries in Romania reacted and adapted to the pandemic. Websites and Facebook pages of libraries were analyzed to determine the activities used to provide notification of services to the public. The results indicated that many libraries assumed the primary role of sharing information about the pandemic for creditable sources. County libraries often reported information for local governments while university libraries disseminated scientific resources. Moreover, libraries adapted how their services were implemented by offering access to digital library materials and

Libraries, Digital Information, and COVID. https://doi.org/10.1016/B978-0-323-88493-8.00003-3

virtual displays. While some libraries only provided access to databases onsite, others provided access to periodicals and databases online. The libraries' online activities included online readings, psychotherapy, classes, and virtual tours (Erich, 2020, p. 341).

Oyelude (2020) notes that libraries played a critical role in disseminating creditable resources during the pandemic. The library community has adapted its regular practices for access and professional engagement because of the pandemic. For instance, Oyelude (2020) has explained how conferences were canceled or moved online. The American Library Association has responded by sharing free online resources. One such resource is Booklist, which offers collection development and readers' advisory tools. The Public Library Association has been offering free on-demand recordings related to digital equity and the pandemic. Another organization, HathiTrust, partnered with academic libraries to provide temporary access to its digital library (HathiTrust Digital Library, 2020). Finally, Oyelude noted that companies with Web 2.0 tools like BrainPOP, Kahoot!, and Pear Deck were offering free access to assist with helping school communities.

While Oyelude (2020) described how libraries offered digital services in general, Ali and Gatiti (2020) focused on the academic librarian's role. They identified three dimensions of the role, including:

1. Sharing public health information for preventing the spread of the virus,
2. Supporting research teams and researchers by providing creditable information,
3. Supporting the fundamental needs of library users.

Ali and Gatiti (2020) further identified how librarians could help the public within these roles. For example, social distancing was clarified as a way to prevent the spread of the virus. Library users needed to know that research was used to draw this conclusion. Hence, they asserted that librarians and other experts could use social media networks such as Facebook, Twitter, WhatsApp, and Instagram to counteract misinformation. Similarly, librarians can use database resources to provide researchers and their teams with the most up-to-date literature regarding COVID-19. Finally, as Oyelude (2020) and Erich (2020) mentioned, library users continue to need the library support that was available to them before the pandemic. Therefore, it is essential to offer document delivery, reference interviews, and other research support accessible prepandemic through virtual means.

Jaeger and Blaabaek (2020) discussed the learning inequities brought forth by the epidemic in Denmark. As with other countries such as the United States, schools were forced to close for social distancing and parents were forced to home educate their children. Jaeger and Blaabaek (2020) cited Andrew et al. (2020) and Bol (2020) when asserting that parents with more education and income can provide more resources, which include homework help and support materials such as digital devices to facilitate their children's educational needs. For that reason, it can be concluded that children with parents of lower socioeconomic status (SES) have received less assistance during the pandemic.

Jaeger and Blaabaek (2020, paragraph 2) utilized public library records for 55 million observations of family library daily checkouts to further examine the disparities in learning opportunities during the pandemic. The results show that socioeconomic variables such as parents' education and income were related to the number of children's books borrowed from public libraries. The researchers observed that children from families with higher SESs checked out more books before the pandemic started. When the pandemic started, the gap between books checked out by families from higher and lower SESs increased, with families from lower SESs checking out fewer books. Thus, the pandemic intensified the disparities that are experienced related to educational resources.

This brief literature review has outlined some ways that librarians are addressing the COVID-19 pandemic. Libraries have adapted their services, with many offering blended and digital activities. Companies and organizations have responded to libraries' need to modify services by granting free access to their resources. While numerous libraries have addressed the pandemic by reworking their services, families with higher SESs are more adept at utilizing library services. Furthermore, the research indicates that digital services are not as effective as they could be because the digital divide compounds the gaps in library usage.

3 Problem statement

The COVID-19 pandemic has been a global catastrophe. Initially, it was compared to the flu, and health professionals believed that it would pass (O'Donnell, 2020). The evolving responses to the virus left governments and university and library leaders pondering how best to handle public services. Libraries were caught in a precarious position as their services are essential, yet gathering in libraries and sharing materials can spread the virus. Based on these factors, this study examines how librarians reacted to the COVID-19 virus using posts in the social media platform Reddit. The questions that guide this investigation include:

1. Based on the posts retrieved by using RedditExtractoR, what COVID-19 pandemic topics were most discussed?
2. Based on the most popular posts retrieved by RedditExtractoR, what strategies did librarians believe were effective for coping with the COVID-19 pandemic?
3. Based on the most popular posts retrieved by RedditExtractoR, what questions did librarians have about coping with the COVID-19 pandemic?

4 Data collection

Woodfield et al. (2013) list some of the benefits of using social media for data collection. According to these authors, social media allows researchers to collect massive amounts of data unobtrusively. Hence, researchers do not need to rely on self-reporting. Instead, they can see interactions in a natural state without worrying about whether the respondent has changed their behaviour to report their responses. Subsequently, retrieving data in its most natural form improves the reliability of the data. Also, there is less bias introduced into the data collection because the researcher collects data from the entire population of individuals who have participated in the selected online community.

A limitation of collecting social media is the restrictions placed on data collection by social media platforms. Reddit limits data collection with its API to 500 comments per thread (Rivera, 2019). It is possible that by using the AI offered by a platform, not all posts will be retrieved. Social media websites frequently use algorithms. A post in Reddit can be buried within the website if it is not commented on or upvoted (liked) by Reddit community participants. Two individuals mining data at the same time may collect entirely different datasets.

There are some ethical considerations for using social media for research. For example, it can be concluded that information openly posted online is public information. On the contrary, some people tend to post information online that can be detrimental to their offline lives. Posters might not post with the intent to have their words used for research. Consequently, it is important to protect the identity of posters by aggregating data and not using usernames, just as one would do if they were writing a report based on traditional means of data collection.

The package RedditExtractoR is described as a "collection of tools for extracting structured data from https://www.reddit.com/" (Rivera, 2019). The pack was used to scrape comments from the subreddit r/Libraries for the term COVID-19. The query was set to be limited to original posts that received at least five comments for this study. By using this approach, 1497 results were retrieved. Next, the researcher removed all references to questions and comments related to advising for completing librarianship studies. After this step, 500 posts remained. The remaining posts were then narrowed down to the comments related to the five most popular original posts, as indicated by the post's number of comments. Narrowing down the comments left the 323 posts that were analyzed for this study.

Posts that were collected using the Reddit API through RedditExtractoR returned comments written between March 9, 2020, and October 20, 2020. The usernames, locations of commenters, and titles of posts and comments were not directly quoted to protect the community participants. After the posts were collected, the top five posts retrieved with RedditExtractoR were analyzed for questions, and the comments were analyzed based on the research questions. The result for Research Question 1 was derived by looking at the total counts for responses to the posts that were retrieved. Research Question 2 was analyzed by reading the posts related to each original comment, coding them, and grouping them into themes using a grounded theory approach (Benaquisto, 2008). The answer for Research Question 3 was found by reading each post and listing the questions that were asked.

5 Findings

1. Research Question 1

Research Question 1 was designed to learn about the topics that were most important to the librarians communicating on the Reddit platform. The following represents the original comments with the most posts.

Libraries open during the COVID pandemic (107 comments). This post was essentially a roll call. The original poster wanted to know how many librarians were still going to work after their libraries were closed to the public. The responses varied with most librarians indicating that they were still at work. Posters debated the need to be closed for various reasons. First, some people needed to work to have their health care. Others felt it was important to serve their populations. By reading the posts, it was clear that librarians are aware of the populations they serve. While some populations can go without services, others will be heavily impacted. The librarians noted that libraries are frequently used as childcare services. In some areas, school-aged students were encouraged to go to the library when their schools closed.

Similarly, during the summer, school-aged children flood libraries for services. Librarians were hoping for a domino effect where schools closed, and children and their guardians were encouraged to stay home to stop the virus spread. Some librarians were desperate enough to want to quit their jobs. The need for health care stopped some from leaving their jobs. Others found safer employment options. The librarians who posted were not sure what they should do. They were conflicted because they wanted to stop offering face-to-face programming, but library services were critical for children who needed access to computers and reading materials.

Telecommuting during the pandemic (67 comments). In this thread, the original poster noted librarians could work from home. Nonetheless, like the "Libraries open during the COVID pandemic" post, librarians in some locations must still go to work in a building that is not accessible to the public. The original poster requested insight on how libraries are handling "work from home" agreements. More affluent neighbourhoods with higher taxes in the United States can close libraries without complaints from patrons. Whether a library was open was also dependent on the type of library. Take for instance medical librarians who benefited from the advice of the medical community. They were working from home because the hospitals felt that the virus could spread through library services. These librarians utilized electronic databases to fill requests for articles. They physically went to work if there was a print document that could not be accessed from home.

On the contrary, academic librarians remarked that they were still working when classes on campus were switched to an online format. Also, numerous public libraries were still open. There were a variety of ways in which libraries differentiated their services. Some limited access by creating appointments, others initiated social distancing, and some made libraries less enjoyable by cancelling programming and limiting services to browsing. Social distancing and disinfecting equipment were also a popular response by librarians that were still working. The responses varied because there were no central requirements regarding how schools, cities, and states should combat the virus.

A library director elaborated on their situation by commenting that having libraries open was saving jobs. Government policies were interfering with prospects for librarians being able to work at home. An example is a poster who commented that people could not be paid in their city if they are not working. There were also a certain number of employees that could be out at any one time. For those that could work at home, they needed to prove that they were completing their shifts. In all, it was easier for part-time workers to work in shifts. Yet these were the people that were the most susceptible to being laid off. Finally, a few comments asserted that the people complaining should be thankful that they have jobs when there are so many people who were furloughed or permanently fired because people were no longer visiting the library. It was not cost-effective to continue to pay them.

Coronavirus on library materials (53 comments). The originator of this post discussed a study that found that the coronavirus could survive on library materials. In responding to this post, the commenters wondered what others were doing to stop the spread of the virus on materials. At some point during the discussion, the commenters noted that there was evidence that the coronavirus is an airborne virus and the implications of being in closed environments with materials that harboured the virus were dangerous. The participants explained that many libraries were quarantining materials. Still, the most popular materials are those that are frequently checked out. Hence, quarantining materials only serves to increase the wait time for requested items. Others responded that they appreciated the study but wondered if it was accurate because of the controlled environment, in which it was conducted. Books are often left in outdoor book drops for long periods of time and in moist conditions.

Libraries and coronavirus (49 comments). Librarians noted that schools are essential, but they had to close and that it is not practical for workers to die so that individuals can have Wi-fi services. The library workers discussed the implications of using libraries as centres for addressing social issues. For example, forum participants asserted that libraries should not be places for treating overdoses, sheltering the homeless, and taking care of children. Nevertheless, the librarians were wary of patrolling patrons to ensure that they followed new protocols for the COVID virus. Tensions were high, and some patrons were abusive when their expectations about access were not met.

The Public Librarian Declaration (47 comments). In this post, the original commentator talked about what libraries do for their communities and how communities should try to reciprocate by protecting library workers. The participants commented that felt that society was failing them. Libraries serve as a safety net, but society did not care about how the pandemic impacted library employees. It was argued that closing would significantly affect the minorities and the homeless that rely on libraries. But librarians are not social workers, and more emphasis should be placed on finding appropriate places for the public to receive social services. Some post contributors felt that they were being described as essential, although they were being paid low salaries like public servants. There was no hazardous pay to account for the risk placed on their lives and the risks they were taking by going to work.

2. Research Question 2

The purpose of Research Question 2 was to determine the strategies that librarians felt were effective for coping with COVID-19. While mining the data to find the strategies that were determined to be effective, recurring themes relating to managerial practices that were disconcerting during the pandemic were noticed. Some subreddit r/libraries community members did not like it when administrators used them to clean libraries after closing. They also disliked it when they were not informed of the plans to cope with the pandemic. In some cases, advertisements were made encouraging students to go to the library after schools closed. In this case, the libraries felt that the library was serving as a Petri dish. Morale was also low when administrators or directors did not leave their offices to interact with customers when the rest of the staff was required to be out in the open. It was also explained that security guards were important for controlling access to the library. In addition to expressing some of the issues taking place during the pandemic, several strategies were offered that they felt were effective. Table 23.1 lists the effective strategies.

3. **Research Question 3**

Using the posts with the most comments, Research Question 3 was designed to determine which questions were asked the most in the community about COVID-19. The libraries' subreddit community asked various questions as members tried to troubleshoot how to respond to the pandemic. Some questions were asked, probably with the anticipation that no one on the message board would be able to answer them. Other questions were asked to find out what other libraries were doing. An example is the question of how many librarians were working from home. Another poster wanted to know how libraries were handling interlibrary loans to report the response to a supervisor. The community members converged on the message board to compare what was happening in libraries, vent about their circumstances, and find solutions to implement in their workplaces. Table 23.2 provides a summary of the questions that were asked.

6 Discussion

6.1 Limitations

A limitation of this study is that it relied on the search term "COVID-19." There are other ways to describe COVID-19, such as using COVID, coronavirus, and pandemic. After selecting the search term, the dataset was further delimited by choosing the top five posts with the most comments. As a consequence, this article introduces how librarians utilized social media to discuss COVID-19. There is more data to be studied relating to libraries, social media, and the pandemic.

6.2 Librarian concerns

For the posts that were examined, systematic issues within the library science professional community were revealed. The library workers were most concerned with securing their jobs while staying safe, finding solutions to provide services while protecting the public, stating their significance in society, and learning about the safety measures that should be followed. Workers struggled to find solutions for navigating the political environments induced by the pandemic, which influenced the decisions that were made about their jobs, and ultimately, their livelihoods. As indicated by the posts, municipalities, schools, and universities waited for directions from government agencies. Frequently, participants stated that they had lost faith in their leaders because decisions were not made promptly, and they felt they were left as community servants without compensation for the risks they assumed for serving.

There were logical solutions for offering quality services, such as remote reference services. Still responses often suggested these solutions were avoided because of the

Table 23.1 Effective strategies for responding to the coronavirus in libraries.

Closing libraries to stop the spread
Practising safety measures by cleaning and using protective wear and protective equipment
Cancelling events
Removing toys, puzzles, and paper from the library
Staggering computer terminals
Practicing social distancing
Limiting the number of patrons with access
Restricting services to checking out books
Cancelling staff meetings
Waiving late fees
Extending loan periods
Limiting onsite staff to accepting material returns and answering questions via phone and email
Having a union representative to advocate for paid leave
Taking paid leave instead of working in dangerous conditions
Creating a plan before there is an outbreak in the community
Communicating daily with administration
Buying cleaning supplies and protective gear in bulk
Rationing disinfectant and sanitizer
Creating a pandemic policy that states adults must accompany school-aged children
Offering curbside services
Scheduling limited shifts for library workers
Using digital libraries to offer reference services from home
Rotating shifts for onsite and offsite work
Focusing on digital resources instead of face-to-face services
Limiting regular staff to utilizing the library for virtual programming equipment while supervisors work in the library and complete dangerous tasks
Offering individuals with medical issues the ability to work from home
Coming to work 1 day a week for hands-on projects (i.e., new books, weeding, and book returns)
Offering no contact returns
Providing case-by-case exceptions for working at home (i.e., elderly parents and child-care issues)
Receiving support from the local Department of Health
Meeting via teleconferencing platforms such as Skype, GoToMeeting, and Zoom
Using outdoor spaces for customers who need Wi-fi and staff for social distancing during breaks
Directing patrons to Listservs to request articles
Quarantining books
Using automated sterilization systems
Sterilizing books with alcohol and Clorox wipes
Using a self-checkout system
Implementing shorter hours and no night shifts
Loaning out laptops
Providing virtual reference services
Implementing extracleaning between library programmes
Touching library cards less
Limiting interlibrary loan to the electronic collection
Giving patrons cleaning supplies to wipe equipment before and after usage

Table 23.2 Questions asked about COVID-19 in libraries.

How will libraries know when to reopen?
How do librarians serve low-income populations that need Wi-fi and computers if they are closed?
How will library closings impact the census?
How will children access Wi-fi for their distance learning if the library is closed?
How will library workers without benefits cope if they must take off from their jobs during closings?
How should librarians de-escalate situations with patrons that appear to be sick?
What policies should be in place for sick patrons?
How will closings impact elections and the ability of community members to vote?
How essential are library services during the pandemic?
How do librarians provide services to immunocompromised and elderly individuals without jeopardizing their health?
Is the surface transmission of COVID-19 something that librarians need to worry about?
How long should books be quarantined?
How does humidity in the book drop impact virus growth and transmission?
Should library workers be focused on aerial transmissions rather than quarantining materials?
Why are librarians at work when they can work from home?
How should library workers handle interlibrary loans when they are working remotely?
What are the benefits of libraries staying open that are more pertinent to stopping the spread of the COVID-19?
If libraries are essential, why are the budgets so low?
What populations are still accessing libraries during the COVID pandemic?

need for libraries to justify their existence. Many librarians sought proof that libraries need to offer in-person services outweighed the health risks to library workers and community members. Ultimately, for numerous participants answers were received when decision makers mandated that the doors were left open to supplement community needs.

6.3 Library education

There were implications for library education. The questions asked by the librarians highlight the need for better disaster training for librarians. The devastation imposed by COVID-19 is atypical because it has caused healthcare and economic crises. On top of that, the effect of the pandemic underscored social disparities and increased social tensions. Librarians are adaptable and have some understanding of coping with crises (Erich, 2020). These crises frequently include natural disasters, community unrest, and bomb threats, from their education and professional resources. Much like the institutions they work for and the communities they serve, librarians were not prepared to face a virus that was asymptomatic in some and produced devastating symptoms in others. Hence, the Reddit posts show that librarians felt that the responses were often not adequate to protect essential workers' lives, such as theirs.

In the future, there needs to be more of an emphasis on managerial training to assist directors in communicating with key stakeholders, building morale, and being transparent. There is a need for people to be culturally aware and understand how to express empathy for others experiencing life-changing circumstances. So many of the posters just wanted someone to care about their viewpoint. Moreover, there is a need to provide guidance on identifying the best resources for learning about a healthcare crisis. The posts on Reddit wavered between stating that everyone should be fine if they washed their hands and the COVID-19 virus being airborne and deadly. It seems that the individuals posting would have felt safer if there was more empathy for them and their needs, administrative transparency, and a unified resource to provide guidance for libraries.

6.4   Service adaptability

According to the Reddit posters, there were notable differences in how libraries adapted the services that were offered. Some libraries closed completely. Others initiated hybrid services, while others were online. Furthermore, there was a discussion about how libraries should not be the places that offer social services. Examples of adaptability included curbside service, appointment-based face-to-face book browsing, and virtual programming.

The difference between the psychological counseling offered in Romania (Erich, 2020) and the library personnel's discussion on Reddit indicates some resistance to providing social services. However, these services are available at various libraries. The discussion suggests that it may be helpful to explore offering social services in libraries by using credentialed professionals. Such is the case of Dominican University (2020) that offers a joint social work and librarianship degree. Perhaps more of these degrees should be available in the United States to assist libraries that address social service needs in communities. On the contrary, Wahler et al. (2020) suggest that having a social worker that collaborates with libraries is an option that should be explored. As indicated by Erich (2020), by the adaptations initiated by libraries during the pandemic, psychological services provided by libraries during crises is a service that could be advantageous.

6.5   Addressing disparities

A theme that arose from the posts was socioeconomic disparities. Librarians were aware that if their libraries closed, their patrons would not likely be able to access materials, the Internet, and services. Patrons cannot use digital services when they do not have the Internet. A lack of Internet is also troublesome for students that were switched to online classes. Libraries are often the sole access point for computers and the Internet for low-income families (Bill and Melinda Gates Foundation, n.d.; Kirchner, 2020). This is especially true during disasters (Young, 2018).

The posts suggest that libraries in lower income neighbourhoods were less likely to close. Still, these libraries were not equipped to maximize services because of a lack of support systems (tax and income) to finance the equipment that their communities needed and to allow staffing to continue the way it was before the pandemic. Families in lower SESs needed more help, to address their educational needs. However, the resources were not available.

7 Conclusion

In conclusion, this study examined how librarians addressed the COVID-19 virus by using Reddit posts with the keyword COVID-19 in the subreddit libraries community. Overall, librarians frequently commented about how to modify services, how libraries are used during the pandemic, safety issues, and strategies that worked in their libraries. Librarians also shared examples of practices that did not work in their libraries and asked each other questions about library services and management. The posts signified that there was no central guidance for librarians. The lack of central guidelines needs to be understood because the COVID-19 pandemic presented circumstances that have never been experienced before in modern history. In addition, libraries are present in various settings such as universities, hospitals, municipalities, schools, and law offices.

Based on this study, it is recommended that library organizations and educational programmes work in collaboration to prepare the workforce for the problematic scenarios presented by the pandemic. Posts by the participants further suggest that cultural awareness and empathy training should be developed for managers of library workers because several posts suggested that a divide existed between management and workers. This training is needed in the public, academic, special, and school library settings. Finally, more joint degree programmes with an emphasis on providing social work could improve library services.

References

Ali, M.Y., Gatiti, P., 2020. The COVID-19 (Coronavirus) pandemic: reflections on the roles of librarians and information professionals. Health Inf. Libr. J. 37 (2), 158–162.

Andrew, A., Cattan, S., Costa-Dias, M., Farquharson, C., Kraftman, L., Krutikova, S., Phimister, A., Sevilla, A., 2020. Learning during the lockdown: real-time data on children's experiences during home learning. Retrieved from: https://dera.ioe.ac.uk/35632/1/BN288-Learning-during-the-lockdown-1.pdf.

BBC, 2020. Covid-19 pandemic: tracking the global coronavirus outbreak. BBC News. December 12. Retrieved from: https://www.bbc.com/news/world-51235105.

Bill and Melinda Gates Foundation, n.d.. First-ever national study: millions of people rely on library computers for employment, health, and education. Retrieved from: https://www.gatesfoundation.org/Media-Center/Press-Releases/2010/03/Millions-of-People-Rely-on-Library-Computers-for-Employment-Health-and-Education.

Benaquisto, L., 2008. Codes and coding. In: Given, L.M. (Ed.), The SAGE Encyclopedia of Qualitative Research Methods. Sage Publications, Thousand Oaks, CA, pp. 86–88.

Bol, T., 2020. Inequality in homeschooling during the Corona crisis in the Netherlands. First results from the LISS panel. Retrieved from: https://osf.io/preprints/socarxiv/hf32q/download.

Denning, S., 2015. Do we need libraries? Forbes. Retrieved from: https://www.forbes.com/sites/stevedenning/2015/04/28/do-we-need-libraries/?sh=4da4e0416cd7.

Dominican University, 2020. MLIS and master of social work dual degree. Retrieved from: https://www.dom.edu/academics/majors-programs/mlis-and-master-social-work-dual-degree.

Erich, A., 2020. Libraries reaction of Romania to the crisis caused by COVID 19. Postmod. Open. 11 (3), 332–343.

HathiTrust Digital Library, 2020. HathiTrust response to COVID-19. Retrieved from: https://www.hathitrust.org/covid-19-response.

International Federation of Library Associations and Institutions, 2020. COVID-19 and the global library field. Retrieved from: https://www.ifla.org/covid-19-and-libraries.

Jaeger, M.M., Blaabaek, E.H., 2020. Inequality in learning opportunities during Covid-19: evidence from library takeout. Res. Soc. Stratif. Mobil. 68, 100524.

Kirchner, L., 2020. Millions of Americans depend on libraries for Internet. Now they're closed. The Markup. June 25. Retrieved from: https://themarkup.org/coronavirus/2020/06/25/millions-of-americans-depend-on-libraries-for-internet-now-theyre-closed.

O'Donnell, J., 2020. Top disease official: risk of coronavirus in USA is 'minuscule'; skip mask and wash hands. USA Today. February 17. Retrieved from: https://www.usatoday.com/story/news/health/2020/02/17/nih-disease-official-anthony-fauci-risk-of-coronavirus-in-u-s-is-minuscule-skip-mask-and-wash-hands/4787209002/.

Oyelude, A.A., 2020. Libraries, librarians, archives, museums and the COVID-19 pandemic. Libr. Hi Tech News 37 (9), 5–6.

Rivera, I., 2019. Package 'RedditExtractoR'. Retrieved from: https://cran.r-project.org/web/packages/RedditExtractoR/RedditExtractoR.pdf.

Rosen, E., 2020. Beyond the pandemic, libraries look toward a new era. New York Times. September 24. Retrieved from: https://www.nytimes.com/2020/09/24/business/libraries-pandemic-future.html.

Wahler, E.A., Provence, M.A., Helling, J., Williams, M.A., 2020. The changing role of libraries: how social workers can help. Fam. Soc. 101 (1), 34–43.

Woodfield, K., Morrell, G., Metzler, K., Blank, G., Salmons, J., Finnegan, J., Lucraft, M., 2013. Blurring the boundaries? New social media, new social research: developing a network to explore the issues faced by researchers negotiating the new research landscape of online social media platforms. Retrieved from: http://eprints.ncrm.ac.uk/3168/1/blurring_boundaries.pdf.

Young, E., 2018. The role of public libraries in disasters. New Vis. Public Aff. 10, 31–38.

No child ignored

24

Sarah Mears
Libraries Connected, London, United Kingdom

1 Introduction

If we could look 3 or 5 years into the future, what would we see? How will today's toddlers fare as they move into education? How will our children be experiencing life as teenagers? Will today's teenagers be settling into fulfilling careers or studies? The impact of the significant disruption children have faced in this strangest of all years is only just beginning to emerge. Public libraries too have experienced unprecedented challenges and have responded with compassion, creativity, and innovation. But the sector now faces an uncertain future with drastic budget cuts anticipated. And yet, more than ever, it feels that public libraries have the potential to make a huge contribution to a better future for the nation's children.

This chapter will outline how public libraries in the United Kingdom have responded to the challenges of COVID-19 and will provide an overview of the emerging evidence of the impact of the pandemic on children. It will set out a vision for the future public library offer to children. It will explore how those children most in need can be supported now and in the coming years to benefit from a reinvented digital and physical library service. Finally, it will present proposals for more systematic approaches to partnership engagement, structural service change, and a strategic focus on targeting library services where they are most needed.

2 Public libraries and community engagement

On March 29, 2020, a headline in the *Surrey Comet* read "Kingston Libraries get creative to keep kids engaged amid coronavirus outbreak" (Bailey, 2020b). The story described how Kingston Library and Heritage Service, reacting quickly to lockdown and the closure of library buildings, set up a live stream on their Facebook page to continue delivering their early years rhyme time sessions and other events. At the start of the first lockdown, Kingston Libraries' digital service reached almost 10,000 people in a week. Many other library services followed their example, developing digital services to keep in touch with their communities, grow new audiences, and engage with children as schools closed and families grappled with the challenge of home learning.

In autumn 2020, two reports were issued which explored community engagement with libraries during the first months of the pandemic. In *Making a Difference: Libraries, Lockdown and Looking Ahead* (Peachey, 2020), the author estimated that around 3 in 10 people in the United Kingdom engaged with public library services during the lockdown and 39% of those participated in online activities. Activities averaged at

Libraries, Digital Information, and COVID. https://doi.org/10.1016/B978-0-323-88493-8.00005-7

around 1000 views each with some reaching over 20,000 views. The second report was commissioned by Libraries Connected (the sector support organization for public libraries in England, Wales, and Northern Ireland). It explored the extent of libraries' digital activity during the lockdown. Over 75% of library services responding to the research (132 services) delivered what became known as "#LibrariesFromHome" services—online activities and events for both adults and children (Holden, 2020).

3 Continuation of digital services

Although libraries are now reopening, the digital services have continued, as social distancing prevents groups from gathering together. Digital events for children include rhyme times; story times; art and craft events; author events; Lego and Science; Technology; Engineering and Mathematics (STEM) clubs; school readiness programmes; live online performances; information literacy sessions and virtual class visits; and Minecraft groups and digital escape rooms. Most libraries celebrated the big national reading events online: World Book Night, Empathy Day, and The Summer Reading Challenge. Publishers have supported libraries by agreeing to the temporary relaxation of permissions to allow filmed stories to be posted online.

Public libraries were thus able to contribute to a diverse and creative digital offer for children. Families who had the capacity to spend quality time together and get online have reaped benefits (Office of the Children's Commissioner, 2020). But libraries were also very aware that some children were (and still are) excluded from the range of digital opportunities available. What of them?

4 Poverty and digital exclusion

Even before the start of the pandemic, child poverty had risen sharply in some parts of the country. The Child Poverty Action Group (CPAG, 2020) estimated that 4.2 million children (or 30% of all children) were living in poverty in the United Kingdom in 2018–19, with children from black and minority ethnic groups more likely to be in poverty (46% compared with 26% of children from White British families). Children in poverty are likely to be behind their peers in education, live in inadequate housing, suffer poorer health, risk chronic illnesses, have shorter life spans, a worse sense of well-being, and lack self-esteem. For these children, the pandemic has deepened existing vulnerabilities and the number in poverty is growing. IPPR, the progressive policy think tank, estimates that an additional 700,000 children face poverty by the end of 2020 as a result of the fallout from COVID-19 (Parkes et al., 2020).

Children and families in poverty are much more likely to face digital exclusion. On April 28, 2020, *The Guardian* reported that 1.9 million households had no access to the Internet (Kelly, 2020). *The House* (the magazine of PoliticsHome.Com) reported that 15% of teachers in schools in the most deprived areas of the country believed that over half of their pupils did not have adequate access to an electronic device for learning (Bailey, 2020a). Only 57% of households have a laptop and many other families can only access the Internet through mobile phones or tablets. As a result, disadvantaged children and students are less able to engage in remote study during school closures. Even for those who own a device, paying for data may be just too expensive. In the Libraries Connected research (Holden, 2020), one librarian said that "people without means to digital have been impacted really negatively … Many children from low-income families were unable to take part in the activities that we moved online or get support to participate in the summer reading challenge." Although the Department for Education and national charities are working to source laptops for the neediest pupils, this will not solve the issue of data affordability. And even where the Internet is available, some parents do not have the necessary skills to help their children.

At the time of writing, in autumn 2020, the impact on the most vulnerable children of the loss of teaching, lockdown isolation, and social distancing is just emerging and revealing the stark disparities between disadvantaged children and their more affluent peers (ADCS, 2020).

5 The impact of COVID on children

In November 2020, the UK's OFSTED published a series of briefing notes presenting findings from visits and other activities carried out in September and October 2020 looking at children's return to school and early year's settings. In standardized tests at primary school, there has been an average decline in the performance of between 5% and 15% with younger children and those from disadvantaged backgrounds worst affected (OFSTED, 2020a).

The National Foundation for Educational Research (NFER) reported in *The Guardian* on September 1, 2020 (Adams, 2020) that the average amount of learning lost for all pupils was 3 months but more than half the pupils at schools in the most deprived areas lost 4 months. Alarmingly, while just 1% of pupils in the wealthiest areas were estimated to have lost 6 months learning to the lockdown, in the poorest areas this rose to more than 10%.

For the youngest children, concerns have focused on the impact on their personal, social, and emotional development. Early years teachers report that children are returning to school less confident and more anxious. Some children's motor skills have declined, and sadly, teachers report children unable to sustain meaningful play and a reversal of existing language development (OFSTED, 2020b). Older children are presenting with anxiety and poorer physical and mental health.

6 A refocus on learning

Since returning to school, children have needed support to refocus on learning and OFSTED report that nearly all schools are prioritizing reading and writing and using stories as a way of settling children. Children seem to be craving stories as a means of escaping the turbulence around them. The National Literacy Trust (Clark and Picton,

2020) surveyed children aged 8–18 about their reading during the lockdown. Children reported a 35% increase in the amount they were reading and a 28% increase in reading enjoyment during the lockdown. Twenty-nine percent of children said that reading made them feel better and 32% said it helped when they felt sad because they were unable to see family and friends.

7 The role of public libraries in children's lives

Reflecting on the importance of reading brings us back to public libraries and the role they should play in children's lives. As we shape the post-COVID-19 public library service, it is vital that responding to the needs of the nation's children is at the heart of the new offer. In this final section, I will suggest some practical and strategic proposals for the public library sector to support children and their families.

7.1 Combating digital exclusion

Firstly, the sector must support the urgent national imperative to improve children and families' access to the Internet, for example, through aligning with the Carnegie UK Trust's 12-point *Digital Exclusion Strategy* (Bowyer et al., 2020). Public libraries have a key role to play, not just in providing the "public safety net" to ensure everyone has access to the technology, but also in supporting communities to develop the skills they need to use the technology effectively. The Good Things Foundation states that providing everyone with the essential digital skills they need by 2028 will lead to a benefit of £15 for every £1 invested and a net present value of £21.9 billion (cited in APLE Collective blog, Joseph Rowntree Foundation, 2020).

7.2 Reconnecting with physical library spaces

As library services begin to open up their physical spaces again, special attention must be paid to reaching out to children. Libraries enable children to physically connect with their local communities, to explore, to empathize, and to better understand the wider world by introducing them to a wide range of reading experiences. When children visit a library, they share the space with other people from diverse backgrounds, cultures and ages, and the face-to-face connections that Eric Klinenberg calls "the building blocks of public life" (Klinenberg, 2018).

In libraries, children learn to be an audience. For the youngest children, the library can play a critical role in social development and communication skills—a simple free weekly rhyme time helps develop speech and language and for children who experience social deprivation, their vocabulary at age five has been found to be the best predictor of whether they will escape poverty as adults (Tucker, 2016). In addition, physical participation in rhyme times helps children develop turn-taking, kindness, and the ability to sit and listen to each other.

For children who have been confined between cramped homes and school, the library is a safe third space in the community, where quiet and reflective relaxation, creativity, inspiration, discovery, and study are all possible.

7.3   Libraries must continue to develop their digital creativity

Despite highlighting the importance of the physical space, we must not lose sight of the digital offer. Libraries have learned so much about digital engagement over the last few months and there must not be a return to pre-COVID-19 services. Customer habits will have changed dramatically, and libraries have the opportunity to become digital leaders. A blended approach incorporating physical and digital services feels both exciting and essential. It will stimulate creativity, engage learners, and allow them to build connections with the wider world and build skills and engagement. Imagine children meeting and talking to each other across the world through their libraries and using library resources to work and create together; games played in both physical and digital environments; opportunities to meet the highest profile authors virtually, followed up by events simultaneously in libraries across the country; virtual reality experiences created in libraries and shared with the community; story times delivered to a physical audience but live streamed to those who cannot attend; children working together to curate digital experiences and collaborating on creative writing projects.

7.4   A combating child poverty plan for libraries

None of these proposals will effectively support those who need them most unless public libraries are recognized as a key tool in reducing inequalities. Libraries already contribute to local poverty programmes, working to address holiday hunger, period poverty, and other challenges, but to be really effective, it is vital that libraries are in the places where families need them most. Although a national library service feels a long way off in the United Kingdom, there should be a national strategy to ensure there is a public library within easy walking distance of the 20% most deprived areas of the country. These libraries should have reasonable opening hours and play a central role in local antipoverty programmes. There should be national investment in a workforce attached to these libraries which is able to provide additional support to children and families.

This workforce could be created by countrywide strategic partnerships with Family Hubs and Children's Centres, as happens in some services already. Joint working would mean sharing resources, skills, and costs and ensure that all families can access the support they need in one place; families in crisis could more quickly be identified. Parents could be supported to learn new skills to get back into employment and the whole family would have access to the universal services around reading for pleasure, learning, well-being, and cultural engagement that libraries provide.

All of this would take initial investment at a time when we know that public finances are facing a bill of seismic proportions. As reported in *The Guardian* on November 21, 2020, the Local Government Association predicts that local councils will face a £4 billion shortfall next year (Jayanetti, 2020). But these early intervention partnerships could enable future cost savings so a small financial investment now could make longer term sense.

COVID-19 has delivered a dramatic jolt to our society. It has placed centre-stage the inequalities that have long concerned us and also highlighted significant gaps in our support infrastructure. But it has also opened doors, in libraries as elsewhere.

It has enabled an explosion of new skills, new ways of working, and creativity to flourish. Libraries are all about people and we must seize this moment to ensure that our services, physical, digital, and blended, provide the best offer for the people who need them most. I will leave the last word to the man who above all others has become the champion of vulnerable children during the pandemic: Marcus Rashford MBE, who tweeted on November 16, 2020: "imagine if all children were on an equal playing field. Imagine if we all started at the line equal instead of 20 yards behind. Imagine children waking up believing that their dreams could come true. Imagine what that belief could do for the future of this country."

References

Adams, R., Gap between rich and poor pupils in England 'grows by 46% in a year', *The Guardian*, 2020, Education, (Accessed 20 November 2020).

Addressing Poverty with Lived Experience (APLE) Collective, 2020. Coronavirus Response Must Include Digital Access to Connect Us All. https://www.jrf.org.uk/blog/coronavirus-response-must-include-digital-access-connect-us-all. (Accessed 1 December 2020).

Bailey, G., 2020a. Out of sight: how do you we protect children in lockdown. The House. https://www.politicshome.com/thehouse/article/out-of-sight-how-do-you-protect-children-in-a-crisis. (Accessed 19 November 2020).

Bailey, S., 2020b. Kingston libraries get creative to keep kids engaged amid Corona virus outbreak. Surrey Comet. https://www.surreycomet.co.uk/news/18343371.kingston-libraries-get-creative-keep-kids-engaged-amid-coronavirus-outbreak/. (Accessed 19 November 2020).

Bowyer, G., Grant, A., White, D., 2020. Learning From Lockdown: 12 Steps to Eliminate Digital Exclusion. Carnegie UK Trust, Dunfermline. https://d1ssu070pg2v9i.cloudfront.net/pex/carnegie_uk_trust/2020/10/14161948/Carnegie-Learning-from-lockdown-Report-FINAL.pdf.

Child Poverty Action Group, 2020. Child Poverty Facts and Figures. https://cpag.org.uk/child-poverty/child-poverty-facts-and-figures. (Accessed 19 November 2020).

Clark, C., Picton, I., 2020. Children and Young People's Reading in 2020 Before and During the COVID-19 Lockdown. National Literacy Trust. https://literacytrust.org.uk/news/our-new-research-with-puffin-shows-a-rise-in-childrens-reading-during-lockdown-has-supported-their-mental-wellbeing-and-inspired-them-to-dream-big/2020. (Accessed 1 December 2020).

Holden, A., 2020. Libraries in Lockdown: Connecting Communities in Crisis. *Libraries Connected*, London. https://www.librariesconnected.org.uk/resource/libraries-lockdown-connecting-communities-crisis.

Jayanetti, C., 2020. We'll have to cut vital services without £4bn help, say England's councils. The Guardian. https://www.theguardian.com/society/2020/nov/21/well-slash-vital-services-if-sunak-withholds-4bn-englands-councils-warn. (Accessed 1 December 2020).

Kelly, A., 2020. Digital divide 'isolates and endangers' millions of UK's poorest. The Guardian. https://www.theguardian.com/world/2020/apr/28/digital-divide-isolates-and-endangers-millions-of-uk-poorest. (Accessed 28 November 2020).

Klinenberg, E., 2018. Palaces for The People: How to Build a More Equal and Unlimited Society. Bodley Head, London.

Office of the Children's Commissioner, 2020. Childhood in the Time of Covid. https://www. childrenscommissioner.gov.uk/report/childhood-in-the-time-of-covid/. (Accessed 19 November 2020).

OFSTED, 2020a. COVID-19 Series: Briefing on Early Years. https://www.gov.uk/ government/publications/covid-19-series-briefing-on-early-years-october-2020. (Accessed 20 November 2020).

OFSTED, 2020b. COVID-19 Series: Briefing on Schools. https://www.gov.uk/government/ publications/covid-19-series-briefing-on-schools-october-2020. (Accessed 20 November 2020).

Parkes, H., McNeil, C., Jung, C., 2020. A Family Stimulus: Supporting Children, Families and the Economy Through the Pandemic. IPPR. http://www.ippr.org/research/publications/a-family-stimulus. (Accessed 1 December 2020).

Peachey, J., 2020. Making a Difference: Libraries, Lockdown and Looking Ahead. Carnegie UK Trust, Dunfermline. https://www.carnegieuktrust.org.uk/publications/ making-a-difference-libraries-lockdown-and-looking-ahead/.

The Association of Directors of Children's Services Ltd, 2020. Building a Country That Works for All Children Post Covid-19. The Association of Directors of Children's Services Ltd, Manchester. https://adcs.org.uk/assets/documentation/ADCS_Building_a_country_that_ works_for_all_children_post_Covid-19.pdf.

Tucker, J. (Ed.), 2016. Improving Children's Life Chances. Child Poverty Action Group, London.

Part Three

Re-shaping society and the future

"Normalizing" the online/blended delivery method into a lasting cultural shift

Paul Kirkham
Institute of Contemporary Music Performance (ICMP), London, United Kingdom

1 Introduction: About ICMP

The Institute of Contemporary Music Performance (ICMP) is a highly regarded small specialist provider of higher education (primarily undergraduate and postgraduate courses) to over 1000 students of contemporary music. Located in Kilburn, north London, ICMP counts on extensive state-of-the-art teaching, performance, studio, and practice facilities, and employs a wide range of expert practitioners, experienced teachers, and respected academics in the delivery of its courses.

Registered as a provider of higher education (HE) with the Office for Students (OfS), the sector regulator, and with over 30 years of experience, ICMP is focused on helping students to realize their full potential and develop rewarding and productive careers, primarily in the music industry. This industry is extremely important to the UK cultural and financial economy, contributing £5.2bn overall, £2.7bn in export revenue, and around 190,000 jobs in 2018, with music tourism generating an additional £4.5bn in the same year, according to UK Music http://www.ukmusic.org/research/music-by-numbers/.

See https://www.icmp.ac.uk for more information about ICMP, its students, its staff, and the courses it provides.

2 Change management and risk evaluation

The first part of this chapter discusses established practices for managing business risk, the limitations of these practices when "low likelihood but high impact" events occur, such as the current COVID-19 pandemic, and the steps taken by the ICMP in dealing with the operational and strategic challenges of this pandemic. The second part examines some of the opportunities that are now arising in the field of English higher education (HE) as a result of this crisis.

Much has been written over the years on change management and risk evaluation and how to deal with unexpected crises. In fact, entire industries and institutes have arisen, not to mention the growth of an extensive field of experts, publishing activity, and consultancy careers, on the back of these concerns. Large amounts of management time are regularly devoted to the assessment of business risk and the

Libraries, Digital Information, and COVID. https://doi.org/10.1016/B978-0-323-88493-8.00002-1

development of action plans that would mitigate that risk. In reality, with most risks and crises experienced day to day, capable, experienced staff and good planning and analysis are sufficient to deal with the consequences and keep a business on track. But even with a great deal of experience, no one really knows how to deal with the most significant crises until they actually happen, and we are confronted with the consequences. For that reason, and regardless of established and documented processes and practices that may have been extensively rehearsed, the most important asset any business should have is its leadership team, working inside an appropriate culture and value set towards the achievement of common goals.

A well-organized business will typically have in place something called a "Risk Register." This lists all the assessed risks that the business might face, in order of magnitude, together with details of contingency plans that have been developed to deal with those risks. The Risk Register would be regularly reviewed, with the management team assessing two variables with regard to each identified risk—the likelihood of a risky event occurring and the impact this might have—and assigning a value to each. These values might be on scales of 0 (very unlikely/no impact) to 5 (very likely/very significant impact). We then multiply these two numbers together (the likelihood of a risk occurring times the impact such an occurrence would have) to create a "Residual Risk Score" (RRS) for each identified risk. For example, if we assessed that a serious flood might be very unlikely to happen, perhaps as a result of the geographical location of the business, it might be assigned a score of only 1 on the "likelihood" scale, but if it did happen it would be extremely disruptive and costly to the business and would therefore have a rating of maybe 4 (out of 5) on the "impact" scale. Multiplying these two numbers together gives us an RRS score of $(1 \times 4) = 4$. The business would then establish its "risk appetite," which is a measure of how risk averse the business is and is stated as a particular RRS score. A business might decide that any risk with an RRS score below 8 wouldn't need any specific contingency plan as it would be either extremely unlikely to happen, of very low impact on the business, or a combination of the two. Risks with low RRS scores are therefore effectively ignored as developing an effective contingency plan would not be considered to be worth the investment of time and resources required. So, in our example, if a flood happened, we would just have to deal with it as best we can.

This simple system works well for most business risks, so long as those who manage and assess risk are experienced and fully understand likelihood and consequences of possible risky events, and good planning procedures are in place to deal with the most likely and impactful events. Where it goes wrong are in the case of "low likelihood/high impact" risks such as our flood example above. These might have a combined score of 0 or 1 (very unlikely) and 4 or 5 (very high impact) and thus would generate an RRS score of <5, probably below the risk appetite of most businesses. The problem arises because events such as earthquakes, wars, terrorist attacks—and global pandemics—are extremely impactful but would probably have such a rating if they were considered by a business at all. We therefore rely on our government (which oversees a national Risk Register) and the wider state to have contingency plans in place for these extreme events, and as has been seen recently, unless a particular government has tangible experience of such events in living memory, even they might not be taking such risks seriously enough.

3 Governments and epidemics

Having said that, there is a long history of epidemics and pandemics that have impacted on the development of human society. These include the Plague of Athens of 430 BC; the Black Death of the 14th century; the Great Plague of London of 1665–66; the American Plagues of the 16th century; the yellow fever epidemic of Philadelphia in 1793; the 1918 flu pandemic ("Spanish Flu"); the Asian Flu of 1957; and regular and still-occurring epidemics of Zika virus, Ebola, AIDS and other miserable occurrences. It would appear that the more successful countries and regions in terms of dealing with the current pandemic, for example, China and South East Asia, are those that have a history, including relatively recent experience, of the particular threat of respiratory diseases (SARS, for example, a viral respiratory disease of zoonotic origin, and a species of coronavirus, identified following outbreaks in the early 2000s). This would suggest that such experience leads to better preparedness for and awareness among the population of such a threat. And it is likely that the risk of an epidemic of this particular kind of respiratory disease sits higher on the national risk registers of these countries as a result.

Of course, differences in the organization and approach of government and state would also have an impact in terms of control of the wider population and effective implementation of national contingency plans. It could be argued that the "liberal democracies" are not well suited to the kind of centrally directed approach necessary to enforce quick and effective action. Putting aside the significant issues in regard to the kind of free, tolerant, and individual-focused society we wish to live in, this may be true, and certainly where there is an effective and accepted leadership with directed, central command and control structures and practices in place, dealing with major crises is arguably more effective. While criticism of the response to the pandemic of various western governments is of course legitimate, if we were to go back to 2019, and the National Audit Office published a report saying that the UK Government had (for example) in the previous fiscal year invested £750m in stockpiling personal protective equipment (PPE) and a range of medical supplies, which had not been used and now needed to be incinerated and replaced, what would have been the press, public, and political reaction? Without real public understanding of the reasons for what would be widely perceived as an inefficient and wasteful approach to public resources, such contingency planning may not be tolerated and it is thus a limitation on the extent to which we can be nationally prepared for low likelihood but high impact risks crystallizing into reality.

4 COVID and higher education: ICMP's approach

As COVID-19 hit in early 2020, those of us involved in higher education were faced with some urgent decisions. The action we took, guided by the needs and views of our staff and students, and the instructions of our government, was intended to address the immediate urgency of the situation without neglecting the medium- and longer-term threats and opportunities that were presenting themselves. Our senior leadership team at ICMP moved quickly into "crisis management" mode, with daily briefings both online and, where possible, face to face. Action plans were put in place, informed by the growing body of evidence that a pandemic was happening and the developing governmental guidance and instruction as we moved into formal lockdown. Our time horizon for operational planning contracted to the immediate "next few days and weeks," and we quickly adapted existing systems for distance learning and communication and put in place immediate training and instruction for users who were not familiar with the technology. In many ways, it was the best time of year for this to happen—most of our courses were nearing their end, and we already had a lot of evidence to enable effective assessment of our students. But we still had modules and exams to complete, deadlines for course work were approaching, we had contractual obligations to fulfil, students and staff were becoming increasingly anxious, and the academic year was not ended.

4.1 Operating principles

As a team, we quickly established some operating principles, which were discussed with student and staff representatives and published widely. These principles guided all actions that we took, and they were as follows:

1. **Health and safety.** We made this our top priority, stating our commitment to maintaining the health, safety, and well-being of students, staff, visitors, and the wider community at all times.
2. **Meeting student expectations.** Conscious of our obligations both moral and legal (under consumer marketing law), we committed to ensuring that our provision would continue to provide demonstrably excellent value-for-money, ensuring that we met students' expectations, including providing appropriate access to our facilities and equipment where safe and feasible.
3. **Providing a high-quality experience.** We committed to continued investment in our teaching, learning, and assessment practices to ensure a high-quality experience, addressing equality, inclusivity and diversity challenges and supporting students to achieve their learning outcomes safely—regardless of any imposed external restrictions.
4. **Honesty and transparency.** We committed to communicating our plans and intentions truthfully and openly, advising staff and students of any changes to restrictions or guidelines and the implications of those changes as soon as they occurred.
5. **No-one will be deprived.** We worked hard to ensure no student would be disadvantaged if they were unable to meet the requirements of their course for reasons outside of their control.
6. **A safe campus.** We made a wide range of necessary changes to campus layout and infrastructure in accordance with public health advice, creating a certified "COVID-secure" work and study space.
7. **Enhanced cleaning and hygiene.** We committed to enhancing and regularly reviewing our hygiene and cleaning protocols and practices, adapting all spaces so they adhered to public health advice, ensuring students, staff, and visitors had confidence in their safety.
8. **Supporting student and staff well-being.** Recognizing that the pandemic would impact significantly on the welfare and mental health of staff and students, we reviewed our support to ensure we met individual and collective needs, for example, by providing enhanced counselling services, doubling the funding available through the "hardship fund" and ensuring regular and effective communications with those most badly affected.

9. **Connecting with international students.** We developed effective processes specifically to support international students and staff, especially during any self-isolation period that they would have to undertake.
10. **Community engagement.** We redoubled our efforts to reach out to our local community and additionally developed a community music platform, "ICMP Together," as a free resource for local people to access and enjoy during enforced lockdown periods.

4.2 Effective communication

In all of this, effective communication was key. We conducted research into our students' views and concerns, using this to guide our approach, and engaged with them directly through their elected representatives and through links to course leaders and other key staff that they could speak to. The Student President and other student representatives were invited to join key project working groups, working alongside management in areas such as the development of our online delivery model and the planning required to return to work with a "blended" model of provision after the summer. We provided regular and clear communications to all stakeholders regarding our planned actions or the changing external environment, utilizing a range of different channels across social media, emails, and direct "town hall"-style briefings to ensure everyone understood what was happening, how we were responding, and what support they needed. We engaged regularly with our regulator, the Office for Students (OfS), and we ensured the direct involvement of our Corporate Board, the principal governing body of ICMP, keeping them fully briefed on our plans and actions, bringing to them our revised operational plans and projections and regular reviews of developing risk, and asking for their support and guidance as required. And we set some clear, short-term objectives that we could focus our activity around and give direction to decisions that needed to be taken quickly and with imperfect information available.

4.3 Maintaining longer-term plans

What we were clear about was that while actions must be taken in the very short term to address the unfolding crisis, these should not wherever possible prejudice our longer-term plans for the institution. Rather, we decided to take the approach that we would make any necessary investments and incur all necessary costs to adhere to the above principles until the pandemic eased, while keeping the medium- to longer-term plans and strategies of the institution intact, albeit in some cases delayed or modified. This meant, for example, no real cuts to our staffing or cost base were considered, and we kept developmental options for business growth and facilities expansion open.

4.4 Financial resources

Crucially, and to enable this approach, one of the first actions of the senior leadership team was to ensure financial resources were in place and adequate to cover at least the next 12–18 months, which was the period we estimated that we would be most impacted for and beyond which we would be able to return to a more normal business model. ICMP is a relatively small, specialist provider and does not count on a large and well-endowed balance sheet. We do, however, have a strong and proven approach to financial management, excellent relationships with our bank and other potential financiers, and an ability to project well into the future to see where financial risks might lie. In this case, given the deep uncertainty that was present during the period March–September 2020, we could not guarantee that either our current student cohort would be able—or indeed willing—to continue with their studies, nor that we would be able to recruit the necessary number of students in September 2020. Focus was given to this matter, and suitable financial arrangements put in place by May—within 2 months of the crisis starting—to ensure the business could count on sufficient liquidity.

This took an enormous amount of pressure off the team and enabled us to make short-term decisions on such things as increasing student hardship funding; investing in the online delivery model; recruiting specialist staff where required; offering a "laptop loan scheme" to students to ensure none were digitally disadvantaged for the new delivery model; investing in our facilities to provide safety and reassurance to staff and students alike; and other key investments. We were also able to provide reassurance to students who would be enrolling from September 2020 that we would be fully operational and able to provide a full learning experience for them. This was critical for business continuity and student confidence.

4.5 Clarifying the offer

It was extremely important to clarify what our offer to students would be over the summer months and into the new academic year. As an HE provider registered with the OfS, we are bound by consumer marketing law, and current and new students had been contracted, or were about to be contracted, based around a package offer which was clearly going to change. We therefore needed to clearly restate our contractual offer to our students, publish it with sufficient time for them to make informed decisions about joining or continuing with a course, and receive their informed consent that they were happy to proceed.

Relevant information regarding our plans and activities was published and communicated widely. We decided that our website would become the central "hub" for all COVID-related information, with regular updating and front-page positioning where normally we would be posting marketing material for recruiting students onto our courses. This was a decision designed not from a commercial standpoint, but from a values standpoint whereby we wanted to reassure a wide range of stakeholders that we were taking their concerns very seriously and were fully aware of our responsibility to inform, reassure, and commit to their needs.

4.6 Summarizing the approach taken by ICMP

This approach can be summarized as follows:

1. Have in place a strong, experienced, and capable leadership team with shared culture and values working to common goals
2. Quickly establish "crisis management" practices and develop communications across a range of media to a range of key stakeholders

3. Establish a short-term plan with clear objectives to give focus to decision making
4. Ensure sufficient resources are available for immediate and longer-term utilization as the impact of cost-saving measures or decisions slowed down by cumbersome approval processes may not be effective
5. Be prepared to take some immediate risk, especially with expenditure, and work flexibly and quickly often outside of normally established practices
6. Engage the entire organization and mobilize other key stakeholder groups, in our case the students, their extended families/supporters and our sector regulator, for example
7. Do not lose sight of longer-term plans and goals—the crisis will pass, and life will return to normal at some point
8. Take time to study any opportunities for growth and innovation that may present themselves as a result of the crisis

4.7 Initial outcomes at ICMP

The result of all this was that we were able to safeguard and in fact enhance our liquidity and overall financial sustainability. We met our September 2020 recruitment targets. We kept our staff onside, without having to make any redundancies or take other negative measures that would impact on morale. The "stress test" applied as a result of the pandemic enabled us to identify areas of the business that were weak and that needed restructuring or more investment. We were able to project a sense of calm, careful control to a wide range of stakeholders even in the most uncertain periods. By not making redundancies or taking significant cost-cutting measures, we were positioned to rebound more strongly from the following year as the pandemic waned. We also took the opportunity to develop a number of ideas about how we might further innovate and grow our provision.

The downside? From a business perspective, really only one—our trading margins were significantly reduced for the 2020/21 period, though we look at that as an investment that will impact positively on the future of the business. But it is essential that we consider the downsides for the people directly involved in this crisis and our response to it.

Our staff, each with a particular personal circumstance and range of concerns and problems, were and continue to be exemplary in their approach to their professional duties during a time of great stress and anxiety. Many had to juggle childcare or home schooling during the lockdown period; many had shielding concerns for themselves, relatives or friends; and some had personal health issues to contend with.

For the students, while we were able to ensure continuity of their academic studies and a stable and effective learning environment was maintained without compromising standards or quality, the impact on their lives and experiences has been significant. Living in lockdown conditions, or with severe restrictions on their ability to socialize and network, especially for first-year students who have moved to a new city and find themselves living away from family and friends for the first time, has been a real challenge. We have seen this in terms of growing demand for counselling services, increased applications to our hardship fund for financial support and a significant number of students who have developed deep personal crises and who need significant interventions.

A key part of the response to a crisis of this nature is the provision of aftercare, managing the "long tail" of the return to normality once the extreme impact (and in some cases novelty) of the first few weeks and months has worn off and the experience becomes one of continued effort, endurance, and hardship. At the time of writing, we are still in this phase, and no doubt it will be some considerable time before we can announce that it is over. This requires patience, stamina, and focus from the senior leadership team in particular. But we have always been clear throughout the pandemic that our goal has been to provide an oasis of stability, security, and confidence in both the present and the future for our staff and students. Wherever possible, we kept to a "business as usual" approach, holding meetings and engaging with planned activities in as normal a way as possible. While our staff and students were navigating their own personal challenges and anxieties, our goal was to present ICMP as something that they could depend upon, that they could rely upon, and that the future of their studies or their careers was the one thing they did not have to worry about.

5   Opportunities and developments arising from crises

5.1   Historical context

Natural disasters, pandemics, wars, and other sources of significant human conflict and suffering have more often than not led to progress, creativity, and innovations—in art, in medicine, in technology, and in our societies more generally. These low likelihood but high impact events force us to take stock of all that we do; we are generally not afforded the luxury to plan our way into them, but must quickly and creatively figure out ways to plan our way out (see http://www.history.com/news/pandemics-advances). These situations therefore often lead to new ways of thinking and increased creativity, driven by need and suffering in the present combined with an aspirational focus to move forward and create a better future.

The Black Death resulted in a significant shortage of labour that empowered workers and arguably led ultimately to the elimination of serfdom. Awareness of the importance of public hygiene and sanitation grew, and practical adaptations that we use today, such as social distancing and quarantining, even then started to become understood and put into practice. The 1918 flu pandemic encouraged new thinking around preventative medicine, the development of more centralized healthcare systems, and the introduction of health insurance in many countries. Suburban planning developed to create less closely packed housing in urban areas. Great novels, including T.S. Eliot's *Wasteland* and William Butler Yeats's *The Second Coming*, were inspired by the 1918 pandemic; Defoe's *A Journal of the Plague Year* was set during the Great Plague of London of 1665–66; Picasso's *Guernica* and Goya's *The Third of May* are just two examples of great art arising from human conflict; the development of vaccines, mass testing, and a wide range of other medical procedures have accompanied the threats and occurrences of epidemics and pandemics over many centuries.

5.2 COVID: The opportunities

Looking at the current COVID-19 pandemic, the question is what innovations, change, and creativity will arise as a result of this suffering and sacrifice? What will we look back on in future years and say, this is the moment that marked either the invention of a new technology, the acceleration of an existing one, a change to the way we live or work, the creation of some great body of art or literature or the transformation of some other element of our culture, our society, or our lives? Some of this is already visible. New vaccine technologies, such as Pfizer's mRNA approach that has recently announced a 90% efficacy in stage 3 clinical trials, are being rolled out in record time, with typical 10-year plus development cycles being compressed tenfold by advances in technology and knowledge. New global accords are being put into place that are evaluating how to deliver vaccines equitably and quickly across the globe. People and their employers are thinking about ways to work together more flexibly and beneficially. And—hopefully—government planners are building on lessons learned to ensure more effective responses next time around.

At ICMP, we have seen the incredible resilience and creativity of our staff, adapting quickly to new ways of working, and our students, finding ways to collaborate, create, and perform great new music. They are building their futures with energy and determination even as the present remains confusing and complicated and the past recedes into a memory of another era. Many of these forced changes will persist as beneficial adaptations and, with creativity, knowledge, and resilience being cultivated across society, we can look forward to significant advancements and further positive change in the years to come.

Of course, adopting a long-term view can be difficult, both practically and psychologically, when we are caught up in the day-to-day reality of dealing with the very real impacts of the pandemic. But as someone working in an English higher education sector that already had some significant challenges to deal with even before the pandemic hit, it is necessary to grasp the opportunities being presented as soon as possible. Whether we are individually or collectively capable of taking advantage of these opportunities is the only question.

6 Lessons for the future

1. Use technology to enhance flexibility and enrich delivery

For a long time, many traditional universities have resisted the online revolution and held out against the advantages offered to their customers by online and distance learning technology. Why? There are three simple reasons for this. First, with so much installed infrastructure and overhead dedicated to the face to face, 3-year, on-campus degree, it is simply not in their interests to revolutionize their provision which could make a large quantity of this expensive infrastructure redundant and require significant change management programmes across a heavily unionized workforce. Second, as any business knows, tying a customer in to a long-term, expensive, and hard-to-leave contract is good for cash flow. Cost of sales is reduced, and the predictability and regularity of revenue makes business planning easy. And third, with continued rhetoric that elevates the 3-year undergraduate on-campus university degree (preferably a Russell Group one) as the ultimate aspirational goal (and even as a "rite of passage"), a regulator that emphasizes the moral obligation of student retention to the end of these long degree courses; combined with the financial benefits to the institution of keeping as many students on course for as long as possible, we have the perfect scenario for the preservation of the existing model, which is not always in the best interests of the student, the taxpayer, or the ultimate employer.

Looking at the impact of the Internet revolution across a range of mainstream industries, one can understand this reluctance to embrace technological change. The Music industry, which is close to the hearts and minds of ICMP students, underwent significant and lasting revolution from the invention of Napster and file sharing in the late 1990s and Apple's invention of iTunes and the reestablishment of the pricing model for music in the early 2000s. A lasting result is the way music is now conveniently and more economically accessed by a much wider range of consumers in a variety of different ways—music consumption increased for the fifth year in a row in 2019, with 154 million albums consumed across streaming and purchasing and 114 billion music streams generated a 3000% increase on 2012 according to the BPI—see http://www.bpi.co.uk/news-analysis/streaming-breaks-the-100-billion-barrier-fuelled-by-exciting-new-talent/.

The publishing industry, bookstores, high street retail, banking, travel, insurance—there is an endless list of major, established, traditional industries that fell prey to the efficiencies and convenience of online technology. Many adapted, but many did not and have disappeared into history. But if there is one industry which is ripe for technological revolution, it is the business of education. Young people—in fact, people of all ages—now conduct very significant parts of their lives online. They make friendships, form relationships, build businesses, develop careers, create art and literature, purchase goods, and generally live a technologically enhanced life that is efficient, rewarding, and valued. Why would their education not be similarly enhanced by technology?

As we are seeing during this pandemic, while some elements of education will always need to be delivered face to face, as we are social creatures and need human contact, practical demonstration, and physical experience, much can be delivered from distance. Blending methods of delivery allow more flexibility and convenience, can reduce costs to the student and the institution, and can enhance and enrich the learning experience. Digital delivery allows for more effective tracking of student engagement, leading to faster and more effective interventions to provide support to the student. And it allows for greater reach, greater efficiency, and greater accessibility. To conclude, from *Digital at the core: A 2030 strategy framework for university leaders*, published in October 2020 and representing a collaboration of several sector and commercial organizations:

> *What [the pandemic] has shown is that developing a long-term strategy for digital is now more essential than ever, despite the evolving and uncertain circumstances we face.*
>
> *(Iosad, 2020)*

2. Develop more flexibility and equality of value around delivery of a range of qualifications

Philip Augar's 2019 review of Post-18 education and funding, among other things, recommended an increase in flexibility and lifetime learning. His panel recommended (Augar, 2019):

> *the introduction of a lifelong learning loan allowance to be used at higher technical and degree level at any stage of an adult's career for full and part-time students. To encourage retraining and flexible learning, we recommend that*

this should be available in modules where required. We intend that our proposals should facilitate transfer between different institutions, and we make proposals for greater investment in so-called 'second chance' learning at intermediate levels.

The use of technology would be of great assistance in the implementation of this idea, and the blended model most of us are now using would lend itself perfectly to such flexibility. But to achieve the necessary flexibility would need two key changes to the current system:

    a. The introduction of credit-based financing, which would enable students to pick and choose the modules they study, and access loans proportionate to their quantum of study, thus avoiding large financial and time commitments upfront

    b. A review of the regulatory metrics used to assess and monitor providers, which are currently geared towards keeping students on fixed courses for as long as possible and which still focus on traditional interpretations of quality and effectiveness of provision

There would also need to be clear and effective communication campaigns around the equality of value of different qualifications and modes of study. With these overarching conditions in place, and without removing the crucial role of the regulator in overseeing quality and standards, we would see providers developing a wide range of innovative products, of short- or longer-term duration, face to face, online or blended, to enable students to build portfolios of credit and qualifications, combine study with work experience and earning, regularly review their progress and where required switch providers or disciplines or perhaps take a break. This would enable them to avoid the monolithic and cumbersome need to make long-term decisions at the outset, incurring significant time commitment and exposure to debt, which is central to the current system. This approach would also be of significant benefit to adult and part-time learners who are simply not in a position to commit to traditional models of higher education.

While the traditional 3-year on-campus degree will always have a central role in higher education, it should not be the only option and in itself is not the answer to achieving true and fair mass access to higher education that provides good value to both the student and the taxpayer.

3. Address the issue of pricing and cost of higher education

Imagine a scenario where, on making the decision to buy a car, one walks into the car showroom to choose a model. Electric or petrol? Small or large? Child friendly or sports focused? Blue or green? There is a range of choices and decisions to be made, tailored to personal circumstances and preferences. But imagine that process of buying a car **without having to consider price—because they all cost the same.** A nice idea, but not possible. Each model will have a different cost of construction, a different brand value, and a different value to the purchaser. They will all take the buyer from A to B, some a little faster, some a little slower, but they will have vastly different prices. This is normal. This is understood. This is what we expect.

So why do the same rules not apply to higher education? In the United Kingdom, why does every degree cost the same, £9250, with few exceptions? Why was the goal of differential pricing hoped for in the sector reforms following the 2010 White Paper not achieved? For the simple reason, it is not in the vested interests of the mainstream providers of degrees to do so. The debates at the time concerning pricing included such class-infused phrases as "the race to the bottom" and were more focused on provider sustainability and reputation, maximizing revenue per student and protecting existing forms of provision as far as possible. These were not consumer-focused debates, and after a short period where a few providers experimented with lower tuition fees, everyone ended up in the same place. And with an income-contingent loan scheme put in place for students, there was further disincentive for the sector to consider the impact of course pricing.

If we take the above example of the music industry pre-Napster, this all looks very familiar. A relatively small number of large, powerful, influential record companies dictated the price of albums and singles and forced us to buy things we did not always want (filler album tracks, for example, when consumers just wanted to buy one particular single). They had absolute control over the means of production and distribution. The industry was effectively behaving as a cartel. Napster and file sharing broke that model wide open and Apple applied the finishing touches. While there are still significant issues today about the value that trickles down to artists, and that is a very important debate, it cannot be said that the previous model was designed to protect the artist either. It was designed to protect the installed infrastructure and vested interests of that small number of large and powerful record companies.

Technology was the key to breaking this dominance, providing wider access more efficiently with differentiated pricing to enhance consumer choice. And technology can now do the same for higher education, with the caveat that proper regulatory safeguards need to be in place and enforced. The "academy," the great and the good of the sector, tell us that a degree is a cherished product and has a value that cannot be varied, that should apply equally to all, and that should not be open to debate. But different degrees have different values to both the graduate and wider society. These values are complex and not simply monetary of course. But we simply have to acknowledge that the costs of different degree courses and the financial, career, and societal outcomes of completing different courses at different institutions differ, that the value equation is different, and that differential pricing, combined with the above-discussed ability to study higher education flexibly, in smaller pieces over variable time periods, is a desirable outcome. And it is not just the tuition cost of the degree—the costs of commuting or living away from home, often in expensive cities, abandoning work for full-time study over a long period, are significant too. The current model of provision will simply not be affordable nor sustainable if we are to meet growing demand for and provide fair access to higher education into the future.

Our experiences during the pandemic demonstrate that we can provide high-quality higher education flexibly using online technology, which should present ways to increase efficiency and effectiveness. This has to translate into differential and more beneficial pricing and delivery models for higher education products. The Higher Education Policy Institute (HEPI) has calculated that there will be over 350,000 more higher education places needed in England by 2035 to keep up with demand (HEPI, 2020). As Jeff Bezos has said, recently quoted in a *Times* podcast, "what happens when infinite demand meets finite resources? Rationing" (Bezos, 2020). In other words, without addressing this issue, we will inevitably return to a system where access to higher education is limited, places are restricted, and individual choice is reduced—and we will all be the poorer for it.

4. Increase the depth and breadth of higher education provision

No-one would doubt that the need for continuous, long-term, and specialized study in specific subject areas should be a prerequisite for much high-quality higher education. Science or engineering undergraduates need face-to-face contact, access to a wide range of practical resources and specialist facilities, and they need a lengthy period of focused and intensive study to become successful and effective. You cannot learn to be a surgeon or a vet by studying piecemeal or exclusively online in the virtual world. The 3-year, on-campus, more traditional degree focused on a specialist subject therefore has a very important place at the heart of our higher education system, as does the extensive investment in research carried out by our universities that supports great teaching. I would like my doctor to have studied long and hard and have a qualification from a very reputable establishment, as I am sure you would. But in a world of increasingly mass higher education, we also have a wider responsibility to educate in a broader sense.

I often use my own example to illustrate this. My father was a tenant farmer in the northwest of England. I was taught good practical skills, pushed hard through my state schooling, and given a strong work ethic. I was the second in my family to go to university where I studied Agriculture and gained a 2:1 degree. On graduating, I joined a large multinational firm and was able to travel the world extensively, gaining a wide range of life and professional experiences that were unbelievable to my parents. I was able to build sufficient resources to be able to transfer from this career to do something different and have been able to apply my extensive experiences and learning to my current project, which is building a university. None of this would have been possible without my higher education degree and the experiences and confidence I gained while doing it. But I do not work in the agricultural industry; the point is higher education more often than not is not about specializing in a particular discipline or career but is about providing people with the flexibility and opportunities to change both their lives and wider society, to adapt and to pursue paths that interest and reward them throughout their lives.

The ongoing pandemic has demonstrated that we all need greater knowledge of the world, of science, politics, and public policy, of government and public health. We need to be able to communicate, and understand communications, and decipher truth from disinformation effectively. We need to cooperate and build strong societies, and work behind shared goals to create better futures. Higher education is a key facilitator of this, which is why we need to examine what we do at every level. This means re-examining our curriculums and considering introducing more science, humanities, or liberal arts-related subject matter into specialized learning pathways. Knowledge of history would be a useful benefit to any decision maker considering pandemic-related planning. "Flipping the classroom" can enable face-to-face teaching to be more productive and relevant, focusing on the development of intelligence, reasoning, and a range of wider transferable skills such as communication and debate, with less interactive content that is nonetheless essential for development delivered more efficiently online with large elements of the whole package captured electronically for continuous reference.

Higher education is an enabler of people's futures, and as such, we need to consider how we educate, what we educate, and why we educate at higher levels. Philip Augar's review panel, mentioned above, recognized that "employment patterns are changing fast with shorter job cycles and longer working lives requiring many people to reskill and upskill." Monolithic higher education, concentrated into three continuous years, early in a young person's life, and with too much specialization, will not suffice for the majority of graduates as they build their futures into what will be a constantly changing world.

5. Reconsider the definition of higher education

I have long argued in the higher education sector that we should be careful about the terminology we use, much of which is loaded with historical prejudice, attitudes to class, and a love of tradition. When we speak of such things as Tertiary Education; Further Education; Higher Education; Oxbridge; Apprenticeships; an "academic" education; a "vocational" pathway; the Russell Group; the "Gold Standards" of "A" Levels and Degrees; or the study of "subdegree" qualifications such as Higher National Certificates (HNCs), we apply a label and establish a sense of who the students studying in those areas might be, where they might come from, and where they might be headed. And we must be careful this predetermined impression is not prejudiced.

As a means to reinforce social class and hierarchy, education has always been a leading tool of choice. Rosemary O'Day, writing in *Education and Society 1500–1800: The Social*

Foundations of Education in Early Modern Britain (O'Day, 1982), captured this idea in a historical context:

> *'The English élite were already reacting against the idea of extending an academic education to all classes well before the [period of interregnum and the Glorious Revolution]: the events of that period merely strengthened their conviction that a little learning was a dangerous thing in the hands of the lower social orders'.*

Even Locke, progressive in so many areas, and quoted in Lawson and Silver's 'A Social History of Education in England' (Lawson and Silver, 1973) was interested only in the 'education of gentlemen…mental culture was not for men of low condition, only for those with means and leisure.

We should not deny that some of these prejudices have permeated through the centuries to the present day, though of course they may be more subtly expressed.

The invention of the printing press in the 15th century revolutionized the dissemination of knowledge and ideas. Enlightenment thought, the translation of the Latin Bible into the vernacular, the impact of more Humanist views which began to undermine the authority of the Church, the Reformation, the scientific and industrial revolutions, and other significant societal changes all drove progress, curiosity, and the development of literacy. This was often hindered by church intervention, and subject to a constant barrage of developing legislation from governments of all ideological colours as the idea of a broad education for all gradually took hold. Gillard, in his comprehensive *Education in England: a history*, is an excellent source for a comprehensive account of this development of English education through history (Gillard, 2018).

So it was that by the late 20th century, we found ourselves in a position where mass education to a reasonable standard was to be expected (and indeed compulsory to age 16 by 1972). But even today we can see the persistence of the resistance to mass education in universities, the long tail of the class system impacting admissions and student choices and driving endless debate over such shibboleths as comprehensive, grammar and public schools, with the constant clashing of ideology with regard to curriculum, parental choice, student ability, and choices and opportunities around academic versus vocational pathways. This is all overseen by authority figures and administrations often not best placed or experienced to provide the right leadership: Two-thirds of Boris Johnson's 2019 cabinet were privately educated, for example, according to research from the Sutton Trust (see http://www.suttontrust.com/news-opinion/all-news-opinion/old-school-ties-the-educational-background-of-boris-johnsons-cabinet/).

Let us therefore take this opportunity to redefine education and learning as a single, continuous, flexible pathway from birth to death that should be facilitated and funded properly and fairly, whether by the taxpayer, the student, endowments, or employers or in a combination of ways, and remove stigmas attached to level or type of study, the name or type of provider, or affordability. The pandemic has demonstrated how equal we all are, so let us provide true equality of access to higher education to all. Let us not venerate and worship the "university," which while an important part of our educational infrastructure is not the only end point. Higher education is and should be much broader than just the university. Let us find and use ways to deliver higher education more extensively, facilitated by technology, adopting the progressive approach of the "dissenting academies" of the 17th and 18th centuries who developed, in O'Day's words, "an education which became much broader than that in the universities and in the schools established by the law and controlled by the church" (O'Day, 1982), and which, according to Ashley Smith (1954) in *The Birth of Modern Education: the contribution of the dissenting academies 1660–1800*, "arguably led the way in developing new subjects and methods of teaching, including such innovations as free discussion, the use of a wider range of texts and the use of the vernacular."

And let us embark on a campaign to remove discriminatory language and beliefs around higher education provision and qualifications, which reinforces stereotypes and limits innovation. Degrees and "A" Levels should not be casually referred to as the "gold standard" and nondegree qualifications should not be termed "subdegree." Nonacademic pathways should not be classed lazily as "vocational," when all learning is to some degree vocational, particularly postcompulsory education. The word "university" should not be elevated as representing the exclusive pinnacle of learned achievement. Flexibility for lifetime and part-time learning should be encouraged and facilitated, and we should seek to reward innovation in the way we deliver higher education. And we should respect, encourage, and be open to a wide range of higher education delivered at a range of levels in a variety of ways from a wide range of providers, including short course, online, and "blended" learning which offer many advantages and should now become the mainstream choice for many subjects.

7 Conclusion

Well-managed and properly resourced businesses will have been able to weather the storm of the COVID-19 pandemic, taking their short-term losses and coming out the other side more resilient and wiser. State-driven support programmes should have supported the majority of those who were particularly disadvantaged and the wider societal challenges that were faced, though the support provided will not have been perfect, and many will have suffered negative health or economic impact as a result of the pandemic's consequences. Some industries will either have taken the opportunity to drive change themselves or will be driven by the changes ensuing from the pandemic, to create entirely different and progressive futures. And some will be lost, a natural and often beneficial process of selection taking place as a result of the crisis. Hopefully, governments will have learned the lessons of planning for low likelihood but high impact events such as this, with rational plans put in place for the future that transcend ideological or political boundaries and are continued beyond the short time frames of the western democratic model.

In higher education, a return to the status quo following this pandemic would be a failure and would ignore the wider lessons of history. It is likely that much of the resistance to online learning among young people will now have been eroded, and the cultural shift in expectations and possibilities around higher education should now be facilitated. This will require progressive providers to grasp the opportunity to innovate and should spur governments and their regulatory bodies to develop a restructured funding and regulatory environment supportive of more flexible and relevant provision that will meet growing demand in an economical and efficient way. Further, we should consider the wider narratives prevalent around higher education, start thinking and talking about it in a different way, and take the opportunity to further dismantle any remaining class or ideological barriers to true mass participation. We must use this progressive approach to deliver in particular our responsibilities to adult and part-time learners—responsibilities that have been badly neglected in recent years—and address the need for lifetime learning that is now essential for all. And we should do this while engaging in honest discussion about costs and fees, driving efficiency and innovation in ways that will achieve the best value for all concerned. These are some of the opportunities presented to us now, and I hope we are able to take them.

References

Ashley Smith, J.W., 1954. The Birth of Modern Education: The Contribution of the Dissenting Academies 1660–1800. Independent Press, London.

Augar, P., 2019. Review of post-18 education and funding. Crown Copyright.

Bezos, J., 2020. Jeff Bezos and the rise of the Amazon empire, stories of our times podcast. The Times. November 11th.

Gillard, D., 2018. Education in England: A History. HMSO. http://www.educationengland.org.uk/history.

HEPI, 2020. Demand for higher education to 2035. HEPI report, 134. October,.

Iosad, A., 2020. Digital at the Core: A 2030 Strategy Framework for University Leaders. Universities UK/JISC/emerge education/salesforce.org, London.

Lawson, J., Silver, H., 1973. A Social History of Education in England. Methuen & Co Ltd, London.

O'Day, R., 1982. Education and Society 1500-1800: The Social Foundations of Education in Early Modern Britain. Longman.

The battered library—Navigating the future in a new reality

26

Stephen Akintunde

National Institute for Policy and Strategic Studies, Kuru, Plateau State, Nigeria

1 Introduction

The idea of a battered library represents a state of volatility. It derives from the dynamic nature of academic library services (Troll, 2001), the changing knowledge and skill requirements of staff (Wynne, 2016), and the obvious unpredictability of the needs of library patrons (Musoke, 2008). Looking back at the idea of a library when it served as the central preserver of knowledge and culture (Too, 2010), what is unfolding today is a remarkable change from what was known. Yet, the change is apparently only just unfolding. The COVID-19 pandemic which became a global and generational signpost highlights the criticality of institutions like health and education in society (de Aranzabal, 2020; Debbarma, 2021). But, how has the changing environment influenced service delivery and the adoption of change by libraries?

Whereas the pandemic resulted in a standstill of social services in many societies, the attention given to libraries in different societies varied. While in some societies libraries invented ways to continue with services (Rafiq, 2021), the experience in countries of sub-Saharan Africa is that of a near-total lockdown (Haider, 2020). The response in many of these African countries is obviously tied to their levels of national infrastructural development of information and communications technology (Asongu, 2017). Poor financing and low levels of digitization of library collections are common features in many of these countries. The immediate response, therefore, was to close institutions of learning. Resources on many institutional websites, for instance in Nigeria, are mere catalog lists, except, perhaps, for a few harvested free online resources. Even then, not many library staff and patrons can afford online services because of the cost of data needed to connect to the Internet. The library in such situations was under lockdown, just as their parent institutions. Librarians and patrons, therefore, waited for the easing of lockdown to resume learning and visit the library again. And, even though the youth population in the majority of higher education institutions is technology-friendly, it had been discovered that they use technology more for mere social interaction and music purposes other than academic (Akintunde, 2020).

The pandemic provided opportunities for individuals and organizations to explore pragmatic ways of communicating and carrying out their work in a new social situation. Many institutions of learning took advantage of their technological status to build and deliver improved online learning environments (Oyedotun, 2020). For such institutions, the pandemic was another opportunity to migrate fully to digital scholarly

Libraries, Digital Information, and COVID. https://doi.org/10.1016/B978-0-323-88493-8.00026-4

communication because of the possibilities of virtual interactions. This comes with its own etiquettes which also have to be defined and refined. Classrooms moved to virtual environments, and participants learned new rules on online interactions (S.E. Shah et al., 2020).

Virtual meetings and conferences followed (Price, 2020), and there was an unveiling of new platforms for both classrooms and conferences and an improvement on existing ones. We now have competing platforms like Google Meet, free conference calls, Hangouts, Webex Meet, and Zoom, which have provided alternatives for digital communication and keep improving. Many professional groups have used some of these platforms to communicate freely with their members and offer free services to the public. Governments and businesses have also used the platforms to disseminate information on the COVID protocol and other matters of governance and business. The situation now appears to be a continuous migration to real-time communication online.

In most cases, equity in access and use of information and communication technology (ICT) by regions of the world is taken for granted. However, this may not be the case as there are inequities in the adoption and use of technology as a solution to social crises, such as the disruption brought about by COVID. The major factors accounting for the inequities appear to be national ideologies, funding, and infrastructural development. This is where sub-Saharan Africa lags. Many countries in the region are yet to implement articulated sustainable national ideologies and policies on technology and other social services which are beyond political identities and patronage (Gillwald, 2010). The challenge posed by the pandemic offers a new vista of opportunity to move forward.

Apart from factors of national ideologies, funding, and level of infrastructural development for ICT, there is also a cultural factor, where there is a disparity in the reading culture between the more developed countries and the countries of sub-Saharan Africa. There is also a poor state of social services which makes the average citizen bother more on how to survive, providing for their households for daily subsistence than creating time to read or desire to acquire knowledge in a crisis situation. This is prevalent in Nigeria.

With these indicators, the physical library in sub-Saharan countries, such as Nigeria, becomes a necessity. So, when there is a social crisis like the pandemic and it is impossible to visit or make use of the physical library, then there is a major challenge needing a solution. This was the situation of libraries in Nigeria during the pandemic. The situation revealed the value placed on libraries as observed in the case of a state government turning the State Library Complex into a COVID isolation center that would accommodate more than 200 beds (Oyelere, 2020). This decision was later reversed after the Nigerian Library Association intervened.

For Nigerian libraries, the pandemic was not an experience to repeat. And, with every possibility of a second wave of lockdown in the future, libraries in developing countries will need to be more creative in order to be relevant in times of national and global emergencies. It is clear now that crisis breeds invention and practical solutions are needed for evolving challenges, not limited to health issues but including war, natural, and other disasters. These are realities of social existence and need to be prepared for since they usually come without a notice, although it seems that each time, the world is caught unprepared (de Amorim, 2020).

In an attempt to assess the response of libraries and patrons of libraries during COVID-19, and project into the future, higher education institutions in Nigeria were surveyed because of their perceived need for library and information services at all times. Nigeria is Africa's most populated country with a projected population of 206 million and the 7th most populous country in the world (United Nations Fund For Population Activities, 2020). The evidence provided by the target population should provide parameters for projections into the future in facing challenges and change.

The chapter proposes a theoretical perspective, states the research problem, and outlines the research questions, then the methodology, results, and discussion. An outline of practical and strategic approaches to challenge and change, based on the findings and discussion, is then given before the conclusion.

2 Theoretical perspective

In carrying out the research, the study adopted the *critical realism* theory. Critical realism recognizes an external objective reality, which interpretation is shaped by the subjective experience of individuals or the interpreters of the reality (Giddens and Sutton, 2017). This subjective experience is usually a result of environmental and historical experiences of individuals. The theoretical perspective supports scientific research as well as sociological interpretation of history. It is a scientific interpretation of Mills' sociological imagination which "enables its possessor to understand the larger historical scene in terms of its meaning for the inner life and the external career of a variety of individuals (Mills, 2000, p. 5)."

In studying the approaches of libraries to the COVID-19 pandemic and projecting into the future, it is imperative to recognize the situational contexts of the key actors—librarians, library patrons, and librarianship students—in particular situations, such as cultural, geographical, and technological. Viewed from this perspective, it is obvious that digitization, the impact of COVID, and approaches to challenges and change would differ from one situation to the other. In a review of Erving Goffman's definition of the situation, Dillon states that "how we initially define the situation will determine how we behave (Dillon, 2014, p. 284)." Applying this to the present study implies that practical and strategic applications and approaches to the challenges and change brought about by the COVID pandemic will be defined by sociocultural, political, technological, and economic situations. The adoption and migration to the digital environment from the manual will also differ according to peculiar situations. This is the extension and application of the critical realism theory.

The **research problem** for this study is therefore the challenges brought upon librarians and library patrons during the pandemic and how these were managed. These include the state of libraries and their readiness to face challenges in service provision, the impact and effect of digitization in critical situations such as the COVID pandemic, and what this portends for the future.

The **aim of the study** is to discover how the target population of librarians, librarianship students, and general students responded to the COVID-19 pandemic and their approach to the change that it has brought. Research questions were:

(1) What was the state of mind of librarians during the COVID-19 lockdown?
(2) How would librarians face another lockdown?
(3) How were library services managed during the lockdown?
(4) What are the new skills and knowledge required for the future?
(5) What tools would be most necessary to navigate the future?
(6) What format for library resources would be most needful in the future?
(7) How would library spaces be used in the future?

3 Methodology

The method of investigation used in this study is a social survey. An online survey of librarians, general students, and librarianship students was carried out among higher education institutions in Nigeria. Social media platforms, such as WhatsApp and Facebook, were used to generate data. This was due to the closure of many higher education institutions in the country, restrictions on physical movements, and the easy accessibility of research population to social media. For the WhatsApp platform, the questionnaire link was shared with the national platforms of the respective target groups. For Facebook, the "status" of assistants was used to fill the questionnaire.

Responses were received from higher education institutions as indicated in Table 26.1.

Librarians were mainly the heads of libraries, while "general students" were drawn from Nigerian higher education institutions studying different courses. It was considered necessary to sample librarianship students as a category in order to determine their interpretation of the situation since they are being trained for the future. It is interesting to observe that in the three categories sampled, there is greater participation of women, which is perhaps normal in librarianship, which could affect the responses on the emotional status of librarians. The responses show a wide distribution and can be considered adequate at the level of research to determine the "practical and strategic application and approach to challenges and change" in the context of the area under investigation when discussing "COVID, libraries, and digital information."

Table 26.1 Respondents by number, institutions, and gender.

Category	Number of respondents	Number of institutions	Female number	Percentage (%)	Male number	Percentage (%)
Librarians	75	50	41	54.7	34	45.3
General students	466	36	255	54.7	211	45.3
Librarianship students	130	2	89	68.5	41	31.5

4 Results

Results are presented using the research questions as a guide.

Research question 1. What was the state of mind of librarians during the COVID-19 lockdown?
Results from the survey show that librarians who are key decision-makers in terms of libraries and digital information were emotionally traumatized during the COVID-19 lockdown, with females feeling more frustrated and unsettled. See Figs. 26.1 and 26.2.
Research question 2. How would librarians face another lockdown?
An overwhelming 71% of librarians would also feel disturbed if there should be another lockdown due to a pandemic or any other reason as indicated in Fig. 26.3, again with the female category tending to feel more disturbed and agitated. See Fig. 26.4. This is a reality of the emotional state of librarians during the pandemic and potentially affects their practical response to an unusual situation.
Research question 3. How were library services managed during the lockdown?
Different countries had different responses to the COVID-19 pandemic based on their levels of digitization and general infrastructural development. In the population sampled for this study, 68% of librarians claimed that they offered services during the lockdown as indicated in Fig. 26.5. Out of those that provided services, 32% claimed that they provided both digital and manual services, 28% only digital, while 6% provided only manual services. Also, 25% of those who could not provide services during the COVID lockdown did not do so because their libraries were shut down during the period, while 16% could not provide any service because apart from being physically shut down, they did not have functional online library services. In sharp contrast to the claim of librarians, only 14% of students agreed that they made use of library services during the lockdown, while 86% said they did not as represented in Fig. 26.6.

Reasons given by 48% of students for not using libraries is that the library was far from where they stayed and so they could not gain access to the library and 23% affirmed that they had no need to go to library for various reasons, while 20% said that the library was locked up.

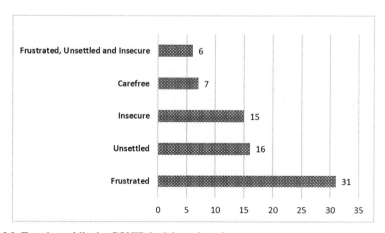

Fig. 26.1 Emotion while the COVID lockdown lasted.

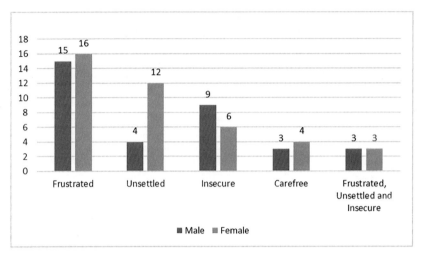

Fig. 26.2 Emotion while the COVID lockdown lasted by gender.

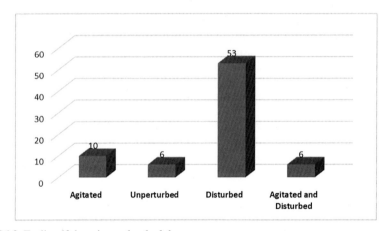

Fig. 26.3 Feeling if there is another lockdown.

Research question 4. What are the new skills required for the future?
It is clear, from responses received, that libraries will experience definite changes in the next 5–10 years. This will affect the way services are delivered with an acceleration in the use of digital resources and the creative use of space. If this would happen, then what skill set would be required for the future? Among librarians, digital literacy, online communication, information literacy, and post-COVID social interaction are top of new skills that would be required to render effective services. See Fig. 26.7.

Among students, generally required skills in the future would be online search, reading, information literacy, and effective web navigation in that order of importance.

Research question 5. What tools would be most necessary to effectively navigate the future?
From responses received, the tools that would be most needed to navigate the future among librarians are mobile devices: smart cell phones (39%), laptops (36%), notebooks/iPad

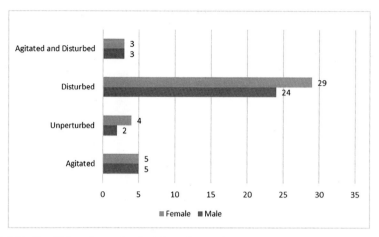

Fig. 26.4 Feeling if there is another lockdown by gender.

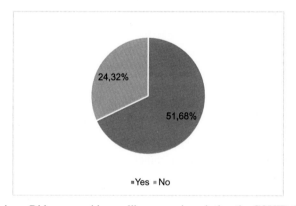

Fig. 26.5 Librarians: Did you provide any library services during the COVID-19 lockdown?

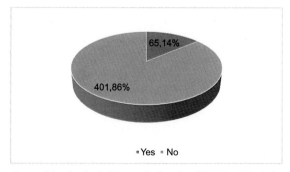

Fig. 26.6 Students' use of institution's library during the COVID-19 lockdown.

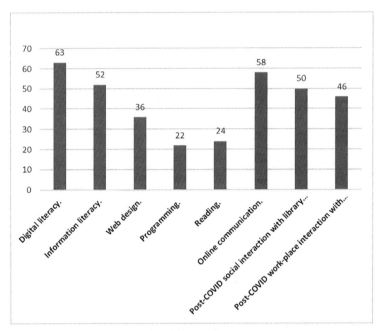

Fig. 26.7 Librarians' skills required after COVID-19.

(21%), desktop (3%), and ordinary cell phone (1%) as most critical. This is the same pattern of responses among students. See Fig. 26.8.

Since the future is projected to be more digital than at present with changes required, librarianship students were asked if they would still choose to study the subject or another discipline, if presented with an option. Results indicate that 70% will still choose librarianship, while 30% would rather change course. Reasons given to want to change the course of study are library schools not catching up with the change in

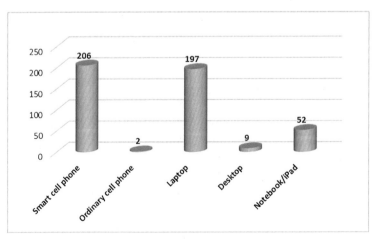

Fig. 26.8 Students: Tools needed the most to access and use resources post-COVID.

the society and workplace, people no longer needing librarians to access information, an uncertain future, and perceived inability to cope with the constant change. Librarianship students were then asked what change they would want to see reflected in their curriculum. The result shows a need for a deeper knowledge and management of the digital environment as indicated in Fig. 26.9.

As reflected in Fig. 26.10, librarians also expressed the need for more training to upgrade their knowledge, most of them needing both formal and informal training.

Research question 6. What format for library services would be most desirable in the future? Considering the present situation and projecting into the future, 91% of librarianship students agreed that the library will not be the same in the next 5–10 years. They affirmed that physical learning resources and digital resources will both be needed, along with full deployment of technology, as reflected in Fig. 26.11. Among students, generally 72% of 466 respondents agreed that online and physical services will be required in the future, with 21% agreeing that only online services will feature and 7% only physical. This pattern of response was also reflected by librarians, with 88% of them agreeing that in the next 5–10 years

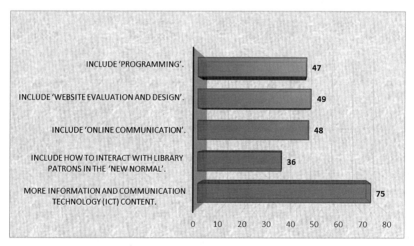

Fig. 26.9 Librarianship students: Change in curriculum expected.

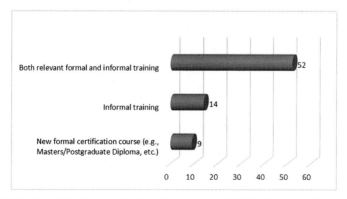

Fig. 26.10 Librarians: Training needed for effective post-COVID library services.

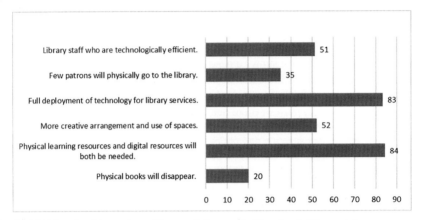

Fig. 26.11 Librarianship students: Expected changes in libraries 5–10 years' time.

library services will be a hybrid of online and physical, 9% suggesting that there will be fully online library services, and only 3% saying that services will be physical only.

Research question 7. How would library spaces be used in the future?

Recognizing the critical role of physical library hitherto in accessing information, respondents were asked whether they would still need to visit the physical library in the near future. Responses from students show that 61% of them affirmed that they would need to visit the physical library. See Fig. 26.12. Among librarianship students, 91% of them agreed that library, though in existence, would not be the same again and only 9% answered that library will not experience any change.

On what use they expected the physical spaces to be used for in the future, responses by librarians indicate that 76% of them expect more flexible and responsive use of library spaces to meet the changing nature of information packaging and service, as reflected in Fig. 26.13.

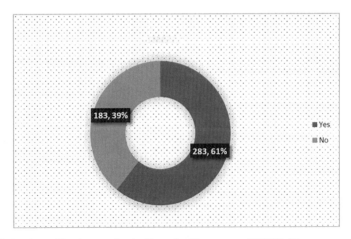

Fig. 26.12 Students: Need to go physically to the library post-COVID-19 era.

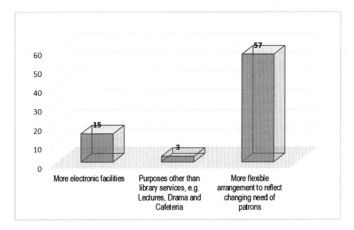

Fig. 26.13 Librarians: How library spaces would be used in the next few years?

5 Discussion

Results from this study which serve as evidence to support projections into the future of the digital environment and future library services require further reflection. This is done by using the research questions as a guide in the discussion.

The *state of mind of librarians during the lockdown of the COVID-19 pandemic* evidently shows emotional instability. When a person is in a state of emotional disequilibrium, it is easy not to think clearly. This in turn affects the exploration of options to confront challenges and bring about innovative and pragmatic solutions. This also probably affected the response of the librarians by not being able to provide creative solutions for the 86% of students who did not make use of their institutional libraries during the lockdown. It is obvious that the COVID pandemic was sudden and most people in all professions were caught unprepared. However, some were able to think through by providing some levels of service using the digital platform. Only 28% of librarians in the survey offered online services during the pandemic. The general psychological impact of the pandemic induced anxiety, stress, frustration, loneliness, and uncertainty in individuals (Serafini, 2020; K.K. Shah et al., 2020).

The *preparedness of librarians to face another pandemic* is also low at this point because it appears that they are yet to recover from the shock of COVID. The ability to recover influences the release of creative instincts. However, since the post-COVID era provides for reflection by individuals and groups on their responses to this novel situation, it is possible that librarians will learn from the practical approaches that their colleagues in other societies have used in facing the challenges posed by the pandemic. And, depending on the time it takes for another pandemic to set in, librarians are most likely to be more emotionally stabilized and produce creative solutions in crisis and postcrisis situations.

The *way that library services were managed during the pandemic* shows that this could be done better. While several more developed economies were able to migrate most of their services to digital platforms, this was not the case in Nigeria because of the low level of infrastructural development. The national backbone for ICT is poor. Each educational institution subscribes to Internet services that it could afford which eventually affects the variety and quality of service (Egoeze, 2014). And, because of the high level of poverty in the country, many students are not able to afford mobile devices that can be used to easily access digital resources online. Moreover, they would need to have Internet connectivity which, for many, is unaffordable. It is therefore not surprising that only 9% of students were able to use online library services during the pandemic.

Recognizing that there is a definite and apparently irreversible change that has taken place and is still happening globally, *the new skills required for the future* are necessarily digital skills in all ramifications. The identification of digital literacy skills as the most required shows that there is an acceptance of a new reality that must be embraced. This upholds the campaign of the United Nations Educational, Scientific and Cultural Organization (UNESCO) advocacy for digital literacy. Digital literacy, according to UNESCO, consists of "accessing, managing, evaluating, integrating, creating, and communicating information individually or collaboratively in a networked, computer-supported, and web-based environment for learning, working, or leisure (UNESCO Institute for Information Technologies in Education, 2011, p. 4)." Deakin University corroborates the advocacy of UNESCO when it affirms that digital literacy promotes the employability of individuals in the new digital world (Deakin University, 2020). The university defines digital literacy as "using technologies to find, use, and disseminate information" (Deakin University, 2020, p. 1). It is therefore a realist solution to present and future challenges for librarians and librarianship students in the population of study to acknowledge their knowledge gap and put digital literacy as a priority need.

It is also interesting to observe that the *tools* identified by both librarians and librarianship students for *future practice* are mobile devices with smart cell phones as the most needed. This confirms the assertion that migration into the digital world is both necessary and natural. It is therefore only reasonable to accept that the new reality of digitalization is irreversible and is already leading to a smart environment, where everything can be interconnected: the Internet of things. This recognition by the population sample also implies that, given the opportunity and an appropriate environment, they can rise up to the challenges posed by any crisis, whether natural or otherwise. It also supports Matheson's thesis (Matheson, 1995) that librarians must be more proactive in terms of training and professional development to meet the challenges of 21st century knowledge-driven library practice.

This is perhaps why both librarians and librarianship students require further training. Organization change requires continuous training for optimum performance of staff. Change in curriculum, as demanded by a majority of librarianship students, is a desire to make their knowledge base synchronize with present and future realities. Librarians who require formal and informal training also acknowledge the need to fill their knowledge gap and be relevant in the future. This finding affirms Chan's statement that "the future of libraries relies on librarians' capacities to continuously transform our roles and skills" (Chan, 2017, p. 80). It also upholds Troll's assertion that "new technologies have rendered traditional measures less effective in explaining what is happening in libraries because the scope of traditional measures is too narrow to encompass the field of change (Troll, 2020)." The need for further training is therefore imperative. Librarians in Nigeria are challenged to, "as a matter of urgency, develop new skill sets tailored toward providing and redirecting library service delivery in support of learning in a virtual environment (Ifijeh, 2020)."

This also, perhaps, leads to the response that the *format that will be most needful for library services in the near future* will be hybrid. It is a realization that physical or manual services can no longer be adequate in meeting the need of patrons in the digital age. This supports the finding that libraries will necessarily adapt to changes in their operating environments if they must remain relevant (Baker and Ellis, 2020). However, the rate of adoption of, or adaptation to, change will depend upon present infrastructure, the preparedness of librarians to embrace change, and the level of adoption of technology in the society.

The *projected use of library space* by respondents as flexible to meet the changing need of patrons is also a reflection of knowledge of the environment, is strategic, and upholds the findings in an earlier Delphi study on the future of library physical space (Baker and Evans, 2016). The intervention of technology in library services has led to a paradigm shift in the organization of library space from traditional arrangements to a more open, flexible, and technologically responsive space. This attracts patrons to the library instead of being content with remote access using smart mobile devices. In creative and flexible learning spaces, there is usually a vast variety of furnishing and facilities supposedly to attract patrons to the library and for them to use the facilities for innovative and learning purposes. In this situation, library staff serve as mere guides by the side of the users. Some of the facilities provided are makerspaces and gaming where technological innovation can be developed in a group or as individuals.

6 Practical approaches to challenge and change

From the results of this study, it is clear that there is indeed a challenge and change in the provision of library and information services in a post-COVID era, at least in Nigeria. The situation of librarians and students in Africa's most populous country requires a practical approach in order to cope and be productive in the new social reality. So, a paradigm shift is required. The paradigm shift moves from traditional library services to a dynamic and adaptable practice. For practical purposes, the following approaches are worth considering:

(1) Redesign present library buildings to accommodate technology.
(2) Create more digital platforms for library patrons to access and use library resources.
(3) Retrain library staff by exposing them to new knowledge and skills required to provide effective and efficient service in the new social reality.
(4) Train library staff and patrons on the most effective use of mobile devices to store, access, and use digital resources.

7 Strategic approaches to challenge and change

Strategic approaches to the growing challenge and change include:

(1) Review of library school curricula to reflect changes in the operating environment.
(2) Mandatory training and retraining of librarians in formal and informal environments on the management of digital resources and digital communication so that they can move with trends in the society and the profession.
(3) Training of librarians and librarianship students on social interaction as the technology, the digital environment, and the effects of constant change in society affect social and workplace communication.
(4) The design of new library buildings to feature technology prominently and provide for flexible uses of space.
(5) Improved funding of libraries to accommodate an increase in the acquisition and use of technology and digital resources.

8 Conclusion

Library today faces a new era of flux. This change is most unpredictable. The COVID pandemic shocked librarians who struggled to adjust to the reality, hoping that it would not be repeated. However, librarians and patrons are compelled to adjust to the new reality: the traditional conception of library and library services has given way to a new paradigm of information storage, access, and dissemination which requires digital literacy for effective and efficient service delivery. Library resources are more digitally available and accessible than before and will continue to be. Physical library will still be relevant but will undergo a fundamental change in the arrangement and use of space. Librarians need to upgrade their knowledge and acquire new skill sets to be able to cope with trends in information formats and dissemination. Good knowledge of the character of the new library patron will be required in order to effectively interact with them and deliver services. Since most of the expected and growing users of the library are digital natives, it is only logical to appreciate their psychosocial situation and provide them with a conducive environment and services that will get them to use both physical and digital spaces of the library. This should also be reflected in a reviewed curriculum of library schools. It is pertinent to note that most of the present librarians and teachers in library schools are digital immigrants and would therefore be relevant only if they embrace the challenge posed by the changing psychosocial and technological environments. The changes are upswing and effecting all institutions that make up the society (Mosco, 2017). They require practical solutions.

References

Akintunde, S., 2020. Digital culture: the dynamics of incorporation. In: Baker, D., Ellis, L. (Eds.), Future Directions in Digital Information. Elsevier, Cambridge, MA, pp. 113–125.
Asongu, S.A., 2017. Enhancing ICT for inclusive human development in Sub-Saharan Africa. Technol. Forecast. Soc. Change, 44–54. https://doi.org/10.1016/j.techfore.2017.01.026.

Baker, D., Ellis, L., 2020. Future directions in digital information: scenarios and themes. In: Baker, D., Ellis, L. (Eds.), Future Directions in Digital Information: Predications, Practice, Participation. Elsevier, Cambridge, MA, pp. 1–15.

Baker, D., Evans, W., 2016. Digital information strategies. In: Baker, D., Evans, W. (Eds.), Digital Information Strategies: From Applications and Content to Libraries and People. Elsevier, Waltham, MA, pp. 1–20.

Chan, D.L., 2017. Using formal and informal channels to update librarians' skill sets. In: Baker, D., Ellis, L. (Eds.), The End of Wisdom? The Future of Libraries in a Digital Age. Elsevier, Cambridge, MA, pp. 75–81.

de Amorim, W.S., 2020. Pandemics, global risks and adaptation: challenges for a changing world. Res. Global., 100023.

de Aranzabal, M., 2020. COVID-19 and Africa: Surviving between a rock and a hard place. An. Pediatr. (English Ed.). 420.e1-420.e6.

Deakin University, 2020. Digital Literacy. Deakin University. Retrieved December 14, 2020, from https://www.deakin.edu.au/__data/assets/pdf_file/0008/1237742/digital-literacy.pdf.

Debbarma, I., 2021. Educational disruption: impact of COVID-19 on students from Northeast states of India. Child. Youth Serv. Rev. 120, 105769. https://doi.org/10.1016/j.childyouth.2020.105769.

Dillon, M., 2014. Introduction to Sociological Theory: Theorists, Concepts, and Their Applicability to the Twenty-First Century. John Wiley & Sons, Ltd, West Sussex.

Egoeze, F.M.-P., 2014. An evaluation of ICT infrastructure and application in Nigeria universities. Acta Polytech. Hung. 11 (9), 115–129. Retrieved December 16, 2020, from https://www.researchgate.net/profile/Sanjay_Misra2/publication/272202390_An_Evaluation_of_ICT_Infrastructure_and_Application_in_Nigeria_Universities/links/55756f3a08ae75363750067c/An-Evaluation-of-ICT-Infrastructure-and-Application-in-Nigeria-Universities.

Giddens, A., Sutton, P.W., 2017. Essential Concepts in Sociology. Polity, Cambridge.

Gillwald, A., 2010. The poverty of ICT policy, research, and practice in Africa. Inf. Technol. Int. Dev. Special Ed. 6, 79–88. Retrieved December 17, 2020, from https://www.itidjournal.org/index.php/itid/article/view/628.

Haider, N., 2020. Lockdown measures in response to COVID in nine sub-Saharan African countries. BMJ Glob. Health 5 (10). https://doi.org/10.1136/bmjgh-2020-003319, e003319.

Ifijeh, G., 2020. Covid-19 pandemic and the future of Nigeria's university system: the quest for libraries' relevance. J. Acad. Librariansh. 46 (6), 102226. https://doi.org/10.1016/j.acalib.2020.102226.

Matheson, N. W., The idea of the library in the twenty-first century, Bull. Med. Libr. Assoc., 83(1), 1995, 1-7. Retrieved December 14, 2020, from https://www.ncbi.nlm.nih.gov/pmc/articles/PMC225988/pdf/mlab00102-0017.pdf.

Mills, C.W., 2000. The Sociological Imagination. Oxford University Press, Oxford.

Mosco, V., 2017. Becoming Digital: Toward a Post-Internet Society. Emerald Publishing Limited, Bingley, UK.

Musoke, M.G., 2008. Strategies for addressing the university library users' changing needs and practices in sub-Saharan Africa. J. Acad. Librariansh. 34 (6), 532–538. https://doi.org/10.1016/j.acalib.2008.10.002.

Oyedotun, T.D., 2020. Sudden change of pedagogy in education driven by COVID-19: perspectives and evaluation from a developing country. Res. Global. 2, 100029.

Oyelere, K., 2020. COVID-19: Kano Govt converts library, sports complex, others into isolation centres. Nigerian Tribune. (May 1). Retrieved October 22, 2020, from https://tribuneonlineng.com/covid-19-kano-govt-converts-library-sport-complex-others-into-isolation-centres/.

Price, M., 2020. Scientists discover upsides of virtual meetings. Science 368 (6490), 457–458. https://doi.org/10.1126/science.368.6490.45.

Rafiq, M.B., 2021. University libraries response to COVID-19 pandemic: a developing country perspective. J. Acad. Librariansh. 47 (1), 102280. https://doi.org/10.1016/j.acalib.2020.102280.

Serafini, G.P., 2020. The psychological impact of COVID-19 on the mental health in the general population. QJM: Int. J. Med. 113 (8), 531–537. https://doi.org/10.1093/qjmed/hcaa201.

Shah, K.K., et al., 2020. Focus on mental health during the coronavirus (COVID-19) pandemic: applying learnings from the past outbreaks. Cureus 12 (3), e7405. https://doi.org/10.7759/cureus.7405.

Shah, S.E., et al., 2020. The technological impact of COVID-19 on the future of education and health care delivery. Pain Physician 23 (COVID-19 Special Issue), S367–S380. Retrieved November 18, 2020, from https://www.painphysicianjournal.com/current/pdf?article=NzEwNw%3D%3D&journal=129.

Too, Y.L., 2010. The Idea of the Library in the Ancient World. Oxford University Press, Oxford.

Troll, D.A., 2001. How and Why Are Libraries Changing. Retrieved 19 December 2020 from https://old.diglib.org/use/whitepaper.htm.

Troll, D.A., 2020. Digital Library Federation. (December 19). Retrieved from DLF https://old.diglib.org/use/whitepaper.htm.

UNESCO, 2011. Institute for Information Technologies in Education, Digital literacy in education. Policy Brief (May), 1–12.

United Nations Fund For Population Activities, 2020. World Population Dashboard Nigeria. 19/12/2020 Retrieved from United Nations Population Fund https://www.unfpa.org/data/world-population/NG.

Wynne, B.D., 2016. Changing the library brand: a case study. New Rev. Acad. Librariansh. 22 (2/3), 337–349. https://doi.org/10.1080/13614533.2016.1156000.

Look to the future now, it's only just begun. The changing role of libraries during and after COVID-19[*]

Martin Hamilton
MartinH.Net Un Limited, Loughborough, United Kingdom

1 Introduction

There was a time when libraries were at the global digital forefront, with initiatives like the United Kingdom's Electronic Libraries Programme (eLib—Rusbridge, 1995) and the joint Digital Libraries Initiative (Griffin, 1998) in America. However, as the Internet and digital technologies have become more and more embedded in our daily lives, it has sometimes felt as though libraries, and perhaps even librarians, may be an endangered species—Blockbuster in a Netflix age.

The COVID-19 era has accelerated and enforced the digital shift that was taking place already, forcing many libraries to move to new operating models—from pure digital to "click and collect," with many other permutations in between. In this chapter, I will look at how libraries can play a catalytic role in helping us to bounce back from the pandemic, and how the very nature of what we think of as a library is changing—perhaps for good.

2 COVID-19: What comes after?

2020 has proved to be an epochal year, with our society and way of life flipped on its head—with new phrases like social distancing and self-isolation entering the lexicon. We have also seen a very British form of "lockdown," complete with rustling net curtains, COVID marshals (Hymas et al., 2020), and police cautioning people for spending time in their own gardens (Stubley, 2020). It has suddenly emerged that millions of people can actually work from home (ONS, 2020a), and now know who the real essential workers are (DfE, 2020). Vaccines are being rolled out alongside therapeutic interventions to reduce the impact of the COVID-19 virus (Peiris and Leung, 2020) in an incredible global science mobilization to contain and perhaps even defeat it. And, increasingly, the question comes: will things ever be the same again?

---

[*]This chapter builds on articles by the author which previously appeared in CILIP's Information Professional and a guest blog for Blackbullion.

Libraries, Digital Information, and COVID. https://doi.org/10.1016/B978-0-323-88493-8.00024-0

When will treatments and vaccines become widely available; when will lockdown eventually be relaxed; and can or should we go back to business as usual? For many of those who have newly begun to experience the freedom of working from home, the idea of returning to spending hours a day commuting is starting to seem unwelcome. And for companies renting expensive premises in towns and cities and facing cashflow crises, it is increasingly attractive to transition to remote working. A Gartner survey of Chief Finance Officers (Gartner, 2020) found that 74% expect to consolidate and normalize the current remote working and telecommuting practices.

Where does this leave librarians and information professionals? Most people's mental model of librarians may well be based on those first, impression-forming, face-to-face interactions in the library back when we were children. But there has been a lot of water that has flown under the bridge since then. Staff at universities, hospitals, and research institutes are already accustomed to working digitally with subject librarians, and perhaps, it will not be that long before this approach is more widely established. With public libraries promoting their e-book services during the lockdown, we have already seen massive shifts towards digital delivery, such as Richmond Libraries' 365% increase in registrations for online access (Richmond, 2020).

But, in this time of upheaval, we also have to ask ourselves what sort of future we want: down one branching path, this could be the final chapter for the library as a physical space; down another, the value of the library as a social glue that binds communities together could finally be understood and properly resourced.

We have seen "fully automated luxury communism" (Bastani, 2020) emerge almost overnight, as governments recognized the need to print money to pay furloughed workers to continue to participate in the economy, whilst also bailing out businesses with grants and loans. At first, the priority has rightly been on the very fundamentals—making sure people can eat and pay or defer bills—although even this has proven fraught (Siddique, 2020). Next, we have to ask ourselves what help is needed for the disadvantaged and marginalized members of our society to get online, access public services and benefits like Universal Credit plus the wealth of stuff that is being made available by everyone from educators to authors and entertainers to keep us all sane during repeated lockdowns and self-isolation (BSG, 2020).

Another lightning-speed shift that we have seen in the research community is the massive global real-time collaboration to share everything that humanity knows about the virus plus potential vaccines and therapies. A whole generation of researchers is now familiar with using Internet collaboration tools to work with their peers, casting aside the traditional reticence about discussing their work before it has been published, and working in the open (Tse et al., 2020).

At the same time, as researchers have grasped the nettle and worked night and day to sequence the virus genome, visualize it, and use data science techniques like computational chemistry to devise potential candidate treatments, we have also seen academic publishers rise to the challenge by opening up their paywalls to make the COVID-19 literature freely available during the course of the pandemic. Sadly, this has only helped to highlight just how much publicly funded research is still inaccessible. Open Science activist Peter Murray-Rust notes that over 85% of articles from a major publisher relating to respirators are behind paywalls which typically charge around $40 per article (Rust, 2020).

We know that diseases like measles and polio ravaged generation after generation before vaccines were developed in the middle of the 20th century (Conniff, 2019). However, whilst rich, developed countries like the United Kingdom managed to largely eliminate them in a matter of years, it is telling that it has taken half a century for these vaccines to reach the majority of the poorest people in developing countries (Gates, 2019). Let us hope that the COVID-19 vaccines will be swiftly deployed to the largest possible number of people worldwide. Let us also hope that the lessons of global collaboration and open science are as widely understood.

3   Public libraries after COVID-19—The great reset?

With the United Kingdom's public library premises largely closed during the coronavirus lockdown, we have seen a surge in ebook loans—Libraries Connected report a 600% year-on-year increase in signups for digital services (BBC, 2020). What could that mean for the future of library services? As I write this in August 2020, some public libraries are starting to partially reopen for "click and collect" and timed booking visits. However, given the extreme pressure on local authority finances created by COVID-19, it is likely that we will see a further wave of closures or libraries transferred to volunteers to run.

This does not have to be the end of the road for public libraries; quite the reverse, in fact. The pandemic has created a once-in-a-generation opportunity for us to consider how to make our lives and communities more sustainable. To pick the most obvious example, millions of people have discovered that they can work from home, saving money and getting time back to spend with their families and on their hobbies. And many of the long tail of employers who have resisted flexible ways of working have now realized that their staff can be productive without having to be in the office, with employers such as Capita closing a third of their offices (Jones and Clarence-Smith, 2020).

The general public may tend to think of the library as a place you go to read or borrow books, but most libraries do not just hold books. From newspapers and magazines to local history collections, CDs, and DVDs, libraries already have a wide variety of items in their collections. And alongside these materials, public libraries often offer their patrons some form of access to photocopiers and scanning, computers, and the Internet. Perhaps, it is now time to ask ourselves what else the library loan model could support, and what other equipment libraries could provide for patrons to use on the premises.

The library of the future could be a much more broadly scoped community resource, a place where you can go to use all kinds of equipment or borrow all kinds of objects—a true "library of everything." Initiatives like the Edinburgh Tool Library (ETL, 2020) give us a glimpse of what that might look like. For a small monthly subscription, Tool Library members get access to equipment that they could not afford to buy outright or would not have a place to store. This does not just help people who are struggling to make ends meet; it could also be a great way to learn a new skill.

When we talk about libraries providing access to tools and equipment, there are obvious parallels with the hackspaces and maker spaces that have sprung up in many of our towns and cities in recent years. The Hackspace Foundation database (HF, 2020) shows around 70 of these in the United Kingdom, mostly in the largest population centres. Whilst some of these have been funded as projects, most of them operate on a bottom-up bootstrapped basis, supported by membership subscriptions and/or pay-what-you-can donations.

Before we get too carried away, dedicated hackspaces and maker spaces often feature heavy-duty equipment such as drills, lathes, and CNC mills. These can be very noisy and so might not be particularly welcome in libraries that are generally viewed as havens of peace and tranquillity. Many of these devices can also be dangerous if not used correctly and are not really suitable for casual use by the uninitiated. Some libraries have experimented with more readily accessible equipment like laser cutters and 3D printers, as part of supporting patrons to develop their digital skills, but these need care and feeding with a regular supply of consumables like printer filament.

With a looming recession and wholesale changes in lifestyles and patterns of working, we need our public libraries more than ever before. The great reset precipitated by the COVID-19 pandemic gives us the opportunity to rethink what the library can and should be. We cannot and will not all become 3D printing experts, but for many communities, there are much more straightforward interventions that could be transformational, like access to sewing machines for dressmaking and clothes alterations, or green screens and studio lighting for budding creators.

Of course, many of the things that we can picture our libraries doing would have ongoing costs beyond staff salaries and premises, like printer filament or software licenses. This could and should be the moment that the central government wakes up to the potential of libraries in supporting their communities to level up and meet the challenges of post-pandemic reconstruction. However, we should not hold our breath, and there is much that libraries can learn from community enterprises like hackspaces about sustainability.

4 All universities are the Open University

There was a brief moment in the Summer of 2020 when it felt as though the pandemic might actually be over, vanquished not by the heroic vaccine-wielding scientists of the Prime Minister's fever dreams, but by good old British common sense. People had kept themselves to themselves for months, drastically limiting the vectors that the virus had to spread. It was all played out, wasn't it?

Against the backdrop of the brewing storm over mutant algorithms (Gibbons, 2020) exposing the inherent inequity in grade quotas for high stakes exams, universities scrambled to prepare for some sort of normality. Online teaching and learning approaches were frantically developed (Weiss, 2020) to cater for those who would inevitably have to self-isolate, whilst institutions simultaneously tried to work out how to reduce the risk to staff and students from unavoidable interpersonal contact on their premises and estates (Greatrix, 2020). Little did all our universities realize how quick and how total their transformation into the Open University would be.

As I said in my talk on COVID-19 and the campus for the Association of University Directors of Estates (Hamilton, 2020), by the time A-Level results came out, it was already too late.

The lesson from American universities which re-opened in early August was that each mass migration of students acted as its own superspreader event. Students would go on to seed infections in hitherto unaffected communities, and dogmatic insistence on face-to-face tuition by some institutions would only make matters worse.

According to the reporting in Nature (Morris, 2020), more than 1000 US 4-year colleges and universities planned to bring students back to campus, with nearly half aiming to teach primarily or fully in person. However, these plans had to be swiftly rethought:

> *The University of North Carolina at Chapel Hill (UNC) announced on 17 August that, because of outbreaks of COVID-19 among students, it would shift all undergraduate classes online, a week after bringing students back to campus.*

This pattern was subsequently repeated at institution after institution across the United States. It then followed in the United Kingdom as Scottish universities welcomed students back in early September, with Edinburgh Napier and St Andrews among the first to report outbreaks on the 17th and 18th of September (Wade, 2020).

There was still time, just enough time, to tell the rest of the United Kingdom's students to stay at home and stay safe. However, by this point, the entire system was set up to operate something approximating a normal Autumn term, and the government had been very clear that this was what universities were expected to do. The rest is history, with this Autumn representing a very different kind of student experience—of lockdowns and food parcels, enforced isolation, and massive fines for transgressing (Batty, 2020).

Office for National Statistics research (ONS, 2020b) showed that COVID-19 had had a disproportionate impact on student mental health and wellbeing, topics that were already a series concern to the sector before the pandemic:

> *Results from three different surveys conducted during November 2020 conclude that more than half of students report that their well-being and mental health has worsened as a result of the pandemic.*

When we look forward beyond 2021, there are two key branching probabilities— on the one hand, rapid testing and vaccine distribution may enable us to return to some sort of normality. On the other, life in lockdown (of one sort or another) will have to continue for some time. And we should keep in mind that viruses keep evolving, so just as we periodically need a new flu vaccine, we are likely to need new COVID vaccines.

Will our universities be able to stop being the Open University and go back to their regular ways of operating? It would be extremely risky to plan on that basis. Instead, institutions need to continue to be prepared to support staff and students who are self-isolating or simply unable to visit campus for a variety of reasons such as more rigorous travel restrictions.

If you are a student who has been affected by all of this, you could be forgiven for wondering what you are really paying for now. It may feel as though you and your peers are simply necessary to stop the whole house of cards from collapsing, however much your university love bombs you with supportive emails.

Universities around the world have been desperately trying to sustain their existing business models as the pandemic has raged around them, but perhaps, it is time to ask ourselves whether some subjects could be taught just as effectively without requiring students to relocate or travel to campus at all. I have already mentioned the Open University, which has been the trailblazer for distance learning, but it is fair to say that there have been a lot of start-ups working in this space, even if none of them have really found their feet yet. These include some quite well-known ones like Udacity, famous for its nanodegree in self-driving car engineering (Davies, 2016) but which also offers more mundane courses in sought-after areas such as data science.

What I think will be really fascinating to see in the coming years is the extent to which hyper-scale Internet companies start to seriously look at online education as a potential market segment. This is just the kind of thing that shareholders would likely welcome from the likes of Facebook, Apple, Amazon, Netflix, and Google— the so-called FAANGs. Already most of the big technology companies offer extensive e-learning programmes for their own products and services, including rigorous certification-based qualifications. It is really not much of a stretch to generalize and diversify if the time and the price is right.

If this sounds fanciful, bear in mind that in summer 2020 Google announced its Google Career Certificate programme (Bariso, 2020), stating that:

> "College degrees are out of reach for many Americans, and you shouldn't need a college diploma to have economic security," writes Kent Walker, senior vice president of global affairs at Google. "We need new, accessible job-training solutions--from enhanced vocational programs to online education--to help America recover and rebuild."

If this wasn't enough to give universities and prospective students pause for thought, Walker also adds that:

> "In our own hiring, we will now treat these new career certificates as the equivalent of a four-year degree for related roles."

Will universities as we know them cease to exist overnight? No, they won't, but some may well struggle to remain viable as they juggle sunk costs and debt servicing with much reduced income from students, conferences, and other sources. For UK universities, the continued uncertainty around what Brexit will look like and entail is also a massive issue, potentially dwarfing COVID-19—hard as that may seem to believe right now.

Will nimble start-ups or Internet giants corner the market in online education? Perhaps not at first, and those that are showing the most promise are focussing on subjects that lend themselves to a virtual digital approach. If I was a betting man, I would take a punt on them for the simple reason that they do not have to retrofit a centuries-old approach and mindset for digital delivery and do not have sprawling campuses to maintain. And, let us not forget that many of those students returning home for the Christmas 2020 break, such as finalists, may never set foot on campus or walk into a lecture theatre again.

5 Conclusion

So, what can we do when Business As Usual is looking increasingly like Mission Impossible? The answer, ironically, is in our hands. For those who are lucky enough to be able to afford them, our phones, tablets, and laptops are highly capable, and connectivity is better now than ever before. And if we get into the habit of fully exploiting the technology at our fingertips, it is an accessibility boon for those people who are living with disabilities and impairments.

But something has changed that takes us far beyond earlier conversations about digital literacy and fluency—people's lives genuinely hang in the balance. The elderly, the infirm, and the immunosuppressed. Most of us have people in our lives who fall into one or more of these categories—family, friends, or neighbours. These are the people who are relying on us not to bring COVID-19 back from a trip to the library or the shops as a piece of unwanted additional baggage.

Hence, I would argue that it is high time we overhauled how we view the digital technologies that now permeate our lives, and with it, perhaps, we can recapture some of that excitement that came with the early days of the Internet. It is time to go jamming with the console jockeys in cyberspace!

References

Bariso, J., August 2020. Google Has a Plan to Disrupt the College Degree. Inc. https://www.inc.com/justin-bariso/google-plan-disrupt-college-degree-university-higher-education-certificate-project-management-data-analyst.html.

Bastani, A., July 2020. The Pandemic Makes it Clear: We Need Fully Automated Luxury Communism. Medium post. https://onezero.medium.com/the-pandemic-makes-it-clear-we-need-fully-automated-luxury-communism-737a756ea1d9.

Batty, D., November 2020. UK Universities Fine Students £170,000 for Covid Rule Breaches. The Guardian. https://www.theguardian.com/education/2020/nov/29/uk-students-fined-more-than-170000-over-covid-rule-breaches.

BBC, 2020. Coronavirus: Libraries See Surge in E-book Borrowing During Lockdown. BBC news coverage https://www.bbc.co.uk/news/uk-england-52368191.

BSG, November 2020. The Impact of COVID-19 on the Digitally Excluded. Broadband Stakeholder Group report http://www.broadbanduk.org/2020/11/02/new-bsg-report-the-impact-of-covid-19-on-the-digitally-excluded/.

Conniff, R., August 2019. The World Before Vaccines Is a World We Can't Afford to Forget. National Geographic. https://www.nationalgeographic.com/culture/2019/08/cannot-for-get-world-before-vaccines/.

Davies, A., September 2016. A \$2,400 Class to Make Anyone a Self-Driving Car Engineer. Wired. https://www.theguardian.com/education/2020/nov/29/uk-students-fined-more-than-170000-over-covid-rule-breaches.

DfE, 2020. Critical Workers Who Can Access Schools or Educational Settings. Department of Education guidance during national restrictions https://www.gov.uk/government/publications/coronavirus-covid-19-maintaining-educational-provision/guidance-for-schools-colleges-and-local-authorities-on-maintaining-educational-provision.

ETL, 2020. Edinburgh Tool Library Website. https://web.archive.org/web/20200809111430/https://edinburghtoollibrary.org.uk/.

Gartner, 2020. Gartner CFO Survey Reveals 74% Intend to Shift Some Employees to Remote Work Permanently. Gartner press release https://www.gartner.com/en/newsroom/press-releases/2020-04-03-gartner-cfo-surey-reveals-74-percent-of-organizations-to-shift-some-employees-to-remote-work-permanently2.

Gates, B., May 2019. An Update From the Fight to Eradicate Polio. Remarks to the Rotary Joint District Conference https://www.gatesnotes.com/health/an-update-from-the-fight-to-eradicate-polio.

Gibbons, A., August 2020. PM Blames Grading Crisis on 'Mutant Algorithm'. TES. https://www.tes.com/news/coronavirus-pm-exam-grades-almost-derailed-mutant-algorithm.

Greatrix, P., June 2020. Universities' Covid-19 Response: No Perfect, but Far From Crack-Handed. WonkHE. http://wonkhe.com/blogs/universities-covid-19-response-not-perfect-but-far-from-cack-handed/.

Griffin, S.M., 1998. NSF/DARPA/NASA digital libraries initiative—a program manager's perspective. D-Lib Mag. 1082-9873. July/August https://web.archive.org/web/20201108081754/http://www.dlib.org/dlib/july98/07griffin.html.

Hamilton, M., October 2020. The Campus after COVID—Rethinking the Role of 'Place' in Higher Education. Presentation to Association of University Directors of Estates https://www.aude.ac.uk/resources/Documents/Content?g=727f0e58-ee0b-48df-b781-e4c52a848488.

HF, 2020. Hackspace Foundation Website. https://www.hackspace.org.uk/.

Hymas, C., Evans, M., Rayner, G., September 2020. Exclusive: Police Dismiss Coronavirus Marshals as 'Covid Wombles'. The Telegraph. https://www.telegraph.co.uk/politics/2020/09/10/exclusive-police-dismiss-coronavirus-marshals-covid-wombles/.

Jones, C., Clarence-Smith, L., August 2020. Capita Plans to Shut Offices as Staff Work From Home. The Times. https://www.thetimes.co.uk/article/capita-plans-to-shut-offices-as-staff-work-from-home-9xvfttmh5.

Morris, E., August 2020. Millions of Students Are Returning to US Universities in a Vast Unplanned Pandemic Experiment. Nature. https://www.nature.com/articles/d41586-020-02419-w.

ONS, 2020a. Coronavirus and Homeworking in the UK: April 2020—Homeworking Patterns in the UK, Broken Down by Sex, Age, Region and Ethnicity. Office for National Statistics statistical bulletin https://www.ons.gov.uk/employmentandlabourmarket/peopleinwork/employmentandemployeetypes/bulletins/coronavirusandhomeworkingintheuk/april2020.

ONS, 2020b. Coronavirus and the Impact on Students in Higher Education in England: September to December 2020. Office for National Statistics. December 2020 https://www.ons.gov.uk/peoplepopulationandcommunity/educationandchildcare/articles/coronavirusandtheimpactonstudentsinhighereducationinenglandseptembertodecember2020/2020-12-21.

Peiris, M., Leung, G.M., 2020. What can we expect from first-generation COVID-19 vaccines? Lancet 396 (10261), 1467–1469. https://doi.org/10.1016/S0140-6736(20)31976-0.

Richmond, April 2020. Boom in Residents Using Digital Libraries, London Borough of Richmond on Thames News Release. https://www.richmond.gov.uk/boom_in_residents_using_digital_libraries.

Rusbridge, C., December 1995. The UK electronic libraries programme. D-Lib Mag. 1082-9873. https://web.archive.org/web/20200730040425/https://www.dlib.org/dlib/december95/briefings/12uk.html.

Rust, P.M., March 2020. Most Scientific Research on Respirators Is behind Paywalls. Twitter thread https://twitter.com/petermurrayrust/status/1240375676085178368.

Siddique, H., November 2020. Marcus Rashford Forces Boris Johnson into Second U-Turn on Child Food Poverty. The Guardian. https://www.theguardian.com/education/2020/nov/08/marcus-rashford-forces-boris-johnson-into-second-u-turn-on-child-food-poverty.

Stubley, P., April 2020. Coronavirus: Police Apologize for Telling Family They Weren't Allowed in Their Own Front Garden. The Independent. https://www.independent.co.uk/news/uk/home-news/coronavirus-garden-lockdown-rules-south-yorkshire-police-rotherham-a9459146.html.

Tse, E.G., Klug, D.M., Todd, M.H., 2020. Open science approaches to COVID-19 [version 1; peer review: 2 approved]. F1000 Res. 9, 1043. https://doi.org/10.12688/f1000research.26084.1.

Wade, M., September 2020. Coronavirus in Scotland: Outbreaks at Universities Add to Strain. The Times. https://www.thetimes.co.uk/article/coronavirus-in-scotland-outbreaks-at-universities-add-to-strain-rgnx35zj2.

Weiss, S., June 2020. This Is Online Learning's Moment. For Universities, It's a Total Mess. Wired. https://www.wired.co.uk/article/university-online-coronavirus.

After COVID? Classical mechanics

28

Graeme Hawley
National Library of Scotland, Edinburgh, United Kingdom

1 Introduction

These are complex times; our minds and social media accounts are filled with complexity. But, are we so busy dealing with the symptoms of complexity that we do not stop to consider the cause of complexity in the first place? I am going to suggest that the cause of complexity and indeed the fundamental issue that we are facing is something that we might call "accelerative change," and what I am interested in finding out is the extent to which COVID-19 has just slammed the brakes on it (triggering rapid deceleration, which will feel every bit as forceful as rapid acceleration) or whether COVID-19 is rather a part of an accelerative change or perhaps even a catalyst for more.

First and foremost, however, COVID-19 is a global disaster, wreaking personal tragedy and distress for billions. It is difficult to consider it as part of anything else other than its own terrifying event. At the time of writing, new strains are causing infection rates to skyrocket in the United Kingdom, South Africa, and Brazil. I am reflecting on the pandemic (as indeed millions are every day) while frontline hospital staff are being harrowed by it and others losing their lives and livelihoods to it. May it be over as soon as possible and all those, however affected by it, recover fully and swiftly. But nothing can happen in isolation (indeed the nonmedical ramifications of the pandemic have been a feature of it from the start—the political, social, and economic has become the medical), and an understanding of the wider implications of it or for it is, therefore, a reasonable thing to dwell on.

Secondly, prior to COVID-19, there was wide global agreement that the Earth was facing an urgent climate and ecological crisis: rising global temperatures, ice melt, extreme weather events, species collapse, resource scarcity, and pollution. That crisis has not gone away during 2020 although the possible environmental benefit of a sudden cessation of typical human activity—the anthropause—is an area of current interest. Many people consider *this* crisis to be the fundamental issue of our time. That being so, it is worth considering that an accelerative consumption of resources and demand for electricity is a probable driver of that crisis and that there is a link therefore worth exploring. I am not a climate scientist, and this chapter will not centre on the climate and ecological crisis, but that is not to say that the magnitude of it is lost on me in any way nor that the considerations discussed here might not also attach to some degree to climate and ecological crises. For the avoidance of doubt, I personally see accelerative change and climate and ecological change as strongly linked.

Furthermore, there are two useful things to know about me before reading this chapter. The first is that, in 2018, I read Alvin Toffler's book *The Third Wave* (Toffler,

Libraries, Digital Information, and COVID. https://doi.org/10.1016/B978-0-323-88493-8.00036-7

1980) and am clearly still to recover from it. It is an exposition on accelerative change and one that has fundamentally affected the way I see the world around me. The second is that I am Head of General Collections at the National Library of Scotland, where I am responsible for publications that date from 1901. I should also say that while my employment influences my thoughts, this chapter is a personal reflection only and should at no point be read as a piece either by or on behalf of the Library. Finally, if at times it feels as though this chapter is trying to address too many topics all at once, that it is going beyond the scope of this book, and that it is overegged, that is a deliberate act of mimesis. I wrote this essay about accelerative change between December 7, 2020 and January 14, 2021, a period of time that history may well record as especially accelerative.

2 Accelerative change

Accelerative change is so much a part of our lives that we may be forgiven for not fully comprehending how much so, but we refer to it all the time in little ways. The constant upgrades of mobile phone technology that frustrate are a good example of this. It took millennia to develop language, hundreds of years to develop systems of communication over distance, decades to work out how to send communication down a wire, years to turn a mobile telephone into a smartphone, and in the last three months I have had to do two software updates to make sure I have the right emojis. In the last week, two new memes have emerged on Twitter that I do not understand but which are dominating the shared creative outputs of the online world that I see. Ditto, everything.

If this rings a bell and you want to delve deeper, then Toffler's *The Third Wave* is absolutely where you should go. What Alvin and his wife Heidi do in that jointly written book is to demonstrate that accelerative change affects everything that we do and think. It changes family structure, society, politics, the environment, and how we work, sleep, and eat. Childhood shortening? Accelerative change. Twenty-four-hour gyms? Accelerative change. Toffler defines the hallmarks of each of the three waves that human society has lived through and focuses in particular on the clash between the second wave (industrial society) and the third wave (technological society) (the first wave was agricultural society by the way). To get to the crux of all this quickly, in an act of self-indulgence I will quote a part of another essay that I wrote on *The Third Wave*:

> *What is interesting right now as opposed to any point over the last, say 250 years, is that younger people particularly are growing up having been born under the terms of a different wave. That's major, and it only happens at the points in history when two waves collide; in other words, not very often at all, and certainly not often enough for the human race to have mastered handling the process.*
>
> (Hawley, 2019)

If things feel difficult, tense, unprecedented, too fast to make sense of, it is because they are. Accelerative change is supposed to feel like this. Enjoying the ride?

3 De-massification

Before I disappear down too many rabbit holes, I want to refer again to the Tofflers and a particular concept they associate with the third wave, that of de-massification. A process of atomization (or de-massification in Toffler terms) has been at work for some decades now. It has been affecting every aspect of second-wave societies. It is fundamental to everything from the development of more media channels and the shift to online music and entertainment, to the disruption of the nuclear family as the default model, to how and where we work, and increasingly to shared ideas and values, and even shared understandings about language. It is crucial to everything because what it ultimately means is the end of majorities, the end of shared reference points, the rise of individuals and individual experience, and everything else that goes with that. Alvin and Heidi Toffler are excellent on this, so if you want to understand the modern world, you know where to go.

4 The library context

The National Library of Scotland's collections are vast and span the centuries. We have approximately one million books and periodicals that were published between 1455 and 1901. We have approximately 15 million books and periodicals that were published between 1901 and now (14 million in print, and several million e-book and journal article parts that equate to about a million-total print-equivalent publications). In the past 7 years we have web-archived, along with the other legal deposit libraries in the United Kingdom and Ireland, more than ten million websites. Charted on a graph, that would be an exponential curve; accelerative even. And, it is not just a case of having more content (scalar change) but more and *different* content (vectorial change). Over the same period, there has been an ever-increasing diversity of formats, subject areas, backgrounds of authors and publishers, and indeed audiences for these ever-increasing works. Our collections *are* accelerative change and *document*…velocity.

5 Initial response to the lockdown

When lockdown started, my instincts, and those of many of my colleagues at the Library and throughout the library and information world, were to do what we could to help. Publishers opened access to science journals; libraries pushed their online resources harder than ever; and, connecting people to knowledge and culture shifted to Zoom and the web. For my own part, I identified e-journal content on three platforms that spoke to what felt to me like the six most pressing broad topics: COVID-19 science; economics, employment, and the environment; health care; international relations; politics; and society. I identified over 60 organizations in Scotland that I thought might benefit from knowing about the remote access they could gain to these resources and emailed them. Eleven of the organizations emailed back to say how grateful they were.

I still think this was the right thing to do and would like to make the time to perfect this kind of direct outreach (it needs some work). But equally, I knew that I was also receiving into my inbox from other organizations more and more online content, more opinions, more facts, more updates, and more information than I was able to keep up with. There were some amazing online events during lockdown I gather, but I missed most of them—there was simply too much to do justice to. The organizations I did not hear back from were very likely as snowed under as I was by an explosion of content and New Things To Contend With.

6 Acceleration in online output

There is no doubt that COVID-19 has triggered a further acceleration in online output (think about how much you read on your phone in March and April 2020 alone), and although there may have been a corresponding decrease in physical publishing (likely, but too early to say), this may be adjusted over the next few years as a bubble of print-only lockdown novels, recipe books, poetry collections, and such like enter the collections. COVID-19 brought further scalar and vectorial change, with new science, new terminology (both official and vernacular), and new social experiences being written about at a totally different scale, especially online. The fact that vaccines have been approved and others are on the way, developed and manufactured at a fraction of the time it once would have taken is another example of accelerative change. In among whatever else that implies, I expect it to impact on science publishing in some way.

Dissemination of information and the broadcasting of culture to those who might benefit were only half of what was going on at the Library during the lockdown. The other half, crucial for a legal deposit library like the National Library of Scotland, was the collection of the information, ideas, data, knowledge, and writing about COVID-19 in the first place, under the terms of the Legal Deposit Act 2003 and Legal Deposit Libraries (Non-Print) Regulations 2013. A collaborative effort with the British Library, National Library of Wales, Bodleian Library, Cambridge University Library, and Trinity College Dublin, we made our focus Scottish publishers, authors, and organizations, in line with the usual collecting practice.

This work is still ongoing. Web archiving was prioritized as soon as lockdown began, because of the vulnerability of publications on the web and the need for pandemic information on the live web to be accurate and up to date. The Library has archived over 4000 COVID-related Scottish URLs since March 2020, and a lot of the content on those sites has been archived multiple times because the content has changed multiple times. If you are looking for a good example of accelerative change, look no further than the Internet itself. We have pages in our digital collections that have not been on the live web for months. When researchers want to look back at what happened in March, April, May, June 2020, these collections will be a vital piece of that story.

Dominant though COVID has been, it is not the only thing I was doing at work in 2020. In July and August, I hosted a remote 6-week internship on the topic of AI-created content. This is a rapidly developing area of publishing and one that I need to keep an eye on. Another chapter would be required to do justice to this topic, but in short, algorithms and (ro)bots are increasingly a part of the thinking and writing process, and humans are already more engaged with this than they realize, from bot-triggered trading that makes pensions exist, to predictive text on your phone, and automatic translation software. Deepfakes of images and video and computer-generated art and music are already established, for good and ill. Over the summer, however, articles started to appear about GPT-3 (perhaps best to Google it), and the process of accelerative change has now kicked in with regard to text. By the time this article is published, you might need to be Googling GPT-4. We are moving very quickly to the point where bot-generated creative writing will be indistinguishable from human-generated content without some additional knowledge about what to look out for. It is a different kind of massive to COVID, but this development is, make no mistake, massive.

7 Defining the COVID-19 collection

In November, I decided to look for evidence of COVID-19 on the collection stacks. Not the actual virus, but evidence of it in some of the publications that had been coming in routinely through long-established legal deposit channels. I went down to level 4 where our new periodicals acquisitions are stored. There was a pile on a shelf awaiting placing; a range of publications in no order other than that they had recently arrived and were to be shelved in this area: *Copper Worldwide* (ISSN 2046-9438), *Furniture and Joinery Production* (ISSN 2396-9024), *Letting Update Journal* (ISSN 1359-9038), *Country Risk Service: Turkmenistan* (ISSN 2051-7440), *The pensioner: the magazine for members of the Civil Service Pensioners' Alliance* (ISSN 2046-9233), *European Pensions* (ISSN 1753-5859), *British Chess Magazine* (ISSN 0007-0440), and *Ice Cream: the magazine of the ice cream alliance* (ISSN 1356-0948). Every single one mentioned COVID-19 on their cover or first page, with many carrying full features about the impact of the virus. Unlike the targeted collecting of websites and material culture relating to the pandemic, I think of this as incidental COVID-19 collecting, and it feels like a genre of its own.

When people ask to see our COVID collection in years to come, will they be expecting to see a trade journal about copper, a periodical about British chess, and the magazine of the ice cream alliance? Perhaps not, but that is the evidence of COVID-19 right there: the transformational impact on literally everything, from copper wire to raspberry ripple. It is highly likely that at least one issue of every periodical-that we have received since March 2020 will have made mention of COVID-19 at least once. Elsewhere, in our life-science periodicals, the density of COVID-19 will be like nothing perhaps we have ever seen before in our collections. I expect it to be genuinely incredible. And then there are the collections of the future that will no doubt come, in print and digital formats: the delayed publications that ended up with new chapters because of lockdown; the poetry collections; the photojournalism coffee table books of clapping for carers; the children's books about germs, loneliness, and loss; the heart-breaking accounts of frontline workers; the stories of those suffering from long-COVID. What is our COVID-19 collection, and when will we have received it?

8 More generates more

2020 was already set to be a year of accelerating change: climate crisis, an extremely bitter election campaign in the United States, Brexit negotiations, and continuing online rage around topics such as free speech and gender identity. COVID-19 at the start of the year, and Black Lives Matter protests in the summer following the killing of George Floyd, opened additional channels of discourse. These significant, multilayered topics, all happening together, generated more complexity, in turn generating more publications to add to our shelves or servers. In simple terms, more tends to generate more. But, is that a problem?

There is a web of complexity that accelerative change creates that is increasingly difficult to process. Even in 1980, the Tofflers were at pains to draw attention to the unsustainable decision-load that was being placed on people and institutions because of complexity. Writing 40 years ago, they were optimistic about the potential for technology to be used to assist decision-making. The processing power of the microchip would simply be better able to compute the exponential rise in complexity. But, computational outputs are dependent on the corpus of data they are fed and the algorithms they have been trained on. If bots inherit the biases of the people and companies that build them (discuss), then welcome to a whole new area of complexity, legislation, and protest.

Complexity is everywhere. Here is a sense of what it looked like the week that I started to write this essay. On Tuesday, December 8, I read an excellent article by Oliver Balch in *The Guardian* (Balch, 2020) about the environmental impact of lithium mining (the Library currently has an internship looking at the climate crisis). There is a lot to understand in this well-researched article, but this section (concerning Maria Carmo, a resident of a village in Portugal in an area earmarked for future lithium mining) nicely gets to the point of complexity:

> *After a three-year struggle, Carmo is exhausted and ready to give in. She feels the government is deaf, and that her fellow citizens aren't interested. "So much destruction," she said. "And for what? So eco-minded urbanites in Paris and Berlin can feel good about driving around in zero-emission cars.*

The answer to petrol-polluting cars it seems is not lithium-polluting cars, but fewer or no cars at all, which in turn could mean: less travel; vehicle-based businesses being at a disadvantage; job losses related to cars and all upstream and downstream businesses dependent on cars and vans; a huge economic hit for some entire sectors; and any number of further unseen consequences and benefits. And the pivot-point of complexity that Carmo alights on, the tensions between those who are shaping the future, those who are paying a price for that, and those who will pay the price for an extension of the status quo, is also at play regarding political and social discourse across dozens of other topics.

9 Agreed facts and shared experiences

I read that article on a rechargeable electric device full of polluting rare metals that I swap every so often, in an online newspaper that I did not pay for, despite knowing that investigative journalism like this does not come for free. Sustainable? Hardly. Also, what I have not done is research the lithium mining industry myself. I have trusted Oliver Balch and I have trusted *The Guardian*. We all do this kind of thing, putting trust in others, all the time. Anything else would be… unsustainable. But as complexity and de-massification makes the establishment of agreed facts and shared experiences less and less likely, knowing who or what to trust is being shaken to the core. Arguments, conspiracy theories, fake news, counter-fake news, and general chaos thrive in this environment and are hot-housed by the accelerative speed of social media, which generates digital publications, which then enter our collections.

Just as an aside within a series of asides, I have been thinking about the extent to which postmodernism might be a product of accelerative change, or a cause of it. I have only the most basic grasp of postmodernism and am not going to take this line of inquiry any further, but I would be delighted to read any thoughts about possible relationships between postmodernism and accelerative change. I would, however, like a moment to dwell on how postmodernism might impact publishing, particularly. The best example I can give here relates to a recent academic publishing hoax known as the Grievance Studies Affair (there is a good Wikipedia entry about it), the essence of which is that some academics submitted deliberately fanciful articles to journals to see if they would be published, and four were before the experiment was rumbled. The point to make here is that hoax and experimentation is everywhere, not just on Twitter, and it is becoming increasingly difficult to know when fake news has become something closer to art or a commentary on our times itself. If postmodernism and accelerative change are feeding each other, then is it any wonder that things are so, for want of a better word, messy?

On Wednesday, December 9, I read an article by Kaitlyn Tiffany in *The Atlantic,* which was a further addition to the growing amount of text that has been written about the trans rights/gender-critical divide. I saw the link to the article on Twitter because of the people that I follow. The article introduced me to several social media and publishing platforms that I was not aware of: Ovarit, Spinster, and Saidit. On Wednesday, December 10, I saw another link in my timeline. That link was to a piece either by or on behalf of Mary Kate Fain, but in the time between seeing it and getting to type my thoughts up for this chapter, it had disappeared from where I had seen it (it has reappeared elsewhere, but I haven't followed up on it yet, and may not get the chance to for a while, or ever—my list of things to read only gets longer). As far as I can remember, the article involved Mary Kate Fain, publishing all the email transcripts between her and Kaitlyn Tiffany (of *The Atlantic*) and a 90-min podcast between Fain and, I think, someone called Meghan Murphy. I think that the Fain piece was going to be a rebuttal of the Tiffany piece. A 15-min article generated a 90-min film in under a day. Accelerative indeed.

10 Collection development and digital publishing

While others may have been agreeing or disagreeing with the articles, I was mostly thinking "Are any of these platforms UK publishers? Are they in scope for web archiving in terms of The Legal Deposit Libraries (Non-Print Works) Regulations 2013? And, are any of these authors Scottish?" because that's what the Library does. My conclusion was that the immediate content that I had seen was not in scope, and no collecting action has been taken yet, but I now have these platforms on my collection development list to look at. We have an ever-growing collection development list just to say, and the exponential growth in digital publishing is largely behind this.

Digital publishing is especially challenging because the Internet itself is atomizing, breaking apart into new platforms that set out to represent particular groups or viewpoints, making the Internet itself more complex. Increasingly, when we talk about the Internet, it will be worth confirming which Internet we are talking about. And as the Internet becomes more complex, the discourse becomes more complex, and so, in turn, do our collections and the work that we need to do to bring them in. It is also worth noting here that what were once stand-up arguments in meeting rooms are all now committed to text on open public platforms. Whatever else social media has done, it has taken what might have been verbal abuse in the street or philosophical musings over pints in the pub in the past and turned them into collection items on the digital shelves (servers) of national collecting bodies. In short, our definition of what counts as a publication has changed radically in the last fifteen years or so.

(Today is January 14, 2021. President Donald Trump has been banned from Twitter and has been impeached for a second time on a charge of incitement to insurrection. He may well take tens of millions of his social media followers with him to brand new platforms. If any further evidence of accelerative change was required, then the first two weeks of 2021 are it. I didn't know where else to insert this piece of breaking news, so I have put it here. It is as good a place as any.)

Even if we accept that social media content equates to a digital publication (I think it does, but I am sympathetic to arguments that are made to the contrary), it does rather feel like what you get on Twitter as well as a finished article are the drafts, edits, publisher spats, and deleted chapters that traditional print publishing would spare you. This is publishing in the open, in the moment, and as tweets often degenerate into nonlinear battles, it is worth asking what it is that we learn from social media publishing. Although I am sometimes left where I began, the things I read introduce me to ideas, experiences, and differences of opinion that I would otherwise not have known about. But, another area of complexity is therefore emerging, between those aware of these discussions and those oblivious to them or turned off by them. Even if you follow social media, there is no immunity to accelerative change: missing a week on Twitter feels like missing a term of school. Factor into this the tendency for social media to form around or spawn echo chambers, and you have a complex scenario indeed. Current discourse on many key topics (including COVID-19) is affected by all the mores of social media, as well as by the matters of the topics themselves.

11   Accelerative language

BAME (Black, Asian, and Minority Ethnic) is a term that has a recent history and a very recent history. In the months since the death of George Floyd in the United States, I saw the usage of the term increase greatly, while also seeing growing numbers of people tweet about their discomfort with the term because of the ownership of it, who is applying it to whom, and the way it obscures the differences within and between the billions of people represented by those four letters. "Increase greatly"; "growing numbers"; not very scientific measurements, but then these observations are based on what I saw on my Twitter timeline. This is my own window on the world because of who I follow and who they in turn follow and what everyone is saying and retweeting. I think there is a good measure of balancing opinions in that timeline, although I might be fooling myself. But the sense that I got was that BAME as a term is already going through a process of rapid change, while other people are only just starting to become aware of it. It is possible that this term will come and go before some people have engaged with the term at all.

LGBT as a term has already changed considerably with the addition (and now also deletion) of letters. The atomizing effect of the third wave is played out everywhere, impacting everything from the economy to sexuality and gender identity. For me, the term LGBTTQQIAAP is not only about sexual orientation and gender identity (I am one of these letters by the way) but is also strongly linked with de-massification, commensurate with the shift to the third wave. All sections of society, including minorities, are atomizing across every facet of their lives. I should of course say that people are also being brought together through atomization and de-massification, just as they are also being broken apart, but there is less predictability as to who is grouping with who, and why. If people were looking for common ground to come together on, their shared experiences of the atomizing impact of accelerative change might be a useful place to begin.

12 The binary bind

I would like to suggest that most people like change up to the point that they do not like it anymore, at which point they would like change to stop or at least pause for a while. Where that point is lies on a personal sliding scale, and accelerative change makes it slide more quickly and without pause. You could map a political spectrum to this sliding scale, but underneath it is the classical mechanics of acceleration, velocity, and friction. On every topic: conservative angles, progressive angles, and every other angle in between and on the extremes of these parameters will continue to enter our collections. At a time when things are at unprecedented levels of complexity, discourse (be it on COVID-19 or any other topic) still tends toward a binary choice: you can have this or that, but you cannot have both. It is easy to see this at work in the debate (and anger) regarding decisions over the economy that put at risk public health/decisions over public health that put at risk, the economy. There is no national agreement on this, and even when the emergency around COVID-19 has passed, we will be left with all manner of unresolved tensions around the relationships between personal freedom, collective responsibility, and government control.

13 Interpreting accelerative change

So, what are the COVID-19 pandemic and related social shifts with regards to accelerative change? When considered in terms of *The Third Wave,* several interpretations present themselves: the pandemic could be another example of a corrective on the second wave (intensive farming and intensive working practices as methods of viral transmission); an example of the flaws of the third (globalization as a means of global transmission); or a catapult back to the first wave (grow it yourself, live local). Discussion about the long-term impact of the virus began very soon in 2020, and the Library's shelves and servers will continue to fill with analysis about COVID-19 for years to come. It would not be too surprising to see more publications about things like universal basic income, social cohesion, and government power in 2021, along with a good crop of "grow your own veg" books. There is going to be a lot to read about the post-COVID world.

Early social and emotional responses to the pandemic were to see it as unifying. Clapping for carers, NHS rainbows in windows, anecdotal accounts of a surge in community spirit, and the shared restrictions on activity that lockdown brought were all seen as good examples of, for want of a better word, *re*-massification. There is no doubt that a restriction on individual freedom meant that people were suddenly forced into doing roughly the same things. But it also quickly became apparent that we were not having the same experience at all. Whether you had a garden or not; whether you had school-aged children or not; whether you lived alone or in company; whether you lived in a city or a village; whether you had Internet access; these all became new ways to de-massify. The preexisting social distance between people in different circumstances was really laid bare in 2020.

Is it a coincidence that all the above seems to be happening at the same time? Are the events of 2020 aligning with Toffler's third wave characteristics of de-massification, the breakdown of majorities, the growing importance of individual identity, the growth in working from home, and so on, because that is the trajectory of our time? We may never know whether home-working would have emerged so dominantly without the sudden need to work from home this year, but now that it has, is it likely to go away? The Tofflers identified home-working, home-schooling, and do-it-yourself as where things were heading 40 years ago. Make of that what you will. Alternatively, has COVID-19 provided an opportunity to shore up the second wave and thwart the third: centralization of government power, emergency laws, massive restriction of personal liberty—all Tofflerian hallmarks of second wave controls but also useful things to do to control the spread of a virus with no known cure. Is COVID-19 a braking action on accelerative change? It is difficult to know. The encouragement or discouragement of homeworking over the next few years might turn out to be an interesting litmus test.

14 Conclusions

So, why is this chapter in this part of the book? The post-COVID-19 world is going to demand changes of us all. But those changes were already upon us or already overdue, not because of a novel coronavirus but because of the overarching trend of our times: accelerative change. And crucial though the response to COVID-19 is, we were already struggling with the rate of change across many fronts long before the virus struck. Back in 1980, the Tofflers warned us in their final chapter to simply prepare for the coming "super-struggle" between the second and third waves. I ask myself, "how did I prepare for the coming super-struggle?" In my professional capacity, what I can say is this: I and my colleagues collected the evidence of it. In my team, in the Library, in libraries and archives throughout the world, we collected this emerging complexity, this accelerative change, over the last few months, and indeed over the centuries as it gradually emerged and continued to accelerate. We are trying our best to keep up with the accelerating pace of it. We were collecting it before we knew what it was and are collecting it before we know what it will have become. But there is a flaw in the plan.

There is clearly no shortage of people generating text, be that in print or digital format, full-length book or 100-word tweet (he says, adding 6300 more words to the pile). We are living at a point of exponential text. There is probably undercapacity to collect it all, but we can do our bit as a global community to collect and preserve representatively and cover as many bases as we can. But, there is absolutely no ability to read it all, let alone make sense of it. Even if we can collect it all, what, or who, are we collecting it for? That is not in itself the Library's problem—our duty is to collect, not to read. If it has not been collected, it cannot be read. But it is still valid to ponder what it means to be producing and collecting more than we can perhaps realistically consume.

What this essay is, therefore, is a squawk from a canary in a coal mine to say that over this year, years previous, and indeed the years to come, our collections (especially digital) have grown exponentially because the world of shared text has grown even more exponentially, and all that shared text is either a product of increasing complexity, a cause of it, or both. Acceleration is locked into our collections. In life, we can observe what happens when things go faster and faster: accidents happen, metal gets fatigued, bolts loosen, and wheels literally fall off. Animals can run fast for a period, but then need to rest. In short, there is usually a corrective to accelerative speed. Unlike COVID-19, which we all hope will soon be treatable and reduced globally to as close to zero as possible, accelerative change seems set to continue its trajectory for the next few months at the very least, and realistically far longer.

There is no agreement (or even any visible public debate) on whether accelerative change is desirable, what the coping mechanisms might be, or what the side effects are for any treatments for it. It may well be that it is desirable, and we may well be incredibly adept at coping with it: the astonishing turnaround of COVID-19 vaccines is reassuring in lots of ways beyond medical treatment alone, as is the widespread anecdotal evidence of community cohesion and human resilience that came with the first lockdown. I would be happy to posit that the Library's collections over centuries are evidence of not only accelerative change but how remarkable humans are at responding to it.

But, because accelerative change is exponential, I think that we need experts on this just as we have virologists studying COVID-19. Libraries need to be working with scholars of classical mechanics and experts on acceleration and velocity. We should be asking: can text output accelerate indefinitely, and what lessons from theoretical mechanics can we borrow, if any? Is it sensible to match accelerative publishing with accelerative reading? Might that simply keep feeding the cycle, and if it does, is that good or bad? Is there a tipping point in exponential text, in the same way that climate scientists are concerned about global temperatures? With exponential text now so closely tied to social media publishing, in the event of a sudden and mass withdrawal from those platforms (the mental health consequences of "doomscrolling" could easily become a tipping point for many), a rapid deceleration of text could take place very quickly. That deceleration may or may not coincide with wider decelerative activity beyond publishing. It could be one way to find out which is feeding which.

My instinct says that if there is more text, then we need more eyes on it, but what is lacking in this analysis is any measure of *quality*. There is certainly more quantity, but how much of it is "useful"? That is not something that legal deposit libraries typically concern themselves with—we are collectors of publications not arbiters of taste or literary or research merit. It also feels questionable to place social media publishing under a different set of standards to other types of publishing that we have been receiving for years. But, after a romp through some aspects of contemporary complexity and a sweep at the vastness of 21st century text output, I find myself considering whether a better approach to exponential growth might be to scale down. Compelling though it is (at least for me anyway) to try to understand the interconnectedness of things and to appreciate scale, it may be that this is now beyond the realm of humans, and that in such a massive dataset, only a computer can see the patterns and trends that are there but otherwise invisible. Perhaps, this is why GPT-3 has emerged at this point; accelerative change has brought with it its own analytical tool. Two years ago, I read a book that I am still thinking about. Perhaps it is time for me to read another. I will leave this chapter there.

References

Balch, O., 2020. The curse of "white oil": electric vehicles' dirty secret. The Guardian. 8 December https://www.theguardian.com/news/2020/dec/08/the-curse-of-white-oil-electric-vehicles-dirty-secret-lithium.

Hawley, G., 2019. Alvin Toffler and The Third Wave. https://digital.nls.uk/1980s/economics-employment/third-wave/. (Accessed 13 January 2021).

Toffler, A., 1980. The Third Wave. Collins, London.

The times they are a-changin': But how fundamentally and how rapidly? Academic library services post-pandemic

Jeremy Atkinson
Jeremy Atkinson Consultancy, Cardiff, Wales, United Kingdom

1 Introduction

The coronavirus pandemic accelerated the move to e-commerce as consumers began shopping online in greater numbers and frequency. Estimates vary, but the pandemic is thought to have speeded up the shift away from physical stores to digital shopping by 4–5 years. During a pandemic, there are the obvious advantages of safety and availability, but other perceived advantages of online shopping for consumers such as convenience, flexibility, and personal delivery or "click and collect" will continue post-pandemic. Perceived disadvantages such as determining quality, choosing the right product for the individual, and the loss of the social aspects of in-person shopping may result in some move back to physical shopping, but a significant, permanent shift to online shopping seems inevitable. This trend has not only occurred in the leading economies. A recent report investigating 3700 consumers in nine emerging and developed economies showed that this shift was apparent in countries as wide-ranging as Brazil, Germany, the Republic of Korea, and Turkey (United Nations Conference on Trade and Development, 2020).

There are obvious parallels between the retail sector and academic libraries. Both have a physical presence and a growing online provision. An interesting question is whether the rapid and permanent shift to online, predicted for the retail world, will also apply to academic libraries. For academic libraries, will the range of online services introduced during lockdown be a permanent feature? Will additional online services be required? Will there be a move back to some of the more traditional face-to-face services? In this small study, views were sought from managers and librarians in the United Kingdom and four other countries in order to try and envision academic libraries post-pandemic.

A short questionnaire was sent out to a small number of the author's contacts in several different countries. These were academic library managers and academic librarians, many of whom had contributed to three recent edited volumes published by Chandos/Elsevier, including a relevant collection of case studies on technology and change in academic libraries, published in 2020 (Atkinson, 2020). Twenty-two

Libraries, Digital Information, and COVID. https://doi.org/10.1016/B978-0-323-88493-8.00019-7

questionnaire responses were received from academic library managers and librarians based in the United Kingdom (England, Wales, and Scotland), the Republic of Ireland, Finland, the United States, and Australia. Given the relatively small sample, it was not possible to make any distinction between responses from different types of academic libraries or responses from different countries, although the responses were often similar.

2 Questionnaire responses

Six simple questions were asked in the questionnaires. The responses are summarized in the sections below.

2.1 How have you delivered services differently during the pandemic, including the provision of services online?

2.1.1 General

Academic libraries reported a strong move to electronic services, with the service model being primarily online during the pandemic:

> *Any services that could be delivered digitally have been moved to that as the primary mode of delivery.*

Some library managers commented that it had accelerated the delivery of a number of online services that were already in development. Some libraries felt well positioned, having moved to online delivery before the pandemic, while others found the switch to online more difficult because of the extent of electronic resources available or the nature of their existing online support systems.

2.1.2 Information resource provision

Many libraries either stopped or had limited purchase of print material during the pandemic. One library manager referred to her library's "e-first purchasing policy," and this was a common approach concentrating on making reading list and course material available online. Liaison with academic staff identified specific online resources required, for example:

> *Drama students were not able to attend live performances and an appropriate database of recorded performances was acquired.*

Many libraries acquired more e-books, with some suppliers temporarily making additional e-books available for free. Some libraries implemented a "scan and deliver" service, where users could request a scan of an article or chapter which, copyright restrictions allowing, was sent directly to their email.

2.1.3 "Click and collect" services

During the pandemic, many libraries did not allow user access to the physical collections, but the setting up of a "click and collect" service was fairly common with users identifying and ordering online the books they wanted access to and then picking them up at an agreed safe collection point in the library building.

2.1.4 Library space

Some libraries were able to remain open where national or local rules allowed, with regular deep cleaning, strict social distancing, use of hand sanitizers, swipe card access, and so forth and with some staff on-site for specific purposes or limited periods. When libraries reopened in a limited way, access to study space was usually on the basis of users prebooking space in specified study zones via an online seat booking system. These arrangements sometimes included access to PCs and printing. When access to study space became possible again, facilities such as group study rooms, computer rooms, and rooms with specialist facilities often remained closed. Typically, continuing restrictions and social distancing resulted in up to half the study spaces remaining unavailable.

2.1.5 Inquiries

Most libraries were not able to offer a face-to-face inquiry service during the pandemic, and there was a move to a virtual support model with the use of telephone support, email, and online chat. Online bookings were implemented to set up appointments with librarians in systems such as Zoom, MS Teams, and Blackboard Collaborate. A lot of queries related to remote access to resources. In some libraries, additional staff time had to be devoted to providing virtual support, sometimes involving staff not previously involved in inquiry work such as library assistants.

2.1.6 Supporting teaching and learning

Most libraries moved their library teaching and induction online wherever possible. This included digital skills, information literacy, and other study skills. A small number of libraries offered a blended approach, with some in-person teaching. A common approach was to have live sessions with a Q&A facility on a system such as MS Teams, supplemented by recorded sessions, online tutorials, and other content. There was some evidence of increased attendance at online sessions compared to prepandemic face-to-face sessions.

2.1.7 Loan arrangements

Many libraries implemented special arrangements including postal loans for users identified as vulnerable. More generally, many libraries extended loan periods, suspended fines, set up book return boxes outside the library, extended laptop loan arrangements for students studying remotely, or made postal loan services more widely available.

2.1.8 Other comments

There were changes in library staff working during the pandemic, with staff often working from home where possible, sometimes for the first time. Some libraries developed guidance for staff working from home, with some workforce development to support the digital shift, including training in the use of online support tools.

Institutions put an emphasis on supporting student wellbeing, with libraries often providing guidance and support as part of an institution-wide student support initiative. There was also a need for libraries to provide increased promotional communications about changes in and the availability of services and resources, via web pages and social media.

2.2 Do you think any of these services will be needed post-pandemic?

2.2.1 General

There were some varied responses on whether new services introduced during the pandemic would be retained post-pandemic. There was a recognition that the pandemic had brought forward some of the services already being planned:

Many of the services were either already planned or being developed. The pandemic accelerated the process and provided a greater focus on the need to deliver them.

Some respondents were more cautious and pragmatic:

The new services introduced might not necessarily be needed but will probably be retained to some extent due to their uptake and customer response.

While others could definitely see some of the new digital services being retained and developed:

A "digital option by default" has become a real priority for us to continue post-pandemic.

2.2.2 Information resource provision

A number of respondents commented that the additional e-resources acquired during the pandemic were likely to be retained and saw a continuing trend to a greater emphasis on the provision of e-resources rather than their print equivalents, including e-textbooks and reading list and reserve material. A library manager commented:

Digital first collection development is likely to become more normal.

However, a number of managers commented on the difficulty in maintaining the spend on e-books because of the funding implications. For those libraries who had implemented a "scan and deliver" service during the pandemic, there was roughly a 50/50 split on the likelihood of the service being continued or stopped post-pandemic.

2.2.3 "Click and collect" services

"Click and collect" services had been taken up widely during the pandemic, but there were differing views on their retention. There was a recognition that the service had been "unexpectedly popular" despite the increased availability of electronic resources and that, as a result, thought needed to be given on whether to continue with the service post-pandemic. Other respondents were definitely not going to continue with the provision, particularly given its staff-intensive nature. One library manager commented:

> Click and Collect also reinforces the perception of the library as a building rather than something far more complex, and that our collections are primarily print, which is not the case.

2.2.4 Library space

Feedback from students in many institutions indicated that they liked being able to book study seats that met their particular requirements, for example to study in a certain area of the library or noise zone. As a result, many librarians thought that they were likely to retain seat booking systems introduced during the pandemic, either as a permanent feature for a percentage of study and PC spaces or at particular times of the year such as examination periods. However, it was recognized that there would be challenges in managing prebooked and open study spaces together.

2.2.5 Inquiries

Most of the libraries felt that the move to a greater emphasis on online inquiry and support services during the pandemic had been well received and would continue. Provision such as extended chat services and bookable appointments with liaison librarians were likely to be retained. These were particularly popular with users not based on campus. Comments included:

> I can definitely see that a blended approach to providing support both on campus and digitally will continue to be needed.
> We may shift the focus of our enquiry service to more remote delivery rather than primarily face-to-face.

2.2.6 Supporting teaching and learning

Online teaching and training by library staff, including induction and information and digital literacy sessions, had been well received during the pandemic with good levels of take up and engagement. The online sessions were thought to offer advantages of inclusivity, flexibility, and interaction. For the future, many students were thought to prefer to attend digital lectures, with, as a consequence, students spending less time on campus with a need for online content and tutorials, including on information/digital literacy skills, to be embedded within modules. It was generally felt that there were would be a move toward greater online delivery of library skills training, both synchronous and asynchronous, than was the case before the pandemic but that there would be some move back to face-to-face delivery where there are advantages for librarians and users.

2.2.7   Loan arrangements

Many respondents thought that temporary loan arrangements would probably revert to prepandemic models, but one service area that was thought likely to be retained and developed was postal loans. It was anticipated that more students may choose to study remotely in the future and that more courses delivered entirely remotely may be developed for which a postal loan service would be required.

2.2.8   Other comments

Permanent changes to the ways in which library staff worked with each other, with other university staff, and with users were thought to be possible. Comments included:

> *Staff may want to continue working from home, some, or all of the time. This might change the way enquiry services are delivered.*
> *It's possible that online meetings will continue to be the default for most types of meetings.*

2.3   In the future, which of your prepandemic services do you think will need to be revised or deleted?

2.3.1   General

In the responses, there was evidence that following experiences during the pandemic, many library managers were now intending to look fundamentally at the nature of their service provision:

> *There is definitely an increased requirement to provide a digital option/alternative for as many of our services as possible. That was a trajectory we were already on, but the pandemic situation has really increased the velocity we need to travel at.*
> *It's about doing things differently that reflect a more flexible way for our staff to work and a demand for greater flexibility from our users in how they access our services.*

2.3.2   Information resource provision

As with the previous question, there were comments about a shift to "e-first purchasing" but with a recognition that the cost of e-resources was generally higher and that this needed to be factored in. In addition, the pandemic had resulted in some library managers reflecting seriously on the value for money of some of their prepandemic library operations, particularly in relation to their print collections:

> *The management of barely used print collections will need to be considered. We knew pre-pandemic that too much time was spent on low-use print collections and not enough time was devoted to high-use electronic formats. We should be under no illusions now about just how little these are used and the poor return on investment we get with this material, in terms of library use.*

2.3.3 Inquiries

Inquiry services were commonly thought to be a service area that would need to be revised post-pandemic. One library manager commented:

> *The staffing of enquiry points is likely to be reduced and the function of this area reviewed. It is unlikely that we will return to exactly the same service we had previously.*

Increased use of chat services and bookable online appointments during the pandemic had proved popular with students, and a number of libraries envisaged providing online options in the future or the partial replacement of previous face-to-face or telephone services.

2.3.4 Supporting teaching and learning

Alterations in the balance of online and face-to-face teaching and training by library staff were envisaged. Face-to-face sessions were likely to continue to be valued by some library staff and students for particular activities, but online delivery was often more convenient and flexible for students. Some librarians envisaged the replacement of some small face-to-face classes which were very labor intensive for the small number of students who attended.

2.3.5 Loan arrangements

Respondents commented that loan services that may need to be looked at in detail post-pandemic included postal loan services, particularly their sustainability, and interlibrary loans. One library manager commented that alternatives to traditional interlibrary loans needed to be investigated and that, in her library, patron-driven acquisition had already been utilized as a partial replacement.

2.3.6 Other comments

There was a recognition that if the move to more digital services continued post-pandemic, there was likely to be a lower library staffing requirement for some processes such as cataloging or the processing of physical items.

2.4 What additional services, including online services, do you think will be required in the future?

2.4.1 General

Many respondents had digital strategies in place with plans to introduce virtual services. These plans had been accelerated by the pandemic, but a number of respondents commented on the need to continue this acceleration. Online services introduced during the pandemic had tended to concentrate on the support of teaching and learning, but other support was now being planned, including for research and enterprise. One respondent commented:

> We are currently transitioning our research support services online. Teaching and learning went first, we're now pushing hard with research support.

Other services envisaged for the future included publishing services, with the library acting as publisher, and online services to the wider community now that so many people had learned how to engage with technology more effectively through services such as Zoom.

2.4.2 Information resource provision

Enhanced provision of e-resources in the future was thought to be key, with open access, through initiatives such as Plan S, being an important element. More emphasis on digitization and digital preservation was also thought to be necessary, in particular, to make rare book collections accessible to a wider audience.

2.4.3 Inquiries

A number of respondents commented on the need to provide online enhancements to existing inquiry service provision, including a live chat facility and the use of chatbots. One library was actively considering being part of a university-wide inquiry management service.

2.4.4 Supporting teaching and learning

A large proportion of the responses to this question related to the need for the library to develop innovative approaches to the support of teaching and learning in an online environment. This included integrating and embedding library content and learning objects, such as video tutorials, alongside academic taught content in VLEs (virtual learning environments) so that they are easily discovered in a need-to-know manner.

Library managers were also reflecting on how there could be linkages between physical library spaces and their online equivalents:

> We are looking at how we can replicate the physical spaces we provide in an online environment, potentially using MS Teams and facilitating areas for group and individual study. This also links to the potential for aligning our physical and digital presence more deeply, to bring together a wider and blended community approach.

There was also a recognition that library websites may need to be revised to reflect changing user needs. One library manager commented:

Definitely a review of our website and how we present the 'window in' to services. It's clear it could be more intuitive and organized differently. I'd like to think we could take a real UX (user experience) based approach to that in the same way we would when reviewing our physical spaces and services.

Other respondents commented on the need to develop face-to-face and online support for students with disabilities, provision of copyright training for users, and potential library involvement in the design and delivery of interactive e-textbook elements in the curriculum.

2.5 Do you think there will be a move back to some of your traditional face-to-face services?

2.5.1 General

Some respondents commented that for a number of library services there was likely to be a blended approach in the future, mixing online and physical services. This would provide flexibility, although there could be resource issues in doubling up provision. The general consensus was that there would be more emphasis on online than was the case prepandemic, although with some move back to face-to-face:

A move back to face-to-face, but not on the same scale. The pandemic has illustrated the number of services that can be operated successfully remotely, in some instances more successfully than face-to-face. At the same time, both staff and users do still find the physical interaction beneficial. Finding the right balance will be key!
Nothing will probably go entirely back to its pre-pandemic model because a blended in-person/digital approach appears to be better, more flexible and futureproof.

2.5.2 Information resource provision

There was a recognition in the responses that in the future there will be many library users who will continue to need access to physical stock. A number of respondents commented that access to and use of special collections is likely to return mainly to its traditional model, although, in time, it could be supplemented by more digital access if further digitization projects can be resourced.

2.5.3 Library space

Physical access to study space was felt to be an important issue. One respondent commented:

Study space will continue to be important. The loss of that, especially for groups, has been the biggest challenge for students.

The importance of individual study space was also recognized, with not all users having a suitable study space at home. A return to the use of individual and group study was envisaged post-pandemic, although maybe initially at a lower level than before. This will have implications for the requirement for face-to-face support and opening hours.

2.5.4 Inquiries

Most of the librarians saw a continuing need for face-to-face support at library inquiry desks:

> A staffed, in-person enquiry service is too valuable to give up. It is the only way to effectively support clients who struggle to find rooms, books, and other physical things in the library.
> I think there will always be a call for face-to-face support at the desks in some form, so we will certainly be continuing with that approach.

There was some evidence of continuing user preference for face-to-face support. In one Australian university, in an area where there had been little community transmission of COVID-19 for several months, staff and students generally opted for face-to-face consultations for reference services when offered an online option.

2.5.5 Supporting teaching and learning

A number of respondents referred to library teaching of information literacy and academic and digital skills being solely online during the pandemic but likely to shift to a blended approach post-pandemic with a mix of online and in-person. Online teaching was felt to offer advantages of better attendance, reach, and convenience, with face-to-face delivery being a "richer, easier to facilitate, collaborative learning experience." It was also recognized that for universities with a strong campus ethos, face-to-face teaching, including library teaching, may become the dominant presence again. A number of library managers articulated the advantages of online library teaching:

> Even though I find virtual training sessions to be better from a management perspective, in terms of offering a consistent suite of training, reaching a bigger number of attendees, and measuring activity, I'm pretty sure that the push from both librarians and students to go back to face-to-face information skills training will be significant.
> For teaching, it's about using the best tools to get the most effective result. Where we can deliver more effectively using online tools and can demonstrate improved impact and engagement, we should continue to use online approaches.

2.5.6 Other comments

It was thought that post-pandemic many more internal meetings would be held online than previously, particularly for multisite meetings or where participants have some distance to travel. Negative comments were made about "mixed mode" meetings where some participants are in a meeting room and others are online. Home working was also thought likely to become more common given positive staff experiences during the pandemic, although one librarian commented:

> *I see some tension between a managerial desire to maintain a friendly in-person presence in the library and pressure from staff to work flexibly and from home more of the time.*

A library manager highlighted staffing issues in developing new service models and approaches:

> *We need to consider how we can facilitate more flexible, creative, and productive working patterns.*

2.6 Have you got any other views on academic library services post-pandemic, including financial aspects and collaborative approaches?

Library collaboration was felt to have been beneficial during the pandemic, particularly in the sharing of information, knowledge, and experience regionally and nationally. Examples were given of collaboration within regional academic library consortia and in national collaborative organizations, such as SCONUL in the United Kingdom.

Considerable concern was expressed about funding constraints post-pandemic. In most countries, it was felt that public spending is likely to come under increased scrutiny which, together with other trends such as reduced international student recruitment, will have a significant impact on institutional staffing and nonstaffing budgets. Post-pandemic, there were considerable concerns over costs and licensing e-content compared to print, particularly with e-books, with the need for new approaches and sector-wide collaboration:

> *There are significant financial challenges around the shift to e-books. The current models are not financially sustainable and we risk locking ourselves into high-cost models which won't ultimately benefit the sector. Sector-wide evaluation of the current models is needed, and lobbying publishers to deliver more affordable business models, or a shift in academic culture to a more open textbook approach.*

Other collaborative approaches referred to include the greater use of systems such as RapidILL for document delivery. Funding constraints and a requirement for efficiencies within institutions were also thought likely to lead to greater collaboration and a continued blurring of boundaries between academic libraries and other support departments.

3 Discussions and conclusions

This small study is based on some rapid responses from academic library managers and academic librarians to a questionnaire sent out in November 2020 during the coronavirus pandemic. The responses were detailed and very thoughtful, but the study had some limitations. It was a relatively small sample, not scientifically selected but focused on contacts of the author. Given time constraints, the survey was also limited to library managers and librarians and, therefore, did not include other stakeholders such as senior university staff, academic staff, researchers, and students. The respondents were probably more experienced and interested in technological solutions and innovation in libraries than academic librarians in general and were also probably more strategic, better linked to senior university managers, and likely to be influential sector leaders. These attributes put them in a good position to be able to help identify and articulate future trends and envision academic library services post-pandemic.

The study clearly shows that there was a large-scale shift to online provision and services in academic libraries during the pandemic. Some libraries found the transition easier than others, depending on the nature of their existing collections and services. For many libraries, the pandemic was an opportunity to accelerate a digital transition already planned and for some a chance to reflect deeply on the nature of their future provision and to innovate and trial new services with their users and their own staff.

How permanent will this online shift be? There is probably no single, simple answer. Some institutions and their libraries have a strong campus ethos extolling the benefits of an in-person student experience. These institutions will probably look to some dialing back to face-to-face delivery and support. Other institutions, who have invested heavily in the production of sophisticated online content and course development, may be looking to extend their reach with a greater development of distance delivery and remote learning, particularly for students in employment or with many and complex nonstudy commitments. Even in campus-based institutions, a growing student preference for digital lectures is likely to continue, with, as a consequence, student time on campus reduced. This is likely to impact the nature of the physical estate, including large lecture theatres and libraries. There will be an increased emphasis on student wellbeing and health—24-hour library study facilities and densely packed study areas may well be frowned upon.

In terms of the digital delivery of courses, one respondent to the questionnaire expressed the view that "the cat is well and truly out of the bag." E-delivery, not just of lectures, is likely to increase in all types of institutions. Libraries will need to reflect on the changing university environments they operate in. Where there is a strong campus ethos, librarians may need to continue to emphasize face-to-face support and provide a range of safe study spaces. Accelerated by the pandemic, academic staff, researchers, and students have had more experience of using online library services, and hopefully, they have liked what they have used and found the services convenient, flexible, and of high quality. Based on the questionnaire responses, it seems safe to say that in most academic libraries there will have been permanent shifts to enhance e-resource provision (costs permitting), to depend to a greater extent on virtual support, to provide more online library teaching both synchronous and asynchronous, to implement online booking arrangements for study space and appointments, and to encourage online meetings and home working. However, in the future, this will need to be tempered with having a blended approach with a physical element, particularly for study facilities, inquiries, and library teaching, where there are clear and identifiable benefits for communication, engagement, social and emotional support, facilitation of learning, and effective individual and group learning.

Academic library managers and librarians will need to be honest with themselves. If they are proposing retention of or a move back to traditional physical services, they need to convince themselves and others that this is not to protect the status quo but is in line with university aims and objectives. If a move to digital is the right thing to do for library users and the university, library managers will need to be confident about the change and invest the time and resources to reorganize and reskill their staff appropriately and embed digital service delivery into their structures permanently and sustainably.

References

Atkinson, J., 2020. Technology, Change and the Academic Library: Case Studies, Trends and Reflections. Chandos Publishing, Oxford.

United Nations Conference on Trade and Development, 2020. COVID-19 and e-Commerce: Findings From a Survey of Online Consumers in 9 Countries. UNCTAD, Geneva, Switzerland. Retrieved from: dtlstictinf2020d1_en.pdf (unctad.org).

Envisioning opportunities and movement for the future of academic libraries

Yi Shen
Independent Researcher, Blacksburg, VA, United States

1 Introduction

In today's challenging and disruptive environments, we must take on shared responsibility and pursue innovative thinking and creative leadership to tackle the many dimensions of contemporary health, environmental, social, and political crises. Academic libraries, as an integral and critical part of scientific research infrastructure, play significant roles in our institutional efforts to deal with and recover from the health crisis, social unrest, and economic downturn of these days. So what opportunities or movements lie ahead that may change the way libraries operate and respond to disruptive events and future challenges? This chapter answers this question with a series of identified opportunities and suggested actions for libraries to deal with the changing environment and a transformative landscape.

2 Opportunities and movement

"Technological innovation and infrastructures have played significant roles in the COVID-19 pandemic, the climate emergency, the global rise in authoritarianism, and a widespread expansion in economic and social injustice" (STGlobal Consortium, 2020). The impact of COVID-19 brings to question how we design intelligent infrastructure for the post-pandemic world—including housing, energy, transportation, and healthcare—that truly serves diverse human communities (Ishida, 2020). This involves embedding intelligence into environments and the physical creation of human-centred communities by incorporating sensing abilities, computing power, and communication capabilities, as well as various AI tools and applications.

So, how were AI tools and robots being used during the COVID-19 pandemic around the world? A recent survey discovered them spraying disinfectants, showing properties for real estate agents, and helping with patient intake and delivery of supplies in hospitals, among others (Hayasaki, 2020). We are seeing a future where assistant robots are on the rise while witnessing how automating certain tasks can keep humans out of harm's way. Taking these examples, now we can imagine the use of robots or AI assistants in a variety of new ways and contexts, for example, to do library disinfection, book shelving, and document delivery, or to provide library tours and

Libraries, Digital Information, and COVID. https://doi.org/10.1016/B978-0-323-88493-8.00028-8

deliver informational services for patrons. The innovative use of advanced technologies represents a promising scenario and important movement to address AI for social good in the library environment.

A recent study envisioned the "smart recommender and virtual assistant" concept of future digital libraries (Shen, 2019). In this concept, intelligent library agents or smart recommenders are capable of personalizing, summarizing, and communicating data, information, and literature for users to support information inquiry and exploratory search, to provide adaptive question-answering and intuitive informational dialogue, and to support proactive information push and knowledge discovery. With the proliferation of personal assistants or digital agents in real-world applications in recent years, we are noticing that AI agents, humans, and physical devices "can cooperate as a community that instantiates, [enriches], and exploits various aspects of collective intelligence" (FedCSIS, 2020). How we embed these technologies in libraries' physical and digital architectures to address human-data, human-computer, and human-environment interactions in support of information needs and inquiries represents a significant opportunity that will change the way libraries operate in the future of work.

Another key opportunity and immediate movement for academic libraries is to showcase advocacy and leadership roles in directly addressing structural racism, social injustice, and systemic inequality in today's politically and digitally polarized atmosphere. As the information bridge and literacy educator, libraries could help cultivate a community of diverse voices that explores these critical issues through creative writing, artistic display, network building, and constructive debate. On top of that, libraries could organize and host interdisciplinary teams to craft creative policy solutions and applicable institutional strategies in efforts to promote and celebrate the diversity of strengths within the academic environments.

Lastly, science, technology, and policy, if strategically organized, can help us be prepared for future disruptive events, including pandemics. So, the importance of taking the long view and funding for preparedness has never been clearer. The library and information communities have a unique responsibility to empower science and technology innovation and to manage intellectual capital and digital assets. We draw on core values of information studies, including access, justice, and inclusion, and use these principles to guide information policies, improve organizational efficiency, and enhance societal responsibility and environmental sustainability. These efforts aim to serve the public interest and social good. To prepare for a resilient and sustainable future, we must actively participate in the value-centered study, planning, and equitable design of technology. These include proactively configuring libraries into sociotechnical systems, infrastructure, and the future of work at the intersection of technology development and social responsibility.

3   Conclusion

We are at an unprecedented stage of social, political, economic, and environmental changes in the wake of the pandemic, with accelerated processes like digitalization and automation, with tremendous opportunities like forging new innovation pathways, reimagining organizational operations, and championing fairness and social justice. These require us to engage in a new strategic visioning and designing practice for the libraries of the future. As such, this paper identifies opportunities and suggests actions for academic libraries to deal with the disruptive landscape and transformative environment. These range from addressing AI for social good in the library environment, to implementing smart assistants or digital agents in support of human information needs and inquiries, and from showcasing leadership role in addressing structural racism, social injustice, and systemic inequality, to participating in value-centered study, planning, and equitable design of technology. At this exceptional time, our library system can boldly demonstrate its resilience and capacity for innovation in the face of unprecedented changes and new demands.

References

FedCSIS, 2020. 1st Workshop on Actors, Agents, Assistants, Avatars (4A'20). https://www. fedcsis.org/2020/4a. (Accessed 25 November 2020).

Hayasaki, E., 2020. Covid-19 could accelerate the robot takeover of human jobs. MIT Technol. Rev. June 17 https://www.technologyreview.com/2020/06/17/1003328/ covid-19-could-accelerate-the-robot-takeover-of-human-jobs/.

Ishida, A., 2020. Rethinking intelligent infrastructure in time of COVID-19. IIHCC Newslett. 3 (2), 5. https://www.provost.vt.edu/content/dam/provost_vt_edu/da-assets/docs/intelli-gent-infrastructure/2020_04_21_AprilNewsletter.pdf.

Shen, Y., 2019. Emerging scenarios of data infrastructure and novel concepts of digital libraries in intelligent infrastructure for human-centered communities: a qualitative research. J. Inf. Sci. 45 (5), 691–704. https://doi.org/10.1177/0165551518811459.

STGlobal Consortium, 2020. Science at Service: Building Inclusive Communities. https://www. stglobal.org/2021-cfp. (Accessed 25 November 2020).

A framework for sustainable success

David Baker[a,b] and Lucy Ellis[b,c]
[a]Professor Emeritus, Plymouth Marjon University, Plymouth, United Kingdom,
[b]David Baker Consulting, West Yorkshire, United Kingdom, [c]University of Exeter,
Exeter, United Kingdom

1   Introduction

This book has looked at the effects of the COVID-19 pandemic with special reference to library and information provision. It has focused on the ways in which libraries and library leaders have responded to the many and varied challenges relating to the provision of access to collections and services; and at a time when many of the traditional, tried-and-tested modes of delivery have not been feasible or required significant reengineering.

Much of the success in meeting the needs of users—and the concerns and aspirations of libraries' stakeholders more broadly—has come as a result of planning, hard work, determination, imagination, and a willingness to think and act participatively and flexibly. However, while the pandemic was an unforeseen event (as evinced by its absence from most institutions' risk registers, disaster planning manuals, staff training, and briefings), libraries which had already made some form of "digital shift" almost certainly had an advantage (if not a head start) as they prepared for life during, if not after, COVID-19. Many lessons have already been learned and no doubt many more will be also. Now is the time to take stock and begin to prepare for the longer term.

> Libraries need a clear strategy and a vision for rapid technology variation. Many libraries have found new ways of maintaining their services – public libraries have had increasing demand for audio books and e-books as well as providing books for collection 'at the door' when buildings have been closed to the public. Similar approaches have been taken by some university libraries and school libraries at least.
>
> *Delphi study, 2021*

> The lessons learned from the pandemic will need to be brought together. Business continuity planning is needed and should include modelling of operations during a virus and pandemic management. Capturing the learning must take place in order to grow and strengthen rather than just suffer. Some people feel more connected than pre-pandemic and my organization has seen its

Libraries, Digital Information, and COVID. https://doi.org/10.1016/B978-0-323-88493-8.00032-X

staff engagement scores go up. The regular briefings and well being support have helped. Having a good working from home infrastructure in place before COVID-19 has helped enormously as the focus can be on social interaction and morale support.

Chief operating officer, national infrastructure provider

COVID-19 and every aspect of the experience of it are challenging deeply held beliefs and philosophies, frameworks, and attitudes. As Sayeda Zain (Chapter 13) and Yi Shen (Chapter 30) both stress that it is now essential that a long-term view is taken in order to plan for life after COVID-19 to learn the lessons from the crises which it has caused and to begin to build the future information landscape as part of the larger rebuilding of our world and our societies, preferably in partnership across sectors, regions, and countries. Lucy Shackleton and Rosa Mann (Chapter 16) in particular draw attention to the "window of opportunity" that can and should be used to "accelerate digital transformation and enhance institutional resilience" as well as to recapture the library's premier position as part of a "rebranding" exercise, as described and developed by Richard Maidment-Otlet in Chapter 12. Paul Kirkham (Chapter 25) points out that this is not going to be easy, given the continuing pressing need to offer some kind of "business as usual," but it will be necessary.

Everything that was there before the crisis is there afterwards, but accelerated and intensified … all of the things we were doing in a slow and incoherent way before the crisis, we need to do in a rapid and cohesive way afterwards.

Tony Blair, quoted in Times Higher Education *7 January 2021*

The present pandemic may not be the last pandemic. Libraries need to be ready for future worst-case scenarios to deal with more challenging situations. But COVID-19 provides opportunities as well as challenges for libraries to step up and innovate to provide better services to their clients. Librarians should continue their roles as professionals, serving our users to the best of our ability for the common good.

Delphi study, 2021

It's made a lot of institutions think about their own infrastructure, their use of the cloud, and their configurations generally which should help to accelerate decisions. This is tricky as such changes can sometimes impact on jobs. This crisis has forced new accelerated thinking about things that were likely to be in strategic plans already.

Chief operating officer, national infrastructure provider, UK

The pandemic may be forcing the world to change, but with purposeful planning, librarians can create opportunities for the optimal development of collections and services, benefitting society at large in the process. Opportunities for libraries and librarians in the next twelve months include: providing customized services for emerging clients; bringing more clients into the physical library by the innovative way they organize the library space; making online presence more interactive; and getting potential groups and organizations to invest in the library.

Delphi study, 2021

2   Moving toward a "new normal" and digital shift

As Rick Rylance comments so ably in Chapter 20, we live in transitional times. But then, humanity has always been in transition. The challenge is the pace at which that transition is happening (and would have happened anyway, but perhaps not as fast as it is now, thanks to COVID-19), together with the nature of the acceleration and its possible end point (Chapter 27). The pandemic was neither anticipated nor desired. Nevertheless, as all the contributors to this volume stress, it has stimulated creativity and resourcefulness in a way that would probably not have been thought possible in 2019. Those organizations, industries, and sectors that are prepared to embrace change are much more likely to stay in existence than those that either refuse to alter their approaches or plan to return to an "old normal" when they believe it is safe to do so (Chapter 24).

Strategy development that responds to external direction and constraints seems set to continue for some time to come. The same is true of museums although not all have developed online resources to substitute in some way for direct access to collections and now there are some in dire straits due to their dependence on income from entry fees and sales.

Delphi study, 2021

In the short term, planning will be directly tied into the priorities of the parent institutions and the constraints that may be placed on them in response to the needs for 'virus recovery' and the likelihood of funding famine. Clearly the wider use of online services must be a focus of attention but decisions about the restarting of the full range of traditional service will require both policy and management decisions.

Delphi study, 2021

Rob May (Chapter 15) talks about the broader issues relating to the major transitions that are now in train and their macrolevel management. While "reforms must be guided by a genuine long-range political process which embraces a multitude of changes, the extent to which innovation occurs and the extent to which it is amplified is subject to political choices." A major problem that has to be faced in many environments—as identified by a number of contributors to this volume—is that of "asymmetric information": caused by "policymakers [who] are disconnected from the realities."

Longer term, the majority of organizations will have their own disaster plans which continue to be important since local issues will likely be the most common issues - flood, fire, pestilence, etc. There remains a significant gap between local developments and the need for national coordination and guidance. In coming years, online services, for example, have to converge nationally and across all collecting sectors to deliver maximum social value to citizens.

Delphi study, 2021

Library and information services have proved their worth and demonstrated their value during the pandemic (as noted, for example, in Chapters 16 and 23). However, while their overall role may have remained much the same as before COVID-19, the contributors to this book clearly believe that reengineering of collections and services that have taken place since late 2019 is unlikely to be reversed, though some authors (as for example Diana Chan and Victoria Caplan in Chapter 2) have noticed, and continue to predict, that there will be a return to physical provision and usage of library materials. This will be in the context of a further, fundamental reappraisal of the value of "just-in-case" stock provision, even in some larger research libraries (Chapter 3), and the "cementing" into the future practice of many, if not all, of the recently adopted online approaches described by Shackleton and Mann in Chapter 16 in terms of online education and Jeremy Atkinson (Chapter 29) concerning the future shape and nature of library provision, at least in developed countries. The Third World may have responded well—if differently—to COVID-19, in terms of library and information provision, as suggested by Lucy Shackleton and Rosa Mann in Chapter 16, but as those authors point out (as does Sarah Mears in Chapter 24), there remains an urgent need to ensure that no one is left behind as the new normal develops. Paul Kirkham (Chapter 25) notes that a key part of the response to a crisis such as COVID-19 must be "the provision of aftercare"; "managing the 'long tail' of the return to normality."

There can be few library and information services that have not already begun a transition to online provision. "Going digital," in fact, has been an almost inevitable trajectory for libraries and librarians for some time—not least as documented and demonstrated in previous publications in the *Advances in Information and Digital Information Reviews* series. Many of the chapters in this book have referred to the fact that the changes now taking place were already in train, but in recent times there has been a "quick pivot" or a "rapid acceleration," as necessitated by the pandemic; some, as for example Sam Brenton and Sandra Tury in Chapter 10 and Stephen Akintunde (from a different perspective, sub-Saharan Africa) in Chapter 26, have suggested that the tipping point in terms of a full digital shift has finally arrived.

While the pandemic will recede, online learning won't. What does each university and college need to make it the best experience, post-pandemic? Secure on-campus connectivity, secure off-campus connectivity, access to the right hardware and software, access to high quality content, digital transformation leadership, data driven decision-making, digital skills for teachers and learners, student experience and employability and innovation. Something similar will be happening for research also which has received less profile compared to the issues facing universities and colleges in relation to post-16 and undergraduate students.

Chief operating officer, national infrastructure provider, UK

Chapter 29 provides a useful summary of which new or reengineered (digital/online) services will remain and be developed, what will possibly revert to prepandemic shape and form in terms of provision, and where an activity or activities may well be discontinued. It is instructive to note that while services might be reintroduced in due course, Atkinson reported that some librarians felt it would be a backward step to reoffer physical access in relation to future library strategy, with users being encouraged to move permanently to digital. Even library skills training is likely to be hybrid if not fully online while recognizing that some groups of users (and staff) will continue to value, and benefit from, face-to-face interaction.

Working from home (WFH) has proved both popular and effective, at least in developed economies. All the evidence points to WFH, therefore, being a basic aspect of the "new normal" and this will impact not only on service provision and library access, but also on the way in which library staff are led, managed, and structured in the future.

'Our homes are now our classrooms; our laptops are our partner; we all are becoming technology savvy'. Library collections and services need to reach users in their private as well as their work and public spaces. Communication between library and users will be more intensive. Embracing contemporary technologies should be practised by libraries and librarians. Collaboration, networking, and learning soft skills are also going to be essential to overcome future obstacles. Critical to future success will be knowledge of the online exchange relationships that take place between user and service, and how to design systems that provide maximum value to the individual.

Delphi study, 2021

Needless to say, reengineered services may be feasible on a lower headcount, especially as developments in artificial intelligence (AI) influence provision. Yi Shen (Chapter 30) in particular looks at the opportunities and movements that could well change the way libraries operate and respond to the significant disruption caused by COVID-19. A "sociotechnical reconfiguration" is proposed for a "smart and resilient future."

In parallel with such advanced technological developments, many contributors to this book refer to the serious economic downturn that is likely to ensue post-COVID and the financial challenges that this will inevitably bring, as enumerated by Rob

May (Chapter 15) in particular. There will be difficult choices to make in terms of new versus existing services in particular. Finding the best mix and balance between preexisting, reengineered, and new and between physical and digital will be key. The need to demonstrate value and return on investment will be more important than ever. Data and metrics will be crucial (Chapter 17).

The VfM case for libraries will be around digital usage, research data management, new digital services, and how they contribute to success/achieving objectives. It will no longer be about print loan and print collections.

University librarian, South East Asia

There is bound to be a long tail after COVID is tamed of fighting funding locally and nationally and for many institutions this may mean battling to sustain what they already have and are doing that is dominant. Library leaders might have to take a 'more with less' approach in providing services to clients, personnel, and partners. In some countries, there currently seems to be limited interest in working to produce national frameworks for online services that bring all types of digital collections within a shared and coordinated framework. How do librarians launch new digital information services so that they reach every user, but possibly with decreasing financial support by governments?

Delphi study, 2021

The new normal
This will be digital-first, physical space-second. Permanently digital-first will, however, need investment in the technology infrastructure of libraries. Pre-pandemic, physical space use was intentionally front and centre, because of the high value attached to face-to-face contact. Libraries don't have a digital workforce, who are curious about new technology and how it can be used in libraries. Nostalgia has largely insulated libraries from the effect of technology.

Of the changes which have taken place because of the pandemic, I would like the following to remain:

- Political and public recognition of the vital role of libraries
- Awareness of information literacy, and libraries as a source of authentic information
- The audience engagement via digital, which has built up
- The emerging practice of using data
- Advances in access to rich digital content e.g. via multi-year licences for e-books.

Building on the above, libraries need to:

- be 'in the boardroom' as part of planning for resilience, rather than information use being a reaction to crisis in the organizations which libraries are part of
- ask for the funding needed to do their work
- get credit for the work they do

Senior library professional, UK

3 Place versus space

Perhaps the single biggest challenge facing librarians as they plan for the future is what to do with their physical space. Problems, opportunities, challenges, and solutions will vary depending on the type of library and its present and likely future purpose.

The closure of the libraries … has had a disproportionate effect on the Humanities compared to Science. This has led to some concerns. Universities traditionally place a lot of emphasis on buildings. 90% of capital spend is focused on new buildings, at the expense of IT and other services. However, during the pandemic, what use was a building? For the most part, the estate was redundant for 7/8 months. People must be thinking less of bricks and mortar and more of the virtual. There needs to be a redefinition of 'the estate'.

Senior manager, national library, UK

Some of these issues apply to all public spaces and have rapidly been dealt with in shops and other places of interaction. To no small extent it will depend on the spaces available and the nature of the user. The small branch library, if open for browsing, will be unable to manage social spacing, while a university library may offer well-spaced seating with required items being ordered in advance while stopping user access to collections. For museums, it is possible to book slots to limit numbers, but since the majority of users will wish to browse collections full management crowd control is pretty much impossible.

Delphi study, 2021

The library as study space: the experience of an engineering undergraduate
Ted O'Hare
Among the many thousands of other university students, in 2020 I found myself jettisoned from a place of relative certainty into a Michaelmas term like no other. Perhaps I was lucky: as a fourth-year student I knew my way around campus by now and, given my MEng research and development project was purely computational, the few contact hours I had were easily adapted to online remote learning. By contrast, many of my peers needed laboratory access, or had to grapple with interactive seminars via conference call. However, it is clear that one thing has affected us all equally to some degree: the closure and subsequent partial re-opening of the university library.

It is rare that my course requires me to seek out books for information; online resources usually satiate any appetite for supplementary reading, and the latest scientific advances invariably take the form of peer-reviewed journal articles or conference papers to be sourced from the Internet. Moreover, in a recent academic writing workshop I was informed that in the hierarchy of veracity – and therefore bibliographic preference – books outranked only 'bloke in pub' and *Wikipedia*! And yet, during more ordinary times, Durham University's Bill Bryson Library played a central role in my studies, the destination of an almost daily pilgrimage.

In my experience, the library provides an excellent environment to study free from distraction, with a collectively perpetuated, palpably non-judgmental atmosphere eager to condemn procrastination. Perhaps simply the very action alone of turning a study session into an *event* to which one has to travel augments productivity; leaving the library having not made progress or produced substantive results is an incredibly disheartening, almost embarrassing position to be in. Unlike other study spaces around the university, for example, the computer rooms in my own department building, the library elicits a certain level of respect from its users which is not to be underestimated, manifesting as a noble silence and an internal determination to achieve something tangible while within the building's walls. Altogether, this makes for an atmosphere perfectly conducive to individual learning and research.

To my mind, the pandemic has lain bare the inherent benefits of the library as a *study space*, rather than simply a repository for books and information. Coming from a discipline where many of the emerging themes of adaptation to the 'new normal' have already taken place to some degree, for example, migration to digital-only principles, the value of physical library space simply as somewhere to work was perhaps already clear to me on some level. But being forced to study from home, where it has been unprecedentedly difficult to focus (and, equally, hard to switch off and unwind) has clearly articulated how indispensable these physical spaces are. I would therefore argue that while over the coming years library and information provision may need to accelerate towards digital, in higher education institutions physical libraries providing collective, reliably *quiet* study space will always be requisite and valuable, forever forming a central part of campus life.

There are several other aspects to this question of space and place. Library buildings will have to be made safe for both users and staff. Trust has been lost, people feel insecure, and it will take some time for the physical library to be seen as space once more. User behaviour has at times been challenging and this has not always helped.

The biggest technical challenge is the development of new protocols for the maintenance of hygiene and biosafety when there is as yet insufficient research to support the management and redesign of indoor environments, the provision of printed materials and the effective safeguarding of users against any infectious material. The pandemic provides an opportunity to create new protocols for the users and design changes such as special sanitizer counters and reading cubicles and disinfection rooms to kill the viruses.

Delphi study, 2021

Libraries might need to set up large indoor rooms with separate spaces for each student, or researcher. The separations could be implemented with a box-office style. Sanitizers are well used already now and there will be enough of these also in the future. In addition, high-tech solutions could be launched to check people when they move around in the building. Health information of all possible clients should be updated every day real time, and this set of information should be at the disposal of libraries and doctors and health care institutions. Air quality inside buildings is an important factor. New virtual spaces could be available via Microsoft Teams, Zoom, and with other similar solutions. In addition practical skills on how to use BrightTALK – type platforms might be useful.

Delphi study, 2021

There is a broader issue that will have to be addressed in terms of social behaviours. It is quite apparent in the depths of the current pandemic many people seem to feel themselves immune from infection. Not wearing masks, meeting in large groups, etc., are the main mechanism for transmission and while the role of service managers is to design delivery systems to meet the needs of users rather than retraining users to use them, in the case of COVID, social behaviours will have to change to beat the virus. In countries where populations are more responsive to advice and regulation – New Zealand, SE Asia – disease control has been far more successful.

Delphi study, 2021

The accelerated shift to digital provision and online access has major implications for physical space, notwithstanding the continued need for face-to-face contact, as noted earlier. Richard Maidment-Otlet (Chapter 12), Sam Brenton and Sandra Tury (Chapter 10), and Sarah Mears (Chapter 24) are four of the contributors who discuss some of the ways in which the best mix of physical and digital may develop, though approaches and solutions will vary considerably depending upon a whole range of variables, as for example the particular and differing needs of public and academic library users. Evgenia Vasilakaki and Valentini Moniarou (Chapter 21) discuss the future for virtual as well as physical library space, not least in terms of the need to provide a "third place." As Ellen Buck and Anna Nunn (Chapter 11) state, libraries must continue to function—whether physical or virtual—as *space and place*: somewhere where people can be, work, and otherwise interact together in one or more ecosystems (social, professional, educational, research, and so on).

Libraries are supposed to bring people together but with social distancing how do they make this possible? User engagement is one of the paramount challenges and the time has come to increase the availability of e-content by establishing virtual libraries and making available more digital content in accessible and affordable manner.

Delphi study, 2021

There is, of course, a broader challenge here: whole industries and sectors have realized that "office working" no longer needs to be the predominant mode of operation and wholesale restructuring of workflows is already in train as a result.

What is the future of working? For instance, how do organizations want to use the office post-COVID and how might this affect employment contracts? Should offices be downsized? Collaborative working has been highlighted. The office as a place where you come and work all day will change. The collaborative working model will change this. If you want to do an agile sprint on something then appropriate space is available for project working. While the offices are closed, refurbishment is taking place such as taking out a lot of the desks and making more collaborative workspaces. Some open plan and 'buzzy' spaces are being made. Collaborative working which is creative has become important as this is harder to do remotely – you need to be face-to-face with people. The creative aspect is very important for how the business wants to work going forward to support members and communities. Caring, connecting and well being is central to the value of the work. It needs to be as flexible as possible.

Chief operating officer, national infrastructure provider, UK

Libraries and librarians need to assimilate these broader trends as they create future library space, whether physical or virtual. Increased demand and usage having gone digital is one trajectory that will need to be considered.

Human nature will drive people back to more face-to-face interaction post-pandemic, but meetings and administrative work will continue to be performed online to a degree. Pre-COVID, my clients were rarely prepared to 'meet' online but now it's the norm using tools like Zoom, Teams and Miro. There will be a greater reliance on digital information, since paper (records) do carry a risk of transmission (like paper currency does). We will certainly move to a paperless health and care system.

Senior management consultant, National Health Service, UK

Physical space investment will be a challenge because work practices used to be around a print-led set-up. The move to digital will not stop, in part because it will take time for trust to be rebuilt and resilience to be developed for a resumption of on-site activity.

University librarian, South East Asia

Libraries must dramatically increase the role of their digital information services in facilitating research and community building in the virtual space. Academic libraries do have broader responsibilities in their mission to help students and researchers to accomplish their work compared to museums, special libraries, national libraries, or public libraries when serving their own customers. Researchers and students use libraries due to their central role in academic education and research. Special and national libraries have a great opportunity now to tighten their relationships with academic libraries. COVID-19 research requires interdisciplinary approaches to identify proper frameworks for mitigating risks associated with everyday life.

Delphi study, 2021

"Mobile" will not always equate with digital, at least in a Third World context, where low-technology solutions may have to be considered, though Stephen Akintunde (Chapter 26) forecasts a future where mobile phones and similar devices will be of significant importance for African digital library provision.

Mobile libraries are appropriate for such challenging times. They have always been of value in public libraries to service remoter communities, but the current trend is for mobiles to be phased out as not being cost-effective. But in a mobile system, the material required can be collected and suitable days and times can be collated via Internet or even phone calls. These could include books, journal photocopies or audio/video resources. This would also be an opportunity to create an awareness campaign. A vehicle with attractive display cases would brighten the day, especially if the users are children or young adults. Outreach activities like storytelling, book reading, competitions can be added attractions. It is easier to sanitize a truck rather than a library.

Delphi study, 2021

Using drones might be effective for remote users. Libraries can use social media as a proactive risk communication strategy to maintain connections with their patrons. Book delivery drones are an effective technology during the lockdown period. Just like Amazon drones can deliver goods to customers, libraries could deliver library collections to patrons. Drones can find users by the location of their smartphone, so there is no need to give a fixed address. Using technologies like chatbots, virtual reality, and artificial intelligence can also support communities.

Delphi study, 2021

Maintaining the technology for an online service requires people and will have a built-in physical aspect. Also, even a completely online service will require staff to maintain it, but this will be a completely different maintenance job from a laptop at home. There needs to be understanding that it takes a lot of work to reconfigure this maintenance and support for online services to enable it to take place off-site. It's not just about machines but also about copyright. When you are not in the building, there are all sorts of difficulties that arise. Data mining services don't work from home in the same way. Text and data mining exemption, for example, requires legal status that requires you to be in your building to define your legal access to collections. On a number of projects, we have found that this does not work once we are working remotely. A lot of things just have not been possible. Prior to the pandemic, we had massively increased its online services and presence. Not all of this is related to access to collections, but also to public events such as children's programmes, schools programmes and student programmes. The latter would have been attended by individuals in their hundreds face-to-face but since being online the attendance is in the thousands. Lecturers may find it helpful to promote the library's programmes to their own students, as readymade content. However, we will continue to be much more than a purely online experience. We have learned a lot of new things about online delivery of content and services, but many things in the future will continue to involve people and physical face to face provision. There are many things that we have not been able to replicate in online environment. Important heritage collections get checked every single day and are carefully environmentally controlled, although they may be accessible online. If you lock the building, the environment does not stay stable, the temperature and humidity is constantly fluctuating.

Senior manager, national library, UK

4   Redefining libraries and librarians

What, then, is the future of libraries? All the authors in this book have responded to this question in their different contexts and ways. There are certainly threats to libraries in the longer term, not only because of COVID-19 and its aftermath but also a result of a whole cluster of trends—massification, atomization, accelerative change, digitization, disintermediation, and so on—which are rendering "the library" invisible and (seemingly) unnecessary in some people's eyes. Hence, Richard Maidment-Otlet's pressing recommendation for a wholesale rebrand (Chapter 12), not least in the context of Education 4.0.

There is, of course, no single, simple answer to the question posed at the start of the last paragraph. The world is complex and will become ever more so after COVID-19. Having said that, this book has demonstrated the ways in which the value of libraries has been rediscovered in a time of major international crisis, with many reports of increased usage, albeit via electronic means for the most part.

It is not clear whether this idea of bringing people together is a fundamental goal of libraries, or museums and galleries. There will be occasions when group activity supports the community – reading groups, volunteering in museums, study groups, etc. but is that fundamental? The following collective mission statement is a far better point of departure: the purpose of museums, libraries, and archives is to maintain and promote collections and services to encourage people's learning and enjoyment and to develop communities.

Delphi study, 2021

Libraries, as social institutions, should be more involved in interacting with society to alleviate the effects of COVID-19. Practical guides that set standards for social spacing and health issues have been developed that could be applied beyond libraries as well as in them. This requires skills in information retrieval principles and methods, distinguishing between correct and false information, being proficient in information literacy skills, programming skills, using statistical software, web design, application software design, and social networking. Consultation could be conducted with specialists, such as sport psychologists, directors of hospitals and regional authorities. Sport clubs, families, and companies in every sector of a society in general could benefit from this process. Information on standard development could be shared online.

Delphi study, 2021

Museums, libraries, and archives in the digital space only have a future if they find a way to work together. Otherwise, they will only be working as 'little pockets of wonder' rather than as a totally integrated digital resource. DPLA (Digital Public Library of America) and Europeana are working this way.

If the future is all about learning, then everything should be easily accessible in one place.

Former public sector chief executive

It is the job of multilateral organizations like UNESCO to come out with a global charter for libraries in view of the new challenges. UNESCO needs to set up a special Global Libraries Fund to support poor countries to implement new measures in view of COVID-19. Without free international cooperation, libraries [in these countries] will suffer. This could lead to a ripple effect in overall human creativity and intellectual and cultural and economic productivity. The future impact on young and new generations needs to be assessed. The global library community need to do lot of hand holding for protecting the future of library and information services sustainably.

The Global Libraries Fund could support governments in implementing practical guides and codes of conduct, helping to create library IT-infrastructure in the poorest countries, supporting monitoring processes and activating metrics for complying with guidelines.

Delphi study, 2021

The critical task will be to demonstrate to governments of all stripes at national level the value of well-funded and well-managed collecting institutions for communities in the short and longer term. However, it will be a big challenge and will cost a lot of money both in exemplars and lobbying.

Delphi study, 2021

Just as there is no simple way forward in terms of the future role of "the library," neither is there a reliable definition of "the librarian." Chapter 21 includes a long list of roles (many with the word "digital" in front of the descriptor) that librarians will need to fulfill in some form, while Ellen Buck and Anna Nunn (Chapter 11) look at the way in which librarians might begin to redefine themselves in the context of education, learning, and teaching, noting the increasingly "porous" nature of past and present boundaries.

Maria Luz Antunes, Carlos Lopes, and Tatiana Sanches (Chapter 14) consider the opportunities that librarians have to show that "even behind closed doors," they provide essential services, albeit remotely. One particular opportunity which they highlight is the placing of library staff "in the flow of the teaching-learning process," especially when so much education is being undertaken at a distance. There are certainly significant opportunities in the context of academic institutions for a much more integrated approach than has often been the case previously and is now happening in an increasing number of educational institutions, as noted, for example, in Chapters 11 and 22. A key role will be to ensure that all users—and library staffs themselves—are digitally and informationally literate in the most comprehensive way possible. This is arguably the single biggest challenge, opportunity, and requirement for librarians in the future.

Users might benefit from e-library studies embedded into every academic degree combining modules from IT system design, intellectual property law, and social psychology. Every student and researcher could have a mentor at an academic library. In the long run a student might opt for working for the library where her or his mentor is located. A company that borrows high quality resources (meeting rooms, e books, etc) from libraries might become an investor of that university later on. In the next 3–5 years, the transformation of the library web page into a fully interactive library space should be considered, with training of staff and Library and Information Studies students on the new paradigm for delivering library services.

Delphi study, 2021

Creative thinking on the future role of librarians will be required, whatever the type of library. Smith (Chapter 23) argues that new forms of management and leadership training will be required in order that library staff are better prepared for the next major crisis, though given the many examples of good practice described in this volume, much has already been learned "by doing," and the important activity will be to ensure that the lessons are codified and disseminated as effectively as possible.

In terms of best practice, the organization has been able to think creatively about people's jobs. What is it that they do and could do more of? This is through necessity at the present time, but this a legacy that can continue. Elements of this thinking were already in the strategic planning, such as upskilling. Wellbeing and work-life balance will be important to be aware of. The organization was already thinking about this more. It is not certain the extent to which the institution will want to structure the thinking around the effect of the pandemic. It's too early to say. There is the question of who would do this. The strategic leadership team has been reflective and is trying to absorb any lessons learned, but it also has to manage the everyday changes as they keep coming. There have been informal discussions in the regular meetings which give people the chance to just talk about it. It's likely that if structured thinking does take place then the whole organization will be involved. During COVID, the organization has strengthened its staff networks around Equality, Gender, LGBT, and BAME issues. These joined the senior leadership team and will be active. The new anti-racism policy was brought out during the pandemic.

Senior manager, national library, UK

Ellen Buck and Anna Nunn (Chapter 11) and Andy Phippen and Emma Bond (Chapter 22) stress the need (along with other authors in this book) to ensure that librarians are well-positioned in the digital environment which is going to be at the heart of future library systems, even if there is also a physical element to provision.

New Zealand's Libraries Partnership Programme includes a $60 million Government funding package to enable public libraries to 'skill up' staff to meet the digital shift. The work will take place over 2-4 years and will support COVID-19 recovery work across New Zealand's library system. It will fund secondments at public libraries to provide librarian jobs and upskill librarians to support community recovery; train, coach, and mentor librarians; provide free public internet to be available through all public libraries; provide relief for New Zealand libraries by the waiver of user charges and procurement costs for collaborative library services; and provide an uplift in specialist library services for schools and young people with the greatest need.

Senior academic, New Zealand

5   Conclusion

COVID-19 is changing the world. It has already affected the way in which we live, learn, plan, and develop and will continue to do so for some time to come. Library and information services around the world have faced hard choices concerning which services to offer and how, ranging from minimal restrictions to full closure. Coronavirus and its aftermath nevertheless offer librarians around the globe the opportunity to demonstrate the worth of their collections and services across a whole range of different environments, sectors, and contexts. The present pandemic may not be the last; services need to be ready for future worst-case scenarios and develop their ability and capacity to deal with more challenging situations.

How should organizations provide services? Without access to print collections, how can digital information replace—whether entirely or partially—original resources? How do libraries open but control numbers? How do they operate self-service? How should they manage staff working from home? How do they prioritize and reallocate resources? What will all this mean for the longer-term future of digital information use and delivery and of more traditional forms of "library" provision? With purposeful planning, librarians can create opportunities for the optimal development of collections and services, benefitting society at large in the process, though buy-in from senior managers and budget holders will be crucial.

This book has attempted to respond to the crucial requirement for information on how to survive and respond positively to the challenges that provides access and services both during and after COVID-19. The opportunity to understand the experiences of others and to compare to one's own experience and to learn and adapt one's own practice is important, and this has been reflected throughout. The pressing need to understand what this experience means—including the rapid pivot to digital learning and whole-scale adoption of online communication—for medium- to long-term strategies and how they should be adapted has also been considered in detail.

The emphasis has also been on how practical guides that set standards for social spacing and health issues can be applied beyond libraries as well as in them. This is necessitating skills development in information retrieval principles and methods, distinguishing between correct and false information, being proficient in information literacy skills, programming skills, using statistical software, web design, application software design, and social networking.

While offering a physical space to read and study will remain important, current events have already triggered a significant shift toward off-site working and study, making online access to information crucial. Already, libraries provide access to digital information. New forms and use of materials all serve to eliminate the need for direct contact in physical space. Even physical environments will be predicated on evolving systems of digital information, as some of our most critical needs are met by remote delivery. Intensified financial pressure will also shape the future, with a reassessment of the commercial value of information. In response, there will be both massification and atomization of provision.

These are just some of the challenges and opportunities presented in this book along with ways in which libraries and librarians have already successfully responded and will continue to respond.

Appendix A: Delphi questions

A series of questions was developed according to the main themes of this book and are listed below. The answers to these questions were collated and turned into a series of statements which were then sent back to the participants for further comment. These responses were then summarized, analyzed, and presented in Chapters 1 and 31.

1. Libraries around the world are facing hard choices concerning which services to offer and how, ranging from minimal restrictions to full closure. Governments themselves are taking different approaches, sometimes ordering the closure of all institutions, sometimes indicating that life should continue as usual, or simply leaving decisions up library directors. Entire public library systems have been closed in many countries and territories around the world.

   To what extent do you think there will be a convergence of action taken by library leaders and governments in their response to the pandemic in (i) the next 12 months and (ii) the next 3–5 years?

   What patterns are emerging across different sectors and countries; where are the differences, and where are the similarities?

   Please insert your answer here…

2. School libraries in 52 countries have been affected by the closure of all educational institutions. In many countries, university libraries are closed, along with national libraries, though some have now re-opened on a limited basis. Others have re-opened and subsequently closed, in response to wider developments.

   What is the future of libraries attached to educational institutions and does this service relationship set these libraries on a different course compared with public libraries, national libraries, museums, and special libraries?

   Please insert your answer here…

3. The present pandemic may not be the last pandemic. Libraries need to be ready for future worst-case scenarios to deal with more challenging situations. The pandemic may be forcing the world to change, but with purposeful planning, librarians can create opportunities for the optimal development of collections and services, benefitting society at large in the process.

   How do you think libraries should be planning for (i) the next twelve months and (ii) the next 3–5 years? What should be the mechanism and where will information professionals get their guidance, ideas, and case studies from? Who will libraries best get advice?

   Please insert your answer here…

4. COVID-19 provides opportunities as well as challenges for libraries to step up and innovate to provide better services to their clients. Librarians should continue their roles as professionals, serving our users to the best of our ability for the common good.

   What do you see as being the opportunities and the challenges for libraries and librarians (i) over the next 12 months and (ii) over the next 3–5 years? What are the distinctive characteristics of librarians and information providers that will be in demand?

   Please insert your answer here…

5. The biggest technical challenge is the development of new protocols for the maintenance of hygiene and biosafety when there is as yet insufficient research to support the management and redesign of indoor environments, the provision of printed materials, and the effective safeguarding of users against any infectious material. The pandemic provides an opportunity to create new protocols for the users and design changes such as special sanitizer counters and reading cubicles and disinfection rooms to kill the viruses.

   Where do you see the research taking us in terms of the management and redesign of indoor environments? How will the evolution of new architectural designs relate to efforts to maintain hygiene on an hour-by-hour basis?

   Please insert your answer here…

6. Libraries are supposed to bring people together but with social distancing how do they make this possible?

   How would you answer this question concerning (i) your own library and (ii) libraries and society in general?

   Please insert your answer here…

7. "Our homes are now our classrooms; our laptops are our partner; we all are becoming technology savvy." Library collections and services need to reach users in their private as well as their work and public spaces. Communication between library and users will be more intensive. Embracing contemporary technologies should be practiced by libraries and librarians. Collaboration, networking, and learning soft skills are also going to be essential to overcome future obstacles.

   In what ways do you see communication between library and users becoming more intensive? Can you give some examples of changing relationships between libraries and their users? Who are the users going to be in the future?

   Please insert your answer here…

8. Libraries, as social institutions, should be more involved in interacting with society to alleviate the effects of COVID-19. Practical guides that set standards for social spacing and health issues have developed that could be applied beyond libraries as well as in them. This requires skills in information retrieval principles and methods, distinguishing between correct and false information, being proficient in information literacy skills, programming skills, using statistical software, web design, application software design, and social networking.

   How do you think that libraries can develop practical guides which set standards for social spacing and health issues? What other sectors would benefit and why?

   Please insert your answer here…

9. It is the job of multilateral organizations like UNESCO to come out with a global charter for libraries in view of the new challenges. UNESCO needs to set up a special Global Libraries Fund to support poor countries to implement new measures in view of COVID-19. Without free international cooperation, libraries [in these countries] will suffer. This could lead to a ripple effect in overall human creativity and intellectual and cultural and economic productivity. The future impact on young and new generations needs to be assessed. The global library community need to do a lot of handholding for protecting the future of library and information services sustainably.

   What do you see as the top three priorities for a Global Libraries Fund and why?

   Please insert your answer here…

10. Mobile libraries are appropriate for such challenging times. A survey of material required can be collected, and suitable days and times can be collated via Internet or even phone calls. These could include, books, journal photocopies, or audio/video resources. This would also be an opportunity to create an awareness campaign, followed by this survey. A vehicle with attractive display cases would brighten the day, especially if the users are children or young adults. Outreach activities like storytelling, book reading, and competitions can be added attractions. It is easier to sanitize a truck rather than a library.

    Is this an example of new users or a new relationship between librarians and users? Should "community" now be given attention as a new unit of analysis in addition to the individual in this pandemic?

    Please insert your answer here...

11. The time has come to increase the availability of e-content by establishing virtual libraries and making available more digital content in accessible and affordable manner.

    Is this the future in the APAC region? How should this be funded and what infrastructure does it need to become a reality?

    Please insert your answer here...

Index

Note: Page numbers followed by *f* indicate figures, *t* indicate tables, and *b* indicate boxes.